JUVENAL THE SATIRIST

Juvenal the Satirist

A STUDY

BY

GILBERT HIGHET

OXFORD
AT THE CLARENDON PRESS
1954

Oxford University Press, Amen House, London E.C. 4

GLASGOW NEW YORK TORONTO MELBOURNE WELLINGTON
BOMBAY CALCUTTA MADRAS KARACHI CAPE TOWN IBADAN

Geoffrey Cumberlege, Publisher to the University

———

PRINTED IN GREAT BRITAIN

PREFACE

THIS book is a study of the life, work, and influence of the Roman satiric poet Decimus Iunius Iuuenalis, known to the modern world as Juvenal.

Its chief purpose is to discuss his poems, both as literary achievements in a valuable though sometimes neglected form and as social documents from an important period of history. It is therefore intended both for classicists and for scholars in other fields who are interested in the man and his time. With few exceptions, quotations in the text are all in English, and citations of sources in Greek, Latin, and other languages are contained in the notes.

The second aim of the book is to propose a reconstruction of Juvenal's personal career and character, in the hope that it may illuminate some of the difficulties in his work. If it is true (as suggested here) that he was exiled to a remote frontier post in early middle life for criticizing court corruption, and that he returned embittered and impoverished, then it is clear why he knew so much of the extremes of both wealth and poverty, and why, even in a period of apparent public happiness, he remained a convinced pessimist, dimly foreseeing the collapse of the Roman empire.

Thirdly, the book tells the story of the survival of Juvenal's work through the Dark and Middle Ages into the Renaissance and down to modern times, showing at how many stages it contributed vital elements to the development of European literature, and what it meant to writers as diverse as Boccaccio, Dryden, and Hugo. In this connexion the book surveys the progress of Juvenalian scholarship during the past 1,600 years. It does not, however, go deeply into the problems of the transmission of Juvenal's text, which have been efficiently covered by Dr. Ulrich Knoche of Hamburg. It deals only briefly with the physical survival of Juvenal's satires, and concentrates on them as works of art and thought, on their literary and social background, and on their continuing influence upon later satirists, teachers, and thinkers.

This is the only modern book of any considerable range in any language which discusses Juvenal as a poet. It is the result of some twenty years of work, often interrupted by other concerns, but sustained by a vital interest in an unforgettable writer whose character was sadly distorted during his lifetime, and whose work has sometimes been sadly misunderstood since his death.

I should like to express my warm gratitude to many friends and colleagues who have advised me, to the authors of many books which I have consulted with profit, and to several institutions which have given me assistance and hospitality. First to the Guggenheim Memorial Foundation, which awarded me a Fellowship to aid in the completion of this study. Thereafter to the indefatigable Reference Department of Columbia University Library; the University of California Libraries at Berkeley and Los Angeles; Harvard University Library; Yale University Library; the Institut de Recherche et d'Histoire des Textes, Paris; the Clark Memorial Library, Los Angeles; the Morgan Library, New York; the Library of Trinity College, Cambridge; and the University of Montpellier, custodian of the Pithou MS. Finally, to the sympathetic and careful staff of the Oxford University Press, with whom it is a constant pleasure, and something of an education, to work.

G. H.

COLUMBIA UNIVERSITY
NEW YORK
1954

ACKNOWLEDGEMENTS

MY THANKS are due to the following persons and firms who have been kind enough to grant me permission to print quotations from works in which they hold the copyright:

Faber & Faber, Ltd., and Harcourt, Brace & Co., Inc., from T. S. Eliot's *The Waste Land*;

Jonathan Cape, Ltd., Henry Holt & Co., Inc., and the Society of Authors (as the literary representative of the trustees of the estate of the late A. E. Housman), from A. E. Housman's *A Shropshire Lad*;

Mrs. George Bambridge, Doubleday & Co., Inc., The Macmillan Company of Canada, and Methuen & Co., Ltd., from Rudyard Kipling's *Barrack-room Ballads*;

The Macmillan Company of Canada, Macmillan & Co., Ltd., of London, The Macmillan Company of New York, and Mrs. W. B. Yeats, from *The Collected Poems of W. B. Yeats*.

CONTENTS

PART TWO

The Satires of Juvenal

CONTENTS   xiii

PART THREE

The Survival of Juvenal's Work

ABBREVIATIONS

The following abbreviations have been used to save space:

ad fin.	*ad finem*: towards the end	init.	*ad initium*: towards the begin-
ad loc.	*ad locum*: in that passage		ning
c.	chapter; and also *circa*: about	n.s.	new series
cc.	chapters	op. cit.	*opus citatum*: the work already
cf.	*confer*: compare		mentioned
ed.	edition, or, edited by	para.	paragraph
esp.	especially	suppl.	supplementary volume
f.	and following lines, or, and	s.v.	*sub voce*: under the heading
	following pages	tr.	translated by
fl.	*floruit*: flourished, was active	v.	verse; and also *versus*: op-
frg.	fragment, or fragments		posed to; and also volume
ibid.	*ibidem*: in the same book or	vv.	verses; and also volumes
	passage		

Figures in italics refer to the Bibliography: thus 'Ercole (*3*) 12' means 'see page 12 of Ercole's *Studi Giovenaliani*'. A small superior number after a date refers to the edition of the book produced on that date: thus '1913⁶' shows that the edition meant is the sixth, issued in 1913.

The sign ∼ placed between two quotations means that the second is some-how derived from the first: thus 'Juv. 5. 138–9 ∼ Verg. *Aen.* 4. 328–9' shows that *nullus tibi paruolus aula/luserit Aeneas* in Juvenal is a parody of Vergil's *si quis mihi paruolus aula/luderet Aeneas*.

Abbreviations of periodicals and standard works are those recommended by the *American Journal of Archaeology*, 54 (1950), 269–72. The most notable are these:

AJP	*American Journal of Philology*
ALL	*Archiv für lateinische Lexikographie*
ALMA	*Archivum Latinitatis Medii Aevi (Bulletin Du Cange)*
AntCl	*L'Antiquité Classique*
AP	*Anthologia Palatina*
ArchP	*Archiv für Papyrusforschung*
BFC	*Bollettino di Filologia Classica*
BonnJbb	*Bonner Jahrbücher*
BPW	*Berliner philologische Wochenschrift*
CAH	*Cambridge Ancient History*
CIL	*Corpus Inscriptionum Latinarum*
CJ	*Classical Journal*
CP	*Classical Philology*
CQ	*Classical Quarterly*
CR	*Classical Review*
CSEL	*Corpus Scriptorum Ecclesiasticorum Latinorum*
CW	*Classical Weekly*

Dig.	Digesta
DOPap	Dumbarton Oaks Papers
EtCl	Les Études Classiques
GGA	Göttingische Gelehrte Anzeigen
GL	Grammatici Latini, ed. Keil
HSCP	Harvard Studies in Classical Philology
ILS	Inscriptiones Latinae Selectae, ed. Dessau
JB	Bursians Jahresberichte über die Fortschritten der klassischen Altertums-wissenschaft
JEA	Journal of Egyptian Archaeology
JP	Journal of Philology
JSav	Journal des Savants
LZ	Literarisches Zentralblatt
MGH	Monumenta Germaniae Historica: Auctores Antiquissimi
MGH/E	Monumenta Germaniae Historica: Epistulae
MGH/PL	Monumenta Germaniae Historica: Poetae Latini Medii Aevi
MGH/S	Monumenta Germaniae Historica: Scriptores Rerum Germanicarum
MLR	Modern Language Review
Mnem	Mnemosyne
NJbb	Jahrbücher für classische Philologie, Neue Jahrbücher für das klassische Altertum (one series)
OCD	Oxford Classical Dictionary
PG and PL	Patrologia Graeca and Patrologia Latina, ed. Migne
Phil	Philologus
PIR	Prosopographia Imperii Romani, ed. Klebs–Dessau–Groag–Stein
PLM	Poetae Latini Minores, ed. Baehrens
PQ	Philological Quarterly
RBP	Revue Belge de Philologie et d'Histoire
RE	Real-Encyclopädie der classischen Altertumswissenschaft, ed. Pauly–Wissowa–Kroll
REA	Revue des Études Anciennes
REL	Revue des Études Latines
RevPhil	Revue de Philologie
RFIC	Rivista di Filologia e d'Istruzione Classica
RhM	Rheinisches Museum
RIPB	Revue de l'Instruction Publique en Belgique
RM	Römische Mitteilungen
RR	Romanic Review
StudPhil	Studies in Philology
TAPA	Transactions of the American Philological Association
TLL	Thesaurus Linguae Latinae
WKP	Wochenschrift für klassische Philologie
WS	Wiener Studien
ZDA	Zeitschrift für deutsches Altertum
ZöstG	Zeitschrift für die österreichischen Gymnasien

PART ONE

The Life of Juvenal

I

INTRODUCTION

The Roman Juvenal was the greatest satiric poet who ever lived. So much we know; but hardly anything else about him is certain. Most satirists give themselves away in their work. Juvenal tried to keep himself hidden, safe, anonymous, remote. And he succeeded. No contemporary writer mentions him by name—except Martial, who speaks of him not as a poet but as a friend. His poetry had no traceable success in his lifetime, and was practically forgotten soon after he died. It was not studied by the chief literary historians and scholars who worked in the two centuries following his death; the first original writer who quoted and named him was the fourth-century Christian propagandist Lactantius; and the first prominent critic to take a serious interest in him was Servius, who wrote the standard commentary on Vergil about A.D. 400.[1] It was only then, when he had been dust for 250 years, that his work first became popular. The historian Ammian, writing about 390, tells us this in a gloomy description of the folly and degeneracy of the Roman nobles. Many of them, says Ammian, are miserably debauched. There are others who ought to be studying serious subjects but hate them like poison, and instead give great care and attention to reading an old historian (now lost) and Juvenal. 'Why they do this' (Ammian goes on) 'I cannot tell; but these are the only books they handle in their deep retirement.'[2] Juvenal himself would have understood. These, his first real audience, were men like him. Condemned, like too many of the cultivated classes under the emperors, to a life of meaningless ceremonies and infertile ambitions, they turned to the poet who had felt the futility of that life most poignantly and described it most bitterly. He was, like them, a man who brooded in deep, wasteful, infuriating retirement.

Although he was writing satire, which is one of the most personal types of literature, he endeavoured to conceal his personality. In one way he succeeded. But in another he failed. It is impossible for an author to conceal himself entirely. Everyone who writes betrays himself—by the subjects he chooses, by his language, by his allusions to people and events, by the energy or gentleness, clearness or difficulty, sadness or humour, of his view of life. For instance, we know that Vergil had to fight the blackest despair when he was writing the *Aeneid*: he told the emperor that he must have been mad to start such a piece of work, and he attempted to destroy it before he died. Yet even without knowing this, we should have divined his character and his attitude to his work from the profound melancholy which darkens every book of the poem until it seems to be not the story of a glorious triumph but the dirge for a defeat.[3] In the same way it is possible to reconstruct something of Juvenal's life and much of his character from his poems themselves. Even the fact that he tried to hide himself is an important feature of his unusual personality. And from silences here and implications there we can build up a picture of his strange and painful career.

MIDDLE LIFE AND OLD AGE

THE clearest part of Juvenal's career is his middle life and his old age. At the very beginning of his poems he speaks of his youth as past, so that by Roman ideas he was 45 or more when he began to publish, while his ghastly description of the weakness and ugliness of old age and his addresses to two elderly friends as his equals show that most of his extant poetry was written far nearer the end of his life than the beginning.[1] Besides, in spite of the furious energy that surges and vibrates through the first six satires, even they are not so wide-awake and contemporary as a young man's poems are. Many of their finest passages deal with situations which were half-forgotten when he was publishing, and people who had long been dead. He gives brilliant and biting descriptions of the fall of Tiberius' favourite Sejanus, which had happened nearly a century earlier, and of the vices of the nymphomaniac empress Messalina, who had been executed two generations before.* Juvenal says this is deliberate policy on his part.† Whatever be the reasons for it —we shall discuss them presently—it is characteristic either of a mild quiet bookish antiquary, which his worldliness shows he was not, or of a still vigorous but ageing man whose most vivid impressions come not from the present but from the past, and who naturally turns towards history to illustrate his words. You can trace the advance of age on him as you read through the satires. The first six, which came out as Book I and Book II, are full of appalling violence and hatred. The three that make up Book III are much milder, more resigned, more general, farther away from life. Book IV, although it contains the fine sermon on the dangers of ambition, is occasionally downright boring; and compared with Book I the Fifth Book is trivial. About 100 years ago the German scholar Otto Ribbeck conjectured that half a dozen of the later satires were not by Juvenal at all but by a forger who copied something of his manner without equalling his spirit. He was right, but the copyist was

* 10. 56–107; 6. 115–32.   † 1. 150–71; and see pp. 9–10.

Juvenal himself, imitating his earlier work after the passion that inspired it had died away.

He scarcely ever speaks of himself. The first person singular is far rarer in him than in any other ancient satirist. But a few things are clear from hints and odd lines in his poems. This is what they tell us.

Juvenal was a free-born Roman citizen.[2] He came from Aquinum, a little hill-town near Monte Cassino, eighty miles down the Latin Road from Rome.[3] He was born about A.D. 60, for his first book came out in or near 110, when he was over 45.* He received the ordinary elementary and high-school education of a middle-class boy, but did not go on to study philosophy, which was the equivalent of attending a university nowadays.[4]

But at this point there is a gap in the story. Juvenal never speaks of his youth.[5] He never tells us what kind of career he followed after leaving school, or where he lived, or whether he was ever married, whether he was rich or poor, happy or un-happy: nothing. Yet we know for certain that he spent some time in Rome during Domitian's reign of terror (81–96), for nothing in the satires is so vividly seen and reported as the characters and the atmosphere of that reign. One satire in par-ticular describes a Cabinet meeting which the sombre emperor held quite early in his reign, and portrays the chief courtiers with such life and clarity that we can hardly keep from think-ing Juvenal was at court then and saw them with his own eyes.[6]

Also, he did at some time in his life visit Egypt: and not for pleasure, since he scarcely ever speaks of the country and its inhabitants without hatred and contempt.†

When he began to publish, it was some time after the murder of Domitian. Juvenal was now middle-aged, grey, and gloomy, with the worse half of his life before him. He had been living in Rome for some time, as a poor dependant of several rich and arrogant patrons.

Two or three hundred years before, there had been some real value in the curious Roman system by which a rich influential man became the 'patron' of a poor 'client'. Originally it had been a sort of feudal relationship. The Roman nobles, like clan chieftains, would gather round them men who supported them

* See pp. 11–12.   † See pp. 28–29.

in faction fights and electoral contests and legal disputes and wars. In return, the nobleman would advise his dependants in difficulties, help them in lawsuits, defend them against the encroachments of powerful neighbours, and throw business in their direction. Often the link was so close that the dependants were part of their patron's household, like squires and retainers in the Middle Ages. They attended the patron in the morning, walking down to the Law Courts and the Exchange with him— much as VIPs nowadays are always escorted by secretaries and attachés; they relaxed or played games with him in the afternoon, and they dined with him in the evening. When the patron stood for office they helped in canvassing; when he was engaged in a lawsuit they appeared on his side of court as a symbol of his dependability and influence; at his wedding, his great public appearances, and his funeral they formed part of the procession; if he went away to govern a province, they might accompany him in minor posts.* Nearly all the best-known Latin authors were either rich men who wrote for their own pleasure—Lucan, Lucilius, Persius, Petronius, Pliny, Tacitus— or poor men who were supported by rich men of taste— Claudian, Ennius, Martial, Statius, Terence. Horace thought it was a big improvement in his standing when he was enabled to give up his job as a minor official and become the dependant of Maecenas, living in his house and going on diplomatic missions as a member of his suite.[7] When he was made entirely independent by Maecenas' gift of a little private estate and income, that was an important step farther, for which he was still more grateful than for the earlier patronage.[8] Just as in the eighteenth century, many men from the lower middle class tried to live all their lives in this parasitic way, either because they hoped eventually to become independent through their patron's gifts and bequests, or because few other vocations were open to them without loss of caste and waste of talent.

However, under the empire, as the sense of public duty dwindled, and the noble houses lost both power and honour, and life became more and more a matter of money, the relationship of patron and dependant changed. Patrons grew colder, less generous, more arrogant; dependants became greedier, less devoted, more hypocritical; it became less of a family relation-

* So Juv. 10. 44–46, 13. 32–33.

ship and more of a business. The dependant ceased to dine with his patron every evening. Instead, he collected the price of a meal from the butler in lieu of dinner.[9] Since the relationship was as cold as this, there was no reason why it should not be made as profitable as possible. Therefore many dependants had a regular list of patrons, called on them all one after another in the morning, drew their dinner-money at each door, and hoped for a present from each at the Saturnalia on 17 December. The entrance-hall of every rich house was crowded, partly with poor men waiting to catch the butler's eye and partly with well-to-do gentlemen calling as a social duty—although Juvenal says they accepted their handout just like the others.* Sometimes it seems as though nine out of ten Romans were living on charity at this time: five of them on the public welfare schemes run by the government, and the other four as dependants of the tenth. This is not true: there was still a solid mass of working people and, especially outside Rome, an equally respectable *bloc* of the middle class. But just as free food and amusements led to the degeneration of the Roman artisans and farmers, so the pur-poseless life, the free meals, and the humiliations of parasitism were encouraging the decay of the middle class. We can see the progress of corruption in the difference between the compara-tive independence of Horace and the servility of later poets. To-wards the end of the first century A.D., Martial was not ashamed to write *and publish* dozens of poetic begging-letters, asking his rich acquaintances for clothes, food, silver plate, and money. Statius, although he was more independent, wasted his talent writing graceful and silly little poems on private parks, statues, mansions with running water in every bedroom, and even pet parrots, owned by millionaires who might be good for a touch.† The life of a 'client' was horrible: without self-respect, without hope of independence unless after long servitude, without any real leisure, and without any real work—a lifetime of standing in waiting-rooms and loitering in corridors and bowing to blind eyes and begging for petty favours, the friend of a man who was neither your equal nor your companion, the dependant of a man who treated you as a useless ornament, the flatterer of a man whom you hated and who usually knew it.

    Scarcely any other writer has ever felt the disgrace of being a

---

* 1. 95–126, 3. 126–30.   † Stat. *Silu.* 2. 3, 4. 6, 1. 3, 2. 4.

dependant so keenly or described it so savagely as Juvenal. Greek and Latin literature has many references to the pathos and shame of poverty, but Juvenal is the first to express the peculiar sufferings of middle-class penury in a world where the rich seem to grow richer year by year and the poor more slavish, while a well-educated bourgeois with no capital must spend his entire life swinging between temporary luxury and permanent squalor, tortured like the wretches whom Ivan the Terrible killed by drenching them alternately with boiling and freezing water, talking civilly to the rich vulgarian and shrinking instinctively from the brutalized poor, striving to hide from both of them the torn overcoat that needs cleaning, the shoe that gapes where the leather has split, and unable even to think straight because his mind is appalled at having to buy a new blanket for the bed.* Two eminent British writers of the baroque age who suffered in the same way would have met Juvenal, not necessarily with pleasure, but with a close and grim fellow feeling. Jonathan Swift, who lived as a dependant in the grand house of Sir William Temple, remembered many years afterwards what agonies he used to suffer 'when Sir William . . . would look cold and out of humour', and some of his inordinate arrogance sprang from his desire to compensate that long-enforced subservience.† In 1749 Samuel Johnson published an adaptation of Juvenal 10 called *The Vanity of Human Wishes*. Six years later, when he thought of asking the Earl of Chesterfield to sponsor his great *English Dictionary*, he was turned away by Chesterfield's servants. True, he had not, like Juvenal, risen from bed at midnight in order to pay his morning call at a respectful time, nor sweated in heavy formal dress as he visited a long series of patrons; but he had starved in filthy freezing garrets, he had been arrested for miserable petty debts, he had made his way by his own efforts, and now he altered a couplet inspired by Juvenal's poetry and his own bitter experience, to read:

> There mark what ills the scholar's life assail,
> Toil, envy, want, *the patron*, and the jail.‡

* Juv. 3. 147–51, 7. 66–67.
† Swift, *Journal to Stella* (ed. H. Williams, Oxford, 1948), i. 231: see the arrogant remark on i. 230.
‡ Juv. 5. 19–23; Mart. 12. 18; Juv. 3. 124–5; Johnson, *The Vanity of Human Wishes*, 159–60—the original reading was 'the garret'.

This, then, is nearly all we know from Juvenal's own poems about his life outside his poetry. He had had a good average education; he hated Domitian; he had been in Egypt; he was a dependant of the rich. One thing more: he was frightened. This is unusual. Satirists are usually bold outspoken men who care for nobody, like Rabelais and Byron, like venomous little Pope and his formidable friend Swift and his formidable enemy Hogarth. Even when their victims threatened them, Lucilius the founder of invective satire and his Greek prototype Aristophanes were both perfectly fearless, gaily daring, and challenging. But they were not living under an absolute monarch who could order them to torture, exile, or execution at a moment's notice. Juvenal had lived such a life. Again and again in his First Book he returns to his fear and loathing of the cruel Domitian.* Others felt that horror too—the proud Tacitus, the mild Pliny, the calm Epictetus—but none recurs to it with so much vehemence.† To it we must trace the strangest thing about his satires—their anachronism. Although almost all satirists write of topical things—the life around them, the people they know, the scandal that has just broken out—Juvenal tries not to do this. At the end of his first poem, which is his introduction to his first and most powerful book, after staring furiously at all the vices and crimes of Rome and declaring he must write of them because he cannot help it, he suddenly hedges. An objector (evidently his own more cautious self) warns him that no one now is brave enough to write as he pleases, with the candour of the republican satirist Lucilius. Put down the name of Nero's vicious friend Tigellinus, he says, and you will be burnt alive, a human torch in the middle of the arena. Juvenal listens. He asks what is the alternative. What must he do? Is he to remain silent when a murderer, rich and haughty, rides past looking down on honest folk? Yes, he must. Even to mention such a man's name is as dangerous as accusing him in open court. Other kinds of poetry, the old mythological stuff, are safe enough, but this is as dangerous as declaring war on crime

---

* 2. 29–33, 4. 37–38, 4. 69–71, 4. 72–103, 4. 150–4.

† Tac. *Agr.* 2. 3–4, 41–43, 45; Plin. *Pan.* 48–49, 52; Plin. *Ep.* 1. 12. 6–8, 4. 11. 5f., 4. 22. 5, 7. 27. 14. Domitian as the typical tyrant in Epictetus is described by C. G. Starr, Jr., 'Epictetus and the tyrant', *CP* 44 (1949), 20–29.

singlehanded. And Juvenal ends unexpectedly by saying, 'I shall see how much I can risk against those whose ashes lie along the highways outside Rome'*—the dead noblemen and millionaires who occupy the big family tombs beyond the city gates.[10] He keeps this promise almost, although not quite, unbroken.† If he wants to write of the disappointments of old age he chooses Priam of Troy and Croesus of Lydia, Marius and Pompey of the old Republic; if he needs examples of debauched nobility, he pitches on Nero, dead fifty years before, and Catiline, who was as far from Juvenal as Louis XVI is from us.‡ The very name of Tigellinus, dead for more than thirty years, is an anachronism. Some of this is due to the habit, common to all those who had had a course of rhetoric in school, of dignifying every argument by citing famous historical examples of its truth. Yet of all those who follow the habit none but Juvenal says he is *afraid* to use real names. Partly he is afraid of them, and partly he cannot become interested in them. He sees the present through the past—a past which almost seems to stop when his poetry begins, soon after the end of Domitian.

Because of this habit it is hard to tell when he wrote his satires and when he published them. Usually a satire can be dated by the latest topical event in it, which must have happened soon before it was issued. But for Juvenal anything which is really topical is dangerous; and on the other hand, anything which is shocking is topical, no matter when it happened. Also, a poem is often written five or ten years before it is published, and altered at intervals while it is still in draft form, so that the only date we can be fairly sure of is the date of its publication, when all the fluid allusions become, for the first time, fixed and unalterable.[11] Greek and Roman poets spent years over their work, retouching, adding, compressing, polishing. As modern Urdu poets still do, as a distinguished French poet§ did towards the end of last century, they read their poetry to friends and circulated it in manuscript for criticism during several years before taking the important, the almost irrevocable step of publishing it to the world. For Juvenal, as for most Latin authors, the date

*   Experiar quid concedatur in illos
    quorum Flaminia tegitur cinis atque Latina (1. 170–1).
† For qualifications see pp. 290–4.   ‡ 10. 246–88; 8. 211–35.
§ José-Maria de Heredia, on whom see p. 226.

of final publication is the date when a poem appeared in book form. He published his satires in five groups, each group filling a separate 'volume' or 'Book' (*libellus*). If we date these Books, we shall have done almost all we can do.

Book I consists of five poems. Two of them are timeless: they are general indictments of the corrupt metropolis of Rome (3) and of the system of patronage on which Juvenal lived (5). Two of them deal directly or by implication with Domitian's reign. Satire Four describes a ridiculous meeting of the imperial cabinet held in 82 or 83; and Satire Two is a blistering attack on hypocrisy and sexual perversion which seems to have been prompted by Domitian's assumption, in 84–85, of the post of censor.* The remaining poem, Satire One, serves as preface, and contains the only certain date in the Book:

> The exiled Marius drinks all afternoon, enjoying
> his own damnation, while the conquering province weeps.†

Marius Priscus was impeached at the request of the province of Africa for corruption as its governor. He was found guilty and banished—although Juvenal says he managed to live like a lord, while the province was no better off after winning its case.[12] The trial ended in A.D. 100. Therefore this Book did not appear *before* 100.

How long *after* 100 it came out, we cannot surely say. Of course we must not place it exactly in the year 100 just because it mentions a notable event of that year. Still, there is one further hint, so vague that it has sometimes escaped notice. In his stinging attack upon noble perverts Juvenal speaks of the emperor Otho taking a mirror on his campaigns during the civil war and depilating his face with a poultice of dough: a trait

> well worth recording in the new Annals and the latest
> History.‡

Now, Otho's campaigns were described by Tacitus in the *Histories*, which came out between 104 and 109; and Otho may

---

* Allusions to the censorship in 2. 30, 2. 63, 2. 121.
† Exul ab octaua Marius bibit et fruitur dis
  iratis; at tu, uictrix prouincia, ploras (1. 49–50).
‡ Res memoranda nouis Annalibus atque recenti
  Historia (2. 102–3).

well have been mentioned again in the *Annals*, on which Tacitus was working after 109. Juvenal need not have read these books in their final form. He may only have heard literary gossip about them and attended pre-publication readings from them. But he obviously knew their contents well enough to make fun of them in this passage and to expect his hearers and readers to pick up the joke.[13] Lacking exact information about the publication of Tacitus' works, we cannot be more precise. But it is a fair inference that Juvenal was publicly reciting the satires which compose Book I at various times during the ten or twelve years after Domitian's death, while the memory of the despot was still vivid; and that he assembled them into a volume and published them in or near the year A.D. 110.

Book II is composed of only one vast satire, the Sixth, against marriage. We are unable to identify the scandalous events which Juvenal retails in it, except a few from the earlier history of the empire, like the nightly excursions of Messalina.* However, there is a clue. One of the objectionable wives Juvenal describes is the gossip and news-analyst.

> The comet threatening Parthian and Armenian kings
> she is the first to sight; she gathers reports and gossip
> at the city-gates, some she invents; Niphates has
> overflowed in foreign parts and covers the country
> in mighty floods, cities are tottering, the earth sinking—
> so she tells everyone she meets at every corner.†

Now, there were two comets which might be said to have portended disaster to the eastern kings, one in 110 and the other in 115.[14] The emperor Trajan invaded Armenia in 113 and Parthia in 116. In December 115 there was a sensational earthquake at Antioch.[15] All these events make good parallels to the gossip reported by the garrulous lady. So unless we can believe that Juvenal invented them all as typical foreign newsflashes

---

* 6. 115–32.
† Instantem regi Armenio Parthoque cometen
  prima uidet; famam rumoresque illa recentis
  excipit ad portas, quosdam facit; isse Niphaten
  in populos magnoque illic cuncta arua teneri
  diluuio, nutare urbes, subsidere terras
  quocumque in triuio cuicumque est obuia narrat (6. 407–12).

before they actually happened, we shall conclude that he published Book II in or not long after A.D. 116, soon after the earthquake, the comet, and the wars.

Book III, vaguer, milder, and more general than its two predecessors, contains only one indication of time. In the introductory poem, Satire Seven, Juvenal describes the poverty and neglect of authors, lawyers, and teachers. Their sufferings are related in a tone of unbroken gloom, and are mainly illustrated by examples from the Domitianic period, like Statius and Quintilian. It is the selfishness of the rich nobles, says Juvenal, which drives poets to starvation and despair.* However, the poem begins with praise for the interest in literature shown by the emperor:

> since only he respects the Muses, now so gloomy.†

The emperor is described simply as *Caesar* and *chief*. He is not named. But he is important, for Juvenal never praises an emperor of Rome anywhere else in his satires, and derides or attacks at least five former monarchs.‡

Who was he? Some have thought he was Domitian; but it is impossible that anyone so fervent and sincere as Juvenal could have attacked Domitian so bitterly in Book I and praised his literary taste in Book III, and highly unlikely that Satire Seven was published in its present form during Domitian's lifetime.[16] Nerva scarcely reigned long enough to make much difference to literary prospects, at least financially. Trajan did give some encouragement to literature, if only by lifting the terror, but he was a soldier rather than an aesthete.§ Hadrian was a good critic and a competent poet, with a genuine love of art and letters. It looks a little more probable that Juvenal is thinking of him, rather than of any other.

However, those who discuss Juvenal's complimentary preface to this poem usually assume that it is a welcome to a new emperor on his accession.‖ There is nothing to justify this.

---

* 7. 36–47, 74–78, 94–95, 104, 178–88.
† Solus enim tristes hac tempestate Camenas
   respexit (7. 2–3).
‡ Julius, 10. 108–9; Augustus, 8. 240–4; Claudius, 6. 621–3, 14. 330–1; Nero, 8. 211–26; Otho, 2. 99–109.   § Plin. *Pan.* 47.
‖ e.g. Duff (*54*) xvi; de Labriolle (*4*) 216–17; Friedländer (*55*) 10.

Juvenal does not greet the emperor, nor speak of a new reign, fresh auspices, a happier age. What he says is that the emperor has turned his attention to literature and is looking for writers who deserve his support. From now on, he predicts with striking emphasis, no poet will be forced to endure work unworthy of his accomplishments.* This seems to refer to some new indication of an emperor's desire to patronize the arts. It is not a coronation poem. It describes not a new personage, but a new attitude. Such a new attitude might well be that expressed in Hadrian's re-foundation of the Athenaeum. Founded by Vespasian as an institute to support and encourage deserving literary men, it was re-established and more energetically patronized by Hadrian.[17] Juvenal may well have hoped to get a fellowship in it, and to enjoy the security that had so long been denied him. Once again here, more sadly than before, he speaks of a poet who has grown too old to go in for trade, soldiering, or farming: and he is thinking, among others, of himself.†

If there is anything in this suggestion, we can place the publication of Book III between the autumn of 118, when Hadrian arrived in Rome for the first time as emperor and set about winning popularity by many grand generous gestures, and the year 121, when he left for a long tour of inspection in the provinces. No doubt such an important act as the new endowment of the Athenaeum took time to carry out, so that we should expect Juvenal's praise of it to have been published a year or so after Hadrian's advent. Let us say A.D. 120.

Book IV contains one or two references to advancing age, including a wonderful hundred-line-long description of the pains, griefs, and squalors of senility which is as grotesque as Swift's account of the Struldbrugs and as violent as *Timon of Athens*.‡ There is no indication of its date, except that Domitian, and his courtier Crispinus, and the bitterness of Book I, are all forgotten in the past.

Book V, the last, consists of three poems, and a fragment. There are only 60 lines left of Satire Sixteen. It stops in the middle of a sentence, although it was obviously intended to be

* 7. 2–12, 17–19, 20–21.   † 7. 32–35.
‡ 10. 188–288 (and cf. 11. 201–4); Swift, *A Voyage to Laputa*, c. 10.

fairly long.* Did Juvenal publish it complete and has it since been mutilated by the loss of some pages in an early copy?† or did he leave it unfinished when he died and was it issued as it stood by his executors? The former explanation is much more probable. The Greeks and Romans did not admire broken torsos or put out works which had not even a pretence of wholeness. They would not issue a poem with a fragmentary pattern ending in a mutilated sentence. Vergil's *Aeneid* and the satires of Juvenal's predecessor Persius were both left unfinished, and were both published after the ragged ends had been trimmed to give them a certain artistic completeness. There are clear proofs that Juvenal's poems were mutilated here and there before the Latin critics began to study them: we shall look into that in a later chapter.‡ Here it is enough to say that the loss of most of Satire Sixteen was probably part of the neglect Juvenal suffered in the generations after his death. We are lucky not to have lost more.

We know also that Juvenal was working on Book V and reciting separate poems from it in and after A.D. 127. There are two exact references to this year. Once, Juvenal cynically consoles a friend who has been cheated out of some money by telling him that at *his* age he might have learnt how unscrupulous people are:

> Are you astonished, *you*, who have left behind you
> sixty years, born in Fonteius' consulship?§

Fonteius is shown to have been consul in A.D. 67. Then again, Juvenal, just before describing a lynching in Egypt, says it happened 'recently when Juncus was consul'‖—which was in the year 127. Further, in 14. 96–106 he declares that some Romans, because of the bad example set by their fathers, are being converted to Judaism and are being circumcised. Now, a terrific Jewish rebellion broke out in 131 or 132, and one of the reasons given for it is that Hadrian had prohibited the practice of circumcision.[18] Therefore Juvenal could not have brought out a book complaining about the custom as being too easy and too

---

* See pp. 158–9, 288–9.   † See p. 287.   ‡ See pp. 94–95, 223–4.
§   Stupet haec qui iam post terga reliquit
      sexaginta annos, Fonteio consule natus?   (13. 16–17).
‖ Nuper consule Iunco (15. 27).

common, if it had been made illegal and difficult before the
book was published. On the contrary, his complaint is probably
evidence of the general disapproval which prompted Hadrian
to enact the law. Therefore Juvenal either published Book V
complete, or died leaving it unfinished, between A.D. 127 and 131.

To sum up, then, Juvenal began to publish his extant poems
in their final form in or near A.D. 110, and ended his work on his
fifth volume in or near 130. Yet it is difficult to believe that he
had not been thinking of satiric poetry for a long time before he
issued Book I. His style has that distinction and individuality
which come from long meditation, and it changes very little
from beginning to end. The early poems are so packed with
material (proper names, parodies, metrical and stylistic tricks)
that they are swollen and strained with the effort of containing
and clarifying it all. Only later in his life does his poetry begin to
thin out. Most of his early subjects and illustrations come from
the age of Domitian, ten or fifteen years behind him at his first
publication. And the leading characteristic of all his work strikes
every reader in its first pages—his absolute clarity, rigidity,
ruthlessness, certainty. Juvenal has made up his mind long ago.
Nevertheless, the first line of the first poem in his First Book
says quite clearly that he has been sitting in silence, that he has
published nothing; and the opening and closing passages of the
same poem discuss his impulse to start a career as a satirist.[19]
He is, or says he is, a complete newcomer in the field. The inference therefore is that he was thinking in terms of satire under
Domitian, but was afraid to publish any complete work. After
the tyrant was killed, he began to polish up the material he had
in his mind, to build it into large-scale poems on single unified
patterns (which he found rather difficult), to recite it at concerts
given at his own expense or at that of his stingy patrons, and
ultimately to assemble it into separate books for publication.
   As we look back over the five Books, we can see one more fact
emerging. The earlier Books are haunted by poverty. Mended
clothes, poor food, miserable lodgings, scanty furniture, gnawing anxiety, a sense of bitter injustice—all these recur often in
the first three Books.* But in the Fourth and Fifth the tone

---

* 3. 147–51; 1. 134, 3. 167, 5 *passim*, 7. 119–21; 3. 166, 3. 200–2; 3. 10,
3. 168, 3. 203–9, 3. 286–7; 7. 34–35, 7. 53–71.

changes. One of the best satires in the First Book describes a meal eaten by a dependant in his patron's house. He and his fellow guests wear darned clothes; they are terribly hungry and they are served cheap and beastly food, while they sit and watch the master's plate, hoping that they may get a chance at a delicacy he has half-eaten and pushed away.* Elsewhere in the First Book Juvenal depicts the wretched 'client', evidently a projection of himself and an epitome of his own experiences, following the patron about all day in the hope of being invited to dinner in the evening; and then, when the summons does not come, buying a cabbage and some charcoal to boil it with.† But in the Fourth Book, the second poem is a charming little monologue in which Juvenal invites an old friend to dine with him at his house in Rome. The place is still simply furnished, with bone-handled knives on the table, and plain fresh country food served by little slaveboys from the farm instead of elegant Greeklings. Still, the note of worry has vanished. Although this is a party for a special occasion, no food has been bought in the expensive luxury shops, no caviare and peaches. It all comes from the farm—a suckling kid, poultry, fresh eggs, vegetables and fruit, and local wine—and there is more where it came from. *At last*, we say as we read, *at last* he has enough to live on in a modest way, instead of sinking deeper into poverty as he grows older. Somehow he has acquired a fair-sized farm at Tivoli, with a staff of slaves to work it—whether by inheritance, by gift from Caesar (Hadrian himself owned a big property at Tivoli, where he built his famous country-house), or like Martial by the long-delayed generosity of a patron.[20] We cannot tell where he got it. He never thanks anyone for it. Only in his latest satires he speaks more warmly than before of the generous impulses of friendship.‡ At least we know that he did not die as he had lived much of his life, in poverty, bitterness, and despair.

Only one of Juvenal's contemporaries even mentions him by name. This is the epigrammatist Martial; and although Martial

---

* 5, esp. 67–69, 103–6, 131, 166–9.

† 1. 132–4, with the contrast to the patron dining alone (let's hope it kills him!), 135–46.

‡ See 12. 10–16, 12. 93–95, 12. 128–30; 13 is a consolation to a friend; 15. 140–58.

says he knew Juvenal well he does not speak of his poetry. Writing in 91 or 92 under Domitian, Martial assails some liar who has been trying to break up his friendship with Juvenal—a friendship, he says, as close as the fabulous unions of Orestes and Pylades, or Castor and Pollux; and a little later he sends Juvenal a present of nuts from his own garden for the Saturnalia.* Then there is a gap of ten years, in which Domitian was killed, Nerva became emperor and died, and Martial himself retired from his old life as a dependant and an occasional poet, returning finally to his native province of Spain. From there in 101 he sent Juvenal a letter in poetry which reads lightly and pleasantly but is in fact rather cruel.† He begins by picturing Juvenal as wandering restlessly through the noisy Subura—a tough, busy street in central Rome, part slum and part Broadway—or climbing the hot hills of Rome to visit the thresholds of the important people . . . as Martial himself had done for thirty years, but now no more. Then he goes on to describe his own country comfort on his farm in Spain after thirty years of city fatigue, sleeping now till 9 or 10 (the equivalent of 12 noon or 1 p.m. for modern people), wearing anything he likes, breakfasting in front of a huge kitchen fire fed with oak logs from the woods and crowned with pots of good stew, hunting in the forest with a handsome gamekeeper, and gradually giving up all his elegant city manners. A vivid little poem, but not wholly likeable. Martial expresses no sympathy for Juvenal still sweating it out in Rome. He could scarcely invite his dear friend to come over and visit him, for he himself had had to touch a rich patron for the fare.‡ But he might perhaps have uttered a word or two of sympathy, or ended on a note of affection, instead of gloating. It looks as though the two men had been estranged. In the earlier poems Martial protests his ardent friendship and sends a gift. In this he stands aloof, without pity, almost with amusement. The only thing common to all three poems is that they each contain a dirty joke. It is a strange and complex relationship, this link between Martial and Juvenal: we shall see more of it later; but it was not wholly a pleasant association.

---

* Mart. 7. 24 and 7. 91.   † Mart. 12. 18.
  ‡ The younger Pliny: see Martial's compliment, 10. 20, and Pliny's obituary, *Ep*. 3. 21.

Martial calls Juvenal 'eloquent' in the second poem. It was a vague word. As he used it, it meant little more than 'interested in literature'.[21] It does not imply that Juvenal had published anything by 91–92, but it does mean that he had a sense of style and could write. Later we shall see that he had an exceptionally keen imitative ear, that he listened to Martial's jokes and read his epigrams, and that he adapted many of them for his own use. Although Martial was a nasty little man, he had a keen brain and quick perceptions, and he was a fine craftsman in verse. It is remarkable that in these little poems he should have hit off several of the salient points of Juvenal's character as it emerges from the Satires: particularly in the two adjectives 'eloquent' and 'restless', which together express the driving forces of his poetry. But Martial does not know Juvenal as a fellow poet.

No one else whom we know ever mentions Juvenal by name during his lifetime. The younger Pliny, who patronized Martial and made a point of naming, in his letters, every person or event which might appear important to his contemporaries or to posterity, never speaks of him. This implies that Juvenal was either very obscure, or else very offensive.* No other author in Latin or Greek alludes to Juvenal until long after his death.[22] He is never quoted by any contemporary. He is not imitated by any extant writer of his own age. His work almost disappeared altogether—for the explanatory notes on his poems which were written for the later Romans to read are so extremely thin that their compilers can have had scarcely any material to work on, and there can have been no regular set of commentaries and personal-interest notes such as grew up immediately after the death of authors like Horace. Strange, that silence. And yet, much later, a thousand or fifteen hundred years after his death, there were many readers who admired Juvenal so much that they learnt his poems off by heart. This discrepancy between the disregard of his contemporaries and the admiration of posterity is one of the chief problems about Juvenal's work. We shall consider it later. Meanwhile, we are trying to reconstruct his life, which was spent, and closed, in obscurity.

* On the relation of Pliny and Juvenal see pp. 292–3.

III

MANHOOD AND EXILE

JUVENAL himself says that when he started to publish satires his life was more than half over.* It is very remarkable for a satiric writer to make his début in middle age: still more so if his work is so expert as Juvenal's. For the First Book of his Satires is not experimental. In many ways it is his best. It is full of immortal phrases, enough to make the reputation of any poet, and the angry, jerky irregularity of Satire One is offset by the skilful structure of the Third and Fifth Satires. And the most remarkable thing about it is the violence of the emotions which break through every one of its poems. Compare their opening sentences with the chatty introductions of Horace's satires, the enigmatic and sententious exordia of Persius' poems. They erupt like volcanoes. Not only are they as violent, but they give the same impression of having been long suppressed and boiling out with redoubled force after some obstacle has been shattered. But later in his career his poems become gentler, more controlled, more generalized; the lava flow slows down, cooling and hardening, the rain of hot ashes stops, the thundering subterranean rumbles die away, the burning clouds clear, with only a few plumes of evil ominous smoke still rising here and there above the black and shattered summit of the crater.

Something very strange and violent must have happened in the first part of Juvenal's life to produce such powerful repercussions in the second. Satirists are even less likely than other kinds of authors to take up writing simply as a way of making money or reputation. Their chief aim is to point out something which they think is fundamentally wrong with society, some clamant injustice, some stupidity so outrageous that it will not let them rest till they have exposed it. Yet other people living in the same society do not seem to notice these crimes and follies, or do not get so excited about them. Therefore the satirists are peculiarly sensitive, and their sensitivity means suffering. They have come into personal conflict with stupidity and injustice, and

* 1. 25; and see p. 4.

their satires are the direct result, the cry of pain and rage their
savage laughter. 'How can you sleep?' cries Juvenal, 'Who is so
iron-hard as to control himself?'* Yet other people seem to
be able to sleep. They remain calm. They may observe the outrages that move the satirist, but they do not feel them. There is
a strange story by Franz Kafka which describes a machine for
inflicting punishment on criminals in a penal colony. The condemned man is strapped down immovably on a flat operating
table in which there are troughs and channels to carry off
blood and sputum. Then a set of sharp needle-like points, like
a harrow, descends on him, and slowly writes, in his living flesh,
the law which he has broken.† Kafka's criminals are gagged.
But the satirist is not. He has felt the steel entering into him,
and what he feels he screams out for us all to hear.

We hear Juvenal's yell of rage and pain. We cannot know
exactly what evoked it, for he never tells us. Evidently it was
something that happened in the earlier part of his life, something
of which the memory, as he grew older, became gradually less
piercing although the scars were permanent. Perhaps we can
reconstruct it. How did he spend his middle years, his young
manhood? What happened then to make him a satirist?

To find out, we must turn to evidence which is much more
confused and less solid than his own poems. This is given by the
biographies and biographical notes which are attached to the
manuscripts of Juvenal's satires. Many of the manuscripts contain explanatory notes, written by scholars in the late Roman
Empire or in the Dark Ages, to help readers who found Juvenal's
style and allusions difficult. (These are called *scholia*, and their
authors *scholiasts*.) Many of the commentaries contain a brief
sketch of his life; and a number of manuscripts include short
separate biographies of him, just as a modern book carries an
outline of the writer's career on its cover. These biographies and
sketches have been studied with considerable care.[1] We cannot
tell exactly how reliable they are—though obviously they cannot all be true, since they often contradict one another. Some
critics reject them all as worthless; some accept them all except
the inconsistencies; some try to select the most probable story
and drop the rest. However, the following facts emerge clearly:

* 1. 30–31, 1. 45, 1. 77.
† F. Kafka, *In the Penal Colony*.

1. The biographies are not complete lives, of the type which was usually prefixed to the 'Collected Works' of many classical authors. They miss out many essential facts, tell us little that is clear and probable about Juvenal's personal life, and contain many wild guesses evidently put in to fill up gaps.[2] They cannot have been condensed from an earlier and fuller biography, or else they would have retained more concrete facts from it. Therefore the main outline of Juvenal's life was largely unknown to the critics who read and annotated his works two or three centuries after his death.

2. As well as being incomplete, the lives are often inconsistent and improbable, disagreeing with one another and conflicting with the facts which emerge from Juvenal's own poems. The statements in them often look like clumsy misinterpretations of passages in Juvenal's own satires, and are sometimes historically impossible.[3] Therefore the intrinsic credibility of the lives is small, and the more details they contain the less reliable they seem to be.

3. The third point is sometimes overlooked. Since no one knows who wrote these biographies it is very hard to estimate their value. But there is one guide. It is this. There are two main versions of the text of Juvenal's Satires. One is much more nearly authentic, closer to what Juvenal actually wrote, than the other—which is full of wrong-headed alterations introduced by well-meaning editors.* (It is as though we had two versions of *Hamlet,* one from the First Folio roughly in Shakespeare's words, and the other bowdlerized and miscorrected by an eighteenth-century critic.) Now, the biographies of Juvenal are all attached to or connected with the inferior text.[4] The truly valuable ancient commentaries do not carry them. Instead, they contain only brief paragraphs covering one or two points in Juvenal's life and leaving the rest in silence. Therefore the external authority of the lives is poor. They should be distrusted, just as we distrust the manuscripts which embody them.

4. The notes in the reliable scholia do not pretend to give a complete account of Juvenal's career. Instead, they contain a remarkably interesting statement about one event in his life.[5] The biographies seem to have been constructed out of this statement with the addition of much padding. Since it cannot have

* For details see p. 300.

been extracted from Juvenal's poems by mere inference, and since the information given by these scholia is generally reliable, this statement should be accepted as the main fact about Juvenal known after his death to the scholars of antiquity.[6]

The statement of the scholia is this. Juvenal, they say, attacked the régime of the emperor Domitian because actors had more power at court than honest men, and Domitian banished him to the remotest settlement in Egypt. The lines for which he was sentenced were those which now appear in the centre of his work, in Satire Seven:

> What nobles do not give, an actor gives: do you
> still court ancestral names and haunt the halls of lordlings?
> Captains and majors are appointed by the ballet.*

We are *not* told that he was banished for writing Satire Seven, which is a fairly innocuous poem; and we are not told how these lines ever got into Satire Seven, if they were not originally part of it. The commentators merely transmitted this single fact. Later the biographers elaborated it, usually by adding weak and anachronistic details.

However, it was also known to two reputable, if dim-witted, scholars of the later empire. Towards the middle of the fifth century, the bishop of Auvergne, Sidonius Apollinaris, speaks of it in a survey of classical Latin literature. After recalling the exile of Ovid, he mentions another nameless poet who

> later, in a similar disaster,
> blown by a gust from the noisy public,
> was banished by an irritated actor.[7]

This is pretty vague to be sure. It might scarcely have been connected with Juvenal at all, if it had not said that an *actor* was responsible for the *banishment* of a *poet* who lived *after Ovid*. The second line looks as though Sidonius had read somewhere that the exile was due to the powerful influence of an actor, but had interpreted 'influence' to mean general popularity rather than favour at court: he is not exact about literary history.[8] Still, we can be sure, from quotations and adaptations in his work, that

---

* Quod non dant proceres dabit histrio. tu Camerinos
   et Baream, tu nobilium magna atria curas?
   praefectos Pelopea facit, Philomela tribunos (7. 90–92).

he knew Juvenal's satires well; and this anecdote is probably derived from the notes in the edition of Juvenal which he used.*

Two or three generations after Sidonius, the popular Byzantine historian John Malalas inserted into his history a very confused paragraph about Domitian, full of evident improbabilities and errors. However, it also contains the irreducible minimum —that Domitian banished Juvenal for attacking him, and that the attack was connected with the court influence of an actor.[9]

That is all the evidence about Juvenal's banishment. He himself never speaks of it directly. This need not surprise us. Several distinguished writers in different times and countries have been turned into satirists by the impact of events so cruel, so unbearable that they never describe them and at most refer to them in general, impersonal terms.† We can be quite clear that the violence, the hatred, the terror with which Juvenal speaks of Domitian's reign make it likely that (as the scholiast says) he was banished then and escaped death with the skin of his teeth.

Can we fill out the story any more, and fit it into the other known facts of Juvenal's career? In particular, can we solve these problems: (1) who was the actor? (2) when was the sentence passed? (3) what was the nature of the offence?

1. Early in his reign the emperor Domitian had a favourite ballet dancer called Paris, who became very influential at court. But in the year 83 Domitian had him killed in the street by a squad of the imperial bodyguards on suspicion of being the empress's lover. The lines which the scholiast says caused Juvenal's banishment are part of a passage deriding the influence of Paris at the emperor's court. Juvenal has been saying that even a good poet, like Statius, can live only by selling a ballet-libretto to Paris; and then goes on:

> He freely passes out commissions in the army,
> hands poets the gold emblem showing six months' service.
> What nobles do not give, an actor gives . . .‡

and so on. The particular point of the attack, then, was that the

---

* See pp. 185–7.
† For instance, Cervantes, Rabelais, and Swift.
‡ Ille et militiae multis largitur honorem,
  semenstri digitos uatum circumligat auro.
  quod non dant proceres dabit histrio . . . (7. 88–90).

dancer Paris had far more power at court than members of the old aristocratic families, and that the best way to obtain a post or promotion in the army was to toady to him. How this affected Juvenal personally we shall see later.

2. The sentence cannot have been passed on Juvenal before 91 or 92, because Martial wrote two friendly poems to him at that time. Martial was so subservient to Domitian that during the emperor's reign he would never have expressed affection for a condemned man; and Domitian was not the kind of ruler to reverse a sentence, so that Juvenal can hardly have been exiled before that, and then recalled. In those later years the reign of terror was growing more terrible. In or about 93, several distinguished opponents of the emperor were executed.[10] We might place Juvenal's exile at that time, and see it as part of a wider purge involving many others.[11]

3. Yet how was it possible for him to be punished *after 92* for writing something about Paris, who was killed *in 83*? What was so offensive about that? This is the reef on which many reconstructions of Juvenal's life have foundered, because scholars have assumed that the attack on Paris must have been made while Paris was still alive.[12] But that assumption is unnecessary. There is an easier explanation.

Let us suppose that Juvenal, in or after 92, wrote a lampoon on someone who exercised undue influence on army promotions, some court favourite who had more power than the nobles; and that, in order to be safe, he called the man Paris. He would think this safe enough. The real Paris had been dead for years. The real Paris had been executed by the emperor's own command for becoming much too powerful at court. Surely it was possible, and might even be politic, to use the name of Paris as a symbol of corruption? Other lampoons were being written and published in Domitian's reign.* What safer subject was there than a fallen favourite?

But the lampoon cut too near the truth. Domitian was a lonely, suspicious man.† He saw what Juvenal's poem really meant—that the imperial court was corrupt, and that the army rolls were filled with useless toadies. He therefore punished Juvenal for writing a covert attack on his own régime.

* Suet. *Dom.* 8. 3, a suggestive sentence.
† See the frightening character-sketches in Dio 67. 1. 1, Pliny *Pan.* 48.

Also, Domitian was a bitter man, who brooded and har-
boured grudges. He loathed the very name of Paris. He had
executed Paris. He had divorced his wife because of Paris. He
killed a sick boy who had been one of Paris's ballet-pupils,
simply because the young dancer looked like Paris.* He even
executed people who dropped flowers on the place where Paris
had been cut down.† It would infuriate him to see ten years
later that the favourite's name and power were not forgotten,
and he would detest the man who recalled them. Even if the
name Paris was not used, even if the lampoon only said 'a
dancer', Domitian would understand that Juvenal meant to
wound him.

There are striking parallels to this in the history of the
empire, and particularly in Domitian's own reign. About sixty
years earlier the poet Phaedrus published some adaptations of
Aesop's fables. They look innocent enough; but some of them
were taken to be veiled criticisms of the powerful minister
Sejanus and of his relation to the emperor: so Phaedrus was
heavily punished.‡ In 93 or so the young Stoic nobleman
Helvidius Priscus produced a farce about Paris—not the dancer,
but the mythical Trojan prince—deserting the nymph Oenone.
Domitian took this as an allusion to his own divorce, and
executed Helvidius.§ It did not matter whether the allusion was
intentional or not. It was sufficient if it was likely to be noticed
and enjoyed by the public. In our own day we have seen
enough of the savagery and suspiciousness of absolute rulers
to realize that such punishments for such offences are not
incredible, or even unusual. The tyrant is lonely: because he
is lonely he is frightened; and because he is frightened he is
cruel.

According to this reconstruction, then, Juvenal was banished
in or after 93, long before issuing any of his satires in their present form. The charge was *lèse-majesté*, and the evidence was
a short lampoon on court corruption.[13] All his property would
be confiscated, and he would be reduced to beggary.[14] In 96
Domitian was assassinated by a palace conspiracy, and all the
exiles were recalled by his gentle old successor Nerva.‖ But
Juvenal's fortune and career were gone. Martial's last letter to

* Suet. *Dom.* 10. 1.   † Dio 67. 3.   ‡ *Phaedrus* 3, prologue 33–50.
§ Suet. *Dom.* 10. 4.   ‖ Dio 68. 1. 2.

him, like his own earliest satires, shows that in 101 he was a morose and impoverished hanger-on, living on the disguised charity of patronage, which he himself felt to be worse than the beggar's crust.*

If this reconstruction is true, it explains two of the most peculiar characteristics of his work. These are, first, the obsession of his early poems with Domitian and Domitian's court—the hatred which dies away in the later Books, but makes several passages in Book I sound like frantic shouts of revenge. And, second, his singular timidity. There is nothing in any of his predecessors to be compared with the passage in which, after announcing that he is eager to satirize the whole world of vice, and contemporary Rome in particular, he suddenly draws back, warning himself to be wary of attacking imperial favourites for fear of being burnt alive in the arena.[15] This apprehension may simply have been part of the general terror inspired by Domitian, but it can be even more easily understood if Juvenal had in fact received a sudden and severe punishment for writing satire on contemporary politics. There are therefore two linked reasons for his strange habit of anachronism. In order to attack contemporary abuses he brings in examples from past history. The reason he himself gives is that it is unsafe to point out living crooks.† But the other reason is that the age of Domitian, because of its crimes and violences, had made such an indelible impression on him that, when he thought of the empire, he thought either of Domitian's reign or of the reigns of Tiberius and Nero, its prototypes. The later emperors, Nerva, Trajan, and Hadrian, he never names.[16] Perhaps, after Domitian, he could scarcely believe in them.

One question remains. Where was he sent into exile? Ovid was banished to Tomis, which is now Constanţa in Rumania, and which was then cold, lonely, dangerous, an outpost among savages, like the Siberian villages. Seneca was sent to Corsica: hot, lonely, partly savage, remote from civilization.‡ Juvenal never speaks of his own exile. The scholia say it was in 'the Oasis, the furthest settlement in Egypt', and John Malalas says

---

* Mart. 12. 18; Juv. 5. 6–11.   † 1. 160–8.

‡ See Seneca's epigrams on Corsica, calling it *barbara, horrida, terribilis, uasta*, a living tomb.

it was in Pentapolis in North Africa.* The biographers guess
wildly.

Now, the only places of which Juvenal seems to speak from
personal knowledge are Italy, Egypt, and North Africa. All his
references to other parts of the world are vague, hearsay, or
hyperbolical.[17] But there is one entire satire about Egypt where,
quite against his usual practice, he mentions his own acquaintance with the country. The poem describes a fight between the
inhabitants of two neighbouring towns who hated each other
for following different religions. One town attacked the other
during a festival; there was a riot; a man fell, was torn to
pieces by his enemies, and was eaten raw. The story is credible
enough, and there are convincing parallels, modern as well as
ancient, to assure us that it was true.[18] But to write a long poem
on it argues a special interest in Egypt, and a special attitude
towards the country. Juvenal's tone reminds us of an old China
hand describing a riot in Shanghai, or a United States observer
telling of a barefoot revolution in Central America. Beginning
his account of the fiesta, he says:

> the sleepless banquet-couches stay there night and day
> sometimes until the seventh morning. Egypt of course
> is crude, yet (I myself observed) in luxury
> its countrymen quite equal its disgraceful cities.†[19]

That 'I myself' is quite unparalleled in Juvenal. It is corro-
borated by one or two other passages where he speaks so vividly
of Egypt and of North Africa that he seems to be drawing from
his own memory.[20] Only in 1895 was this really confirmed.

The two towns which fought each other are called Ombi and
Tentyra. Juvenal places them carefully: near enough each other
to be handy for a fight, and 'above the walls of warm Coptos'.‡
Now, as soon as modern scholars began to look for Ombi and
Tentyra, they found one in Kom-Ombo on the right bank of the
Nile and the other in Dendera on the left bank. But these two
towns were about 200 miles distant from each other, on different

---

* See n. 9 on p. 239.
† Peruigilique toro, quem nocte ac luce iacentem
   septimus interdum sol inuenit. horrida sane
   Aegyptos; sed luxuria—quantum ipse notaui—
   barbara famoso non cedit turba Canopo (15. 43–46).
‡ *Finitimos* 15. 33, *uicinorum* 36, *super calidae . . . moenia Copti* 28.

sides of the river, and only one was 'above . . . Coptos'. The inference was obvious: Juvenal did not know Egypt, was writing on a hearsay description, and had made a bad guess at the topography of the feud.[21]

However, the opposite proved to be true. In 1895 the eminent archaeologist Flinders Petrie discovered the ruins of the real Ombi, only ten miles from Dendera, on the same side of the Nile. It was a cult-centre of Set, the god of darkness, the evil principle, donkey-headed, pig-headed, the murderer of Osiris and the enemy of the sky-god Horus. Dendera was the home of Horus' consort, the goddess of love and gaiety, Hathor: she had a huge temple there—Domitian himself built two gates for it, and it survives little injured to this day. There was bound to be a constant feud between the worshippers of cruel Set and the worshippers of kindly Hathor. The British excavators actually found the remains of a wall built between the two sites, as though the men of Dendera had been trying to keep off the attacks of their fierce neighbours. This helped to confirm Juvenal's description, and to make it even more likely that (as he said) he had visited Egypt personally.[22]

That Juvenal despised and detested the Egyptians there is no possible doubt whatever. The first bad man he names, at the beginning of his first poem, is the Egyptian Crispinus who became commander of the imperial guards. There and elsewhere part of Juvenal's hatred of him is that instead of being a Roman he is a filthy Egyptian.* Soon afterwards, following a patron to the Forum, Juvenal is outraged to see that *another* Egyptian officer has dared to have a triumphal statue of himself set up among the statues of Roman generals: he suggests it ought to be used as an open-air lavatory.[23] Nearly all foreigners he disliked; but he loathed Egyptians. Yet he had lived in Egypt, and knew not only the big cities but (on his own testimony) the life and customs of the countryside.† Remembering his bitter, resentful character, we shall not find it hard to infer that he knew Egypt so well and at the same time disliked it so violently because (as the scholiast says) he had been banished to Egypt by the emperor Domitian—perhaps even by the Egyptian colonel of the guards, the scented and arrogant Crispinus.[24]

Is it possible to go farther and discover to which part of the

* Juv. 1. 26 and 4. 23–33.   † 15. 44–46, and see p. 28.

country he was sent? Perhaps it is. We can be certain that it was
not to one of the cities. The emperors did not send their enemies
to such enjoyable places, but to remote spots where they would
be (a) out of touch with their friends except by letter, (b) so
isolated as to have no opportunity to make propaganda, (c)
easily kept under surveillance, and (d) extremely uncomfort-
able. Ovid in his Gothic 'Siberia', Seneca among the burning
crags of Corsica we know. But Augustus himself sent his own
bad daughter Julia to a Devil's Island in the Mediterranean
where she could receive no visitors, see virtually no one but her
guards, and have no comforts.* Compared with that, her accomplice Ovid got off easily. For less important exiles the
easiest way of maintaining security was to send the prisoner to
a garrison post where the commander could be made responsible
for him. We should therefore expect Juvenal to be ordered to
one of the distant frontier villages of Egypt where an outpost
was always maintained.

Several of the ancient accounts agree with this. They even
name various remote spots; but they differ with one another.
For instance, John Malalas says Juvenal was assigned to Pentapolis in Libya—but that was part of the province of Crete and
Cyrenaica until Diocletian rearranged the provinces.[25] The
good scholia say he was transported to 'the Oasis':† they mean
the Great Oasis, Waha el-Khârga. Exile there was indeed a
heavy punishment, which we know was legalized under the
later emperors.[26] When the philosopher Hero returned after
serving a four-year term there, Gregory Nazianzen said he was
like Lazarus recalled from the tomb‡—and we remember that
Dostoievski described his own Siberian exile in the same terms,
as *The House of the Dead*. The third possibility is the Roman
frontier post in the extreme south, Syene, which is now Aswân,
the site of the mighty Nile dam. There were three cohorts
stationed in Syene: at one time a friend of Martial's was the
commanding officer.[27] Between these three places there is
hardly any way of choosing. The Great Oasis lies out in the
desert opposite Ombi and Tentyra: to reach it or return from
it Juvenal would have had to pass through the very region

* Suet. *D. Aug.* 65. 3; Tac. *Ann.* 1. 53; Dio 55. 10. 14.
† Schol. ad 1. 1, 4. 37.
‡ Gregory, *Or.* 25. 14. 62–67 (*PG* 35. 1217).

where the fight described in his Fifteenth Satire occurred. Again, Juvenal once says that in Meroe, the Ethiopian island far up the Nile, the women have breasts bigger than their fat babies. It is a vivid detail, which looks as though it came from personal observation; and it is not mentioned by anyone else, so that it is not simply a geographical cliché.[28] If he had been deported to the sub-equatorial frontier post of Syene, he would have seen many of the Ethiopian negroes from the south, coming in with the ivory trade. It is impossible to be definite. That he was exiled to Egypt we may feel sure; probably to a frontier post, and possibly to Syene with its garrison rather than to the Oasis.

But wherever he went, it was certainly to an endless term of loneliness, surveillance, silence, hardship, and poverty. The emperor might have lived on for many years, as deaf to appeals for mercy as was Augustus to Ovid's plaintive flatteries. The emperor's successor might have kept Juvenal in exile, as Augustus' successor kept Ovid in exile. In some hut on the edge of civilization Juvenal might have rotted away like Dreyfus in Devil's Island, forbidden to write or publish, dying of loneliness, disappointment, and 'barbed-wire fever'. Dostoievski —to whom we have already compared him—was sent into exile also, and lived for years in Siberia. But before that he was actually sentenced to death. He was driven to the execution ground with many other condemned men. He was lined up beside a scaffold and a row of coffins. He was stripped to his shirt, or shroud. He heard the death sentence on himself and on all the others read out. He heard his funeral sermon preached and he was offered the cross to kiss. Then, when he thought he had only five minutes more to live, an officer galloped up with a reprieve. So must Juvenal have felt when, three or four years after his banishment, the emperor was assassinated, and from barren rocks and lonely villages the exiles began to return— still dazed and incredulous, and, like the prisoners released from concentration camps, unable for years to speak directly of their sufferings.

IV

YOUTH

THERE is one further piece of evidence which may help us in reconstructing Juvenal's singular career.

During the eighteenth century several antiquarians read and copied two inscriptions on broken marble tablets in or near the church of St. Peter near Aquino. They are gone now—apparently stolen by 'modern barbarians'. When Henzen inquired about the more important one in 1846, it was missing; and in 1876 Mommsen was told by the mayor that it was still lost.*

However, the copies remained. Mommsen reconstructed them and published them in his great collection of Latin inscriptions.† Here is his restoration of the more important inscription (the italic letters are those which were missing and were filled in by conjecture):

*Cere*RI SACRVM	THIS OFFERING TO *Cere*S
D. *Iu*NIVS IVVENALIS	D. *Ju*NIUS JUVENALIS
trib. COH *i* DELMATARVM	*captain* OF THE *first* DALMATIAN BATTN.
II VIR QVINQ FLAMEN	MAYOR IN THE CENSUS YEAR, PRIEST
DIVI VESPASIANI	OF THE DEIFIED VESPASIAN
VOVIT DEDICA*vitq*VE	VOWED AND DEDICA*ted*
SVA PEC	AT HIS OWN EXPENSE.

The other inscription, which was apparently attached to the first, contained a vote of thanks from the people of Aquinum to 'their benefactor' and recorded their resolve to set up a bronze tablet perpetuating it, together with a statue 'as a lasting memorial' of their friend.[1] Evidently this Juvenal, whoever he was, had given something to the goddess Ceres which also benefited the people of the town: a new shrine, or a new temple.

There was heavy fighting in and near Aquino in 1944—it is only a few miles from Monte Cassino—and the chances of finding either of the stones again are very slim. But we can infer a good deal from the copies.

To begin with, they were probably not forgeries. A forger

---

* See Mommsen in *CIL* 10, p. 531.   † *CIL* 10. 5382 and 10. 5426.

would have taken some trouble to make the stones say clearly
that they had been put up by *the* Juvenal, since only that would
give them value in money or prestige. But it is not at all clear
that Juvenal the poet is the man referred to—in one inscription
the name is incomplete, and in the other there is no name at all
—and several scholars have declared that he had no connexion
with them. No one knows. All that we can do is to show, *if*
he was the man of the inscriptions, how they fit in with the
other details of his life. Let us look over them.

The first inscription was evidently part of a dedication. The
Juvenal who set it up had vowed, if Ceres granted a prayer of
his, to give her a new altar, shrine, or temple. He got his wish,
and made his dedication 'at his own expense', which shows
that he was fairly well-off. Small offerings were not announced
in such terms.

It was associated with the temple of Ceres Helvina, now the
church of St. Peter near Roccasecca. Ceres was the goddess
of fertility and marriage, order and virtue, and prosperity: her
surname means that she was especially worshipped by the
family of the Helvii or Elvii, whose tombstones are found here
and there near Aquino.* Now here is the first link with the poet
Juvenal, and it is a close one. In his Third Satire, he says good-
bye to a friend who is leaving Rome and going to live in a little
seaside town. The friend, Umbricius, means never to return to
the wicked and cruel capital, but he does not wish to break off
his friendship with Juvenal; and so he says:

> Good-bye, remember me: whenever Rome
> returns you, eager for rest and peace, to your Aquinum,
> invite me over to Helvine Ceres and your Diana
> from Cumae.†

The shrines of Helvine Ceres and Diana were the two main
temples in the town. Juvenal makes his friend mention them to
show that Aquinum really was Juvenal's home, which he knew
well and could characterize by its main features. Also, if we
look all through his satires, we shall find that, although he is

---

* *CIL* 10. 5477 and 5585.

†   Ergo uale, nostri memor; et quotiens te
Roma tuo refici properantem reddet Aquino,
me quoque ad Heluinam Cererem uestramque Dianam
conuerte a Cumis (3. 318–21).

generally pretty off-hand about the gods, making fun of the
sexual adventures of Jupiter and the helplessness of Mars, he
does believe that Ceres stands for the important virtues whose
loss he laments: chastity, and a disinterested love of mankind,
and truth.[2] If Juvenal had been a gentle, pious, rather milk-
toast character like Pliny, or a complete cynic like Martial, his
mention of the goddess would mean much less. But he has ideals,
and Ceres is the only goddess he chooses to represent some of
them. Now it was to Ceres that someone called Juvenal, in
Juvenal's own home and in the temple known to Juvenal personally, once vowed and dedicated an offering.

The second line of the same inscription gave the name of the
man who worshipped Ceres in this way. We cannot tell whether
it was our Juvenal. Although some of our manuscripts say that
the poet's first name was Decimus and his other names are
known to be Junius Juvenalis, we cannot match these names
exactly with the stone: for it is broken, and does not show the
donor's first name. But, since the last two names coincide,
we do know that the stone was put up either by Juvenal the poet
or by some close relative.[3]

The third line tells us that the donor of the stone was once
the commanding officer of an auxiliary unit in the Roman
army. We do not know his precise rank or the number of his
unit, because of imperfections in the stone; but we see that his
men were 'Dalmatians', tough fighters from the north-west of
the Balkan peninsula, where the Jugoslavs now live.[4] Still, the
mere fact that he held such a post tells us much more about
him. These auxiliary commands were a preliminary stage of the
'knight's' career, the regular pattern of upper-middle-class service by which a man with some money could, without entering
politics, make his way up through army appointments and
governorships and administrative jobs until, with luck, he
might become one of the most powerful officials in the empire.*
At the very top were posts such as the vice-imperial governorship of Egypt and the colonelcy of the household troops. At the
beginning of the career were these auxiliary commands, where
the aspirant could gain experience. We know, from the pattern
followed by other officials and recorded on their tombstones

* Details in O. Hirschfeld, *Römische Verwaltungsgeschichte* (Berlin, 1877),
247-50; and see the whole chapter, 'Die procuratorische Carrière'.

and dedications, that the commanders of auxiliary units were either young men at the beginning of their official careers, or middle-aged men at the end of their regular army service. Sometimes a senior centurion who had risen to the top non-commissioned rank in his regiment (*primus pilus*) was admitted to the order of knighthood and given one of these commissions, to close his career most honorably after twenty or thirty years of service. But if the man of the Aquinum inscription had been a veteran, he would most certainly have recorded his previous service on the stone, as others did. More often the aspirant was a young man of free birth who had £4,000 capital, and had been granted the rank of knight.[5] (All the officers in this governmental branch of the imperial administration were knights, members of the class which in the early days of the Roman army had been able to meet the expense of serving as mounted troops. Their service was therefore still called the 'equestrian' or 'knightly' career.)[6]

There were two other possibilities. Sometimes the officer might be a youth of good family trying to get on to the equestrian ladder of promotion by serving as a centurion and then going on to this auxiliary post; or he might have been a commoner elevated to knighthood by the special gift of a knight's gold ring or a certificate equivalent to six months' army service from the emperor or one of his advisers. But in either of these cases it is again most likely that he would have signalized, in the inscription, the privilege he had been granted.

Therefore the Juvenal who made the vow to Ceres was a young knight with an independent income, at the beginning of his career, in the emperor's branch of the administration of the Roman empire.

The next line of the inscription calls him *duouir quinquennalis*. The *duouiri* were the two men who headed the local government board of a town of Roman citizens (a *colonia*). They were roughly equivalent to joint mayors and sheriffs. To be on the board (as a town councillor, a *decurio*) one had to possess some capital, £1,000 or so. To head it, as one of the *duouiri*, was an honour. The extra title *quinquennalis* signified a special honour, for it meant that one had been chosen to hold the rank in the year when the five-year census was taken and more responsibility was laid upon the two mayors. From other inscriptions we know also that such a man was usually 25 years old, or else had served several campaigns in the army with commissioned rank.[7] Therefore the Juvenal of the inscription was rich (by the standards of his town) and was by this time one of the most prominent persons in Aquinum.

The inscription goes on to say that he was priest of the deified emperor Vespasian. It was in A.D. 79 that Vespasian was taken ill and said, 'Oh dear, I think I'm becoming a god'; but he did not formally become one until some time between February and mid-June of 80.* Men in charge of the worship of the deified emperors in the townships like Aquinum were prominent and responsible local personalities: they had to be municipal magistrates, ex-officers, or knights.† This man was a municipal magistrate, had been an officer, and must have been a knight. It is tempting to suggest that he could only have been granted this particular dignity between 80 and 81—because Vespasian's son Titus died and was deified in 81, and if the municipality had wished to honour this Juvenal later, it would surely have made him priest of the newest imperial divinity, of Titus and not Vespasian.[8]

Now let us sum up the picture which the inscription gives us. It was put up by someone called Juvenal, in the poet's own home, to a goddess whom the poet knew and revered. The man who put it up was rich and prominent in local affairs. He was either an old soldier, or (much more probably) a well-off young man starting his career in army and government service as a knight.

But, when we first meet the poet Juvenal, he is old, poor, and bitterly disappointed. He has no hope for the future and never mentions his career as a young man. How is it possible that this elderly sponger, trudging about from one rich man's house to another hoping for a meal, could ever have been the comfortable young officer who was honorary mayor of Aquinum? Many scholars have felt that these two figures were utterly irreconcilable. They have concluded, therefore, that the inscription was put up by some relative of the poet, and that it tells us nothing of the poet's own career.[9]

* Suet. *D. Vesp.* 23. 4; A. Chambalu, 'Flaviana 4', *Phil* 1 (1889), 571.
† See De Chaufepié (*11*) 69–72.

Yet we have one more fact about Juvenal, which makes it not only possible but likely that the two men are identical. We know that he was banished and reduced to poverty. *When* this disaster fell upon him, no one can be sure; but we have suggested (in the reconstruction on pages 24–27) that it happened *before* he began publishing his satires, between A.D. 92 and 96. Now, suppose that he was the man who put up the stone and made the dedication in Aquinum, in A.D. 80 or so. If so, he was then young, rich, and ambitious, with the chance of a great career before him. Ten or fifteen years later his career was blighted and his wealth confiscated. When he emerged from banishment he was the gloomy rancorous middle-aged man we know from the satires.

Chronologically, this is perfectly easy. Can it be supported by anything in Juvenal's poems?

If we look more closely at the early satires, we shall see that it can. They are dominated by two emotions—fear, which we have already discussed, and disappointment. The disappointment appears as a profound and bitter sense of social injustice. Yet it is not the purest hatred of injustice as such. Juvenal is not really sorry for the very poor, or for the working class.[10] He is sorry for middle-class men like himself who cannot get advancement. And he has a particular grievance about unworthy men who get ahead in the equestrian career. The man he hates most, next to the emperor Domitian, is the Egyptian Crispinus, who rose from being a fish-peddler to hold one of the two top posts open to knights, the command of the imperial guard.* At the very beginning of his survey of vicious and corrupt Rome, he describes Crispinus waving a fat hand in the air to cool it, and also to show off his gold ring, the essential symbol of knightly rank.† Later in the same poem he sneers at the Egyptian Jew who got the other equestrian plum, the governorship of Egypt.‡ The magic figure of £4,000, the capital sum which was necessary for knighthood, is mentioned enviously several times.[11] And once there is an attack on the law excluding ordinary citizens from the knights' seats at the theatre—an attack which looks out of place, as though it were dictated by a personal grudge. Juvenal has been saying (through the mouth of his friend

* *Princeps equitum*, 4. 32.   † 1. 26–29.
‡ 1. 129–31; see p. 29.

Umbricius) that honest men in Rome can barely get enough to eat, and have to wear torn clothes and battered shoes. Then suddenly he adds 'And another thing!—we are kept out of the knights' seats, though the sons of rich pimps and prize-fighters can sit there!' A really poor man, struggling to keep body and soul together, would not think he had any right to enter those special seats. The complaint makes sense only if it comes from one who had once been a knight, and through some injustice had lost his money and his rank.[12]

Another theme, closely related to this, is the unworthiness and ineffectiveness of the Roman nobility. Juvenal loathes and despises the representatives of the great families for being selfish, vicious, irresponsible, and weak. Again and again he repeats his charges in different forms: the nobles will not patronize literature, they grudge a meal to their dependants, they will not even pay their children's tutors, they will not help the deserving, they will not resist tyranny.* He stands well away from them. He is not a noble, and does not pretend to be. He calls the nobles 'sons of Troy', laughs at their follies, and rages at their vices.† One of the few men he admires is Cicero, who put down the noble traitors: *municipalis eques*, the knight from the country-town.‡

Suppose, then, that Juvenal himself was the man who set up the inscription, a young knight from a country-town. Suppose that he had entered the army, and hoped for promotion in the equestrian career. How could he get it? Only by very exceptional merit and good luck—or else by the recommendation of someone so noble or so powerful at court that he wielded great influence. Such recommendations were called *suffragia*: certain inscriptions actually mention them in describing a successful career, and there are many cases of their being given or even sold.[13] Without them it must have been difficult, if not impossible, to obtain promotion. Now imagine that Juvenal had vainly tried to secure such recommendations.[14] Would he not gradually become more and more bitter, as he saw good posts going to wastrels and upstarts? He would haunt the vestibules of all the noblemen to whom he could get an introduction, and he would find the nobles deaf, and gradually decide that they were

* 7. 1–97; 1. 132–46; 7. 150–214; 4. 150–4; and see all Sat. 8.
† 1. 100 and 8. 181.   ‡ 8. 238.

all worthless. He would loiter about the imperial court itself.
Satire Four, which takes place in Domitian's court at Alba in the
early 80's, and describes the gathering of the imperial Cabinet
as seen by a spectator just outside the inner sanctum, looks as
though it was conceived while Juvenal waited for the interview
which was never given, the appointment which never came.

Now let us recall the story of his banishment. The ancient
tradition is that he was sent into exile for writing a short lampoon about unfair influence on promotions in the army. The
actual lines are preserved: they say that it is useless to expect
promotions from the favour of the Roman nobility, but that a
ballet-dancer with influence at court will get you advancement
in the knight's career.* If Juvenal was the rich young officer
of the inscription, his failure to obtain promotion and his resentment at the injustice which was delaying him in his career
and wasting his life would be an amply sufficient motive for
him to write such a lampoon. And the lampoon, if circulated
under Domitian, would be a more than adequate pretext for the
emperor to condemn him to degradation, beggary, and exile.

* 7. 88–92; see the discussion on pp. 23–27.

V
RECONSTRUCTION

Here then is the complete story, as far as we have been able to piece it together. Juvenal was born of a well-to-do family in the small Italian town of Aquinum, about A.D. 60. After leaving school he joined the army, in order to make his career in the imperial service. He was well-off, and as a compliment his townsfolk elected him honorary mayor and priest of the deified emperor. After completing his preliminary military service, he failed to obtain a new appointment. He passed some time at the court, hoping to be noticed, and he tried to persuade the Roman nobles to recommend him for a post. But years passed, and he was ignored.

When he watched the unworthy methods by which such posts as he hoped for were actually distributed, and when he saw foreigners rising to the very heights of power in the empire, he grew bitter and lost hope. To fill in his time, he interested himself in literature. He became a friend of Martial, who was himself a knight by grace of the emperor; but he published nothing substantial. However, after his chances of advancement had finally gone, probably in 92 or 93, he made up a little lampoon on the fact that military commissions were handed out by the influence of unworthy court favourites such as actors. Perhaps he used the name of Paris, thinking it would be safe because Paris had been killed ten years before. But Domitian was offended, confiscated all his property, and exiled him to Egypt.

He returned after the emperor's death in 96, and led the life of an impoverished ex-gentleman for some time. But his sense of injustice and his still burning hatred of Domitian combined with the stimulus he had received from Martial to make him attempt satire. In the poems he first recited he drew partly on his memories of Domitian's era, partly on his new experiences of poverty and insult. After he had been reciting and publishing for ten or fifteen years, he was saved from poverty by a gift from the emperor Hadrian or from a patron of the arts, which once more made him independent. The tone of his satires grew gentler as he grew older—although he still remained a pessimist, and could be stirred to fury by a report of an atrocity in the hateful land of Egypt. He published his last Book in or near 130, and died soon afterwards.

This reconstruction is a hypothesis. It explains all the established facts, but new facts might well be discovered which would overthrow it. Also, there are peculiar silences and shadows over Juvenal's life. He never speaks of his career, nor does his friend Martial. The ancient authorities are confused and uncertain about it. The inscription may not have been set up by the poet, but by a happier and more successful kinsman.

Yet it is possible to combine all the available data into a consistent picture of a tormented life, and by doing so to find a convincing explanation of that peculiar personality, harsh and cruel yet timid and evasive, indignant about the past, withdrawn from the present, despairing of the future, lonely and defeated, furious at first and gradually growing resigned in pessimism, brilliant and cultured but poor and embittered, whose fierce denunciations and harsh broken laughter we can hear from every page of Juvenal's satires.

PART TWO

The Satires of
Juvenal

VI

INTRODUCTION TO THE SATIRES

Juvenal's life-work consists of sixteen poems. They are arranged in five books, which were no doubt published separately, at intervals of several years. Altogether, they contain something under 4,000 lines of poetry. There are a few bogus lines, interpolated after his death; there are gaps now and then where some genuine lines and even whole passages have dropped out; and the last satire is mostly lost. But the total cannot have come to much more than 4,000 lines in all.[1] It does not seem much, for the work of thirty years. Yet it contains the experience of a lifetime. It reflects a great part of the Roman world.

Does it reflect that world truly? Does it distort the reflection? Can we look at it and say we are seeing the truth? And, whether true or distorted, are the poems good? Are they worth reading and remembering, not only as documents but as works of art? In order to find out, let us look at them separately, and then try to measure their art and their truth.

All but one of the sixteen poems are monologues. One alone, the ninth, is a dialogue. There are occasional interludes of conversation in the others, and we often hear Juvenal arguing with more or less imaginary opponents, cross-questioning them, confuting them, advising and persuading them, and at least once consoling them. But the pattern of fifteen out of the sixteen satires is the monologue. Juvenal speaks to us. Even when he is ostensibly addressing a rich young nobleman or a fellow dependant, even when (as in the third poem) he puts his own hatred of Rome into the mouth of a disappointed friend, it is always his voice that we hear. Several times in the First Book, he breaks out into passionate speech to the general public, without caring who hears him. He shouts:

> Oh, to escape beyond the Eskimos and the frozen ocean!*

---

* Vltra Sauromatas fugere hinc libet et glacialem Oceanum . . . (2. 1–2).

or, like a showman with a travelling monster, he cries:

> Here is Crispinus again! and I shall often recall him.*

But later he gives up these dramatic openings. His monologue becomes an address to a friend, or sometimes a soliloquy which we are allowed to overhear.

A monologue without a purpose is tiresome. Juvenal's monologues are not purposeless. He means to show us something, or to persuade us of something. Therefore three of his satires are narratives, in which he tells a startling story, and two are descriptions, in which he paints a vivid picture. The other eleven are arguments, in which Juvenal sets out to prove a point, laying it down clearly in the first few lines and then hammering it home with argument after argument to prove it. Of course there are fine descriptions and brilliant narratives and snatches of dialogue here and there in the eleven argumentative satires, but they have no central story and no unbroken chain of description: they are held together by the continuous thrust of Juvenal's persuasion and denunciation.

The poems, as we have seen, are arranged in five books. No doubt they were composed separately, and 'privately published' separately by being read at recitals or circulated in manuscript. And we need not expect all the poems in one book to have been composed consecutively, or completed at the same time. Careful, meditative workers like Juvenal usually write slowly, brooding over their poems for months or years. But we can be fairly sure that the five books were published, as five units, at separate intervals; and that they marked five different stages in his career as a poet. After 1,800 years it is difficult to get the proper perspective. Sometimes critics make the mistake of thinking that all sixteen poems were conceived and published *en bloc*, as the 'Complete Works of Juvenal', so to speak; and they conclude that there ought to be no important variations in manner or matter between the individual satires. Others seem to think of the poems as sixteen quite independent entities —without reflecting that when Juvenal published a book of them he designed it as a group, knowing what was in it and what collective effect it would produce. But no one would try

---

* Ecce iterum Crispinus! et est mihi saepe uocandus
  ad partes . . . (4. 1–2).

to discuss Beethoven's music without distinguishing the nine symphonies from one another, or to write on Shakespeare by mixing up the early comedies with the late tragicomedies; and so, on a lower level, it is not possible to estimate Juvenal's work without treating the five books of satires as different but equally interesting expressions of his talent.

VII

SATIRE ONE
The Satirist Announces Himself

BOOK I, a far louder, broader, and more vehement protest than anything we know of in previous Latin satire, is made up of five poems. Its general subject is the decay of the Roman upper class. But this decay is seen from several different points—from above, below, and within—and explained by several different though convergent reasons. The total picture is of a society whose leaders are—physically, mentally, and morally—dying off, being killed or committing suicide.

Satire One, which is an uninterrupted shout of fury from the beginning until almost the end, is Juvenal's introduction to the Book and to his own work as a satirist.[1] It falls into four parts, which form a single logical and emotional development.[2] But before we look at it more closely, we should note that here, as in many of his poems, Juvenal spoils his structure by highlighting his details. This is both a merit and a defect. It means that he gives us a series of brilliantly vivid pictures, perfectly realistic even when we feel they are so hideous as to be barely possible; but also that his attention is so fixed on the separate pictures that he tends to neglect, or at least to obscure, the central structure of his poems. His critics have often been very severe on him for this. Yet it was in the tradition of Roman satire, which affected spontaneity and (as we can see from the satires of Horace) eschewed the artificiality of logic; and there is no doubt that it helps Juvenal to sound sincere, even when he is hard to follow. He sounds like an angry man pouring out his just grievances, and not like a moral essayist who has subheaded and paragraphed his subject by (a), (b), and (c), and is wondering what to say next.

Juvenal begins with a half-humorous cry of protest against literature. Too much is being written, he groans, everybody is a Bard, the air rings with poetry:

> For ever must I be only a listener? never reply?*

* Semper ego auditor tantum? numquamne reponam? (1. 1).

In his place we should talk of hundreds and thousands of books loading the booksellers' shelves. He speaks of something rather worse—of recitals by aspiring poets, hoarse with declaiming their own epics, reading on and on until the very pillars of the recital hall writhe and split with boredom. All you need to write, he says, is a high-school education. I had that. Why shouldn't I write too?

It seems an odd way to begin one's career as a poet, by abusing poetry and complaining that too much is being written anyhow. But this first page contains a fundamental distinction which runs all through Juvenal's work and which we today would heartily approve. Most literature, he says, is superfluous, because it has nothing to do with real life. Most poetry is merely long-winded reconstruction of Greek myths, of stories which were often pretty silly in themselves and have now been so hackneyed that they are revolting. The two most ambitious types are epic and tragedy—both unrealistic, both inordinately long-winded, both packed with conventions, the Family Crime, the Terrible Storm, the Battle of Heroes. The minor genres like love-elegy and comedy are less ambitious but equally bogus. But Juvenal himself holds that the only kind of literature which has any genuine reason for being written—now, in his own day— is satire. Satire deals with real life, and real contemporary life is so horrible and so absorbing that other subjects are worthless.

In later poems Juvenal recurs to this distinction. Once, before describing the Grand Council held by the emperor Domitian, he calls on the Muse of History to utter—and then qualifies it:

> Calliope, commence! You can sit down, you needn't
> sing: this is just the truth.*

Several times when describing a disaster which really happened in his own lifetime, he adds that it was as dreadful as the tremendous climaxes of epic poetry, but real as well. And there is a key passage at the end of his most ambitious satire, the Sixth, in which he speaks of mothers murdering their own sons for money, and then stops to say:

> This is all fiction, satire wears the tragic mask,
> no doubt, and leaving the tradition of our elders

---

* Incipe, Calliope. licet et considere: non est cantandum; res uera agitur (4. 34–35).

we are now raving out the widemouthed songs of Athens?
I wish it were all false! But the murderess shouts 'Yes!
I did it, I confess, I made poison for my children . . .'*

He goes on to say that women as bad as the fiendish villainesses
of tragedy meet you every day, you can find a Clytemnestra in
every street.† Taken together with his other treatments of the
theme, this passage shows that Juvenal did not only claim that
satire was more true than epic and tragedy. He was prepared
also to avow that its truth made it quite as valuable a form of
literature. Of course, it could not equal the mighty masterpieces of the past; but in Juvenal's own day, he maintained,
satire was at least as much worth writing as tragedies and epics.[3]
He raised it, then, from a second-rate literary form to the first
rank, and as Wordsworth said of Milton's transfiguration of
the sonnet:‡

in his hands
The thing became a trumpet.

However, in this his first satire Juvenal makes no such bold
claims. He begins with ironic modesty by saying 'Everybody
writes poetry. Why shouldn't I?' Then (after catching his
audience's attention and tickling their humour) he goes on to
explain the most important question, why he should write
satire.

He draws a deep breath. And then, in one continuous speech of
over fifty lines, he describes the world, he describes his world
of Rome as he sees it, from the point of view of the intelligent
man in the street who is jostled by the attendants of millionaire
criminals, who has to step aside while a successful forger is
carried past lolling among cushions, who can stand at every
busy street-corner and count the crooks, the perverts, and
the murderers who have risen to wealth while he is still poor,
who cannot open his eyes without seeing burning injustice and
who cannot sleep for thinking of the boiling corruption of his

* Fingimus haec, altum satura sumente coturnum,
   scilicet, et finem egressi legemque priorum
   grande Sophocleo carmen bacchamur hiatu. . .
   nos utinam uani! sed clamat Pontia 'Feci,
   confiteor, puerisque meis aconita paraui . . .' (6. 634–6, 638–9).
† 6. 655–6.
‡ Wordsworth, *Miscellaneous Sonnets*, 2. 1.

city, Rome the capital of the world. Material? There is more than enough, wherever you look there is Vice triumphant. And the need to write? It is not only the wish to retaliate on other poets, to read rather than listen. Juvenal says it is impossible, when you look at the world, *not* to write satire:

If nature cannot, indignation will make verses.*

It is a splendid tirade. In two pages it puts us in the streets of the rich, busy, corrupt city, energetic, ruthless, cruel, the stony-hearted stepmother. Juvenal does not make us watch it from a distance. He places us in the crowded thoroughfare where we are shoved to the wall by the dependants of a crooked politician, where we the ordinary public are ignored and dominated by barbers, gigolos, and poisoners; and the thick closely packed sentences, filled with drastic and shocking words, themselves carry us along as though we were being pushed and buffeted by the crowds of Rome. Scholars have made several attempts to discover, in this fine passage, a symmetrical arrangement, some classification of the injustices to which Juvenal chiefly objects.[4] But that is impossible, and the attempt is doomed to failure. The satirist is not showing us a procession, but plunging us into a mob. Every new figure he sees rouses him to fresh fury, for every new figure typifies a different kind of outrage on normal feeling. The first group he shows us contains (a) a soft eunuch who is marrying a wife— some ex-slave from the east who has gained his freedom and made a fortune and now wishes to pose as a complete man;[5] (b) a lady who has become so expert at big-game-hunting that she appears in public, in the arena, to fight a wild boar on foot with short spears—and wears the theatrical costume of a bare-breasted Amazon huntress;[6] (c) a hairdresser who clipped Juvenal's beard when Juvenal was younger (and richer) and has now become as wealthy as any Roman noble;[7] and (d) the revolting Crispinus, colonel of the emperor's life-guards, negligently wearing the rich crimson military cloak and waving a sweaty hand on which he displays a special light summer-weight gold ring— thus showing both that he is a knight, and that he is delicately bred.[8] Two of these are perversions of sex and two are corruptions of wealth and rank; but the eunuch and the lady are also

* Si natura negat, facit indignatio uersum (1. 79).

examples of the misuse and maldistribution of money. They are followed by a *nouveau-riche* lawyer who has puffed and bluffed his way to success, and by an agent of the emperor's secret service. By the end of the speech we have seen well over a dozen figures passing, with others behind them in perspective, and so variously vicious that it would be a falsification of art and truth to try to fit them into one system. Some are criminals. Some are sexually abnormal. Some are men who were once poor (because of low birth or extravagance) and are now rich. Nor is there any particular social interpretation to be drawn from the description. Juvenal does not say that the poor are exploited by the governing class or that the middle class is being crushed out of existence. He does not say that 'the system' should be changed to put a different social class on top. He merely says that the whole thing is wrong, wrong, wrong.

The proof of his superior art is that he convinces his readers. If we analyse his complaints we soon see that his chief objection to these people is that they are rich while he is not. True, he would not commit their crimes for all their wealth.* But we feel that he would not be nearly so indignant about them if he were not poor. Since he is poor—or has been impoverished†—he cannot stop thinking about money; the final source of his gnawing and sleepless indignation is the formula:

wealth = crime, or vice, or corruption.

Yet although his motives are not the highest, although his perception has been sharpened and possibly distorted by poverty, although he may not be telling the whole truth, it is impossible to read this passage without feeling that he is telling at least part, and an important part, of the truth.

The poem is half over now, and Juvenal, who began by telling us that he might as well write poetry, has explained, in accents of unchallengeable energy and conviction, why he must write satire. Next he tells us what satire is, and how he will interpret it. The name *satura* simply means 'medley'. When the Romans first worked out the possibilities of satire as a literary form, it was simply varied, personal, and improvisatory. It was Lucilius, Juvenal's model,‡ who first gave it its function of social criticism

---

* 3. 41–57.   † See pp. 37–38.   ‡ 1. 19–20, 153–4.

which it has never since lost.⁹ Juvenal is aware both of the original meaning and of the new function of satire. Therefore, having announced that he must write satire, he now defines it. From earliest times, he says, from the beginnings of history at the great Flood:

> Whatever mankind does, their hope, fear, rage, and pleasure,
> their business and their sport, are the hotch-potch of my book.
> And when was there a richer crop of vices?*¹⁰

By mentioning the Flood (although he does it with a joke) Juvenal means that he is taking not only the present but the past into his range as a satirist. This was another of his important innovations. He was the first satirist to blend the past with the present, to see the crimes and follies of the past as though they were still contemporary. Sometimes it takes an effort for a modern reader to realize, in the midst of a description of the overthrow of Sejanus or the debaucheries of the empress Messalina, that Juvenal is describing, with amazing vividness and a genuine sense of outrage, something which happened before he was born. It was this sense of history that made him, not merely the scourge of a single emperor, but the satirist of all Rome.

All human life, then, is the subject of satire, from the remotest past to this moment. The field is as broad as the world and as long as time. But Juvenal immediately narrows it, by asking:

> when was there a richer crop of *vices*?

It is vice that chiefly interests the satirist—although he looks at it against the spacious background of the rest of life. Or, to put it another way, he portrays the whole of life exactly as it is, without idealization or concealment, in order to punish vice by displaying its horrors. To pillory vice will help to destroy its power. It is a difficult transition, this, and the passage has been much discussed by critics;¹¹ but it was probably easier for a Roman audience who had the definition and aims of satire more clearly present to their minds.

Juvenal has already dealt with an assortment of vicious and

---

* Quidquid agunt homines—uotum, timor, ira, uoluptas,
 gaudia, discursus—nostri farrago libelli est.
 et quando uberior uitiorum copia? (1. 85–87).

criminal characters. He therefore narrows the field still further. He points to the two most violent vices of Rome. In modern times we are always surprised to hear their names; perhaps we even feel embarrassed when the Roman moralists denounce them; we expect the Romans to be scolded for cruelty or for debauchery, for the blood in the arena and the rose-lipped girls. But their critics all say, and Juvenal agrees with them, that their besetting sin was Money. It had two sides, greed and extravagance. Either is bad enough, but taken alone it is not so grave; greed alone is a kind of perverted thrift, while extravagance finally disappears like water spilt in the sand. But to be greedy and extravagant, to wring millions out of a subject world and throw millions away on useless and senseless luxury, that is to climb an endless spiral away from ordinary life into the madness of unlimited desire. Nowadays we have people who make themselves mad with drugs, or drink themselves into asylums. In the Middle Ages there were many men who lusted for cruelty. The Romans were masters of the whole western world, and they went mad about money: getting and spending, they laid waste their powers.

So the particular vices which thrust themselves upon the Roman satirist were greed and extravagance.[12] These, says Juvenal, are my special subject, for they have now reached a height unequalled in all history. He devotes the third section of his poem to money and its misuses:

> since among us the holiest divinity
> is Wealth, although there is no temple yet for deadly
> Money, we have not yet put up a shrine to Cash.*

What angers him most is the maldistribution and misuse of money in the patron-dependant relation. Patrons are rich. Their dependants are poor. But patrons will not share their wealth with those whom they call their dependants; they dine in luxury, alone. And needy dependants are elbowed aside by nobles, by great ministers of state, by parvenu ex-slaves from the East pushing ahead of everyone, all eager (says Juvenal) to collect the silver shilling which is handed to them in lieu of a

---

* quandoquidem inter nos sanctissima diuitiarum
  maiestas, etsi funesta pecunia templo
  nondum habitat, nullas nummorum ereximus aras (1. 112–14).

dinner invitation. After paying their respects and collecting their 'box', the other callers leave. The regular dependants wait to escort their patron to the Forum. No doubt he goes down to discuss business and politics with his equals, and he takes his dependants with him to keep off the crowds and to show his eminence. But Juvenal says nothing of that: his dreary hours of duty and idleness are summed up in a few lines about the statues in the Forum. In the good old days a dependant would escort his patron home from these hours of business and then join him for dinner. But now

> the old and weary clients leave the anteroom
> abandoning all hope,*

going miserably home to buy cabbage for dinner and charcoal to cook it with, while the patron dines alone on the richest foods, peacock and wild boar—and let's hope his solitary guzzling, his extravagant greed, brings him to a sudden and a drastic end![13]

Juvenal has now announced himself as a poet (why not?), explained why he chooses satire (what else?), and defined the subjects of his satire. He could have stopped here. But he adds one more passage which qualifies everything he has already said, altering it in the strangest way. It is as though a symphonist, after a busy and argumentative opening, had moved into a loud and tumultuous development building up great hopes, and then shifted his key, diminished his orchestra, and ended, not on a triumphal chord but on insistent discords of harrowing anxiety.[14] Juvenal repeats as an assertion what he has already said as a question:

> every vice has stopped at a dizzy height.†

In such a world the satirist can use all his powers.

But suddenly here an objector appears. He is the imaginary opponent, descended from the interlocutor in Plato's dialogues. He is common in satire and in its ancestor the philosophical propaganda-speech; he is the opposite side of the dialectic; and usually in such a personal form of literature as satire, he is another aspect of the author's own self. Generally he is defeated

---

* Vestibulis abeunt ueteres lassique clientes,
   uotaque deponunt (1. 132–3).
† Omne in praecipiti uitium stetit (1. 149).

and converted. Here, unusually, he wins. He asks Juvenal where any poet can get the frankness of the early satirists like Lucilius: how, even with a heart on fire with rage, anyone would dare to name names. He warns Juvenal that, if he does venture to mention Tigellinus (favourite of the emperor Nero, of any absolute monarch), he will certainly be burnt alive in the arena. Juvenal resists. He has already said that his indignation will not let him sleep, that he has only to stand at a street-corner to fill a notebook. He recalls this now, and asks:

> So he who gave three uncles aconite can ride
> on a feather-cushioned litter, and look down on us?*

His alter ego says Yes. It is not dangerous to write epic poetry and idylls about mythology; but if you make war on vice and crime, beware.

This is a very strange and significant passage. It means either that Juvenal had already suffered for writing satire, or that he had been so deeply horrified by the corruption of Domitian's reign that he could never, even under a kind emperor, expect anything better. If the story of his exile is true, this cautious qualification was its result. If it is not true, the result for us is the same, for it means that he thought the whole Roman empire was permanently and incurably corrupt. Whether by exile, or by fear, he had been converted into a bitter, distrustful, pessimistic man, whose world was out of joint. Nowadays, if we were told that a man might be burnt to death for writing satire against powerful politicians, we should shake our heads and smile. Or rather, we should shake our heads: for in some countries, instead of the arena, there is the concentration-camp. But among us it is impossible. It would have been impossible in Rome, until a century or so before Juvenal wrote this poem. It had become possible only with the entrenchment of a powerful bureaucracy headed by an absolute ruler. But by Juvenal's time it was possible. He had seen it. Perhaps he had been threatened by it. For it is notable that he does not attempt to deny it—although, since this satire was to be recited and this book of satires was to be published under the liberal emperor Trajan, it might have been tactful to cry, 'No, no, impossible!'

---

* Qui dedit ergo tribus patruis aconita uehatur
pensilibus plumis, atque illinc despiciat nos? (1. 158–9).

Instead, he asks, 'What can I do, then?' His adviser replies, 'Careful, think well, do not attempt to emulate Lucilius' frankness and to point out the guilty as he did.'

Here the satire closes, abruptly and unsatisfyingly. Apparently Juvenal had two choices open to him. He could have said, 'Nevertheless, I cannot keep silent, I *will* write satire, and I *will* be heard.' Or perhaps he could have said, 'In that case, satire is impossible, vice has finally triumphed.' But he chooses neither alternative. He compromises.

> I'll try what may be said against the men
> whose ashes lie beside the highways north and south.*

These are the dead—not the ordinary dead, but the dead who were rich and noble enough to have a large tomb built facing the highroad. Since it is unsafe to write satire about the living, Juvenal says he will *try* writing satire on the dead—the implication being that even that might be visited by the revenge of their descendants, but that he will risk it. He says no more. The satire ends, not with a bang but a whisper. The last point is a very strange one, which would have repaid some development. But he will not speak of it any further. He stops, as though he were ashamed.

Yet it is an important announcement of his policy as a satirist. It needs, therefore, a little more examination. Juvenal says that, in writing satire, he will speak of the dead: the rich and noble dead. This is a new invention of his. Satire in Rome had always prided itself on being contemporary, on hitting at living people, the more powerful the better.[15] No Roman satirist known to us had undertaken to write exclusively about the dead. It does not sound very promising. We should find it difficult nowadays to care much about a satire on Teddy Roosevelt, or W. E. Gladstone, or Napoleon III. It could hardly have been successful if Juvenal had not been a great artist.

What exactly does it mean? It might mean that he intends to write only about *topics* drawn from past history, as we might choose to write of the Teapot Dome scandal or the Dreyfus case. Occasionally that is what he does. One of the best satires in this very book describes the emperor Domitian presiding over a

---

*   Experiar quid concedatur in illos
quorum Flaminia tegitur cinis atque Latina (1. 170–1).

Cabinet meeting early in his reign.* But still, most of his satires are on subjects which are not bound to any particular time—the haughtiness of patrons, the impossibility of being happy though married.†

Therefore, it might mean that he intends to use only *names* taken from the past, so as to avoid the offence of naming living criminals. Tigellinus in this very passage is such a name, and a little later Juvenal uses Verres, a figure of the republic, for a corrupt provincial governor.‡ The name of a vicious aristocrat recently dead would serve instead of the name of a living example of vice. This is probably what Juvenal chiefly intends. He has already said that the crimes and vices of Rome cry out for exposure and punishment. He has been told that it is dangerous to point out the living criminals. He replies, 'Then I shall use names drawn from the past.' The vice will be living, but it will wear a death-mask.[16]

Juvenal's readers have usually believed him on this point. They have taken his assurance that every man and woman he named was dead—or else insignificant or imaginary.[17] It is possible, however, that he was lying, and that he made this assertion simply to protect himself. Later we shall examine the characters in his satires, and see how far they can be identified.§ Meanwhile, it would be best to take this simply as his professed programme, and suspend judgement on it.

But, as a programme, it is exceedingly interesting. It shows us something valuable about the Roman empire. In the first place, it is important that, under the empire, at a time when according to Juvenal vice had reached an unparalleled height, it was unsafe to write frankly about it. Juvenal's apprehensions tell us as much as he himself could put into an entire poem. And in the second place, it means that Juvenal saw the empire as one long continuous process of degeneration. One evil emperor to him was like another. Every corrupt nobleman resembled his ancestors, having merely grown worse. Over a century earlier, Horace had pointed to this process, and said, in one of the gloomiest of his poems, that the morals of his countrymen were

* Satire 4: see pp. 76–82.
† Satires 5 and 6: see pp. 83–88 and pp. 91–103.
‡ 1. 155, 2. 26, 3. 53.
§ See pp. 290–4.

growing worse from father to son, uninterruptedly.* Now, looking gloomily back, Juvenal saw the long slope reaching to his
feet.† He realized (although perhaps his audience did not)
that it would be trivial to satirize only the men and women of
his own time. They were end-products of a process which began with the lash of Julius Caesar and the wet sword of Augustus,‡
which ran on through the lunatic Caligula, through Nero and
the civil wars, to the fiendish emperor of yesterday and perhaps
another monster tomorrow. This realization was one of his chief
contributions to satire. Sometimes it is necessary for a satirist
to stigmatize one man, one act, one abuse: then Swift writes
The Drapier's Letters or Byron *A Vision of Judgment*. But sometimes a thinking man looks at a whole age, at all his world, and
sees that it is bad. Then, if he is a historian, he writes a bitter
and pessimistic work like the historical books of Juvenal's
contemporary Tacitus. If he is a novelist, he writes a study of
a moribund society like the novels of Proust. If he is a satirist,
he writes sixteen strange poems in which the past is inextricably
mingled with the present, where a vicious empress of sixty years
ago is grouped with wealthy harpies of his own day, where the
badness of the past is both a preparation and a proof of
the vileness of the present; and he is Juvenal, the satirist of the
Roman empire.

To sum up, then, the First Satire is Juvenal's own justification
as a satirist. It falls into four parts: 1 (1–18) Why I write poetry;
2 (19–80) Why I choose satire; 3 (81–146) The chief subjects of
my satire are the greed and extravagance of Rome; and 4
(147–71) But my illustrations must be taken from the past.

* Hor. *Carm.* 3. 6. 45–48.   † 1. 147–9.
‡ Caesar, 10. 109; Augustus, 8. 242–3. Elsewhere Juvenal says the process
began even earlier: 6. 286–300.

VIII

SATIRE TWO
The Faerie Queenes

THE subject of Satire Two is homosexuality.[1] One or two generations ago it would scarcely have been possible to discuss the
poem unless in 'the obscurity of a learned language'.* But within our lifetime there have been many medico-legal and psycho-
analytical examinations of the problem, which have reached a
large part of the public, and a number of contemporary writers
have produced more or less sympathetic studies of homosexuals
and their peculiar life. Juvenal is not a bit sympathetic. He
treats them as ridiculous and disgusting.

Homosexuality among women was known in Rome and in
Juvenal's own time, but he never attacks it. His friend Martial
sneers at a female athlete with Lesbian inclinations: in adapting
the epigram, Juvenal cuts out the perversion.† It is probably
the only vice of which he does not accuse women in his enormous Sixth Satire. He thinks women are oversexed, but
'normally oriented'.

Among men, homosexuality appears to take two chief forms
which have very different psychical roots and products. Some
men find women unattractive, and prefer making love to other
males. This attitude often appears among groups of men who
are separated from women for long periods, and does not seem
to make the male lovers less vigorous, less brave, less manly in
fact. It has been known as a fashion among closely knit com-
panies of *élite* fighters—for instance, the Spartans, the Theban
aristocracy, possibly the Knights Templars, and certainly the
Prussian nobles in this century, not to mention the imitation
élite of Roehm and the S.A. officers under Hitler. Sometimes it
is apparently induced by a dislike of women—Juvenal himself,
at the beginning of his satire against women, speaks of it sym-

---

* Gibbon, *Decline and Fall of the Roman Empire*, c. 40 (Everyman ed., vol. 4,
p. 155).

† Martial 7. 67 ～ Juv. 6. 418–33; and cf. Juv. 1. 22–23 and 2. 49.

pathetically from that point of view.* Sometimes it has deeper origins, hard to enucleate: for example, in the eminent French writer André Gide, who produced several books praising it, but could never explain how he acquired it.

The other form is more difficult to understand. Some men prefer not to be men, but to be women. They do not wish to be active partners in love-making, but to be mastered by a male lover. They cultivate a partly feminine appearance, dress, gait, manner of speech, and habits, and can go to remarkable extremes of abjection when the habit gets a grip of them. This was the group to which Marcel Proust belonged, and much of his novel, *Remembrance of Things Past*, is devoted to describing the excitements, dangers, and humiliations of its members. There is one scene, quite as good though not as vivid as anything in Juvenal, which shows the proud and unapproachable Baron de Charlus paying to have himself held down and lashed with wire whips by a vulgarian who despises him and insults him for enjoying his surrender.†

It is against this second type that Satire Two is directed. A few of them, says Juvenal, are pardonable or pitiable, because their perversion is a congenital affliction. They were born with it.‡ But for the others he has no pity whatever, nothing but contemptuous disgust.

He attacks them in six bitter pages. As he exposes them, they do not seem to belong to one single tightly organized clique. Instead, we are introduced to them in four stages,[2] the disease growing worse in each, as in the later volumes of Proust where almost all the characters, the hero's mistress Albertine and his stalwart friend Saint-Loup and so many others, are gradually revealed as being corrupt beyond corruption.

The first section shows us a peculiarly Roman group, which disgusts Juvenal on several different counts.§ Many men, he says, pose as being philosophers of the sterner sects: not lax Epicureans, but taciturn Stoics, with their scalp clipped short in a 'crew-cut', with arms and legs covered with bristly hair, and with the severe look of the hard-willed Superman.[3] Yet for all their show of stern morality they are utter hypocrites, practising

* 6. 33–37.
† Proust, *Le Temps retrouvé* (Paris, 1929), i. 165 f.
‡ 2. 15–19: *fatis, morbum, furor.*   § 2. 1–63.

perverts, and must shrink from the contempt even of a hearty whore.

The girl, bold and shameless but honest, retorts to their moralizing in a spirited speech, and puts them to flight. But after them another hypocrite appears.* He is not a professed Stoic, but still a professional moralist; a lawyer, who specializes in prosecuting wicked women and convicting them of offences against the laws protecting marriage. He is as stern as any conservative of the old republic, and yet while making his speech he chooses to wear a thin transparent gown. He says the hot summer weather makes it necessary. Juvenal tells him to speak naked rather than wear chiffon:

> madness is less disgraceful.†

The metaphor of disease reappears here in a strong sentence which was quoted from Juvenal hundreds of times during the Middle Ages and thereafter:

> infection caused this taint
> and will spread wider, as a whole herd in the fields
> will fall sick of the scab from a single pig's mange,
> as a grape will draw ripeness from the sight of a ripened grape.‡

And yet the affected lawyer has still not reached the depths;

> no one becomes depraved in a moment.§

After some time, he will join the third group.‖ This is a secret society of imitation women. Behind closed doors, they dress like women. They even hold services to worship the Good Goddess, who can be worshipped only by women and to whose rites men may never be admitted. They make up like beauties in the powder-room, lengthening their eyebrows with pencil and putting in that telling shadow with trembling eyes upturned. They wear gilt hair-nets and fashionable fabrics. One carries a looking-glass handed down to the sorority by an illustrious

---

* 2. 64–81.
† Nudus agas: minus est insania turpis (2. 71).
‡   Dedit haec contagio labem
  et dabit in plures, sicut grex totus in agris
  unius scabie cadit et porrigine porci,
  uuaque conspecta liuorem ducit ab uua (2. 78–81).
§ Nemo repente fuit turpissimus (2. 83).
‖ 2. 82–116.

pervert, the emperor Otho, who worried about his make-up even during his campaigns—unlike other warrior queens. The high priest or priestess of the group is a white-haired shrill-voiced shaman, who has almost made himself a eunuch for the Mighty Mother's sake.[4]

Yet these three grades of homosexuality are all partly hidden. The orgies are still secret. The thinly dressed orator is merely affected. The sham philosophers attempt to conceal their in-clinations, which show through only faintly—as the Baron de Charlus, when Proust first met him, wore a quiet dark tie in which there was 'a patch of red as faint as a liberty that one does not dare to take'.* Worse than these is the perversion which displays itself in high places.† A man belonging to one of the most distinguished families of Rome, a Gracchus descended from the Republican house which once bred the people's champions, became a woman and put on bridal dress and was married to a man in the publicity of a formal wedding. He brought his 'husband' a rich dowry, enough to make the lucky bridegroom a knight.‡ There was a huge wedding banquet, and all his friends were there. That this should be done, almost in full public view, by a Roman of high rank, descended from the honest herdsmen and children of Mars who founded the city, makes Juvenal certain of the complete degeneracy of his fellow Romans. It was this same Gracchus, he goes on, who appeared as a half-naked gladiator, the net-caster who throws his net and runs away, pursued by his opponent, if he misses.[5] It is difficult for us to think that the effeminate young man who dressed as a woman would be bold enough to fight against a heavily armed man in the arena, and it is difficult to understand how his public appearance as a gladiator struck Juvenal as worse than his semi-public perversion. But gladiators were the lowest form of life for the Romans: short lived and brutalized, they were not even free but could be treated as slaves; to become a gladiator was not like being an amateur boxer nowadays but was something parallel to prostitution. Gracchus' rank and family were felt to make it worse—just as we should be out-

---

* Proust, *A l'Ombre des jeunes filles en fleurs*, 2 (Paris, 1927), 211.

† 2. 117–48.

‡ *Quadringenta*, 2. 117: once more the sum which fascinated Juvenal (see p. 37).

raged if a Cabinet Minister appeared professionally as a clown in a circus. And as for the bravery involved, one perversion demanded as much courage as the other, and as much willingness to outrage accepted standards of morality.

The noble names of Gracchus and of his peers who watched his degradation carry Juvenal's mind back to the great days of Roman history. There is of course, he says, no underworld as described by Vergil and other poets, thronged with shades of the mighty dead. But suppose there were. Imagine that instead of being visited by Aeneas, the Roman heroes like Camillus and Scipio were confronted by the ghost of a perverted descendant like this Gracchus: would they recognize him? No, they would think they were polluted by the very sight, and try to purify themselves, to disinfect their shades.[6] It is not (Juvenal goes on) that the Roman empire is shrinking. No, it is spreading wider in the east and in the west—and here he mentions the conquest of North Britain by Agricola.[7] But the Romans are degenerate, and although conquering they are corrupt. A young Armenian nobleman who came to Rome as a hostage, once brave and simple like a cossack or a gaucho, has already been seduced and won by a Roman officer. No doubt when he returns he will teach his friends the vices of Roman youth, and so the infection will spread throughout the world.*

Although this satire reads like a general denunciation of Rome, it is a quite carefully aimed and calculated attack. Its one target is the Roman aristocracy. Gracchus, with his wealth and his proud name, is obviously a nobleman.† The celebrants of the secret orgy are expensively dressed and have connexions with the former emperor Otho. The lawyer preaching against vice bears the proud name Creticus—which means that one of his ancestors was a general who had had a triumph after conquering Crete: it was a real name, borne by the Caecilii Metelli. The hypocrites, admirers of Cato and Hercules, are not everyday philosophers, but Stoics, and Stoicism was the doctrine of the aristocrats who opposed the empire and upheld republicanism: the passage contains a sneer at Horace's praise of Cato.[8] There are several side-blows at the emperor Domitian, who,

---

* 2. 159–70.

† *Quadringenta sestertia dotem,* 117; *ingens cena,* 119–20; *clarus genere atque opibus,* 129.

like the mock Stoics, lived an immoral life while setting himself up as a moral censor.* The motive of the satire is the hypocrisy and degeneracy of an entire class, unworthy of the names they bear, a disgrace to their ancestors and a source of infection for the simpler world outside Rome, the world which they conquer and corrupt.

* 2. 29–33; *censura*, 63; *censore*, 121.

IX

SATIRE THREE

Babylon

AFTER the Second Satire, it is a relief to turn to the Third. This is one of the finest satires ever written. It deals with an important theme; it is full of variety; it is well arranged; it is alive with brilliant epigrams; and, unlike many stirring satires, it is very largely true. It was true in Juvenal's day; it has been true in several different periods and places since he died; and it is true today.

The theme is the power and the vileness of the big city.[1] This thought recurs again and again in the greatest poets, philosophers, and preachers. In the Bible it appears very early, where Abraham pleads with the Lord to spare the wicked place if it has as many as ten good men within it; and a little later, lo, the smoke of Sodom and Gomorrah goes up as the smoke of a furnace.* At the very end of the Bible it reappears in a denunciation, written during Juvenal's own lifetime about Juvenal's city of Rome:

Come out of her, my people, that ye be not partakers of her sins, and that ye receive not of her plagues. For her sins have reached unto heaven, and God hath remembered her iniquities. . . . How much she hath glorified herself, and lived deliciously, so much torment and sorrow give her: for she saith in her heart, I sit a queen, and am no widow, and shall see no sorrow. Therefore shall her plagues come in one day, death, and mourning, and famine; and she shall be utterly burned with fire.[2]

It is heard here and there in the seventeenth and eighteenth centuries, and grows much louder in the nineteenth century; De Quincey wanders through London, the 'stony-hearted stepmother', and finds scarcely a living soul to befriend him but a young prostitute; Cobbett fulminates against the Great Wen that sucks the vitality out of England; Balzac shows us Rastignac declaring war on the huge and ruthless enemy he

* Gen. xviii–xix; cf. Juv. 13. 26–27.

4213.4   F

sees from the cemetery of Père-Lachaise, the city of Paris;
novel after novel in Europe and America tells us of the trans-
formation worked in country boys and girls who come to the
city full of hope and ideals, often to lose both, while others describe the distorted souls of men and women born and brought
up within the hell-like world of the slums; within our own day
it appears as part of a nightmare vision:

> Under the brown fog of a winter dawn
> A crowd flowed over London Bridge, so many,
> I had not thought death had undone so many.
> Sighs, short and infrequent, were exhaled,
> And each man fixed his eyes before his feet.[3]

However, it is not all cities that are denounced in this way.
The little cities dedicated to art and thought have few to hate
them—Athens, Florence,[4] Edinburgh, Geneva; and the cities
set in provinces and smaller countries, whether ugly like Leeds
or beautiful like Stockholm, do not have the same masterful
quality that characterizes the Babylons of the world. There is a
good deal of shooting in Kansas City, and some expert razor-
slashing in Glasgow, but neither of these places has the irresis-
tible attraction that draws souls into them to be ruined and
cast away. The city which the poets and prophets denounce
is what Spengler calls the World-City, the Cosmopolis, the
Megalopolis—the international city which is more than a
market, factory, and administrative centre for its own nation or
region, and has become a focus of attraction for a large part of
the world, which is filled with a Babel of languages so that half
the people in it seem to be foreigners, which consumes far more
than it produces, which grows bigger year after year, four million, five million, six million, ten million, and which as it grows
bigger seems to grow more complicatedly wicked.* For the
wonderful thing about such a city is its magnetic force. Even
those who hate it feel its pull. Those who denounce it sometimes
sound almost sad as they think how man's perversity ruins one
of his most ambitious works, full of riches—

cinnamon, and odours, and ointments, and frankincense, and wine,
and oil, and fine flour, and wheat, and beasts, and sheep, and horses,
and chariots, and slaves, and souls of men.†

* O. Spengler, *Der Untergang des Abendlandes* (Munich, 1921), 1, Einleitung
§ 12, pp. 44–47, and 2. c. 2, §§ 4–5, pp. 113–27.   † Rev. xviii. 13.

The denunciation of city life therefore does not appear, or at least reach its full force, until the city has grown so rich and populous that, instead of being part of a healthy regional complex (city-towns-villages-countryside), it has become an international megalopolis, a floating island, a world in itself. In the Greco-Roman world we hear it first in the age of Alexander, who founded the megalopolis of Alexandria. As long as Rome resembled the Latin market-town which she had once been, such complaints were rare; they began when she was unchallengeably the capital of the western world and was changed from brick to marble.

Resistance to unnatural city life takes two chief forms. One is idealization of the village and the country. Pastoral poetry was first made into an art by a poet who lived partly at Alexandria and partly at the rich court of Syracuse, and it has always been most popular at courts or among fugitives from the megalopolis. It is the escape from megalopolitan life nowadays which has filled the countryside with week-end cottages, rustic furniture, square dances, converted farms, and even imitation ranches where city folk can pretend, for two dollars an hour, to be cowherds on horseback. This need not be laughed at, for it is an attempt, often successful, to restore that balance which is the law of nature.

The other form of resistance, less healthy, is produced by more violent hatred. This is absolute renunciation of the city and the wish for its destruction. The Cynics, who called all social conventions silly and preached the life according to nature, naturally despised the refinements of city life: Diogenes refused to live in a house and have unnecessary furniture, but slept in a barrel and drank from his hand. But they still lived most of the time in the city, if only to scold it and bark at its citizens. Later, men began to feel that it was foolish, wrong, impossible, to live among such corruptions, and that the only possible safety lay in the destruction of the city or in flight to complete loneliness. Both these solutions appear in the Book of Revelation, but the voice from heaven begins by saying, 'Come out of her, my people.'[5] The desire to escape into the deserts from the vileness of the city made many early Christians become hermits: the word is *eremite*, which means an inhabitant, not of the country, but of the desert. Not only Christians felt like this:

for the historian Rostovtzeff held that the later Roman armies, mostly recruited from the farms and the remoter provinces, grew to hate the parasitic cities so much that in any disorder they turned to looting and destruction, not only willingly but with a sense of belated retribution.*

These are the lines of thought which run together in Juvenal's Third Satire. But, like all good poems, it has not merely one simple message. Other ideas, almost equally strong, give it complexity and strength. To his denunciation of city life, Juvenal adds another of his bitter contrasts between rich and poor (although as usual 'poor' does not mean 'working-class' but rather 'rootless middle-class') † as well as a furious attack on the foreigners who have poured into Rome from Greece and the Near East to ruin its society and its morals.

The poem is a monologue, its theme 'Why no one can live well in the City'. But it has a graceful introduction, to set the emotional tone and make the speech more plausible. Although the ideas are largely Juvenal's own, although the experience of disappointment, renunciation, and relief was partly his and his friend Martial's, it would have been absurd for a satirist to stay in Rome and recite a dozen reasons for leaving.[6] The monologue is therefore couched as a farewell speech made not by Juvenal himself but by his friend Umbricius.[7] Like Juvenal, he has been a dependant of the rich. Now, middle-aged, poor, and a failure, he is quitting the city for ever, moving to the old, quaint, deserted seaside village of Cumae—as a Londoner might move to a lonely Cornish hamlet or a New Yorker to a sandspit on Cape Cod. He is not destitute. Juvenal's 'poor' men always have just enough to keep them going in leisured indigence, and their chief struggle is not to keep from starving but to avoid the degradation of having to work.[8] He has a little capital, not enough to keep him as a dependant in Rome, but enough to live on in frugal comfort in the country, where he can buy an excellent house and a little garden for the amount he now pays out yearly for a dark attic at the top of a rickety apartment-house.‡ Now he has hired a mule-drawn wagon to move his furniture to Cumae, miles away on the coast, down the Appian Highway. His servants have carried the things to the city gate (for wheeled

* M. Rostovtzeff, *Social and Economic History of the Roman Empire* (Oxford, 1926), 443 f.   † See p. 244, n. 10.   ‡ 3. 23–24, 223–5, 193–6, 197–202.

vehicles were not allowed to enter Rome during daylight hours) and are now loading them on the wagon. Juvenal has walked with him as far as the gate to say good-bye. The two friends turn off the road into a little park, Egeria's Glen, outside the city walls, to talk in peace.

Once it was a sacred spot, holy and enchanted, where the ancestral priest-king Numa met the goddess Egeria and learnt songs and spells from her. Now, says Juvenal, it has been ruined in two different ways. The little grove has been rented by a settlement of Jews—who are not, as we might expect, merchants, but something much poorer and less stable, beggars and fortune-tellers like gypsies in modern times.[9] And the cave of the nymph—

> that deep romantic chasm which slanted
> Down the green hill athwart a cedarn cover—

has now been spoilt by modern improvements, the grass and the native stone overlaid by expensive marble in the baroque style, gorgeous and unreal.[10] Thus, by describing the setting of the monologue, Juvenal has given us its emotional tone. He and his friend hate the city so much that they will not even stop to talk within its walls, but turn their backs on it and look for the quiet of nature; and the only spot they can find has been ruined by foreigners, by greed, by tasteless extravagance, and by the destruction of fine old traditions.* Similarly, the satire ends with an allusion to Juvenal's departure from Rome for a holiday in his little native town of Aquinum; Umbricius will come to see him there, but never return to the loathsome city.†

In this grove, then, among the marble and the beggars, Juvenal's friend Umbricius begins his farewell to Rome. It opens with a long carefully worked sentence which reminds us at once of the opening of the tirade in Satire One,[11] and although it never grows so intense and violent as that poem, it keeps up a steadier, stronger pace. Although the details make the figure into Umbricius, the voice is clearly the voice of Juvenal.[12]

The monologue falls into two main sections. The first describes the poverty in which Umbricius has been living, the

---

* Foreigners, 14; greed, 15–16; tasteless extravagance, 18–20; destruction of tradition, 12–18: these being four of Juvenal's chief complaints against Rome itself.

† 3. 318–22, ending with a pleasant contrast to the crowded city, *gelidos agros*.

second details his discomforts and dangers; or the first describes the impossibility of making a living, the second the impossibility of enjoying life.[13]

Each of these is arranged under three heads. He begins by asking what the difficulties are in the way of making a living in Rome. He replies, first, that honesty is not rewarded; second, that Greeks and foreign immigrants elbow out the native Romans; and third, that a poor dependant is universally despised and rejected, because money is the only standard on which people are judged.*

'Let others stay in Rome', says Umbricius, 'men who can make money by rapid speculations, no matter how undignified they may be.' It is strange to see how bitterly he despises transactions which we should think honourable and creditable, and which many of the Romans themselves must have approved: for instance, contracting for the building of a harbour or the control of a river or the erection of a temple. The Romans were fine builders and engineers, and cannot all have looked down on such activities. But Juvenal speaks from the point of view of the old-fashioned gentleman who believes the only honourable income is that derived from land. Only a century ago gentlemen in Britain were apt to think the same, and their wives would not receive the wife of anyone who made things instead of owning land. The Romans were more devoted to tradition than even the British, and Juvenal speaks here as the last descendant of the elder Cato, who said there was only one truly safe and honourable way of making money, which was farming.†

Also, he distrusts the mushroom rapidity with which a fortune can be built up by a few big contracts, just as a modern banker will distrust a speculator who makes millions on a lucky turn in the market or corners a critically needed material. These people, says Juvenal, will do anything, however dirty or disgusting, if there is money in it. They will contract to clean up sewage (or flood debris, which came to the same thing), to bury the dead, they will put money into public lavatories and make fortunes from the admission fees; and, in an enigmatic line, he adds that they will even sell themselves into slavery for

* 3. 21–57, 58–125, 126–89.
† Cato, *De Agri Cultura* init. See the treatment of the ironmaster in Dickens's *Bleak House*, and of the 'dust-contractor' in *Our Mutual Friend*.

money—not permanently, but as a quick though degrading way of making a profit. Evidently they expected to buy themselves out again and would ignore the degradation, since they had got some capital by it.[14]

This is not for me, Umbricius goes on; I am not the man to make money out of dirt. Then, in a famous speech, he asks:

What can I do in Rome? I can't tell lies. . . .

nor praise bad books, or pretend to forecast the future, nor assist a political crook in his chicaneries. So I have no hope of a career. In the energy of this tirade, we forget the other possibility, that the speaker might have turned his hand to honest work. There is no such thing as honest work, he makes us believe, no one can ever get ahead except sharpers and their accomplices.[15] This speech was much admired in the Renaissance, often copied in satires against court life and *arrivistes*, and found its latest echo in the fine harangue where Rostand made Cyrano consider the ignoble rungs on the ladder of Success, and to each cry:

No, I thank you!*

Where I fail, Umbricius continues, others succeed. These are the greedy Greeks—and the Asiatics who have poured into Rome like the Oriental river Orontes (which flows through Antioch) debouching into the Tiber. The Greeks are clever, the Greeks are bold, the Greeks are talkative, the Greeks are versatile, the Greeks lie and flatter their way into great houses, and seduce the master's wife, or his daughter or son-in-law or son, or failing that his grandmother. Soon after they have established themselves, the honest Roman client, who cannot lie and flatter, is shown out.[16]

Xenophobia was not marked in the world of Greece and Rome. Greeks and Romans alike despised barbarians, as most of us despise savages who (however 'integrated' their culture) cannot read and write, cannot cure their own illnesses, and have no standards beyond those of a tiny tribe. But anyone who learnt the Greek or Roman language and became part of that wide and millennial culture—however remote or barbarous his origins—was welcomed as an equal member of the world-

* Rostand, *Cyrano de Bergerac*, 2. 8,

society. Those who were in it but not of it, like the Jews, were distrusted.* The origin of its other members scarcely mattered —Terence was a dark African, Diogenes the Cynic came from the Sea of Marmora, Zeno the Stoic from the Semitic town of Citium, no one cared.[17] But within the empire there was a permanent division between the conquered Greeks and their Roman conquerors. The Greeks despised Roman crudity and violence, the Romans distrusted Greek versatility, elusiveness, lack of principle. The Greeks borrowed few ideas from the Romans. The Romans learnt much from the Greeks, and some of the high points of their aesthetic achievement were works in which they blended the masterly Greek style with Roman gravity and moral sense. Still, there had always been Romans who distrusted Greek influence. Cato (while accepting part of it) fought against it all his life.[18] Some of the central facts of Roman society—religion and politics, social relations and duties —were only superficially touched by Greek influence; others, such as sexual morality, were deeply affected, and suffered for it. Although in the late republic and in the early empire the educated Romans had been practically bilingual, yet Greek did not penetrate deeply into the western provinces, and Latin asserted itself but little in the east. The division between the Greek-speaking eastern half and the Latin western half of the Mediterranean world was always important, and became fundamental when the empire was divided in the fourth century. It is reflected now in the division between the Roman Catholic and the Greek Orthodox churches, each of which has excommunicated the other as heretical; and between the nations like Serbs and Croats, Czechs and Slovenes, Poles and Russians who were converted by rival churches, along a line prolonging the old rivalry of Greece and Rome. Juvenal is therefore not venting merely a personal prejudice or the spite of a disappointed competitor. His words reflect a fact, and voice a feeling, which were very deeply implicated in the life of the Roman empire, and it would not be too much to say that here once again he has put his finger on one of the causes which brought the empire to its collapse.

But quite apart from the competition of the Greeks, Umbricius goes on—and this is his third point—it is impossible for a

* p. 283.

poor man to make his way in Rome. However honourable his character, however faithful he may be as a dependant, he will be neglected if he is poor—or worse, laughed at:

> The harshest punishment of wretched poverty
> is that it makes men look ridiculous.*

The result is that everyone in Rome lives above his means. Umbricius, now surely speaking for Juvenal (who came from a small town), looks beyond the walls of Rome to the pleasant little towns where no one ever wears the full-dress toga except to be buried in it.[19] At all other times, even in grand festivals when the grass-grown theatre is opened for strolling players to produce a favourite farce, the ordinary public and the town officials alike are content to wear clean white shirts. There is no spite, only a little ironic respect, in the tone with which Juvenal refers to their excellencies, the town councillors. He may himself have been co-mayor of such a little town, and the vivid picture could be a reminiscence of his youth. But in Rome, he concludes, we all live in pretentious poverty: even to be a dependant of the rich costs money, paid out in tips to the haughty slaves who have their master's ear and favour. The torments of poverty are, then, that it holds poor men down, subjects them to contempt, and makes it impossible for them to live even on their own simple scale.

Looking back over the first part of this passionate monologue, we soon see that it is, like most angry complaints, not very consistent. Logically, it could be exploded fairly easily. But emotionally, it makes good and cogent sense. Umbricius, or Juvenal through him, has given three reasons why he cannot make a living in Rome. The first is that he will not be a crook (a term which for Juvenal includes business-men); the second is that there are too many Greeks; and the third is that 'slow rises worth by poverty depress'd'.† Put them together, and they make a single complaint, which accounts for the drive we feel behind this part of the satire. The complaint is that no one can make a living in Rome if he is honest, poor, and Roman.

That proved, Umbricius now turns to show that life is not worth living in Rome anyhow.

---

* Nil habet infelix paupertas durius in se
  quam quod ridiculos homines facit (3. 152–3).
† Johnson, *London* 177 ∼ Juv. 3. 164–5.

First, the houses keep falling down or burning up. (Affectionately he names three or four quiet country towns like Bolsena and Tivoli where one could live for years without ever thinking of such a thing.) Building laws were inadequate, or could be evaded as they are in modern slums, and a tottering tenement could be shored up with a few props, its cracks plastered over. If it did not fall, it was liable to catch fire—and in a fire the poor attic dweller, living up among the tiles and the pigeons,[20] is most apt to be burnt alive and to lose all his goods. The rich, by contrast, if their mansions should burn down, are presented by eager friends with books and bookcases, statues and silver plate, to help them in refurnishing. The richer they are, the more they get, until a childless millionaire is suspected of burning his house down on purpose.[21]

And next, it is impossible to get any peace, because of traffic and crowds all day and disorders and crimes all night.* This is a splendid passage which could be adapted to modern conditions and applied with scarcely a change to any modern megapolis. There is hardly any satiric exaggeration in it. In fact, exaggeration is unnecessary when the satirist is describing the New York subway (or the Paris Métro, or the London Tube, or conceivably even the Moscow Subway) during the rush hour; or an August holiday crowd at a railway station. Juvenal merely tells us truly what it feels like to be in the middle of the crowd:

> pushing on, we are stopped
> by the wave ahead, and the mighty mob following shoves
> at our hips: an elbow hits us here and a hard pole
> there, now we are smashed by a beam, now biffed by a barrel.†

Or of course there is always the chance of being run over by a truck full of heavy blocks of building-stone, and utterly erased. If you survive the dangers of the day, there are the perils of the night: going home from dinner, you may be hit by dishes, or their contents, thrown from windows; you may be held up by

---

* So also, but more mildly, Horace, *Ep.* 2. 2. 65 f.; Mart. 5. 22, 12. 57.
†   Nobis properantibus obstat
      unda prior, magno populus premit agmine lumbos
      qui sequitur, ferit hic cubito, ferit assere duro
      alter, at hic tignum capiti incutit, ille metretam (3. 243–6).

a drunk, forced to quarrel, and beaten up in the ensuing fight;
or attacked by armed thieves or burglars. This last danger,
which modern city-dwellers would probably think far the most
formidable of night terrors, seems less real to Juvenal, though he
uses it for a climax, than the row with the bully in which he is
insulted and thrashed and made helpless: partly because his
pride is his most sensitive organ, partly because there was apparently much less organized crime in those dark and quiet
streets than among our lighted and moving avenues.

All this section is most carefully orchestrated. Its subject is
simply the traffic in the streets, but it is so planned as to cover
a complete twenty-four-hour period—from the insomnia of the
small hours, through the morning crowds, past the lunch-time
rush, towards the afternoon traffic whose victim sits shivering
on the banks of the Styx while his household prepares his bath
and his dinner; then into the dark hours punctuated by a few
lighted windows, slashed by the long trail of torches which
escort a great man in his crimson cloak home from dinner,
among his clients, and then threaded by the brief candle which
lights Umbricius homewards, while the drunkard waits at the
corner and the picklock picks at the locked lock.[22]

So Umbricius ends his denunciation. His little household has
been loaded on the wagon. The driver waves his whip to signal
that he is ready. The sun has begun to slope downwards, so
that the tiny emigrant train can set off in comfort down the
highway, 'Good-bye' says Umbricius, 'do not forget me. And
whenever you return to your little town of Aquinum for a much-
needed holiday, invite me over. I shall come to hear you read
your satires. Surely your poems won't be ashamed of me,
although I don't wear city dress but come as a countryman
striding with heavy boots through the cool fields.'*[23] There is no
reply. Umbricius turns his back on the city for ever. Juvenal
drifts away under the dripping arch of the gate, to merge in

the smoke, the wealth, the noise of Rome.†

*   Ergo uale, nostri memor; et quotiens te
Roma tuo refici properantem reddet Aquino,
me quoque ad Heluinam Cererem uestramque Dianam
conuerte a Cumis. saturarum ego, ni pudet illas,
auditor gelidos ueniam caligatus in agros (3. 318–22).
† Fumum et opes strepitumque Romae (Hor. *Carm.* 3. 29. 12).

X

SATIRE FOUR
The Kingfish

THE Fourth Satire belongs to quite a different period and milieu.[1] Satire Three was all about poverty and degradation. This is all about wealth, pomp, and power. It is the only satire we have which takes us inside the court of a Roman emperor.

It is in two parts, an introduction and a story.[2] They do not seem to have much to do with each other, except superficially. The introduction is a short but searing attack on the Egyptian colonel of the emperor Domitian's bodyguard, the former fish-peddler of Canopus, riddled with vice and loaded with wealth.* One of his exploits was to pay £60 for a six-pound fish, the rare red mullet which is seldom caught above a pound or so.[3] Juvenal says he could have bought the fisherman for less than the fish.

The main body of the poem is another fish-story. A turbot of gigantic size was caught in the Adriatic, and sent to Domitian as a royal fish. Since it was too large for any vessel in the palace kitchen, he summoned his Cabinet to discuss how to cook it. It would have been a barbarism to chop it up and stew it.[4] An old gourmet among his ministers proposed that a potter be called to make a special jumbo broiler, calculated to fit the fish; and the council was dismissed.[5]

Logically, the connexion of the story and the introduction is plausible, though pretty thin. They are both about fish, and expensive fish at that, phenomenal fish. They are both about folly and extravagance. Crispinus wasted his money: he paid £10 a pound, says Juvenal, and then did not put the red mullet to any diplomatic use by presenting it to a rich old gentleman or a dear young lady, but idiotically ate it himself. Domitian wasted the time and energy of his Cabinet, which hurried together at his summons as anxiously as though he had a new dispatch from his northern wars to discuss with them. And finally, both the introduction and the story deal with

* See p. 37.

Domitian and his court, showing different sides of its evil
nature. If we read only the story, we might think that the
emperor was a vile tyrant, all of whose courtiers were to be
pitied because their lives were in constant danger from his
caprices. The introduction is therefore meant to show that a bad
ruler selects bad men to help him, and that Domitian's leading
courtiers were not only frightened but evil.

But the real link between the two parts of the satire is emotional. They both vibrate with hatred for the régime of Domitian. And they both presuppose this hatred in the hearers or
readers of the poem. If recited in the years directly after Domitian's assassination, when the blood of his victims was still wet
and the mourning of their families still fresh, it would have a
formidable impact. We know from Pliny and Tacitus how
vividly men remembered the reign of terror, and how they
talked over it with amazement, indignation, unbelief, and
horror—as we recall Hitler and the bodies piled up like logs for
the burning in Buchenwald, although the modern tyrant's atrocities were far worse than those of the Roman emperor. But a
few years later Juvenal's vituperation against Domitian would
come to seem a little *passé*, under a good régime a little unnecessary: salt in old wounds. And now the satire looks to us
like two pictures instead of one, so that we must make an effort
to bring them into the same focus. Yet for some readers their
lack of unity is compensated by their incomparable vividness.

Modern readers also find it hard to understand why the
Romans of the empire prized certain kinds of fish so highly
and were willing to pay such enormous prices for them. It was
partly a competitive fashion—what Thorstein Veblen called
'conspicuous waste'—partly a craze, like the tulip-mania in
seventeenth-century Holland, and partly a genuine refinement
of taste. Meat is seldom good in the hot Mediterranean countries, and the ancients had no fine breeds of beef cattle and
sheep like our Herefords and Southdowns. The Homeric
Greeks were tremendous meat-eaters and never seem to have
touched fish—one proof that they were recent immigrants into
the Mediterranean area from a nomadic or pastoral north. But
their successors in 'classical' Greece lived largely on fish. The
common people of ancient Rome got most of their protein from
pork—the jokes about ham and sausage in Plautus' comedies

were put in to suit his Roman audience, and the vulgar millionaire in Petronius shows his vulgarity by having one course, which is apparently composed of fancy dishes like fish and capon, really made wholly of disguised pork.[6] But the rich and refined wanted something less coarse, and turned, like the Greeks, to fish. Gourmets paid highly to have it fresh: they arranged special relays of messengers to bring it to them still 'tasting of the sea'[7]—as we fly early spring flowers to the cities from hundreds of miles away, or as the Incas of Peru had runners to carry fish from the Pacific up the Andes to their capital in time for dinner. (The Prince de Condé's chef Vatel killed himself because he thought his system had broken down and had failed to provide fresh fish for Louis XIV.*) Certain species, particularly dainty, were sought after and competed for: lampreys, or more probably morays (caught among dangerous rocks or specially bred), red mullet (still a rarity in Italy), turbot, and sea-bass.† So in our own day a party is sometimes built around caviare brought all the way from Russia.

The introductory sketch on Colonel Crispin is quite short.[8] It follows a pattern which Juvenal loves to use for his villains, and which has sometimes been misunderstood by serious-minded scholars. The most famous example is in the Eighth Satire, where he says that Orestes, like Nero, murdered his mother —but did not also murder his sister and his wife, poison his relatives, sing on the stage, or write epic poems.‡ So here Juvenal begins by calling Crispinus a monster redeemed by not a single virtue, and goes on to say that he seduced a Vestal virgin who was then buried alive for violating her vows—but he concludes with the story about the phenomenally rare £60 fish. Juvenal remembers what some of his critics forget: that ridicule is as powerful a weapon as invective, and that it is more properly the arm of satire. Many a great scoundrel will be unmoved if he is called a villain, and some impressionable people may try to emulate him. But if he is shown to be a fool, he will wince, and those who might have admired him will turn away

---

* Mme de Sévigné, *Lettres*, 161 (26 April 1671).

† D'Arcy Thompson, *A Glossary of Greek Fishes* (St. Andrews University Publications 45, London, 1947), 264–8, 223, and 140–2.

‡ 8. 215–21.

with a grin. When Napoleon asked Talleyrand what he thought of the execution of the Duc d'Enghien, Talleyrand replied, 'It was worse than a crime. It was a blunder.'* In the same way, Juvenal shows that his worst-hated butts were not merely knaves; they were also fools.† During the transition from Crispinus the fish-lover to his master, Juvenal plants one final banderilla, more wounding than all. He recalls Crispinus' origins, as a poor peddler wearing a flimsy loincloth of papyrus, and how the luxurious fish-fancier once used to bawl:

> while selling off his catfish, born like himself from mud.‡⁹

Then Juvenal calls on the Muses, adding that they needn't stand up and sing, just sit and tell the truth; and he begins the tale of the Miraculous Turbot. The story itself is nothing, and is meant to be nothing. It was chosen because of the ridiculous disproportion between the trivial subject and the portentous importance of the emperor's deliberations.¹⁰ Instead of showing Domitian as a fiendish murderer, it merely mentions his murders in passing, and concentrates on showing him as a thrice-double ass.

The plot is nothing, then. The style and characterization are everything. To heighten the contrasts implicit in the theme— the Emperor and the Flatfish, the Terror and the Trifle—the story is told in a mock-heroic tone, with noble epic cadences, a comic invocation to the Muses, and lofty phraseology far removed from the simplicity of prose or the nonchalance of satire.¹¹ In all probability it is a parody of part of a contemporary epic poem by Statius, one of Domitian's favoured poets. We have only four lines of that poem, and we do not know its scheme and scope; but the four lines introduce three of the Cabinet Ministers who appear here, describing them in similar terms, while the tone of bogus reverence adopted by Juvenal towards the emperor looks very like a sneer at Statius' real adulation.¹² This satire is the sole ancient ancestor of many modern satires written in mock-heroic style, such as Dryden's *MacFlecknoe* and Pope's *Dunciad*.

---

* But Fouché, the Crispinus of his time, also claimed the phrase.

† Crispinus, 4. 1–33; Domitian, 4. 69–71, 150–4; Nero, 8. 211–30; Sejanus, 10. 61–64.

‡ Iam princeps equitum, magna qui uoce solebat
    uendere municipes fracta de merce siluros . . . (4. 32–33).

But there is another element of parody in it. The emperor Domitian decided to call himself God while he was still alive, instead of waiting for deification after death like any well-conducted monarch. His imperial missives began *Your Lord and God Domitian*. Now, one of the signs of divinity is the power to perform miracles, and there were many stories in antiquity about superhuman heroes who exercised a miraculous power over animals—very like the legends of medieval saints who ploughed with lions and preached to attentive birds. Domitian was credited by his flatterers with possessing this power. So here the fisherman who presents the turbot to the emperor says, 'It came to capture willingly', and at the words Domitian's cox-comb stood erect, he loved to hear himself praised as 'a power equal to the gods'.* Later the fish, which is huge, foreign, and spiky like a warrior, is interpreted as an omen of the capture or death of a hostile foreign chieftain, an omen presumably sent by divine favour.† The satire therefore ridicules Domitian's claims to be a heroic general and his aspirations to be a god.[13]

The persons of the satire are the emperor's Cabinet Ministers. We count eleven of them. Nine are senators, apparently all of very high rank. Two are commanders of the imperial household troops, who although only knights ranked with the senior senators because of the importance of their post. It may be only chance, or perhaps by Domitian's time the number of the Roman Politburo had been fixed at twelve.[14]

Their characters are very various. Some, the oldest, are mild and accommodating politicians like the Abbé Sieyès, who, when asked what he did during Robespierre's Terror, answered 'I survived'. There is one astonishing old rascal who dates back fifteen or twenty years to Nero's time: he was one of the chief gourmets at that lavish court (no doubt arguing with Petronius about a new fish-sauce) and has lived through a terrible civil war, the reigns of five subsequent emperors, and who knows

---

* 'Ipse capi uoluit.' quid apertius? et tamen illi
surgebant cristae: nihil est quod credere de se
non possit cum laudatur dis aequa potestas (4. 69–71).

†   'Ingens
omen habes' inquit 'magni clarique triumphi.
regem aliquem capies, aut de temone Britanno
excidet Aruiragus. peregrina est belua: cernis
erectas in terga sudes' (4. 124–8).

what private threats and dangers? But there he still is: Juvenal shows him to us, waddling in slowly, 'delayed by his paunch', and it is he who—in terms of elaborately studied courtesy— makes the proposal that carries the day:

> bring clay quickly and bring a wheel; but from this time
> forward, Caesar, let potters be attached to your headquarters.*

The five who hurry in first are apparently good men trying to do their best for the empire though crippled by the times in which they live: the youngest, Acilius Glabrio, was to be executed a few years later, probably as a Christian convert. And there are at least two 'informers', the deadly Catullus Messallinus, all the more horrible because he is blind like Pew, and the even more ruthless

> Pompeius, who could slit a throat with a thin whisper.†

Such men did not, like modern informers, make money out of denouncing ordinary lawbreakers. They specialized in ferreting out prominent men who had voiced, or hinted, or thought opposition to the emperor, prosecuting them for high treason, and collecting a large proportion of their property as a reward. In effect, therefore, they were a high-level Gestapo, and their chief target under bad emperors was the old republican aristocracy. They were the arm used by the ruler and his circle to destroy the nobles who could be neither seduced nor cowed. One of the main differences between the reign of a hated monarch like Domitian and that of an admired monarch like Trajan was that Domitian favoured such men and apparently used them as an instrument of policy, while Trajan and his like refused to tolerate them.[15]

But they all have one characteristic in common. They are all terrified of Domitian. This is shown by a number of vivid details; first, by the fact that he calls them to discuss such a trivial subject without compunction, and that they do not laugh but examine it seriously; then, by the pallor and gloom of their faces; and by the nervous haste with which they rush in, not to keep the tyrant waiting, hurry, he has taken his seat, hurry; and by the elaborate, almost Oriental courtesy with

---

   * 'Argillam atque rotam citius properate; sed ex hoc
     tempore iam, Caesar, figuli tua castra sequantur' (4. 134–5).
   † Saeuior illo | Pompeius tenui iugulos aperire susurro (4. 109–10).

which they address him.[16] They were Caesar's 'friends', says Juvenal: so they were always pale.

What of the detestable emperor himself? He is not described. At the very beginning of the story he is called 'the bald Nero' (he hated any reference to his baldness, for the Romans associated baldness with clowns), but that gives us no clear picture of him. We never see his face or hear his voice, until the last member of the Cabinet has panted in. He listens. He says four words. Fat Montanus makes the final speech, and the council is over. Juvenal hated Domitian so much that he could not describe him fully. But also he was too good an artist. He had set out to describe a man with unlimited power using it for bad and silly purposes. The idea of debating about a fish is silly; but the terror Domitian inspires in his councillors shows he is also bad. We never see him, behind his closed doors. We hardly hear his voice. But we are conscious of his power, and of his brooding incalculable dangerous character, silent and unpredictable like a snake.

On this impression the satire ends rapidly and efficiently. Juvenal adds a final double cut by saying that this was all a trifle compared with Domitian's murder of so many noble Romans—which went unpunished. 'He fell only when the working men became afraid of him.'*[17] The contrast is untrue, for his murderers were not members of the working class, nor had the workers any reason to be afraid of him. He was actually killed by retainers of the palace, set on by his own wife. But the nobles, as Juvenal says, were impotent. They gave the bald tyrant either their willing flattery or their lives unavenged. This is another proof of the degeneracy of the Roman aristocracy. We have seen them, through Juvenal's eyes, as greedy, extravagant, and perverted. Now he shows that they are also cowards.

---

* Sed periit postquam cerdonibus esse timendus
    coeperat. hoc nocuit Lamiarum caede madenti (4. 153–4).

XI

SATIRE FIVE
Snobs and Snubs

IN Satire Five we are back again in the world of poor, rootless
hangers-on; but now the poverty is exacerbated by a sharp and
bitter contrast with great wealth. The poem simply describes a
dinner-party.[1] The host is a wealthy and proud Roman, Virro.[2]
There are three groups of guests: a few rich men like the host,
the host's freedmen (once his slaves, now members of his
household acting as secretaries and the like), and a few 'clients'.
Virro invites these poor dependent 'friends' only out of a sense
of duty, once every two months or so, and they go only out of
greed, for there is no real hospitality, no trace of friendship.
The dinner is described, course by course, detail by detail.[3] At
every course, Virro and his special guests are served particularly fine food, in elegant dishes, by chosen servants. The dependants are given inferior food, cheap wine, tough bread,
poor and insolent service. No one speaks to them. The freedmen, resenting their presence, quarrel with them. The host
himself gives them no word and will not even exchange a toast
with them. The entire dinner is a calculated snub.

The general theme, a description of a dinner, was a favourite
one with satirists in the Greco-Roman world. Dinner was the
chief social function, and the arts of cookery and entertainment
were highly developed, so that there were many different points
of view from which good observers could describe a party.
Sometimes a modest dinner was pictured, in order to illustrate
the moral of Sweet Content, or Plain Living and High Thinking.
Sometimes a pretentious and vulgar meal, which tortured the
guests with embarrassment, could be portrayed so as to satirize
the parvenu host: the most famous of these meals is the Dinner
of Trimalchio, which occupies thirty-four pages in Petronius'
satire, and which a few naïve readers still take to be an account
of an ordinary Roman banquet instead of a description of a
monstrous but comical offence against every law of taste.

Sometimes a terribly poor meal, almost uneatable, practically invisible, is set forth so that its readers squirm and laugh at the same time. The satirists of the Renaissance loved this theme: the Italian Berni and the Frenchman Régnier did deliciously horrible descriptions of meagre meals.* Juvenal's present poem is a blend of two such variations, for the host dines in the utmost luxury and the dependant in the utmost squalor, and the two are, if not cheek by jowl, at least face to face.† Is it improbable? is it exaggerated? Apparently not. Juvenal's contemporary, the younger Pliny, says that the rich used to give these two-level dinners, and he makes a special point of serving the same food and wine to his social inferiors as he eats and drinks himself.‡

The purpose of the poem, as well as the combination of the themes, is new in Juvenal. It was written in order to satirize the relationship of patron and dependant still more completely and still more bitingly than Juvenal had done in the earlier satires of Book I. Therefore, although it is a monologue like the other four poems, he made it a monologue addressed to a poor dependant like himself. Technically it is a 'persuasion', because its aim is to convince the hearer that life as a dependant is not worth living.[4] No doubt the poor hanger-on (whom Juvenal calls Trebius) is really drawn from Juvenal's own experience, and the poem is like the Third Satire, in which Juvenal's friend tells Juvenal a hundred reasons for leaving Rome. But here the bitterness and disillusionment of the poem gain extra force from the fiction that Juvenal is addressing a friend who has still to be convinced. Why not be a beggar? he cries—

is no street-corner vacant? §[5]

And at the end he foretells for Trebius, if he will not listen, a fate far worse than beggary.

From another point of view this is a satire on the rich. It shows their utter selfishness, their absurd wastefulness, their empty-headed sensuality, and their half-unconscious, half-calculated cruelty. Perhaps it is not deliberate. Perhaps the host never even thought of his unimportant guests. Marcel Proust describes a similar situation in the Grand Hotel at Balbec, where the poor

---

* See Berni, *Capitolo* 48, and Régnier 10.
† This variation is found elsewhere only in Martial and Lucian.
‡ *Ep.* 2. 6.   § Nulla crepido uacat? (5. 8).

tradesmen and fishermen who inhabit the town stand at night outside the great glass walls of the dining-room, watching the wealthy visitors at dinner, and feeling themselves as strange and remote as though they were scrutinizing a set of marvellous fishes and molluscs in an aquarium;* and Mr. Creevey once publicly protested against the cold neglegence of his host, 'King Jog', exclaiming that 'if it was not for the fuss and jaw of the thing' he would 'leave the room and the house this instant'.† But Juvenal is convinced that Virro's conduct is not merely careless. He believes that it is deliberate, and that the poor man who is snubbed and insulted is being purposely tortured so that his agonies can spice the rich man's banquet.

The Fifth Satire therefore is so designed and so placed as to bring us closer than before to the chief subject of Juvenal's first book: the rich. Through the patron-dependant relationship we saw them in the First Satire, remotely handing out a few coins in lieu of a dinner invitation, and then banqueting alone; and in the Third Satire, accepting the flatteries of greasy Greeks and turning away old dependants. Now we see them face to face. A two-word invitation to dinner and three hours of torture, that is how they repay their retainers' dutiful attendance.[6] Again, we saw the rich in Satire Two as debauchees and perverts, in Satire Four as cowards. We see them now as cruel and callous. We knew they loved only themselves. Now we see that they hate everyone else. The Fifth Satire is the climax of the entire book.

But the poem is almost equally a satire on the poor, and particularly on the middle-class parasites of whom Juvenal felt himself to be one. We met them, these educated men without capital or a profession, in the First Satire, and we were sorry for them as they turned away from My Lord's vestibule to go and dine on boiled cabbage.‡ Then in the Third Satire we shared their wry humiliations, the torn overcoat and the scarred and mended shoe.§ But here what happens to them is not sad. It is disgusting, because it is disgusting to see any human being humiliated; but it is funny, because they have brought it upon themselves. Juvenal does not speak of them as 'we'. He says 'you'

---

* M. Proust, *A l'Ombre des jeunes filles en fleurs* (Paris, 1919), 2. 112–13.
† *The Creevey Papers* (ed. Sir H. Maxwell, London, 1903), 2. 91–92.
‡ 1. 132–4.   § 3. 147–51.

and 'people like you'.* With him, we watch them writhing on
the hook, and smile sardonically at the cupidity—or stupidity—
of men who will go through so much for a free dinner. The
servants are insolent, the freedmen guests resentful, the host
proud and distant. They dare not even raise their glass to him or
speak his name, so far beneath the status of real friends are they.
Still, they sit there, with their bread drawn and in readiness like
a weapon, and watch the host's plate, in case he might be going
to leave them a capon or send down a hare half-eaten.† The
climax of humiliation is to know how low one has fallen. And so
Juvenal adds this last degradation—he explains to them exactly
how much they suffer, and how the host enjoys their suffering,
and how vile their motives really are in enduring all this.
Technically (as we have pointed out) the poem is a 'persuasion'.
But Juvenal shows very little expectation of convincing Trebius
himself, the poor guest, to abandon his life as a hanger-on. It is
we, perhaps it is Juvenal himself, whom Juvenal hopes to convince. To Trebius he begins:

> If you're not yet ashamed of following this career
> and think the height of bliss is eating another man's bread
> I'd be afraid to trust your honour even on oath.‡

Then he exposes Trebius' degradation, describing the insults
heaped upon him by his patron. And then, in the last four lines,
by a masterly stroke of satiric indignation, he shifts the weight of
his attack from patron to guest, from the cruel and haughty
Virro to the abject Trebius. Virro has more brains than you
have, says Juvenal:

> He shows good sense to treat you so. If you can endure
> the worst, then you deserve it. Later you'll shave your head
> and offer it to be slapped, you won't shrink from the cruel
> lash of the whip, to earn such a dinner and such a friend.§

* *Tu* and *te* throughout; *uos* and *uestrum* in 5. 52 and 129; a phrase such as
omnia ferre si potes, et debes (170–1) is cold and distant compared with *clientes
cogimur* in 3. 188–9.   † 166–9.

‡ Si te propositi nondum pudet, atque eadem est mens
   ut bona summa putes aliena uiuere quadra, . . .
   quamuis iurato metuam tibi credere testi (5. 1–2, 5).

§ Ille sapit qui te sic utitur: omnia ferre
   si potes, et debes. pulsandum uertice raso
   praebebis quandoque caput, nec dura timebis
   flagra pati—his epulis et tali dignus amico (5. 170–3).

These two further degradations are worse than any free man
could contemplate. It was the professional clown who shaved his
head to look ridiculous and allowed himself to be beaten, to
raise a laugh at his own deformity and helplessness, like the
final humiliation of Emil Jannings as the clown in *The Blue
Angel*.[7] The clown was to the ordinary freeborn educated man
in Rome as a strip-teaser is to the ordinary lady today—something not to be imitated without losing all self-respect. To sink
lower still was to rank with slaves. That is what Juvenal foretells for Trebius. He will, voluntarily, endure the cat-o'-nine-
tails which was kept for the punishment of unruly slaves.
Rather than be a free beggar, he will make himself a slave *by
choice*, and become truly worthy of a 'friend' such as Virro. The
normal link of rich patron and poor retainer had been a democratic one at least. One was host, the other was guest, but they
were still friends and equals.[8] But the relationship had degenerated so deeply by Juvenal's time that he says both parties were
now corrupted. The host was becoming a slave-owner, and the
dependant a slave.

From the point of view of style this is one of Juvenal's more
brilliant poems. Not nearly as big as Satire Three, it is quite as
vigorous. It is a small brightly lit picture like the Fourth. Like it,
this poem gains an impression of both truth and moral force
from the drastic vividness with which every detail is painted.
Juvenal will have none of those bold slapdash satires with vague
settings and huge grotesque effects. They are jolly, but they are
too enjoyable. He wants to make our flesh creep and our gorge
rise. So we can see the jumbo crayfish carried through the
hall to the master's table, with its tail curving upwards as
though to look down upon the canaille, and long thick stalks of
asparagus flanking it on each side; we can see the black and
bony hand of the negro servant coming over our shoulder, and
taste the tough mouldy bread:

> exercising the jaws but not admitting a bite.*

The master's special carver gesticulates (in Greek terms like
the *entrechats* and *jetées* of the ballet) at the sideboard, cutting
up the master's special dishes with graceful sliding flourishes.

---

*   . . . solidae iam mucida frusta farinae
quae genuinum agitent, non admittentia morsum (5. 68–69).

The eel on our plate looks like a snake. The African oil in our cruet smells like kerosene. All is clear, memorable, and revolting; but everything happens in silence. There are some drunken squabbles, and the servants growl, and the hungry guests whisper as they watch the host's table, but for all the hours all the courses take to serve, no one speaks, there is no conversation, no enjoyment, nothing but silence, hauteur, and greed. The vividness of these impressions is increased by their antithetical arrangement. Since the satire is a contrast of rich and poor, the contrast will be best emphasized if the extremes are put abruptly together, so that our eye can move from the host's amber goblet to the guests' cracked glasses, so that while we chew at our impenetrable bread we can watch the basket of fine rolls going past to Virro's table. Look at that, and now at this; he takes that, he gives you this, back and forward swing the antitheses, poverty in the midst of luxury, stingy extravagance, cruel hospitality, slavish friendship. These contrasts are the essence of the Fifth Satire. And they have all arisen, Juvenal implies, from wealth, which has driven a deep wedge between people who should have been friends, and between classes who were once partners and are now, to each other, either hateful enemies or masters and slaves.

XII

RETROSPECT OF BOOK ONE

As we look back over Book I, we see that the five poems in it fall into a simple, bold arrangement. The First, Third, and Fifth Satires deal with the conflict of wealth and poverty. The Second and Fourth deal with the corruption of the nobles and of the emperor Domitian's court. The five are set out in a climactic scheme, so that the indictment of cruel wealth and the exposure of hopeless poverty grows sharper as the book proceeds. Satire One introduces us to a number of possible themes, then narrows them down to those which Juvenal prefers. Satire Three, long and finely constructed, is placed in the middle for the maximum effect, Satire Five sharpens the focus and drives home Juvenal's point about the corrupting power of money, with no remorse and no possible escape.

We notice also that the First, Third, and Fifth are written from the point of view of a poor man looking up, while the Second and Fourth are written from the point of view of a rich man—or of a man on almost the same level as the rich and noble. This adds completeness and authority to the general picture. In one book of just under a thousand lines Juvenal takes us through many different social strata of Rome, all the way from a poet's sparsely furnished attic to the emperor's summer palace, from street-corner brawlers to a secret meeting of wealthy perverts, from the crowded streets of the city to the quiet garden of a country town.* Yet it is a little difficult to understand how the same man can have written both groups of poems, unless he had been both rich and poor. In our reconstruction of Juvenal's life we have suggested that he was well off at the beginning of his career, and that as a young knight he sought for influence and promotion in rich men's houses and in the emperor's palace; but that late in Domitian's reign he was banished and reduced to beggary.† Should this be accepted as

---

* 3. 197–209; 4. 60 f.; 3. 286–301; 2. 83–116; 1. 22–80 and 3. 236–67; 3. 226–31.

† See pp. 40–41.

true, then the Second and Fourth Satires reflect the earlier part of his life, and the First, Third, and Fifth the later period of poverty and disillusionment, ending on a note of bitter abnegation and self-reproach.*

* This is not, of course, to say that Satires 2 and 4 were written down (far less published) in or near the period of the 80's to which they refer; but that the ideas and the impulses which produced them came to Juvenal at that time, growing into poetry much later, after Domitian's death.

XIII

THE SECOND BOOK: SATIRE SIX

Advice to those About to Marry

BOOK II is even more ambitious than the First Book. The entire thing is one single poem, the Sixth Satire, running to the extraordinary length of nearly 700 lines. As far as we can tell, this was unique in Roman satiric poetry. Juvenal's immediate predecessor Persius wrote poems averaging just over 100 lines each. Horace has some only a page or two in length, and his biggest does not reach 350 lines.* We cannot tell the size of Lucilius' satires, but we should probably have heard of it if he had ever produced such a leviathan as this. The first book Juvenal published was a bold attempt to dominate the whole field of satire. This is a second attempt, even bolder.

The subject is a tremendous expansion of the theme of one of *Punch*'s most famous jokes, 'Advice to those about to marry: Don't.' The poem is sometimes called a satire on the female sex, 'A Legend of Bad Women', and the like. It is not. It is a satire on marriage: it is a denunciation of wives, and in particular of rich wives. Poor wives are mentioned now and then, there is an extravagant Bovary who spends more than her husband can afford, but the vast majority of the women in the poem are rich, and most of them have claims to social prominence.[1] In the First Book Juvenal showed us very few women—a poisoner here, a prostitute there, but only here and there.† All his chief characters were men—though some were unworthy of the name. Now, as though to complete the picture, he shows us a vast gallery of Roman society ladies, some beautiful, some ugly, some young and some old, but each and all distinguished by a particular affectation or folly or vice.

Like the Fifth, and in a way like the Third, this satire is a 'persuasion'. Juvenal addresses a friend called Postumus. 'Are

---

* *Serm.* 2. 3.   † 1. 69–72, 3. 133–6.

you getting married?' he says, '—married, when ropes are so cheap and suicide is so easy?. . .' Then he proceeds to give almost every possible reason against marriage, by describing all the appalling types of wife the unfortunate man is liable get. Vicious, extravagant, quarrelsome, sex-crazy, drunken, gossipy, affected, domineering, lying, treacherous, murderous —the horrible catalogue goes on, and on, and on. Quite early in it, Juvenal disarms one possible objection by saying that, even though one woman out of a million might be perfect,

> the rarest bird on earth, unique as a black swan,*

she would be so proud of all her virtues as to be quite intolerable.

This theme, the Torments of Marriage, is a very old one in western literature.[2] It first appears about the eighth century B.C., in Hesiod's story of Pandora. The gods made a being endowed with all the qualities of an ideal woman, and sent her down to be the wife of Epimetheus, Afterthought; but the dowry she brought him was a casket containing all the diseases and troubles that have plagued mankind ever since.[†] Then Semonides, about 630 B.C., wrote a poem comparing wives to various kinds of animals and natural phenomena: sow, vixen, bitch, and so forth; only one is good, the busy bee. Similar attacks appeared from time to time thereafter, for instance in the dramatists (Euripides, Aristophanes, Menander) and in the mime-writer Herodas. In Latin literature the topic first emerges in Lucilius,[‡] and often recurs, passing eventually into the writings of the sterner church fathers. To judge from the stories which appear in Petronius and Apuleius, there was a large popular tradition about the lusts and tricks of women. Similar tales occur in the *Arabian Nights*, and became common again in the west during the Middle Ages—for example in the popular French *fabliaux* and in Chaucer's *Canterbury Tales*.[§] On the whole, this attitude to marriage seems to belong to the working class and the middle class. There is no trace of it in Homer, where even the unfaithful Helen is portrayed as a great and lovable lady: aristocratic literature generally idealizes women or else ignores them. It is the hard-working Hesiod ('get a woman and a ploughing ox')[‖]

---

* Rara auis in terris nigroque simillima cycno (6. 165).
† Hes. *Op.* 50–105.   ‡ Lucil. frg. 678–86.
§ *The Miller's Tale* and *The Merchant's Tale*.   ‖ Hes. *Op.* 405.

who begins it; and even in Juvenal we feel that many of the bitterest complaints come from a man of the middle class, indignant at the caprices of upper-class ladies and their imitators.

The theme was also discussed by philosophers, who treated it as a moral problem: 'is marriage good or bad?' and 'how can marriage be made to work successfully?' Sometimes also they argued about a special case: 'should the philosopher marry or not?' On the whole, the Stoics recommended marriage, as a duty to the state and mankind; the Epicureans viewed it with distrust;* and the Cynics opposed it. Juvenal has often been called a Stoic, but here as elsewhere we see that he either did not know or did not accept their basic teaching on certain important matters.

Rhetoricians also used to debate the pros and cons of marriage, and prided themselves on finding trenchant objections to it and then overthrowing them. A good deal of what Juvenal says here was apparently selected from the arguments of the rhetorical schools, and some of his examples, too, come from their catalogues.

Quite apart from his own experience, then, Juvenal seems to have been drawing on a large reservoir of working-class and middle-class misogynistic propaganda, on philosophical discussions of marriage (in which he largely ignored the general arguments but used the psychological descriptions), and on the debates and illustrations of popular schools of oratory.

The structure of this enormous poem has been much canvassed. It must have given Juvenal a good deal of trouble to fit all his dozens of wounding arguments, bitter epigrams, and savage character-sketches, into any single scheme; and no one would say that he has been wholly successful. The poem has a beginning, and a middle, and an end—which are clear enough.† They make a good structural skeleton. But the subordinate sections sometimes appear disconnected, and it is not always clear why one section belongs to one of the main parts of the poem rather than to another.

Similar difficulties appear in other satires of Juvenal—for instance, in the First (see n. 2 on p. 246) and the Fourth (see pp. 256–7), and later in the Seventh and Eighth and Fourteenth.

* e.g. Lucr. 4. 1058–1287.   † Details on p. 267.

Many critics have written about them, sometimes in terms of great acrimony and sometimes with proud and half-deliberate blindness like an eighteenth-century aesthete describing a Gothic cathedral. Now that we are discussing Juvenal's most ambitious poem, this is the right place to say something of the structure of his satires in general.

All readers agree that his poems do not follow regular and predictable patterns; that he wanders away from the point (although usually to some other almost equally interesting point) and returns with a perceptible jolt; that his transitions from one part of a poem to another are apt to be sudden and illogical; that he gives some subjects far more space than they seem to need; that he occasionally announces a new theme with some emphasis, and then drops it before working it out; that he creates a general impression of ill-applied energy and planless excitement. Most readers add that the poems such as Satire Three and Satire Ten which have a clear structural plan prove him to be a fine craftsman; and then they try to excuse the unevenness of his other satires. A few, however, call him an inferior artist who could work in detail but had little sense of plan.

Why are Juvenal's satires irregular? The easiest answer was given by Ribbeck in 1865 and echoed in various forms by other scholars. The poems (they suggested) were all right when Juvenal wrote them, but were tampered with later. Scribes miscopied them, or editors transposed passages to suit their own taste, or subsequent readers inserted lines and whole paragraphs of their own with the idea of improving the poems. Ribbeck called nearly all the later satires downright forgeries.[3] A variant of this explanation has also been put forward. It is suggested that Juvenal himself brought out two successive editions of his satires, altering or restating certain ideas in the second version, and that what we now have is a blend of the two different versions made by some numskull after the poet died; or else that Juvenal left, in the margin of his own copy of his poems, variants on several passages, which were incorporated into the text after his death.[4] All these theories are built on one simple and incontrovertible truth—that Juvenal's text has suffered some serious cuts, dislocations, and additions.* But there

* The best discussions of this are by Cremer (*42*), Jachmann (*43*), Knoche (*45*), and Vianello (*52*).

is no evidence to support the idea that what Juvenal really wrote was something very far different from the poems as we have them; and in particular, the theory that he himself issued two editions is improbable and unproved. To produce a new edition of a book of poems in classical times seems to have meant rearrangement and excision much more drastic than anything hitherto suggested for Juvenal. When we find repetitions in his poems, they are either meant to add punch to some point he wishes to drive home, or else intended as explanations of something difficult. The first type he probably wrote himself. It is likely that he wrote much of the second, and that helpful readers added the rest. Gaps in the poems have certainly been introduced by editors and scribes. But there is at present no evidence whatever for widespread dislocation in Juvenal's poetry, corruption which would justify us in breaking up his satires and reassembling them in a form closer to our heart's desire. The danger of this kind of criticism is that it expects an emotional poetic monologue to be as well-balanced, straightforward, and economical as a scientific paper. We can imagine such a critic turning to Hamlet's first soliloquy—

> Oh, that this too too solid flesh would melt,
> Thaw, and resolve itself into a dew—

and cutting out the second line as 'weak repetition', in spite of its melody and in spite of its essential truth to Hamlet's character and Shakespeare's style.

Another answer to the problem is that Juvenal was simply a bad poet and that modern readers could better his work.[5] Critics bold enough to say this proliferated in the confident nineteenth century: they would scold a Latin writer as freely as they would improve an eleventh-century church or bowdlerize a Renaissance play. Many of them were displaced scientists, trying even in literary criticism to make the facts fit the theory. Some were Hegelians, who felt that all the Real ought to be Rational. Some were promoted school-masters who enjoyed rebuking people like Juvenal and putting them in their proper place. Some, no doubt, were believers in the inevitability of Progress, so that they considered that any nineteenth-century critic was bound to be wiser than any second-century poet. We are perhaps less sure of our own rectitude these days, and we look at the slashing affirmations of such critics (in Housman's words), 'less with envy than with fright, like Sin when she gave birth to Death'.*

Other critics, however, are less blunt. They say that Juvenal was a poet with good ideas, but that he wrecked many of them by false emphasis; and they explain that this was the result of the habit he had acquired as a 'declaimer', while making speeches on general themes, as a hobby carried over from his youth.[6] Such speeches, delivered to emotional but easily bored audiences, resembled the essays and articles of much modern journalism. Like essays nowadays, they were part of a regular school education. Many men with literary interests continued to produce them after leaving school, much as a modern writer fills in his time by turning out critical papers and brief imaginative articles. But since they were spoken rather than read, they leant heavily on sudden brilliant effects—paradoxes which made the audience gasp, epigrams which dazzled it, antitheses which dizzied it, images which, even if inappropriate, excited it.

This point also is true, but exaggerated. It is based on a remark in the ancient lives of Juvenal, that he 'declaimed until middle age'—which is likely to be a false deduction drawn from the first two pages of the Satires, and has little if any real ancient authority.† But we do not know that display speeches of this type were usually delivered year after year by grown men, unless they were professional teachers of rhetoric. The truth more probably is that (as Juvenal says himself‡) all poetry in the empire was read aloud to recital audiences, and was therefore filled with brilliant effects which, even if they distorted the structure of the whole, would be applauded when read aloud. The big speeches in Seneca's tragedies, the stentorian apostrophes in Lucan's epic, and other high lights of Silver Age poetry, all suffer from the same fault. Like Juvenal, they all tend to sacrifice the whole to the part, to elaborate an irrelevant point for its own sake, and to prefer a succession of fireworks to a rich sun-like glow. Juvenal's friend and closest inspiration was Martial, who wrote nothing but tiny epigrams, one sure if another failed.

A clearer and simpler criticism of the structure of Juvenal's

* A. E. Housman, *Manilius* I (Cambridge, 1937²), pref. xliv.

† *Ad mediam fere aetatem declamauit* = Juv. I. 15–17 + I. 25. On the ancient lives see pp. 21–23.   ‡ I. 1–13.

poems is to say that they are not always logically coherent. Scholars have rearranged them, using phrases like 'This parenthesis is here unnecessary' and 'Here Juvenal indulges in a digression'.* But most of these criticisms are misapplied. In the first place, Juvenal is a poet, and the arrangement of a poet's ideas is not always governed by logic, but often by emotion. Logic is equable, emotion is violent and irregular. Often Juvenal wishes to give full play to his emotions and to go on and on describing some infamy even when logic requires him to look elsewhere. Often he wishes to surprise his readers with a sudden unexpected side-development: often to relieve the tension by a joke or a quiet description or a recapitulation. Then, in the second place, Juvenal is a satirist, and maintains the tone popularized by previous satirists—the tone of improvisation, of half-humorous, half-indignant conversation, the tone of the brilliant talker half of whose brilliance lies in the fact that no one knows what he is going to say next, not even himself.† This is the tone we know from the fantastic chatter of Rabelais, the whimsical indirection of Sterne, the reckless hiccuping energy of Byron; and Juvenal's readers knew it from Horace, from Seneca, from Petronius, and from his other predecessors. Finally, a sympathetic analysis of many of Juvenal's poems will show that they are in fact built on a firm logical substructure, which has been concealed from many readers by his energy, his speed, and his air of nonchalance.[7] But scholars do not always appreciate the art which conceals art.

In Satire Six, then, as in other satires, Juvenal is not merely trying to make a logical sequence of thought, and failing. He is trying to create emotional conviction and to do so within the manner of satire, which always posed as being sincere because it was unaffected and careless. Yet even allowing for this tradition of incoherence, it is true that the Sixth is among his less successful poems if looked at as an exercise in form. It is possible for an apparently artless discourse, shaken by gusts of indignation and buffeted by gales of savage laughter, to be so unobtrusively arranged that each part grows out of its predecessor

* 'Digressions' are a favourite notion of Hartmann (21).
† So T. Birt, 'Der Aufbau der sechsten und vierten Satire Juvenals', *RhM* 70 (1915), 524–50.

and into its successor, forming a whole which we remember as much for its structure as for its content. Juvenal contrived that in other poems, such as the Third and the Tenth. Here, something got in his way. It may have been the absence of any kind of model for such a huge work. It may have been his lack of practice in abstract and logical thought. It may very well have been the intensity of his emotion, which made him hate all wives indiscriminately, whether they were prigs or poisoners, public speakers or public harlots. (Towards the end of his life Shakespeare seems to have suffered from a similar obsession—the theme of adultery. He wrote several plays which turn on it, and he made his heroes denounce it with a hysterical and disorderly violence that reminds us of Juvenal in this poem.*) Therefore, although every reader remembers some of the pictures and descriptions in the Sixth Satire, few can grasp its underlying structure, and none can relate all the parts to the scheme of the whole.

Sometimes Juvenal makes us think of the Flemish satiric painter, Pieter Bruegel. Many of Bruegel's pictures are clearly and calmly planned, with a central theme which is supported by all the details. The theme is usually bitter even when the details are idyllic or gay, but still it is clear: such pictures are *Icarus, The Merry Way to the Gallows, The Country Wedding*.† But there are also some pictures of wildly imaginative subjects in which Bruegel reverts to the older style of his master Bosch, and fills a canvas with dozens of groups of people exemplifying proverbs or children playing games, but makes no effort to relate them to one another except by their compresence in the same place within the same frame. There are others again where, shaken by some overpowering emotion, he allows an explosion of horror to burst out upon a canvas which is packed with shapes of death and torment, fiends and fiendish animals, impossible monsters, skeletons and flames and yawning hell-mouths, pictures as compelling and incomprehensible as a nightmare. Such are his *Triumph of Death* and *Mad Meg*. In the same way,

---

* See, for instance, *Cymbeline*, 3. 5, *Othello*, 4. 2, *Timon*, 4. 3, *Troilus*, 5. 3. 134 f., and *Winter's Tale*, 1. 2. 129 f. A comparably deep hatred of women runs through most of the work of Strindberg.

† See G. Highet, 'Bruegel's Rustic Wedding', *The Magazine of Art*, 38 (1945), 274–6.

Juvenal sometimes paints a wry little domestic scene (e.g. Satires Nine and Eleven) in colours as bright as Vermeer; but now and then his emotion carries him off and he breaks into a nightmarish, maniacal, almost incoherent violence of invective. Such a poem is the Sixth Satire.

The theme is 'It is madness to marry'. Juvenal works it out in four big sections.[8]

In the first he says that no man should think of marrying, because chastity has left the world and all women are impure. This section ends with a searing description of the empress Messalina slipping out of the palace in disguise to spend the night in a brothel—from which (Juvenal characteristically adds) she returned unsatisfied.[9]

The second section is built round a series of questions from Juvenal's interlocutor Postumus, the man he is dissuading from marriage. He asks if married love is an illusion and if no woman is worth loving. The answers are that 'love-marriages' are built on money or the temporary attraction of a pretty face, that a perfect woman would be impossible to live with, and that if you do fall in love with your wife she will dominate you, intimidate you, and finally deceive you with someone else.[10]

Juvenal has now shown that a pure and happy marriage is impossible. This assertion, which might be rejected as an absurd exaggeration, he supports in his third section by a powerful general statement, and in his fourth by a horrid series of examples of its truth.*

But what produced these monsters? do you know their origin?
It was humble poverty that kept the Latin women chaste
so long ago. . . .
Now we have the sickness of long peace: harsher than war,
luxury preys upon us and avenges the conquered world;
every crime and shape of lust has appeared since the age
when Roman poverty vanished.†

* 6. 286–351 and 352–661.
† Vnde haec monstra tamen uel quo de fonte requiris?
praestabat castas humilis fortuna Latinas
quondam. . . .
Nunc patimur longae pacis mala: saeuior armis
luxuria incubuit uictumque ulciscitur orbem;
nullum crimen abest facinusque libidinis ex quo
paupertas Romana perit (6. 286–8, 292–5).

Marriage was once good and women were once virtuous—
long ago. At the beginning of the poem, jokingly, he said it
was in the Golden Age, when we all lived in caves—and even
then he contrasted the rugged big-breasted cave-mother with
the degenerate women of Rome like Propertius' emancipated
Cynthia and Catullus' passionate Lesbia.[11] Now he says seriously
what many other Roman thinkers said before him, that Roman
morality was ruined by the accumulation of wealth, by the
removal of that challenge which Carthage (and other enemies)
once offered, and by the influx of foreign customs. This may
sound like an obvious commonplace, but it was hard for the
average Roman to accept and it was earnestly believed by
many of Rome's finest minds. The elder Cato saw the process
gathering strength and tried to halt it. Sallust was an observer
and perhaps himself a symptom of its increasing power. Juvenal's
predecessor Horace made it the theme of several of his most
powerful lyric poems. A long succession of legislators, from
the censors of the Republic to the emperor Augustus and
Juvenal's foe Domitian himself, attempted to arrest the degeneration by restrictive laws. For us, Juvenal stands almost
at the end of the process. He said in his First Satire that vice
had reached its zenith, that posterity could add nothing worse.*
Elsewhere in the First Book he repeated that life in Rome was
hopeless and unendurable.† Now he makes the point once
again, on an equally important topic, and—if we can judge
by the predictions of earlier writers—with a great deal of truth
on his side.

So then, disorderly as the satire may seem to be, exaggerated
as its theme may at first appear, it is in fact a serious attempt to
describe the results of a long and violent revolution, the collapse
of family life and sexual morality in what had been one of the
most puritanical societies of the ancient world. What Juvenal
here denounces is what Horace foresaw, and what the Christian
fathers a few generations later were to attack and, fortunately
for the world, to overthrow. After giving that short account of
the causes of this catastrophe, he hurries on, in two pages of
unequalled vigour and unbelievable brutality, to describe the
debauched women of contemporary Rome as forming a secret
society of their own, free from all restraints of family duty or

* 1. 87, 1. 147–9; see pp. 57–58.   † Satires 2, 3, and 5.

thoughts of virtue, drinking themselves into a frenzy, defiling the altar of Chastity, dancing the hula at the secret festival of the mysterious Good Goddess, and polluting all the religious ceremonies which had once bound Roman women together for good and now served as an excuse for exciting intrigue.[12] All this passage, which grows directly out of his account of Rome as ruined by wealth, strikes us with the same revolting unreality as the account of the men's homosexual society in Satire Two, and its details are unconfirmed by other writers: so that it might all come from Juvenal's own angry conviction that Roman women were hopelessly corrupt, and be rather inference and invention than true evidence. We have no way of checking. All we can say is that nothing Juvenal describes is impossible and that worse things are known from both ancient and modern times.

The fourth, last, and largest section of the poem is a catalogue of the vices which have resulted from the process of degeneration Juvenal has mentioned.[13] He proceeds to describe the various fads and follies and corruptions and crimes to which Roman wives are addicted. Beginning quietly, after the terrible account of the secret orgies, he speaks first of the spendthrift wife, then of the wife who insists on having homosexuals and eunuchs on the household staff,* then of social affectations ranging all the way from an unnatural interest in foreign politics to a passion for face-cream. So far the offences are domestic and social. Juvenal moves on from them to the extravagances of the wives who accept imported religious cults, who practise Yoga and obey the Swami, or, still worse, become astrologers and Madame Blavatskys themselves. Last of all—we might think that no climax would be possible after the outrages described in the third section, but we should never underestimate the power of a woman—last of all he speaks of wives as criminals, those who procure abortions when pregnant, those who drug their husbands into imbecility, those who kill their stepchildren, and their children, and their husbands.

The four sections of the poem therefore form a climax. In the first, Juvenal says that wives cheat their husbands; in the second, that they tyrannize their husbands; in the third, that they despise and ignore their husbands; and in the fourth, that they torment and kill their husbands.

* On this passage ('the O fragment') see pp. 335–6.

That is only a brief outline of this powerful poem. The innumerable brilliant pictures in it cannot be reproduced. They must be read in Juvenal's own words, and then they can never be forgotten. Some of them are perfectly modern; the wife who

> knows what happens everywhere in the world,
> what the Chinese are doing, and what the Bulgars . . .*

and who discusses foreign affairs with generals in full uniform; . the wife who consults the stars on every action; the wife who gives monologues on the appreciation of poetry till she could silence a lawyer, an auctioneer—even another woman; the attentive wife who tells her husband what friends he should cultivate and whom he should mention in his will.† Others are, thank God, creatures of a different age: the virago who has her noisy neighbour beaten up and the sadist who tortures her slaves; yet even so they are recognizable, and not even improbable.[14] Of course the satire is overweighted. Of course it has seemed false in ages when family life and sexual relations were well adjusted. Yet because of the long degeneration of Roman morals it was probably close to the truth in its own time; and so many quotations and imitations have been inspired by it in the last 1,500 years that it must contain a large proportion of permanent truth.‡ It is strange to look back on it and to compare it with the other satires of Juvenal. They so often speak of the decadence of Roman society as manifested in weakness: men dressed as women, nobles unable to resist tyranny, true citizens helplessly driven from their homes, defeat and surrender everywhere. But in the Sixth Satire there is no weakness. All the women are strong characters, stronger than their husbands, possessed by furies of ambition, wilfulness, and lust, utterly selfish, boldly irresponsible, courageous, ruthless, remorseless. Evidently the profound spiritual maladjustment from which Rome suffered in Juvenal's day had sucked away the strength of her men and intensified the passions of her women.[15] They were no longer partners, or members one of another, but rivals, or deadly enemies.

       * Haec eadem nouit quid toto fiat in orbe,
         quid Seres, quid Thraces agant . . . (6. 402–3).
    † 6. 398–412; 553–81; 434–56; 212–18.
    ‡ See p. 265.

Such a poem, with all its acute observation and sometimes overloaded description, clearly took Juvenal many years to mature and compose. Yet if we ask to what period of his life it mainly belongs, we shall have to answer that it originated in some time when he was comparatively well off, when he was fairly young, and when he was full of idealism. There is no trace in it of the pinching and scraping that make up a dependant's parasitic life. The marriages which Juvenal shows us are mainly upper-middle-class and aristocratic. Censennia has a dowry of £3,000,000; Bibula's husband buys her huge estates and vineyards and historic diamonds; others have emerald necklaces and pearl ear-rings and gold-trimmed dresses; even the religious loonies are rich enough to be asked for a sacrifice of 100 sheep. They are nearly all well off, and Juvenal has seen them from their own level though his standards are different.[16] On the other hand, this satire must be later in conception than Satire Two, which is rather kind to women and says they disgrace their sex much less, and much less often, than men.* Recalling our reconstruction of Juvenal's life,† we might suggest that, after coming up to Rome from his country town, he had an unhappy experience with the proud and selfish Roman ladies. It looks as though, while waiting for the appointment in government service which never came, he had married a lady of superior rank and pretensions, and found her intolerable. When he was sent into banishment, she would surely divorce him—so that he would lose not only his career and his money but his home and his family too, and would return from exile some years later to become (like Umbricius) a disillusioned and saturnine old bachelor.[17]

* See Juv. 2. 36–65.   † See pp. 40–41.

XIV

THE THIRD BOOK OF THE SATIRES

Book III shows the beginning of a failure in Juvenal's powers. He was getting on in years—he must have been about 60 when it came out; he had said much of what he originally had to say; his initial impulse was growing fainter and farther away, for Domitian had been dead for a quarter of a century; and he had had no success whatever. Books I and II were bold bids for fame, an attempt to raise satire to the level of high poetry. They can scarcely have succeeded; Juvenal's contemporaries received them with complete silence. The reason, no doubt, was that they were too good. The Roman upper classes did not care to hear themselves so trenchantly attacked: so they ignored the attacks. In addition, as we shall see, Juvenal took care to alienate some of those who could have been his most distinguished patrons.* The result was, almost everywhere, a disdainful silence. He had already suffered a great deal. This new blow did not numb him. He was able to accept it and to convert it into his later poems—in particular, into the fine Tenth Satire which states a sombre, convinced, but courageous pessimism.

The Third Book is short—three satires, about 700 lines—and leaves a rather ugly impression on its readers. Although it is carefully balanced, the final effect is unpleasant. Its opening and closing satires deal with unemployment and poverty and the central satire with the proper employment of the rich. That is symmetrical. But the Seventh Satire, which opens the book, describes the crisis of the intellectuals, whereas the Ninth, which closes it, describes, rather more gaily and vividly, the impoverishment of a professional pervert. That is a skilful and interesting poem, yet—both for ancient and for modern taste—it is almost as twisted as its subject. It tends, therefore, to disguise the fact that in this Book, for the first time, Juvenal becomes not

* See pp. 290–4.

only a negative critic but a positive teacher. For the long
Eighth, the centre of the book, contains some really good advice
on two of the biggest problems of the Roman empire—how to
employ the rich nobles and how to govern the provinces. This
Book, then, marks the beginning of another change in Juvenal's
perspective, but the inequality of the poems in it shows that he
had not yet managed to adjust his vision to the new focus.

XV

SATIRE SEVEN
Poverty and Poetry

THE Seventh Satire, like the Fourth, is made up of a brief introduction and a detailed study of one particular social class.[1] The
opening passage praises the emperor as the only active patron
of literature. The rest of the poem describes the hopeless de-
pression and poverty into which literature and allied pursuits
have sunk, an abyss from which only the monarch's powerful
help can save them.

This theme, the misery of the intellectuals, always appeals
to artists and critics, and seldom to anyone else. Much had
been written on it before Juvenal's time.[2] His Greek contemporary Lucian suffered from the same hardships and wrote
about them in his own clear, rather shallow manner. In certain
stages of civilization this maladjustment is a familiar complaint.
It was one of the chief bases of the gloom which afflicted so
many in Elizabethan and Jacobean England, and which produced Burton's *Anatomy of Melancholy*.* In the eighteenth century it was experienced and described by Samuel Johnson and
others, and amusingly caricatured in Hogarth's *Distressed Poet*.
The Grub Street of baroque London has become a symbol of the
life of starving hack writers. Perhaps we should take it more
seriously if we had not been accustomed, by Mürger's *Bohemian
Life* and Puccini's opera *Bohemia*, to think that most artists are
happy in slums and attics. But Bohemia is a state of mind proper
to youth alone. To give up your whole life to a valuable profession like teaching or a difficult ambition like poetry, and then
to remain poor all your days and die poor, is really miserable.†

The intellectuals of whom Juvenal writes are a curious lot.

---

* Burton, *Anatomy of Melancholy*, Part 1, Sec. 2, Mem. 3, Subsect. 15;
J. M. Murry, *Countries of the Mind* (1st series, London, 1931), c. 3; L. C.
Knights, 'Seventeenth Century Melancholy', *Criterion*, 13 (1933), 50.
97–112.

† So says Juvenal himself, 7. 32–35.

He begins with poets, who get the most space. Only the loftiest types of poetry are mentioned—epic, tragedy, and lyric.* But here is another change in his outlook. When he wrote Book I, he was derisively unsympathetic towards serious poetry; now he thinks of it as a noble aspiration which deserves encouragement. He said then that it was a useless occupation, and added that the results bored him to death. Now he admires the poet who pawns his overcoat and dishes to keep him alive while finishing his tragedy, and he expresses kindness for the poet laureate Statius who had to write ballet-scenarios in order to pay the grocer's bill.[3]

After poets he goes on to historians, who get a meagre seven lines;[4] and to lawyers, who get forty-four. The satire ends with a memorable description of the miseries of schoolmasters, both on the elementary level and in high schools. As we read on, we almost forget how limited this picture is. Very few types of poetry are mentioned, and only one kind of prose, which is brushed off in a paragraph. Prose fiction and essays do not appear. Philosophy is not spoken of—Juvenal distrusted professional philosophers, and anyhow most of them were Greeks. There is no trace of science; there are no painters; there are no sculptors. All these were Greeks, so that Juvenal both expected and regretted their success. There are musicians—one of them with a Greek name—but they are so rich that they form a brilliant contrast to the poverty of the teacher: so nowadays a Horowitz or a Heifetz makes as much in one evening as a professor in a year.† The poem, then, does not give us a complete picture of the intellectual and aesthetic life of Rome. What it shows us is distorted by Juvenal's hatred of foreigners and limited by his own strong but narrow interests.

The misery of these intellectuals Juvenal treats in his own cold and realistic way. Repellent as this may be at first, it still reveals some unexpected and unconventional truths. He does not complain that the intellectuals are neglected. He does not say that their poems are ignored or misunderstood by the stupid bourgeois. On the contrary. He says their poetry is loved dearly

---

* Epic, 7. 27, 66–68, 79–81, 82–86; tragedy, 7. 12, 72–73; lyric implied in 7. 58–65.

† 7. 175–7. Chrysogonus appears in 6. 74 and Polio in 6. 387; the latter is mentioned in Mart. 3. 20. 18 and 4. 61. 9; otherwise both are now unknown.

and applauded with enthusiasm.⁵ He says the schoolmasters are
kept busy, with crowded classes. His main complaint is that
they make no money out of it. Their work is truly appreciated.
High standards, intellectual and moral, are set for the teachers.
The whole city flocks to hear a recital by one of the best poets.
But there is no cash in it. The elementary schoolmasters have
to pay a commission to each pupil's guardian slave; the higher
teachers have to sue the parents for their fees; poor lawyers get
no money at all but are paid in kind—

> a dried-up ham and a mason jar
> of tuna-fish, or a sack of onions fit for convicts,
> or local wine from up river, five whole quarts.*⁶

The poets have to write hack stuff, or else give up their art
and take to business, speculative and degrading as that is.† In
itself, art will not provide enough to live on. Only glory. But
what is glory, if you are hungry?‡

The poverty of the intellectuals is well described. Here as
elsewhere Juvenal shows us far more of the life of the middle-
class poor than any other ancient writer. I remember when I
first read one of his phrases in this satire, I thought it forced and
incomprehensible. He says that to imagine and write an epic
poem is

> the work of a mighty mind, which is not aghast at the thought
> of buying a blanket.§

As an undergraduate I could not conceive how anyone could
be aghast at the thought of buying a blanket. But later, I joined
one of the groups of which Juvenal writes, and found that the
monthly bill for electric light or the cost of a new rug was a very
serious problem. Then I understood that the line made good
sense and the antithesis good poetry. It is pretty clear that
Juvenal himself had suffered. He mentions hardships which
are similar to those of a musician trying to get ahead nowadays,
but which we should never have known about, had he not written.

---

* Quod uocis pretium? siccus petasunculus et uas
  pelamydum, aut ueteres (Maurorum epimenia) bulbi,
  aut uinum Tiberi deuectum, quinque lagonae (7. 119–21).
† 7. 87, 3–12, 17.   ‡ 7. 81.
§ magnae mentis opus, nec de lodice paranda
  attonitae (7. 66–67).

Your patron, he says, will grant you some help if you are giving a recital—but not much. He will let you use an old studio with creaking doors and damp-stained walls, and will tell his freedmen to attend and applaud. But the benches in the centre, and the high seats on scaffolding at the back, and the armchairs in the front rows—*you* have to pay for hiring them.[7] It reminds us of the pathetic little concerts nowadays, half-filled with free-ticket-holders; the one-man exhibitions in booksellers' back parlours; the poems privately issued in limited editions by unknown publishers; the little magazines printed on miserable yellowing stock and filled with misprints; the plays performed in dusty barns with hideous lighting and improvised properties, in an aura of gallant despair.

But the poverty of these intellectuals would not deserve our sympathy if they were getting their fair share. Therefore Juvenal takes care to emphasize the fact that their rewards are unjust. He does this by showing how the rich grudge money to a poet or a professor, and squander it freely on silly and degrading expenses. One millionaire refused (he says) to send a cheque to a deserving writer on the edge of starvation. But he bought a tame lion to feed on raw meat—

> that animal is less expensive,
> no doubt, and the belly of a poet is far more capacious.*

Another paid Quintilian, the finest literary critic and teacher of his day, £40 for tutoring his son; and then spent astronomical sums on building a huge country house with a private swimming-pool, a marble-pillared dining-room, and a long portico in which he could drive even in wet weather without soiling his mule-team's polished hooves.[8] The poem ends with another such contrast: a year's pay for a schoolmaster, with all his responsibilities intellectual and moral, is equal to the bonus given to one jockey when he rides one winner.[9]

There are two other contrasts which make the poor intellectuals feel their poverty more bitterly. The lawyers complain that they cannot get a start without being noble or rich, or at least pretending to be rich. If they are poor, they get miserable petty cases to plead, they might as well emigrate. The big fees

*   Constat leuiori belua sumptu,
    nimirum, et capiunt plus intestina poetae (7. 77–78).

go to the nobly descended Aemilius, who has a triumphal statue of his ancestor the general in his hall, and a slightly decrepit sculpture of himself near by, dressed as a victorious warrior to show his skill in attack. No one can meet such competition unless by putting on a tremendous display of wealth. Like the young lawyer who became the judge in *Trial by Jury*, who had

> A swallow-tail coat of a beautiful blue, . . .
> And a ring that looked like a ruby,

the rising barrister must hire a jewelled ring to attract the eye while he speaks, and wear rich clothes, and have a large retinue of slaves and secretaries and dependants—even if he risks going bankrupt by straining his credit.[10] To him that hath shall be given; from him that hath not shall be taken away.*

Juvenal does not deny that a few intellectuals are prosperous and successful. There was Lucan, who was rich because his father had made a fortune in the imperial service.† There was Quintilian, who became a millionaire as professor of rhetoric and as barrister. Yes, Quintilian was rich; he was also lucky, and handsome, and brave, and wise, and noble, and sang well even if he had a cold, in fact one in a million, a phoenix, so lucky that he cannot be set up as a model. He was phenomenal. But without such luck, most teachers have to fight to keep off starvation.‡

What, or who, is to blame for this misery? The question has often been asked, whenever there have been many ragged-trousered intellectuals, and it is not so easy to find the answer. It is not always the social system which is at fault. Sometimes it is merely an economic readjustment that is needed, like the rise of modern publishing methods. Sometimes there are too many mediocrities writing and composing when they would do better as farmers or fishermen—and perhaps Juvenal's earlier contempt for the poets of his own time was justified, for most of what they wrote seems to have been miserably imitative and dull. But Juvenal himself has no doubt who is at fault. The rich, it is the rich Romans again, who applaud and pose as culture-lovers, but allow the poets and the teachers to starve, while they build vast mansions and keep tame lions and waste

---

* Matt. xxv. 29.   † 7. 79–80 and Tac. *Ann.* 16. 17.
‡ 7. 188–202.

their fortunes. It is the same contrast of extravagance and meanness, of callousness mixed with hypocrisy, which Juvenal has
shown us before in other contexts.

Against this background, the dedication is a remarkable
compliment to the emperor. Thanks to Caesar, distinguished
poets *now* need no longer face the choice of starving with their
art or throwing it up and turning to commerce. Caesar is the
only hope, Juvenal repeats; and he has *already* taken steps to
save the declining arts:

> Attention, then, young men! Our ruler's kindly favour
> is looking round encouragingly for new material.*

This can only mean that the emperor had formally signified his
interest in literature by doing something concrete and permanent, looking far into the future:

> none of us will be compelled to submit to labour
> unworthy of our art, *henceforward*.†

Most probably the occasion was Hadrian's re-establishment of
the Athenaeum, with chairs and pensions for deserving writers.
We have already suggested this, but it is worth hazarding one
further suggestion. The position in which this complimentary
passage appears, at the beginning of a new Book, makes it
virtually a dedication to the emperor. And the succeeding poem
shows a new and positive interest in the efficient administration
of the empire, for it advises a young nobleman how to behave
as governor of a province. After years of bitter and utterly destructive criticism of both the imperial house and the rich
aristocracy, Juvenal now comes out boldly on the side of the emperor. In the Fourth Book, immediately following this, we find
him for the first time relaxed and in comfortable circumstances,
with an income and a small property. In Book III, an emphatic
expression of gratitude to the emperor Hadrian, who favours
literature. In Book IV, signs of ease and confidence, and an
estate at Tivoli, Hadrian's favourite resort. It looks as though

---

* Hoc agite, o iuuenes! circumspicit et stimulat uos
materiamque sibi ducis indulgentia quaerit (7. 20–21).
† Nemo tamen studiis indignum ferre laborem
cogetur posthac (7. 17–18).

Hadrian had—on the strength of Books I and II, and not without an eye to the neglect Juvenal had suffered from the nobility —given him a place on the endowment of the Athenaeum, so that a generous emperor might undo some of the harm done by his bitter and vindictive predecessor Domitian, whom Juvenal never mentions again.

That is only a guess. We know too little about the Athenaeum and about Juvenal's life to prove or disprove it. What is certain is that the Seventh Satire contains his first dedication to any individual, and his first complimentary reference to any emperor. It is wrong to represent him as a wholehearted opponent of the imperial system;[11] but he is, and remains, a wholehearted enemy of the extravagant, greedy, and selfish rich.

XVI

SATIRE EIGHT
True Nobility

UNTIL Satire Seven, Juvenal had never had a good word for any emperor. Then, quite unexpectedly, he praised Caesar for favouring literature. He always hated and despised the aristocrats of his own time. But now, in the Eighth Satire, we are even more surprised to find him talking in terms of friendship to a Roman noble.[1] It is a young man called Ponticus—a name which implies that he is descended from a general who triumphed after a war in the east. The height of nobility (as Juvenal often tells us) was to have such eminent ancestors.[2] Ponticus is making his way up in the senatorial career, and is now within sight of being appointed governor of a province. The core of this poem is Juvenal's serious advice to him on his conduct as governor.

It is strange somehow to hear a Roman advising another Roman to maintain justice in one of the provinces of the empire. It is stranger still to see how long a view Juvenal takes of this problem. His main point is that young Ponticus owes it to himself to be fair and incorruptible. But he says something else which did not occur to many Romans. He points out that long ago it used to be easy to plunder the recently conquered 'allies' of Rome, when they were rich to overflowing. But now that they have been impoverished, it is becoming dangerous to rob them. And, in words which Edmund Burke once quoted against a proposal to starve out the American colonists, he adds:

Beggared, they still have weapons!*

Stranger still is it to hear Juvenal addressing a nobleman as a human being who has good in his soul, who can listen to advice. This is the first time he has even hinted that he thinks the nobles are curable. Until now he has shown them to us as a group of weak and affected perverts, cowardly, selfish, and impotent. They were the helpless victims of Domitian and

* Burke, *On Conciliation with the Colonies* (22 Mar. 1775) ∼Juv. 8. 124.

I

his agents: the agents gnawed away at them like rats at a caged animal, the emperor slaughtered them until he dripped with their blood.* The few who were strong were hard and bitterly selfish, as we have seen through the eyes of their dependants. When we dined with Virro, we dared not even raise a cup to toast him; we had to bribe a slave to get a wordless nod from Veiento.† But now we hear Juvenal talking in a tone, not quite of friendship but of genuine interest, to a young nobleman with a triumphal name and a long tradition of aristocratic descent. All his earlier satires were utterly negative: the only solution they proposed was suicide or beggary or escape to the wilds.‡ But the Seventh Satire at least began on a hopeful note, and now the Eighth offers positive advice to a young man who wishes to make his character and to help his country.

In form, naturally, the poem is a 'persuasion', like the Third, Fifth, and Sixth.³ The obvious way to persuade a young nobleman to lead an upright life would be to remind him of his magnificent ancestry, to describe the splendid examples of wisdom, temperance, courage, and piety which they had set, and then to encourage him to equal and perhaps to surpass them. That approach is summed up in the phrase *noblesse oblige*, 'nobility means duty'. But it would not do for satire, not for Juvenal. It would not allow enough invective or enough mockery for a satiric poet, and it would have irked Juvenal by making him praise the great old houses and the ancestral portraits. So he inverts the argument. Instead of assuming that noble descent is good, and advising Ponticus to live up to it, he declares that

> although your hall is lined on every side with ancient
> portraits, the only badge of noble rank is virtue.§

Instead of saying that aristocratic origins inspire good conduct, he says that they cast a lurid light on wickedness. And most of the poem is taken up with vivid descriptions of foolish and vicious aristocrats. One of these, particularly brilliant, is placed by design next to the positive advice Juvenal gives to Ponticus

---

* 1. 33–35, 4. 96–103, 4. 150–4.   † 5. 125–31, 3. 184–5.
‡ Suicide, 6. 30–32; beggary, 5. 6–11; escape to the wilds, 2. 1–2 and 3. 1–9.
§ Tota licet ueteres exornent undique cerae
atria, nobilitas sola est atque unica uirtus (8. 19–20).

on his service as governor. It is a character-sketch of a dandy of
Nero's reign, Plautius Lateranus, who liked to drive a fast
chariot down the public highway like a professional jockey,
and haunted the stables, and swore by the barbarous horse-
goddess Epona, and preferred the lowest taverns—not as a
youthful prank, but as a rooted perversion of his rank and
obligations.[4]

> Send down to the docks, your majesty,
> send men to find your general in a huge saloon:
> you will get him lying near a gangster, cheek by jowl,
> mingling with lascars, thieves, and convicts on the lam,
> among the undertaker's men and the builders of coffins
> and the idle bongo-drums of a lolling eunuch fakir.*[5]

After another attack on the noblemen who appeared as clowns
on the stage and gladiators—no, as the most barefaced kind of
gladiators, the half-naked helmetless net-casters who threw and
missed and ran away—Juvenal moves into a climax with Nero
himself, the emperor who lost the empire through his follies as
well as his crimes, and then Catiline and his accomplices who
died as traitors.

It would not do to end on this note. Juvenal therefore re-
asserts his main thesis. Catiline was nobly born, but was the
enemy of his country. Who thwarted him? It was the consul
Cicero, a knight from a small Italian town; and with Cicero
Juvenal begins a list of great Romans who distinguished themselves although born of low families: Marius the democratic
general; the Decii who devoted themselves to death to bring
victory for Rome; the slave-girl's son who became king; and the
lowly slave who revealed a plot made by young nobles against
the republic. It is difficult in this passage not to feel that Juvenal
is thinking of his own merits, long ignored and now perhaps
recognized for the first time. Like Cicero, he was 'a knight from
a little town': he was a patriot too, and he thought much of
saving the state.

*   Mitte Ostia, Caesar,
        mitte, sed in magna legatum quaere popina:
        inuenies aliquo cum percussore iacentem,
        permixtum nautis et furibus ac fugitiuis,
        inter carnifices et fabros sandapilarum
        et resupinati cessantia tympana galli (8. 171–6).

The poem ends with a short paragraph which delivers a final blow to the idea that noble descent is a value in itself. Better to be a hero born of a fool than a fool born of a hero, says Juvenal; but after all, since Rome was first peopled by nomads and runaway criminals,

> the founder of your family, whoever he may be,
> was either a herdsman or—the thing I will not name.*[6]

It is a curious poem, astringent and sour. It can scarcely have been very soothing reading for young Ponticus, but it may have been more genuinely stimulating than exhortations to remember his great-grandfather. At any rate it is a novelty for Juvenal to take such apparently sincere interest in any nobleman, and to give such positive advice, even although he surrounds it with destructive criticism. He is mellowing as he grows older. All the important examples in the poem are drawn, not from life, but from books: several of them are evidently inspired by the contemporary success, Tacitus' *Annals*, although Juvenal has typically given his characters a different interpretation.[7]

But the most important thing about the piece is its genuine interest in the central problem of Juvenal's world, the administration of the empire. Trajan had devoted much time and energy to its military expansion. Hadrian, to whom Book III is dedicated,† spent far the greatest part of his reign, not in Rome, but on tours of inspection and consolidation in the provinces. His successors were to do the same. Trajan, and Hadrian, and Antoninus Pius, and Marcus Aurelius, were not Roman nobles. They were 'small-town knights' or provincial gentry, like most of their best helpers. Therefore in this satire, which at first sight looks like a cross between a rhetorical commonplace and a handful of historical examples, Juvenal has stated an important truth about the destiny of the Roman empire and the civilized world.

---

* Maiorum primus, quisquis fuit ille, tuorum
  aut pastor fuit aut—illud quod dicere nolo (8. 274–5).
† See pp. 13–14 and 111–12.

XVII

SATIRE NINE
Ah, Corydon, Corydon*

THE Ninth Satire is one of the most shocking poems ever written.[1] It is a dialogue between Juvenal and a pervert, in which the pervert complains of the troubles of his profession. Juvenal listens to him with apparent sympathy—but his sympathy is an ironic screen for bitter mockery and scorn.

'Why do you look so miserable, Naevolus?' Juvenal begins. 'You used to be the smoothest, wittiest, happiest of men about town, haunting the temples to pick up women and making love to their husbands too. Now you look unkempt and anxious. What can be wrong? Have you changed your way of life?'[2]

In two brilliant pages, in sixty lines equivalent in perception to many a modern psychological novel, Naevolus replies. His monologue exposes and incriminates himself; but he does not know it, because he is quite dead to shame. He has been living with a corrupt millionaire called Virro. He has been the strong male 'husband', and Virro has been the weak 'wife'. Marcel Proust (we are told), after he was 'separated from Mummy', became such a 'wife' and had a series of secretaries to live with him as his 'husbands'.[3] But Proust at least was never married to a woman. Virro was. Being weak and perverse, he could not consummate his marriage. His 'husband' Naevolus did the job for him, even produced a child. And now, after such multiple services, Naevolus has been discarded. Like a skilled craftsman whose trade has suddenly dwindled, he sees unemployment, and poverty, and a destitute old age.

Before consoling him, Juvenal asks about Virro. Oh beware, says the sodomite, please do not mention all this, for Virro is quite capable—if he knows his secret vices have been exposed —of having me murdered. Juvenal laughs, and replies that no

* Juv. 9. 102, parodying the homosexual passion of Vergil, Buc. 2. 69.

rich man, however careful, can keep a secret, however disgraceful, from his servants.

> Close the windows,
> curtain the cracks, draw the doors, remove the light,
> send everyone away, let nobody sleep near by—
> yet what the rich man does at three o'clock in the morning
> the corner grocer will learn by dawn. . . .*

But still, what am I to do, says the pervert, and how am I to
live? Don't worry, says Juvenal in a single short paragraph
which distils all the acid of many years, as long as the Seven
Hills stand there will be pansies who will employ you. They all
come to Rome. Just wait!

I wish I could, replies Naevolus; all I want is a little invested
capital; and some good silver plate; and some slaves to work for
me: not much, although it means my happiness; but my luck
has died on me, Fortune plugs her ears when I call her. Poor
Naevolus sees nothing ahead. He would not dream of working.
The only choice is beggary or vice.

So the satire ends—like many of Juvenal's early satires, in
tragedy, although it is a ludicrous tragedy.[4] In spite of its
repulsive subject it is a masterpiece. Economy and force, subtle
irony and broad laughter, cheerful colloquialism and beautiful
poetry,[†] brilliant parodies[‡] and startling original phrases, all
are combined within a handsomely constructed dialogue of
150 lines to expose a vile man living as a parasite on an equally
vile society. The neatest thing about it is that Juvenal allows
the pervert to expose his own vileness and corruption, merely
by asking him a few leading questions. This is a device he has
not employed before on such a scale. It was used in several
different literary types both in Rome and in Greece.[§] We find
it in comedy, where a fool or a scoundrel will appear on the
stage and in one scene or even one speech show the audience

---

    *   Claude fenestras,
    uela tegant rimas, iunge ostia, tollito lumen,
    e medio fac eant omnes, prope nemo recumbat:
    quod tamen ad cantum galli facit ille secundi
    proximus ante diem caupo sciet . . . (9. 104–8).

† e.g. 9. 126–9.
‡ 9. 37 and 102; note also the epic parodies in 64–65 and 149–50.
§ On the sources and analogues of the satire, see n. 1 on p. 274.

how foul or foolish he is. It appears in the literary mimes, where a vicious woman or a coward or a rascal, merely by talking, shows the fault which consumes him or her. Very early in the history of Roman satire we find it in Ennius, who made a professional diner-out boast of his own ability to sponge on his hosts. The comedian Terence borrowed the idea, and put a confidence-man on the stage in a role where he appeared slightly drunk and obsessed with his own cleverness in living on others: a splendid part for a good actor, who could make the audience both laugh at the parasite and despise him. Long afterwards, Jack Falstaff was to be the heartier but scarcely less perverted descendant of these follies and vices, openly displayed.

Two of Naevolus' weaknesses strike us in everything he says. One is that he has no moral standards whatever—except that he despises ingratitude, especially to himself.* Again and again he boasts of his own vices, explaining at length how complicated they are, what an effort they cost him, how completely they fill his life. The other is that he does not even enjoy his vices much. They cost him too much trouble. It is really exhausting to preside over the perversions of an entire family. He speaks with all the pathos of a drug-pedlar explaining that things have got very difficult since the police doubled their narcotic squads and set a stronger watch on incoming ships. What Naevolus really loves is not his vices, but money. Everything he does is convertible into cash or real property. If it were not, he would have no interest in it. Therefore he is another of the many characters in Juvenal's satires who have been ruined, partly by their own weaknesses, but chiefly by money. All he wants—he says pathetically—is to get a steady independent income. That is why he became a pervert and the utensil of a pervert.

Poor Naevolus is not the only subject of the satire. Behind him is Virro, his patron and accomplice, a much more sinister figure. Like the tyrant-emperor in the Fourth and the host in the Fifth Satire, the vicious employer is only obliquely seen and scarcely heard. The vicious Naevolus reveals himself. Virro is not directly described; but his vices come out with remorseless clarity.

* 9. 82: ingrate ac perfide.

First, lust. He is what the Greeks and Romans called a pathic: as soon as he sees a strong young man he showers him with love-letters and slobbers with longing to become his 'wife'.* Not an exaggeration, this. Seneca describes perverts even more outrageous, and one of the chief characters of Proust's novel, though his first appearance is more discreet, ends in more extreme and obvious degradation.†

Then, weakness. He cannot even make love to his own bride on the wedding-night; he cannot become the father of his own child, although he registers and boasts of its birth. His wife has to be married and his children begotten for him by his dependant Naevolus, while he stands snivelling at the door.‡

Third, secretiveness and vindictiveness. His discarded donkey Naevolus must not be thought to have described their amours: for Virro is quite capable of having him murdered, violently or cunningly.§ His catlike secrecy and vengefulness are the obverse of his softness and weakness.

Fourth, meanness. He fell in love with Naevolus to begin with, but he immediately reduced their affair to money, and then counted out the money as though it hurt him. Naevolus observes that he himself took care to buy tactful and dainty and expensive presents for his lover: a green parasol and pomander-balls of perfumed amber, sent on the traditional day for making presents to lady-friends. But his returns were almost nil: a meagre income, and no capital which would make him an independent gentleman.‖ Virro remains rich. Naevolus, cast off and poor, realizes that the millionaire was (as Macaulay said of Marlborough) 'thrifty in his very vices'.¶

The poem is therefore a satire not on one type of man, but on two: the rich canny pervert and his cold shallow accomplice. But if we look at it again, we see that it is also Juvenal's last attack on the relationship of patron and dependant. This is made absolutely clear by several pointed descriptions of the link between the two men. Naevolus has been the rich man's

    * 9. 34–37.
    † Sen. *Ep.* 87. 16 and *N.Q.* 1. 16. Proust on Charlus, *A l'Ombre des jeunes filles en fleurs*, 2. 208–12, and *Le Temps retrouvé*, 1. 165, 226–35.
    ‡ 9. 70–88.   § 9. 93–101.
    ‖ 9. 28–31, 40–42, 50–69.
    ¶ Macaulay, *History of England*, c. 4 (Everyman ed. 1, p. 354).

'client'. Like Trebius in the Fifth Satire he has been subjected to neglect and humiliation; like Umbricius in the Third and others in the First he has been kept on short commons and is finally discarded with no provision for his old age.[5] To make the point still clearer, Juvenal uses the name of the insolent host in the Fifth, Virro, for this even more disgusting monster.*

Although this poem was published in Juvenal's Third Book, it looks like a product of his younger days. One of its subjects, male homosexuality, connects it with the Second Satire; but although Juvenal still hates the vice described, he appears to have overcome the earliest horror he felt, which makes the Second Satire a trifle incoherent, and to have settled into a steadier contempt. The other subject, the patron–dependant relationship, we have met before in his poems, and shall scarcely ever meet again.† The impulses which produced the satire come then from the earlier periods of his life, and its style, its wit, its vivid immediacy of perception, its daring, its urbane conversational tone, and its desire to shock all indicate that it was conceived and largely created early in his working career as a satirist. But its meanings are serious enough. There is not a virtuous person in the whole poem. Everyone is weak or vicious or both. The first four lines contain an obscenity so startling that classical editors tried to replace it by something milder and nineteenth-century editors sometimes failed to understand it.[6] Mentioning the temples of the gods, Juvenal adds, 'Of course women prostitute themselves in every temple, don't they?' and his last words are, like the last words of Satire Two, the hideous assertion that Rome is now the centre of corruption for the whole civilized world.‡

* See n. 2 on c. 11, p. 262.
† Clientship is mentioned again only in 10. 44–46 and 13. 32–33.
‡ 9. 24, 130–3.

XVIII

SURVEY OF THE FOURTH BOOK

Book IV is the work of an ageing man. It is a strange blend of sombre melancholy with tenderness and even gaiety. We have seen glimpses of Juvenal's tenderness before,* but the gaiety is something new. And there is a new note in the melancholy. Hitherto he has protested against certain aspects of life, such as marriage and poverty. Now, in his Tenth Satire, he speaks more universally. He denounces *all* the externals of life. All the machinery of happiness that men try to work is useless. Nothing is worth hoping for except courage and health. The poem reminds us of the meditations of some medieval mystic on the worthlessness of human existence, on the vileness of all human actions—except that it does not close with the ascent of the soul to God. Yeats felt the same dark pessimism towards the end of his life, but though he blended his sorrow with gaiety like Juvenal, his sorrow was less measured and his jollity more febrile. Not all, he says, not all of us can bear to realize

> That if their neighbours figured plain,
> As though upon a lighted screen,
> No single story would they find
> Of an unbroken happy mind,
> A finish worthy of the start.
> Young men know nothing of this sort,
> Observant old men know it well;
> And when they know what old books tell,
> And that no better can be had,
> Know why an old man should be mad.†

---

* 3. 172–9 (especially the pleasant little picture of the frightened child, and the geniality with which the country folk are treated, instead of being shown as ill-dressed boors), 5. 139–45, 7. 207–10.

† Yeats, *Why Should not Old Men be Mad?*, from *Collected Poems* (New York, 1951), 333. The rhymes in the Irish accent (plain: screen; start: sort) add something indefinably touching to the poem.

Yeats consoled his fanatic heart with little tunes on a one-stringed fiddle or a beggar's pipe.* Juvenal found another consolation, the pleasures of friendship. It is to these that the other two satires in Book IV are devoted. This is again something quite new for the gloomy rebel. He has never before spoken to anyone, or of anyone, in terms approaching affection. But now he begins, as it were, to build a little world of his own, where he can escape from the unendurable vices and the contemptible follies of society, where with a friend or two he can take his ease at a modest table, enjoy poetry, chat in the sunshine.† This emphasis on friendship was one of the foundations of Epicurean ethics. Put together with his renunciation of external goods (not as hindrances to virtue, but as seeds of trouble and suffering) in the Tenth Satire and with other indications elsewhere, this seems to mean that, after having had no very clear philosophical attitude throughout his earlier career, he was now turning towards the Epicurean philosophy, which, if it cannot cure the ills of life, at least provides a palliative for them, or a drug.‡

The relaxation in the tone of this Book may not be due to old age alone. In Satire Eleven Juvenal invites a friend to a dinner which is, though not luxurious, certainly comfortable, with three or four servants and wholesome cooking and good fare sent down from his own farm in the country. In Satire Twelve he sacrifices two lambs and a bull-calf in honour of another friend's escape from death. This shows that he was now in easier circumstances than the poverty which stamps Satires One, Three, and Five. He may (as we have conjectured)§ have received this leisure and comfort from the emperor, as other Roman poets had done. At least he did not, like Swift, drop down a spiral of bitterness and hatred into silence and madness; but rather, like Horace, lived out his last years in good cheer and comfort. He enjoyed his ease, not as proof of the goodness of life, but as consolation for its agonies and stupidities. We shall see in Book Five that he retained his conviction that the world

---

* 'Here's a Montenegrin lute, / And its old sole string / Makes me sweet music': Yeats, *The Statesman's Holiday* (*Collected Poems*, 334).

† 11. 64 f., 11. 180–2, 11. 203–4, and pp. 136–7.

‡ The philosophical 'conversion' of Juvenal is discussed more fully in Highet (22).   § See pp. 111–12.

is much more evil than good. However, like the ageing Yeats, he could now say:

> Much did I rage when young,
> Being by the world oppressed,
> But now with flattering tongue
> It speeds the parting guest.*

* Yeats, *Youth and Age* (*Collected Poems*, 208).

XIX

SATIRE TEN
From Hope and Fear Set Free

'THE lapse of ages', said Byron once, '*changes* all things—time—the language—the earth—the bounds of the sea—the stars of the sky, and everything "about, around, and underneath" man, *except man himself*. . . . The infinite variety of lives conduct but to death, and the infinity of wishes lead but to disappointment.'* He was talking of a famous adaptation of Juvenal's Tenth Satire, and thinking of the satire itself. What he said was a good summing-up of the poem. Modern readers, following Dr. Johnson, usually call it *The Vanity of Human Wishes*.

What should we pray for? That is its theme.¹ A lofty question, and deep. It was answered by Jesus himself when he taught his pupils how to pray. 'Your Father', he said, 'knows what you need before you ask him.'† Juvenal answered it in the same way, and very nearly in the same words:

> Nothing, then: shall we pray for nothing? Let me suggest—
> leave the gods alone, let them determine what
> will be most suitable and help us in our lives;
> they give, not what is pleasant, but what is right for us.‡

But first he examines all the things that men and women usually pray for. He finds them all useless—or, even worse, dangerous.

It is a beautifully constructed poem, far clearer than most of his other satires.² With the remorseless lucidity of pessimism, Juvenal scrutinizes one wish after another, and discards them all. Wealth, the least noble and the commonest prayer, he touches in a brief introduction, only to dismiss it. The rich man

---

* Journal, 9 January 1821 (T. Moore, *Life, Letters, and Journals*, London, 1920, 475). † Matt. vi. 8.

‡ Nil ergo optabunt homines? si consilium uis,
permittes ipsis expendere numinibus quid
conueniat nobis rebusque sit utile nostris:
nam pro iucundis aptissima quaeque dabunt di (10. 346–50).

is in constant danger. A tyrant will liquidate him. A relative will poison him. Even if he lives, even at his most pompous and circumstantial, superhuman in rich clothes and gold and jewels, he looks a ridiculous ass. That is a fine page, which we can scarcely transfer to the life of our own century. It might have been easier, in Edwardian or Victorian times, to find a parallel to the haughty Roman official presiding in the amphitheatre at the opening of the games, proud though almost bankrupt, dressed as a victorious 'general, carrying an ivory sceptre with the eagle of Jove carved on it, elevated above ordinary life by a golden crown held over his head, parading in a splendid chariot amid trumpeters and white-clad dependants ('friends,' says Juvenal, 'because their allowance is safely locked away in their cash-boxes')* high in the dust of the circus. Not many Romans could bear to satirize the mighty men of their empire so trenchantly. Nor could many moderns.

Then the other prayers. Power? Its possessor prepares his own downfall. In a marvellously vivid passage less than fifty lines long Juvenal describes the moments just after the denunciation, degradation, and execution of the emperor Tiberius' favourite Sejanus.

> Down come the statues, following the rope,
> and next the crashing axe breaks up the chariot wheels,
> fracturing the legs of the poor undeserving horses.
> Now the bonfires roar, now under bellows and blasts
> glows the head once adored by the public, and crackles the mighty
> Sejanus: out of the face once second in all the world
> are moulded jugs and basins, pans and chamber-pots.†

Death, and a violent death, is the expected end of all the powerful.

Death too with violence and insults was the reward of Demosthenes and Cicero when they aspired to fame and influence,

---

*   . . . niueos ad frena Quirites,
   defossa in loculos quos sportula fecit amicos (10. 45–46).
†   Descendunt statuae restemque sequuntur,
   ipsas deinde rotas bigarum inpacta securis
   caedit et inmeritis franguntur crura caballis.
   iam strident ignes, iam follibus atque caminis
   ardet adoratum populo caput, et crepat ingens
   Seianus; deinde ex facie toto orbe secunda
   fiunt urceoli, pelues, sartago, matellae (10. 58–64).

to be won through their genius as political orators. Cicero's
head and hands were nailed to the platform where he used to
speak. Death also, abrupt or ignoble, is the end of military power
—like that of Hannibal, and Alexander the Great, and the
emperor Xerxes sailing home through the seas strewn with the
corpses of his Persian fleet. The paths of glory lead but to
the grave.

Think too of another prayer which we constantly utter,
whether we are sick or sound: the prayer for long life.[3] It is
only a prayer for old age—and old age is both degrading and
painful. Now, in a hundred lines, Juvenal gives us one of the
earliest and one of the greatest of the many denunciations of old
age which have come from ageing poets, lyric or satiric. It is
ugly, he begins—and we see the decrepit friends of Proust, as
they appeared to him when, after a long absence, he returned
to Paris and went to a reception given by 'his oldest friend' the
Duchesse de Guermantes. All his friends and enemies were
there; but they appeared to him to be in fancy dress, hidden
by the absurd and hideous wrinkles, the seemingly false beards
and white hair, the ridiculous trembling hands and shaking
heads, the vile disguise of old age.* Old age is weak and sickly,
Juvenal goes on: crippled; deaf; blind; paralytic—and we hear
the frantic indignation of Yeats, tortured by sickness and by
impotence ill-matched with hot desire, yet trying hard to make
his soul, in spite of

this caricature,
Decrepit age that has been tied to me
As to a dog's tail.†

Relentlessly Juvenal continues, saying that old age is forgetful
and crazy—and we see the miserable Struldbrugs of Swift, who
'forget the common appellation of things, and the names of
persons, even of those who are their nearest friends and relatives.
For the same reason they never can amuse themselves with
reading, because their memory will not serve to carry them
from the beginning of a sentence to the end'; we even see the
haggard face of Swift himself, like a tree cankered or lightning-

---

*   10. 191–202; Proust, *Le Temps retrouvé*, 2 (Paris, 1927), 83 f.
†   10. 203–32; Yeats, *The Tower* (*Collected Poems*, New York, 1951, 192),
and see *Sailing to Byzantium* and *Politics* (ibid. 191–2, 337).

blasted, beginning to 'die at top'.* Last and most powerful of all his indictments of long life, Juvenal points out that it only increases our sufferings by bringing us the death of children, wife, brothers and sisters; of all we love; and finally the overthrow of whatever personal power or happiness we thought we might have established—and now we hear the voice of Ecclesiastes, the Preacher, speaking sombrely of the day 'when the grasshopper shall be a burden, and desire shall fail: because man goes to his long home, and the mourners go about the streets . . . then shall the dust return to the earth as it was; and the spirit shall return to God who gave it'.†

There is one other prayer. We do not usually utter it ourselves. We pray for long life when we are mature. But mothers, when their children are young, pray for them to be beautiful. Yet the beautiful girl is seduced, the handsome young man is corrupted—like Silanus, on whom the eye of the lustful empress Messalina once fell. He could die; or else sin and die; but his beauty surely meant his ruin.‡

What then shall we pray for? Nothing? Nothing outside ourselves, Juvenal replies. Our prayers may be profitless, or even dangerous. As Shakespeare puts it in a passage perhaps adapted from this very poem:

> We, ignorant of ourselves,
> Beg often our own harms, which the wise powers
> Deny us for our good; so find we profit
> By losing of our prayers.§

We should leave all that to the gods, who know best what is good for us:

> We pray for marriage, pray for our wife's delivery: God
> knows what the children and what the wife will be like.||

If we must ask for anything, we should

> pray for this: a sound mind in a sound body.¶

Pray for courage to ignore death and to scoff at the power of

---

* 10. 232–9; Swift, *Voyage to Laputa*, c. 10; E. Young, *Conjectures on Original Composition* (ed. E. Morley, Manchester, 1918), 29.
† 10. 240–88; Eccl. xii. 5–7.   ‡ 10. 289–345.
§ *Antony and Cleopatra*, 2. 1. 5–8. || 10. 352–3.
¶ Orandum est ut sit mens sana in corpore sano (10. 356).

chance. All that is external is irrelevant. The mind is its own place and in itself can make a heaven of hell, a hell of heaven.

So ends this noble treatment of a tragic theme. Philosophers and satirists before Juvenal had treated the problem of prayer, but none at such length. He enriched it by blending it with another favourite subject, the mutability of fortune. So far, the themes of the satire are 'commonplaces'. What makes it distinguished poetry is the vividness with which he describes the concrete results of all the mistaken prayers (the trembling friends of Sejanus deciding to run and kick his corpse, 'but let the servants see us', the general's tomb split by the roots of a barren fig-tree) and the steely sharpness of the epigrams, such as the famous *mens sana in corpore sano*, or Byron's favourite:

> put Hannibal on the scales: how many pounds will you find in the mighty marshal?*

It is not deeply thought out, and it is not wholly filled with noble truths. Instead of being called 'The Vanity of Human Wishes' it should be named 'The Dangers of Ambition'. Often Juvenal, as a gloomy and disappointed old man, seems merely to be grumbling 'Nobody can win, so why worry?'; and when he says that he would rather be the author of bad poetry like Cicero's than of the great speeches which brought the orator's death, he is lowering his own standards in order to make a point. But on the whole the brilliance of the detail, together with the breadth, clarity, and simplicity of the treatment, raises the theme far above the level of a debater's cliché, and makes it a memorable and powerful poem on the tragedy of human hopes.

* 10. 85–88; 143–6; 356; and
    Expende Hannibalem: quot libras in duce summo
    inuenies?   (10. 147–8).

XX

DINNER AT HOME

THAT powerful Tenth Satire takes up more than half of Juvenal's Fourth Book. To balance it and to relieve its pessimism, Juvenal composed two shorter, lighter satires combining gravity with gaiety, serious thought with pleasant relaxation. Together, they form a sort of consolation for the scarcely-relieved gloom of the Tenth. They are linked not only by their tone of cheer and sympathy but by their subject—for both deal with aspects of friendship, and each describes a little celebration which Juvenal intends to share with one of his friends. This, as we have already pointed out,* was a special mark of the Epicurean philosophy, to which he had now been converted. And as we look more deeply into these two poems we see that he had come to feel the Epicurean ethic very genuinely and strongly: for the lesson which they both, in various ways, direct and indirect, set out to teach is the Epicurean lesson, that happiness lies in moderation.

The subject of Satire Eleven is (like that of Satire Five) a dinner.[1] Its theme is simple. Juvenal is inviting his friend Persicus to have dinner at his home in Rome.[2] He chats for a while, describes the modest menu he has planned, and ends, as it were, by slipping his arm through that of Persicus and walking him off to the baths to spend a few hours of ease and sunshine while dinner is being made ready.[3] As an additional inducement, an extra mark of comfort, he observes that the baths will be delightfully empty because this is the festival of Cybele and all Rome is at the races.

Out of this simple subject Juvenal draws a series of meditations which all fall into the pattern of contrast.

It would be rude and unrestful to begin abruptly by saying 'Come and have a meal!'—so before offering his invitation he discourses for a little. The whole city was gossiping about the same subject: a young man called Rutilus who had just spent his entire property on luxurious living and then, penniless, had enlisted as a gladiator. And he is only one of many (says

* p. 123.

Juvenal) whose 'eyes are bigger than their pocket',* who spend
their inherited cash and sell their inherited property and lose
their rank of knighthood and borrow more money and spend
that and finally go bankrupt, all for the sake of eating fancy
foods. Ridiculous and wicked, this contrast between expensive
tastes and limited incomes, the combination of poverty and
gluttony.†

I do not live on such a scale, Juvenal goes on. You shall see
for yourself when you enjoy my modest dinner. He describes
it—good plain food sent down from his own farm, a young kid,
eggs and chickens, asparagus and grapes and apples and pears,
with local wine from Tivoli. He makes a point of saying that
none of it has to be bought. Everything is home-grown. (That is
why there is no fish-course.)‡ The furniture and dishes are as
simple as the meal: no tortoise-shell couches and silver plates,
no ivory-pedestalled tables of precious wood, not even ivory-
handled table-knives.§ And the servants too will not be highly
skilled carvers or spoiled pretty boys imported from the East, but
simple youngsters from the farm, the sons of Juvenal's herdsmen, shy, awkward, and honest.‖ Finally, the entertainment
after dinner will not be provided by a troupe of girls singing
lewd Spanish songs and dancing naughty dances (he calls them
'music of Cadiz', and every description of them makes them
sound very like the shows put on today by the gypsies of southern
Spain, even to the castanets); it will simply be readings from
Homer and his rival Vergil.⁴ This then is another contrast,
between the modest meal given by Juvenal and the luxurious
banquets of wealthy gluttons. We see them in the background
from time to time, these spoilt sybarites—they have no appetite
for their turbot and venison unless it is served on costly tables,
they need the hulas of the dancing-girls to stimulate their flag-
ging sexual energies, and instead of drinking wine normally
they merely taste it and spit it out on the marble table.⁵

With this a third contrast is interwoven. While describing

---

* The Scots say of a glutton that 'his eyes are bigger than his belly'.
† The introductory chat, 11. 1–55.
‡ The menu, 11. 64–89. Fish had to be bought in the market and were
expensive: see 4. 15–33, 5. 92–102.
§ The furniture and dishes, 11. 90–135.
‖ The servants and the wine, 11. 136–61.

his plain meal and service, Juvenal adds that it would have been a luxurious feast for the great Romans of the early republic, who lived on porridge and vegetable-broth, with meat only on holidays and special occasions, who had no silver dishes but used any silver they won in battle for decorating their armour. Strong, brave, sober, and simple, they were the extreme opposite of their greedy, extravagant, silly, sickly descendants.*

One further contrast is implied. Juvenal is the host, and Persicus is the only guest. As the poem closes, we see the two old gentlemen sitting peacefully in the sunlight, listening with amusement to the roars of applause which boil up like explosions from the racecourse.[6] This is one aspect of the contrast of crowds and loneliness, or rather solitude, which appears in this poem from time to time. In the early satires we saw Juvenal always in the midst of the mob, standing at busy street-corners or shoving his way through packed streets.† Now he is getting old, and prefers to avoid the many-headed beast. His slaves and his food alike represent the country, and are almost out of place in the loud city. The rich man's banquet is fussy and exciting and noisy, while Juvenal's is carefully controlled and peaceful, almost like a Chinese philosopher's meal. And its essence is escape, from the bawling mobs and the thronging cares of daily life.

Within Juvenal's own work this poem forms a striking contrast too. Do you remember the painful Fifth Satire, which described a dinner given by a cold-hearted snob to his friends and his dependants? There everything was a blend of luxury and meanness, drooling greed and tormented disappointment. It had to be borne, that kind of prolonged insult, by anyone who loved the life of a rich man's 'client'. The dinner was narrated at length. It was all hateful. Now Juvenal describes another dinner, at which he is not a tortured guest but a friendly host. This contrast marks a change in his circumstances and in his character. Then he was a parasite. Now he is independent. Then all parties hated the dinner, both the host who gave it and made it an opportunity for degrading his social inferiors, and the guests who suffered humiliation, disappointment, and hunger.

* 11. 77–119; porridge (*farrata*) 108, vegetable-broth (*holuscula*) 79.
† 1. 63–64, 95–101, 128; Umbricius shares his experience in 3. 243–67.

Now it is a meeting of true friends, so pleasant that it will be, for one day at least, an escape from the anxieties of life, from woman's infidelity and man's ingratitude.

Genial as it is, the poem ends on a note of pessimism. The Epicurean creed is defeatist, its essence is making the best of a bad job. Withdrawal, avoidance, limitation, are its keynotes. And so Juvenal concludes his invitation by saying:

> You could not do this for five days
> running, for even such a life can come to bore us
> terribly. The spice of pleasure is its rarity.*

This is true Epicureanism, the doctrine that pleasures should be spaced out in order to be appreciated. It is in the same vein, therefore, as the Tenth Satire, with its stern limitation of the aims and hopes of life:

> since the world has still
> Much good, but much less good than ill,
> And while the sun and moon endure
> Luck's a chance, but trouble's sure.†

*   Facere hoc non possis quinque diebus
continuis, quia sunt talis quoque taedia uitae
magna: uoluptates commendat rarior usus (11. 206–8).
† A. E. Housman, *A Shropshire Lad* 62.

XXI

SATIRE TWELVE
For Love or Money

SATIRE Twelve begins charmingly. It is a happy morning. Juvenal is about to make a sacrifice of thanksgiving. Three altars of green turf have been set up, for the ruling deities of the Capitol. They make a pleasant picture, and so do the two white lambs and the fighting bull-calf who are being given to the gods.* Juvenal's home too is all decorated with lights and green leaves and flowers.† This day marks his fulfilment of a vow, and another assertion of the primary value of friendship.[1]

Juvenal vowed to offer this sacrifice if one of his friends, the merchant Catullus, came safely through a dangerous voyage. Some weeks before, Catullus had sailed for Spain, and perhaps for Greece also, to buy luxury articles for import—fine cloth and silver plate.[2] On the way home, however, his ship was caught in a violent Mediterranean storm, the mast was struck by lightning and had to be cut away, and all the precious cargo had to be jettisoned. When it finally limped into the harbour of Ostia, the ship was only an empty hull; but the lives of the crew, and of Juvenal's friend, were safe.‡

The poem closes with a reflection like that which opened Satire Eleven. Lots of people (says Juvenal) offer sacrifices on behalf of their friends. But very few will do so unless the friends are likely to leave them money. Catullus will leave nothing to me—he has three young sons—therefore this is a gesture of true friendship. Others, the parasites and legacy-hunters, will invest only if they can foresee a return. Then, for a rich childless old lady or gentleman, they will vow sacrifices of a hundred animals, elephants if obtainable, boy and girl slaves, even their own daughters! Clever fellows, shrewd investors: rich, but loveless.

Like many of Juvenal's satires, this poem cuts two ways. The closing theme is the favourite Roman attack on legacy-hunters —that strange class of schemers who would court the childless

* 12. 1–9.   † 12. 87–92.   ‡ 12. 17–82.

rich in the hope of being left a substantial legacy. The best-
known description of them is in Horace (*Serm.* 2. 5), and the
funniest is in Petronius (*Sat.* 141), where three crooks are successful in persuading a millionaire to leave them a huge legacy,
but find that he has attached a condition to the bequest. Before
they can touch a penny, they must publicly cut up his body, and
eat it. One of the cruellest pranks of the fate which has destroyed
so much Greco-Roman literature is that, unless we find another
manuscript of Petronius, we shall never know how this adventure
turned out. As the present text ends, on the very last page, one
of the three is trying to persuade the others. 'Close your eyes',
he says, 'and just imagine you are eating a hundred thousand
pounds. . . .'

The legacy-hunters, then, pretend friendship for the sake of
money. Let them have the money, says Juvenal. Friendship is
better.[3]

However, the body of the poem, which looks like a straight
description of a storm and a near-shipwreck, is also satiric in
intention. For it tells how a wealthy merchant, rich enough to
charter an entire ship, and engaged on importing extravagant
luxuries to Rome, was forced to throw all his wealth into the
sea to save his life.

But who else is there, where in the world would anyone dare
to value his head above silver, prefer his life to his cash?*

It is implied, therefore, that the merchant has paid no more
than the just penalty for his greed. Once more this is an Epicurean point of view. Most men (according to Epicurus) are
fools when they allow themselves to be led by unlimited desires
into unnecessary efforts and dangers.† The true Epicurean
actually thinks it is pleasant to watch their struggles.‡ Juvenal
is not quite so cruel as that. He remembers that Catullus is his
friend; still, he lets us know that Catullus deserved all his folly
brought to him.

Once again, as often before, Juvenal is looking at the world
of business and finance, and dismissing it with contempt. In
earlier poems he said pretty bluntly that all business men were

---

* 12. 48–49.
† Epicurus, *The Extant Remains* (ed. C. Bailey, Oxford, 1926), fragments
68–72, p. 136.   ‡ Lucretius 2. 1–6.

crooks, or at least that commerce was unbearably vulgar.* Here, since he has grown milder and since he is talking of a friend, he says only that the importing business is both stupid and dangerous. You see, he is an old Italian countryman. Since his ideal is the farm which supports its owner in modest comfort (or the estates which make a man a knight), he does not realize that Italy now lives by imports. And he will not understand that the Greco-Roman world was built up by the efforts of the shrewd, energetic, competent men who made harbours, highways, aqueducts, drainage-systems, and baths; who cleared the forests and set up the trade-routes; who exchanged the products of the far parts of the globe and ventured on innumerable dangerous voyages. Most commerce (Juvenal believes) is the exchange of silly luxuries,† or else the import of grain and fruit for the city mob.‡ This short-sightedness was not entirely his fault. He shared it with his spiritual ancestor Cato and with his new teacher Epicurus; and, like them, he made it his ideal to cultivate his garden.

Sometimes Juvenal was ahead of his time in diagnosing a weakness in his own civilization. Here he himself, with his ignorance of the importance of world-wide commerce, is a symptom of a vital weakness which helped to wreck the western empire: for if more Romans of intelligence and competence had engaged in trade and manufacture, in the exchange of goods and services, the financial disasters of the third and fourth centuries would have been long postponed.

The Twelfth Satire, then, is another poem on the theme of greed, interwoven very cunningly with the theme of friendship false and true. It marks a further softening in Juvenal's nature. In the early satires he was supremely lonely, obsessed with the humiliations of poverty and the dominance of wealth. But twice in this poem he says that wealth is useless and meaningless. And his final curse on the successful toad-eater is a sincere one:

> may he pile his gold as high
> as Everest, but love no one and be loved by none.§

---

* 1. 103–9, 3. 29–40, 7. 13–19.   † 11. 124–7, 12. 38–47.
‡ 8. 117–18, 3. 83.
§   Montibus aurum
exaequet, nec amet quemquam, nec ametur ab ullo (12. 129–30).

After the almost intolerable violence and hatred of the first two Books, it is a relief to see the old man—though still a pessimist— mellowing a little and sitting at his ease with a few disillusioned but faithful friends. He himself, like the merchant, has just escaped a shipwreck by jettisoning the burdens he was carrying. Persicus can forget his vicious wife, Catullus can abandon thoughts of huge profits, Juvenal can relinquish for ever the hopes of his youth, if they have a little comfort, sunlight, and loyalty.

XXII

THE LAST BOOK

Signs of age were visible in Juvenal's Third and Fourth Books. Book III was weaker. Book IV was mellower. But as we reach his last body of work, Book V, we are surprised to hear the old lion roaring away with a new access of vigour. There are four satires in it, more than in any Book except the First; and although it is badly mutilated at the end, it still contains over 800 lines, more than any Book except the First. It would be longer still if we had the middle and the end of Satire Sixteen, which in all our manuscripts is broken off at line 60, half-way through a sentence.* The old man who had started writing only when he left youth far behind, and who had brooded so long on the crimes and stupidities of his world, had enough material and enough energy to produce nearly one quarter of his work when he was approaching his seventieth year.

The chief weakness which we notice in this Book is that, like the Fourth and some of the Third, it lacks topical interest. Satire at its best always has its eyes fixed on contemporary life, it walks the streets with a notebook and draws illustrations from its own time and place. Juvenal did this in his early satires. Whether the names of his victims were disguised or not, they stood for well-known contemporary figures, still alive or very recently dead.† But as age and disappointment grew on him and as he turned away from the crowded streets of Rome to his own home and his little circle of friends, he lost sight of the actual persons and came more and more to satirize only the qualities. Illustrations, when he used them, he took more and more from the collection of stock mythical and historical examples known to every schoolboy.‡ This diminishes both the vividness and the variety of these later poems. Like

* On the mutilation of Satire 16 see pp. 156–9.
† For a discussion of this point see pp. 56–58, 290–4.
‡ Details in De Decker (*18*) 107–9; see also his pp. 35–36 and 42. At least fifteen contemporaries are named in 150 lines of Satire 1 and only four in 150 lines of Satire 14.

many old men, indeed like some other satirists (for instance Boileau) in advancing age, he came to live in the world of memory and of abstract thought. His mind was as strong as ever, but his eyes, withdrawn from the outer world, were growing dim.

XXIII

SATIRE THIRTEEN
Crime and Punishment

MONEY and friendship were the themes of Satires Eleven and Twelve. Money and friendship are the points of departure for the first poem in Book IV, the Thirteenth. But the poem itself is really a discussion of crime. For it is a consolation to an old friend who has been cheated out of £200.[1]

This particular variety of crime was one which we seldom see nowadays, although there were some cases of it among refugees from Europe in the 1930's and 1940's. A man who wanted to put money or valuables in safe keeping, instead of entrusting them to a bank or storing them in his own house, would—perhaps before going on a journey—deposit them with a friend, who took a solemn oath to return them when requested. Then, if the friend succumbed to temptation, having the property in his hands, he had only to perjure himself, break the oath, if necessary swearing another oath that he had never received the valuables and denying his signature on the receipt; and he could keep them. You know how often in nineteenth-century novels unhappy gentlemen got into debt because they 'backed a bill' for a friend, endorsing his promissory note and then having to shoulder his obligations. (There is a comic version of this catastrophe in *David Copperfield*, c. 28.) Now the type of fraud Juvenal is here discussing seems to have been quite as common in Greece and Rome, for it is often mentioned. The Christians of Juvenal's day took a special oath to practise virtue—an oath which was apparently based on the Ten Commandments; but they included an explicit provision against this action, and swore 'not to deny a deposit'.[2] Ordinary larceny or cheating was somehow more endurable, because it involved merely stealth; while the essence of this was the denial of friendship and perjury against heaven.

The purpose of Satire Thirteen is to console Calvinus, the victim. He is an elderly man, for Juvenal says explicitly that he

ought to know better 'at sixty years of age'.³ Evidently he is one
of Juvenal's little circle of friends like Catullus in Twelve and
Persicus in Eleven. But we know nothing more of him, and do
not even hear the name of the embezzler. This means that the
poem is a general discussion more than a personal address. Anyone who has met treachery and perjury may read it, and find
good in it.

Notice the shape of the poem. It is a 'consolation'. Greek, and
later Roman, philosophers and rhetoricians worked out this,
among so many other patterns: a list of the most suitable things
to say or write to anyone who had, by death or exile or impoverishment, suffered a grievous loss—together with a method
of arrangement which would make the arguments attractive
and persuasive. We know little about the art of persuasion now,
and find it difficult to frame a letter even to a dear friend when
a disaster strikes him; but the Greeks and Romans had found
the best methods. Basically, the 'consolation' was only a variety
of the persuasive speech, directed to the special purpose of
persuading the sufferer to conquer his grief and resume normal
life. Hard it is, hard, to do this in illness or bereavement. It is
a good deal easier when the victim has simply lost money; and
the amusing satiric twist about Satire Thirteen is that Juvenal's
opening argument is 'Why, what else did you expect? *nowadays?*'*

There are very few things you can say to console a sufferer,
although they can be comfortingly elaborated. Just as you can
recommend a decision to a deliberating assembly only by saying
that it is *right, necessary,* and *advantageous,* so you can give comfort to a mourner only by showing that the loss was *inevitable,*
that it is *usual—*

Thou know'st 'tis common, all that live must die—†
that it will become *less painful* in time, that it is his *duty* to be
brave, and perhaps one or two other arguments. Juvenal cannot use all these points here, but he is careful in choosing and
disposing those he selects.⁴

How can you console a man who has just lost £200 to a false
friend? And, at the same time, how do you teach your readers
that money and the loss of money are negligible?

Juvenal begins by the sour consolation we have already
seen: that things like this happen all the time, so why grieve,

* 13. 13–70.   † Shakespeare, *Hamlet,* 1. 2. 72.

why even be surprised? The world is steadily growing worse.
Once before, we recall, he said that the Golden Age lay far
back in the past, and at least once before he proclaimed that vice
was at its high noon now.* Here he restates this in another allusion to the myth of the ages: after that of Gold, and then those of
Silver and Bronze, came the cruel Iron Age. Ours, says Juvenal,
is worse even than that era of crime and violence; it is an age in
which, as in Sodom and Gomorrah which Jehovah destroyed,
there are not ten, not even seven, just men to be found.† Most
of us believe so wholeheartedly that Progress is continuous that
it is a shock to see how wholeheartedly Juvenal believed the
opposite. Yet he was sincere. It is in moments like this that he
takes his place among the world's great pessimists: Swift, and
Palladas, and Nietzsche, and Bernard of Morval,‡ and Ecclesiastes.

The second argument he uses to console his friend is that the
loss was inevitable, since money is now all-powerful, the supreme
inducement, stronger than fear of the gods who punish perjury.
We might think that the force of pagan religion was gradually
dying away by Juvenal's time, that intelligent men believed
Jupiter to be (as Queen Elizabeth's enemy Maitland of Lething-
ton held God) 'ane bogle of the nursery',§ and that perjury
therefore had no spiritual terrors for them. Yet Juvenal says
No. There are atheists, of course, who perjure themselves
freely and easily. But there are also perjurers with strong religious convictions, who think:

> Great though it is, yet the anger of the gods is slow:
> so if they take the time to punish all the guilty
> when will they ever reach me? yet perhaps I'll find
> that God is merciful, *c'est son métier.* Many
> commit the same crimes and meet different fates:
> one is rewarded by the gallows, one by a crown.‖

* 6. 1–20, 1. 147–9; see pp. 100 and 52–54.
† 6. 23, 13. 26–30; cf. 13. 38–52 on the Age of Saturn. Gen. xviii. 23–33.
‡ On Bernard see p. 308–9.
§ So G. L. Strachey, *Elizabeth and Essex,* c. 2.
‖ Vt sit magna, tamen certe lenta ira deorum est:
  si curant igitur cunctos punire nocentes,
  quando ad me uenient? sed et exorabile numen
  fortasse experiar; solet his ignoscere. multi
  committunt eadem diuerso crimina fato:
  ille crucem sceleris pretium tulit, hic diadema (13. 100–5).

Thirdly, Juvenal points out that the loss is relatively easy to bear: the offence was small compared with the far more atrocious crimes, gangsterism, arson, sacrilege, poisoning, parricide, which crowd the courts. Crime in Rome, he says, is as normal as goitre in Switzerland, big breasts in upper Egypt, and blue eyes in Germany.

His friend still lacks one consolation: revenge. In the second part of the satire Juvenal clears his mind of this obsession. Sensibly he begins by telling Calvinus not to brood over retribution:

> only a small
> and weakly, poor and narrow soul enjoys the pleasures
> of vengeance: you can be sure of this, since no one
> loves revenge more than a woman.*

Then he adds that the tortures of conscience and of fear will punish the guilty man constantly, with perpetual anxiety, sleeplessness, and horror at every storm or every disease which may be a messenger of God. It is a splendid passage, one of those which in the Christian Middle Ages gave Juvenal his reputation as a vigorous moralist.†

Last of all—last of all, there is an anti-climax. Juvenal consoles his friend by pointing out that the embezzler will surely commit another crime and suffer execution or exile, and then Calvinus can rejoice in his overthrow.‡ This from the man who has just delivered a warning against the petty pleasures of revenge! Yet it is of a piece with Juvenal's character. He was vindictive and hateful himself, as we can see from the venom with which he pursues his dead enemies; and his character had been so twisted or crippled that he often praises the second-best and enjoys the less admirable pleasures. Satirists are not happy, noble, well-balanced men. They are twisted, because their world is out of joint.

So ends this strange poem, with the declaration that although the world is steeped in the dregs of corruption and although crime is rampant and apparently triumphant, there is still a

---

*   Quippe minuti
  semper et infirmi est animi exiguique uoluptas
  ultio: continuo sic collige, quod uindicta
  nemo magis gaudet quam femina (13. 189–92).
† 13. 192–239.   ‡ 13. 239–49.

fundamental and divinely ordered justice in the scheme of things. The minority suffer, but they will be avenged. It was this firm conviction which made the Christian writers of the Dark and Middle Ages ready to accept Juvenal as a wise teacher and a sympathetic thinker.*

* See Chapter XXX.

XXIV

SATIRE FOURTEEN
Training in Avarice

THE Fourteenth Satire is the third largest of Juvenal's works.[1] Of course the longest is the Sixth, on marriage. It is a fair inference that a poet spends time and effort on themes which he thinks important.[2] We conclude therefore that the chief preoccupation in Juvenal's mind was the corruption of family life: for, as Satire Six dealt with wives, so Satire Fourteen deals with parents and children.

He was a hard man, Juvenal, but one of his few soft spots was his love for children. It comes up again and again;* and the proof that it is genuine is that it forces its way into his poetry against his will. For example, in the satire about the rich man's snobbish dinner-party, Juvenal observes that, if Trebius, the penniless dependant, only had some capital, he would become a favoured guest—all the more so if he were childless, for then he might leave the host some money. But *as it is* (since Trebius is poor) his host will be charming to his children and give them little presents.† Now, the host is the cruel Virro, the patron who takes a fiendish delight in torturing his poverty-stricken guests. In fact, he would have been as cold and beastly to 'the infant parasite' as Mr. Dombey was to Florence.‡ If he would not even speak to the father, he certainly would not play with the children. But Juvenal, even at the cost of breaking the consistency of his character-sketch, cannot bear to think of any man's being cruel to a child. His friend Martial, 'so witty, profligate, and thin', shared the same tenderness: his only poems of disinterested affection are about children.§

The opening theme of Satire Fourteen is a sad one. It is wrong education—which spoils children. Every teacher and

---

* 3. 175–6, 6. 629–42, 11. 152–5, 15. 134–40.   † 5. 137–45.

‡ Dickens, *Dombey & Son*, cc. 6 and 18.

§ e.g. 5. 34 and 37. Edward Young said to Voltaire 'You are so witty, profligate, and thin / At once we think you Milton, Death, and Sin' (*DNB* s.v. Young, p. 1284).

most parents have felt that there must be something wrong with our methods of bringing them up. They are so charming when they are young, and they usually grow up so dull or so disappointing. But at least we can feel we taught them what was right. Juvenal's complaint is that in Rome they are taught what is wrong.

There are, he says, two aspects of this fact.

Children readily imitate their parents: therefore they copy our vices and follies.* Gambling, gluttony, cruelty, lust, these and other sins they will pick up from their parents' example, however earnestly their fathers and mothers may cry, 'Do as I say, don't do as I do.' This is one of the strongest arguments to make us virtuous in adult life, that we owe it to our young family.

> A child deserves the maximum respect, whenever
> you meditate some wickedness: don't overlook its youth:
> a little speechless son should call Stop to your sin.†

Juvenal writes a noble page here about the responsibility of parents towards their children, and adds two contemporary examples: the ambitious spendthrift who wasted much of his capital on erecting enormous showy houses, and whose son outdid him, building still more stately mansions and bankrupting the entire estate; and the man who was attracted towards Judaism, observing the sabbath and eating kosher food, after which his son had himself circumcised and maintained all the exclusiveness of the chosen people.[3]

These, and other such divagations, children acquire spontaneously from their parents, simply by copying them without instruction. But (continues Juvenal) there is one vice which we in Rome teach our children deliberately, as though it were a virtue. This is the typical Roman vice of greed:

> the insatiable hope of making more and more and more.‡

And now, for the remaining two-thirds of the poem, Juvenal delivers a trenchant sermon against greed, first as a deleterious

---

*   14. 1–106.
†   Maxima debetur puero reuerentia, si quid
          turpe paras; nec tu pueri contempseris annos,
          sed peccaturo obstet tibi filius infans (14. 47–49).
     There is a warning hiatus in 49, *peccaturo // obstet*, whose effect I have tried to render by the warning alliteration in *s*.
‡   Acquirendi . . . insatiabile uotum (14. 125).

quality to implant in the young, and then as a dangerous vice in itself. Obviously it was a subject on which he felt very deeply: so that his treatment of it ranges very widely and his examples are taken from all over history—Croesus (550 B.C.) and Licinus (20 B.C.), the imperial freedman Narcissus (A.D. 50) and a recent case of temple-robbery in his own time.* Rambling as it may seem at first, the sermon has a clear structure.[4] Money, Juvenal declares, brings no happiness.† The love of money breaks up traditional morality—a point which he drives home by one of his favourite contrasts of the degenerate present with the simple life of the yeomen who were the strength of early Rome.‡ When taught to the young (he goes on), greed produces crime—from which the parents themselves inevitably suffer, since it is their wealth that tempts their children. To the rich father of a greedy son he says:

> Now, would you like to pick next autumn's figs,
> to handle next spring's roses? Buy an antidote,
> to take before each meal.§

Finally, Juvenal broadens his discussion into a general denunciation of avarice. He shows that it is ridiculous, because of the fantastic contortions which it makes people indulge in.‖ (His typical case is the merchant who is shipwrecked on a trading voyage after loading his vessel down to the gunwales, and who is last seen clinging to a plank with his right hand and gripping his money-bag with his left hand and his teeth;¶ in modern times he might have substituted a miser like Hetty Green, who, when many times a millionaire, dressed her son and herself in paupers' clothes to get the boy free treatment at a hospital.) Finally, wealth is not only ridiculous, it is painful.** The penniless hermit lives far more comfortably than the millionaire surrounded with fire-alarms and night-watchmen and private detectives. Enough is plenty.

---

* 14. 328, 306, 329, and 261–2, the last being apparently another allusion to the sacrilege mentioned in 13. 147–53.
† 14. 107–37.   ‡ 14. 138–88.
§   Si uis aliam decerpere ficum
    atque alias tractare rosas, medicamen habendum est
    sorbere ante cibum quod debeat et pater et rex (14. 253–5).
‖ 14. 256–302.
¶ 14. 288–97. Contrast Juvenal's friend Catullus in 12. 37–51 with this far more desperate greed.   ** 14. 303–31.

No satire better illustrates Juvenal's original gifts and supervening defects as a poet. His special talent is to take ordinary thoughts and express them with extraordinary vigour. The two themes which he treats here, education and materialism, were often handled by his predecessors and contemporaries. But he felt the importance of them both with real sincerity, spoke of them with unusual force, and blended them into a unity which was original. The care with which he worked out the poem is shown by several skilful little adaptations of passages from eminent forerunners and by several epigrams which have become immortal.* One of these in particular became a favourite with the men of the Middle Ages, who are constantly quoting it:

Your love of money grows as fast as your bank account.†

However, in spite of his undoubted sincerity and many flashes of his old satiric humour, in spite of the energy of his rhetoric and the vividness of his phrases, Juvenal is not wholly successful in this poem; largely because he fails to combine its generalizations with memorable and striking topical pictures. A sermon must be wise and broad, but a satire must appear immediate and spontaneous. This is more a sermon than a satire.

But the issues with which he was dealing were of vital importance. They still are. Any nation which neglects its responsibility to its children is doomed. Any nation which believes that material wealth is the supreme end of life is doomed. In the second century of our era, when Juvenal was writing, the world of civilized Europe was far richer and far more prosperous than it was ever to be again until the nineteenth century. And, just as it did in the nineteenth century, it brought on its own downfall largely by the hypertrophy of its wealth and power and greed. The terrible third century, with the vultures tearing at one another over the bleeding body of the empire, is beginning to look more and more like the age that began in 1914—filled with wars and rumours of wars, inflation and bankruptcy, epidemic plagues and reasonless outbreaks and the threat of barbarian conquest. Juvenal could not foresee all that. What he saw, he said: that careless education and limitless materialism were ruining his country. He was proved right.

* e.g. 14. 34–35, 47, 109, 207, 321.
† Crescit amor nummi quantum ipsa pecunia creuit (14. 139).

XXV

SATIRE FIFTEEN
The Fanatics

THE themes of Satire Fifteen, Juvenal's last complete poem, are cruelty and religious fanaticism.[1] The story we know—it is the grisly tale of a religious feud between two Egyptian villages, in which a man was knocked down by a mob, torn to pieces, and eaten.* The rest of the poem is Juvenal talking to a friend and to us about this act, more beastly than any lynching.[2]

Was the story true? Yes, there can scarcely be any doubt that it was. To begin with, the two hostile villages have now been identified, one inhabited by worshippers of the sinister god Set, spirit of darkness and cruelty, the other by devotees of Hathor, the goddess of beauty and merriment. They lie close together in a bend of the Nile, with a wall between them; and Juvenal evidently knew them personally, better than all historians and Egyptologists did until towards the end of last century. Then there are records of similar hatreds and similar barbarities in Juvenal's own time, from Egypt and North Africa. During a Jewish revolt in Cyrene about ten years before the date of this incident, the Jews are stated not only to have eaten the flesh of the Gentiles but to have skinned them and worn the skins.† In modern times it would not be fair to point to the cannibalism of prisoners in the German concentration-camps, for Juvenal himself clearly distinguishes the frenzy of starving men from this Egyptian atrocity, which was an act of cruelty and hatred.‡ Yet we have recently seen lampshades made of human skin, and ornaments made of human bones.

Admitting that the story was true and not exaggerated or isolated, we can still see certain oddities in Juvenal's treatment of it. First, it is a little odd that he does not know, or does not think worth mentioning, the other incidents of the same kind which had happened in his own lifetime. Then, it seems strange

---

* Details on pp. 28–29 and related notes. † Dio 68. 32.
‡ Juv. 15. 93–115.

to modern readers that he does not speak of cruelty in Rome itself. At the gladiatorial games, men fought wild beasts and men killed men, to make a Roman holiday. Other Roman writers openly express their disgust at such butchery.* Many of the Greeks (whom Juvenal so despised) shrank from it with horror: when the city council of Athens proposed to introduce gladiatorial shows, the proposal was routed by the philosopher Demonax, who observed that before they did so, they should first destroy the altar of Pity standing in the market-place.† Even the ordinary Romans sometimes felt it: for once, when a herd of elephants was being hunted in the arena and seemed to beg for mercy by raising their trunks in supplication, the Roman crowd protested, and cursed Pompey for putting on such a spectacle.‡ But apart from the games, we find it impossible to forget the cruelty which had been shown at Rome in persecutions of the Christians, whom Nero made into living torches after the fire of Rome, and who, like St. Paul, fought with beasts, or were thrown to hungry lions. Why does Juvenal mention none of those monstrous practices?

The Christians he never mentions at all. Very few writers of his time do. Twice he speaks with sympathy and horror of the types of torture to which they were exposed.§ But apparently he did not know that the Christians existed as a separate body. And since they were foreign in origin, and Eastern, and Jewish, he would scarcely have been capable of taking any interest in them. He was not alone in this. The church in the west only became strong when it became naturalized and began to speak and think in Latin; and the division between the Greek Orthodox church and the Roman Catholic church reflects the deep disharmony (which Juvenal felt keenly) between the eastern and the western parts of the empire.|| Furthermore, all early pagan writers who paid any attention to the execution of Christians believed that, although cruel, it was justified—since the Christians were not merely another religious sect but a group which hated the whole Greco-Roman world and prayed for its destruction. Juvenal's contemporary Tacitus, after describing how Nero

---

* e.g. Seneca, *Ep.* 7.   † Lucian, *Demonax*, 57.
‡ Pliny, *N.H.* 8. 7. 21; Dio, 39. 38.
§ Burning alive, 1. 155–7; fighting wild animals, 4. 99–101, on which see note 14 (4) on pp. 259–60. || See pp. 71–72.

tortured Christians to death, observes coldly that the crowd was sorry for them 'although they were guilty and deserved the utmost'.*

The games Juvenal often mentions, and always with contempt. He did not feel that they were cruel so much as vulgar.³ For him, a gladiator was the lowest type of man, far beneath slaves. He regarded gladiators as a well-bred woman regards prostitutes. He speaks of men becoming professional fighters as a lady might speak of a girl who deliberately chose to enter a brothel; and the depth of his hatred is kept for the aristocratic men and women who take up the same profession as amateurs, without even the excuse of poverty. He describes Eppia, the senator's wife who eloped with a tough, scarred, blear-eyed old gladiator, as comparable to Messalina.† We should not therefore expect him to lament the cruelty of killing such a man, any more than we nowadays should shed tears over the woes of the side-show freak who drives pins through his lips or eats live frogs.

But why does he speak of this single incident in Egypt, without citing any parallels? There is only one likely reason. As we have seen, in his old age he was turning more and more away from the outside world, and paying less and less attention to contemporary events. Probably he had not even heard of the revolts in Cyrene and similar barbarities elsewhere. But this atrocity happened in Egypt. In Egypt, that loathsome country —the land he hated far more than any other Roman who has left a record, perhaps the land of his early exile.‡ At once, when he heard the story, his old loathing revived, and he wrote a satire which was not simply a general discourse on man's inhumanity to man, but also a particular attack on the barbarism of the Egyptian nation.⁴ What he finds specially detestable in them is a feature which many other travellers have noticed—the paradoxical character which combines feebleness with violence, worships animals and kills men, sometimes abstains from certain vegetables and sometimes eats human flesh.⁵

If this was a special personal hatred, does it invalidate Juvenal's satire? Surely not. Satire teaches, and sets out to tell the truth even though it is warmed by gaiety and darkened by

* Tac. *Ann.* 15. 44.   † 6. 82–113 and 115–32.
‡ See pp. 27–31.

hatred. Lampoon merely sets out to wound a personal enemy, whether he is a good man or a scoundrel. The frontier between satire and lampoon is vague, and broad, but it exists. Probably there should be something of the lampoon, some wish to hurt an enemy, in all satire. Probably it would be impossible to write effective satire without personal loathing. Still, there should be much more than that, and certainly there should be a general truth. We may only feel its heat, in laughter, and see the shadows it casts, in hatred. But it should exist, and irradiate the satire.

The particular driving force in the Fifteenth Satire, then, is Juvenal's personal hatred and contempt for the Egyptians. The general theme, however, is the barbarous cruelty which is always pressing in upon civilization from just outside its frontiers, or from beneath the surface of its mind. Juvenal could not foresee that comparable barbarisms were to invade Rome and Greece themselves soon after his death. Indeed, he contrasts the conduct of these Egyptians with the age-old ideals of Greco-Roman civilization, in words which are more like those of a philosopher than a satirist.[6] But he implicitly connects this outbreak of savagery with the softer vices of his own country, by saying it is another proof that *in his time* 'evil has reached the zenith', new precedents for wickedness have been established, and an era worse than the ages of Bronze and Iron has begun.[7]

In Satire One Juvenal explained that he had set out to write satire because other kinds of poetry—even the highest, such as epic and tragedy—were unrealistic and irrelevant. Satire tells the truth. He repeated the same thought in later poems, sometimes emphasizing it by naughty parodies of epic pomp and tragic grandeur. Occasionally he varied it by declaring that, bad as the crimes of tragedy might seem on the stage, those of contemporary life were worse. Clearly this idea connects with that outlined in the previous paragraph. This is not the Heroic Age now, says Juvenal. This is worse. This tale I am telling is not an epic fiction. It is the truth, it happened a few years ago in the consulship of Juncus, in Middle Egypt, up river from Coptos.* And the fact was far more terrible than anything told of in tragedy. For it was the crime of a whole people, changing

---

* The date was established by Borghesi, 'Intorno all' età di Giovenale', *Œuvres complètes*, 5 (Paris, 1869), 49–76.

themselves from kindly men into savages, worse than the beasts which refuse to eat their own kind.[8]

Not many critics like the Fifteenth Satire. Some believe it is a forgery,[9] and many think it is artificial and silly. Perhaps it seemed silly in the nineteenth and early twentieth centuries because no one could believe that such outbreaks of savagery within ostensibly civilized nations were a serious possibility; it looked as though Juvenal had been wasting his time, inventing subjects, beating a man of straw, laboriously imagining a horror to make our flesh creep. But, since 1914, savagery worse than that of any Egyptian village has not only broken out in civilized lands but been converted into a political weapon, organized as a social institution, and even elevated into a moral code. I for one, after reading the records of the past forty years, cannot feel justified in despising the old man who so violently denounced a bloody murder, and who—although he had never heard the precept *Love one another*—still said that sympathy was the essential virtue which the creator gave the human race, to distinguish us from animals.*

* 15. 131 f.

XXVI

SATIRE SIXTEEN
The Luck of the Army

SATIRE Sixteen is the last, and it is not all there. Only the first sixty lines are left. Then it breaks off, in the middle of a sentence.

Yet it begins interestingly. It is on quite a new subject, something no other Greek or Roman social critic discusses at any length; and on a very important subject—an issue which, some generations later, was to become one of the central problems of the western world. The subject is the Roman army.[1]

This was a carefully organized and highly efficient institution, the strongest and most continuously effective fighting force in all human history. In Juvenal's time it was divided into two groups with dangerously different duties and powers. There were the legions, standing armies stationed in those provinces which faced a potential enemy: Roumania, Armenia, Britain, and others. These were composed of long-term soldiers who were always recruited in an area far away from their post, but who usually settled down and formed a resident occupation and defence force, 'the German legions', 'the army of Syria'. Then there were the praetorian guards, an *élite* corps stationed just outside the city of Rome. Technically they were the body-guard and household troops of the emperor in his capacity as commander-in-chief ('emperor' means 'supreme commander'); they were also the garrison of Italy and of its capital, Rome. These two duties gave them immense power, for in practice no one could become emperor without either defeating them in battle (like Vespasian) or being peacefully accepted by them through choice (like Trajan) or caprice (like Claudius).

But the praetorian guards and all those legions were numerically a very small part of the population of the vast empire. It was, on the whole, a prosperous, peaceful, orderly realm. There was no military conscription. Most men of Juvenal's time never thought of joining the army, any more than we should think of becoming detectives or test-pilots. Well-to-do young men of good family would serve as temporary junior officers as a preliminary to entering politics or the imperial administration; strong and ambitious youths would join up to make their fortunes and see the world; friendly aliens often came in to acquire Roman citizenship; but the average man was a civilian. So much had Rome changed since the days of the republic, when the legions that beat Hannibal and conquered the world were villagers and farmers drafted year by year from their homes. The very word 'legion' means 'levy'.

A standing army is always privileged. Sometimes only the officers enjoy the privileges, while the private soldier has to say:

> I went into a public-'ouse to get a pint o' beer,
> The publican 'e up and sez, 'We serve no red-coats here.'*

Sometimes, again, all ranks regard themselves as far superior to civilians, claim precedence over everyone not in uniform, and are loaded with comforts and rewards which are given all the more readily because they might be taken by force. And furthermore, in a large and rich country, service in a standing army (given a lucky war or two) is a route to fortunes otherwise unattainable. Vespasian, founder of the second dynasty of Rome's emperors, began his career as a junior officer just like Juvenal and finished it by becoming ruler of the western world.† Thousands of inscriptions still remain, set up by Romans of humble origin, who after years of service found promotion coming to them more and more rapidly, and who ended, not indeed as emperors, but as administrators of powerful services and governors of great territories, powerful and respected.‡

These privileges are the theme of Juvenal's last satire, 'The Luck of the Army'. If you enlist under a lucky star, says he, your rewards will be innumerable.§

But first (he goes on) let us look at the ordinary privileges enjoyed by all soldiers, lucky or not. If they are involved in a police-court case, they are not tried by the ordinary magistrate but by a court martial—and what civilian is going to venture into camp among all those heavy boots to lodge a complaint and

---

* Kipling, 'Tommy', in *Barrack-room Ballads*.
† He was *tribunus militum* (Suet. *Vesp.* 2. 3); cf. pp. 34–35.
‡ Examples in A. Stein, *Der römische Ritterstand* (Munich, 1927), 142 f.
§ 16. 1–6.

appear before a bench of tough old sergeant-majors? If they have a lawsuit, it is always taken at the head of the calendar, while civilians have to endure the law's delays. They are absolute owners of their military pay and appurtenances, and (unlike civilians) can will such property to anyone they choose, even during their fathers' lifetime; and some are rich, through bonuses and awards for distinguished service:

> In fact the general himself is surely interested
> to see that every hero should be prosperous too,
> that all who proudly wear orders and decorations . . .*

—and there the satire breaks off.

What happened? Why have we only sixty lines of this interesting poem? It is possible to give a clear, though hypothetical, answer.

There are several hundred manuscripts of Juvenal. Every one stops at this point. Not one has a single line or word more. The ancient commentary tails off in the Sixteenth Satire, and stops altogether a few lines before this break. No Roman scholar ever quotes or mentions any of the rest of the satire. Therefore, either the remainder of the poem was never written; or it was lost at a very early time, between Juvenal's death and the appearance of the basic text and commentaries which we now have, and which were copied in all those manuscripts.

Now, Juvenal himself would not have published a sixty-line fragment which begins by announcing an ambitious treatment of a big topic, and stops before reaching the main point. After three complete satires ranging between 170 and 340 lines, this prelude, halting in the middle of a bar, makes an intolerable anticlimax to the Fifth Book.

Was it censored, then? No, for Roman censorship, like that of other absolutisms, was thorough, and would have deleted the entire poem, if not the entire book.

Did Juvenal die, leaving it unfinished? This is the usual modern explanation. A number of distinguished Greek and Roman writers died before completing their work, and it was then edited and published by their executors: Thucydides,

* Ipsius certe ducis hoc referre uidetur
  ut qui fortis erit, sit felicissimus idem;
  ut laeti phaleris omnes et torquibus omnes . . . (16. 58–60).

Vergil, Persius the satirist, Lucretius the philosopher-poet. But the editors always did their best, without adding anything, to give the work the appearance of artistic and intellectual *completeness*. Vergil felt his draft *Aeneid* so unsatisfying that he wanted to burn it; but his executors made it into an almost satisfying whole.* Persius died without publishing his collection of satires; his two editors trimmed off some lines from the end of the book 'so as to make it look complete' before publication.† The poem of Lucretius contains six books on the universe, the structure of man, and the physical constitution of this planet. We know it was read, and St. Jerome says it was edited, by Cicero after Lucretius' death; there are many traces of interruption and repetition in the argument of the poem, as in every draft work; and some scholars believe that it was planned to be much longer, embracing the ethics of Epicureanism as well as its preliminary physics. But it looks complete enough; there is not an unfinished verse in it: many critics think it is virtually finished as it stands. Even in Vergil the fragmentary lines nearly always make sense. No editor in Greece or Rome would have published a broken fragment like Satire Sixteen.

We forget this now, because, since the breakage of classical harmony which began late in the eighteenth century, we have come to think that a fragment is as beautiful as a whole, and perhaps more interesting. Maillol and Rodin produce statues which look like relics of Greek figures mutilated by age.‡ Coleridge publishes fifty-four lines of *Kubla Khan* with the explanation that he completed it in a dream and was interrupted before he could write it all out.[2] We play Bach's *Art of the Fugue* and pause at the unresolved chord where the master laid down his pen for ever. But the Greeks and Romans never did this. They would not publish drafts or fragments (although their great authors must have left many such sketches); they did not care for ruins, and torsos, and unfinished symphonies. Therefore,

---

* Serv. ad Acn., init.: 'Augustus . . . Tuccam et Varium hac lege iussit emendare ut superflua demerent, nihil adderent tamen.'

† *Vita Persi de commentario Probi sublata* (see Owen, *61*, xv): 'Hunc ipsum librum imperfectum reliquit: uersus aliqui dempti sunt ultimo libro ut quasi finitus esset.'

‡ e.g. Maillol's *Torso* (1910), headless, armless, partly legless; his *Spring* (1910), armless; and his last work, *Harmony* (1944), armless. An armless Harmony!

even if Juvenal died before completing Satire Sixteen, his executors would either have suppressed it altogether or else published it in a shape which read continuously and made sense, and not as we have it now.

Only the fourth explanation, then, is possible. The poem was mutilated and largely lost at a time when Juvenal was scarcely known. There was only one copy of his work which survived. It was a book written on parchment, and it lost its last pages, containing the final few hundred lines of this satire.[3] The first scholars who started to study Juvenal intensely (some generations after his death) could not replace the lost passage. So they copied out these sixty lines and handed them on, adding a few, a very few, notes. It is strange to think how close we came to losing the whole of Juvenal's work, if a section of it could vanish thus completely.

The ancient commentators added a note saying that some people believed the Sixteenth Satire to be spurious; but they gave no reasons, and in fact the vocabulary, the rhythm, and the whole manner are unmistakably Juvenal's.[4] The one difficulty which has sometimes troubled me is that here Juvenal speaks as a civilian—whereas (if our reconstruction on pp. 34–35 and 38–39 is valid) he had spent some time in the army as a young man. Still, even if he had, he would have been a civilian for about half a century before publishing this satire, and he cannot in any case have believed that his short service as a junior officer in the Balkan auxiliaries put him on a par with the long-term professional soldiers of the regular army.[5]

It is possible to conjecture how the poem went on. The surviving sixty lines explain that soldiers are superior to civilians in legal privileges. It is likely that the satire then discussed other privileges possessed by soldiers—for instance, social superiority, financial security. All these Juvenal calls 'general advantages'. Now, in the opening lines he said that his main theme was the great *special* advantages brought by good luck in the army: so no doubt, in the main part of the satire, he would go on to describe the rewards which fell to a really lucky soldier—plunder; and promotion (as the junior officers of the Royal Navy used to drink to 'a bloody war or a sickly season'); and, above all, power. Therefore, the Sixteenth Satire was meant to be a big catalogue-poem like the Third (320 lines), the Sixth (693 lines), and the Tenth (366 lines). It is even possible to conjecture its length. Many of the manuscripts of Juvenal's poems seem to have had twenty-nine or thirty lines to the page. If the sole surviving copy of his satires was written on this scale, and lost the last quire of eight pages (as vellum manuscripts often did), then the Sixteenth would have been about 300 lines long ($60+8\times30$). If it lost *two* quires, then the poem would have been a giant of some 540 lines. Of course, we cannot tell how it ended. But we do know that the most remarkable reward of soldiering in the Roman empire was the chance to become emperor of the western world—the prize won by Julius Caesar, and by Vespasian, and by Trajan. Juvenal was always so occupied with ambition and reward that he could scarcely have avoided this theme, which would make a striking, though slightly dangerous, peroration for his Fifth Book. (Was it unofficially censored, after all?)[6]

The subject was important enough to justify this large plan. For it either covered or implied some of the most vital issues in the decline and fall of the western empire. Soldiers were now no longer ordinary citizens, obeying the universal call of duty. They were a special caste, which despised the soft civilians—even this small fragment of the Satire begins with a brutal picture of a civilian who after a brawl with a trooper

> dare not show the judge the teeth that are knocked out
> and the black lump on his face among the swollen bruises
> and the eye left in place but despaired of by the doctor.*

This division between soldiers and citizens was to grow ever wider, until the army came to feel it was not an organ of the Roman government but was in effect the Roman government itself. The praetorian guards had already made two emperors. Only a few generations after Juvenal wrote, they were to auction off the throne to the highest bidder. The legions out in the provinces had already clashed in one civil war, and the victors had battled their way right into the streets of Rome to make their commander Vespasian the new emperor. Seventy years after

---

*   Dissimulet, nec
audeat excussos praetori ostendere dentes
et nigram in facie tumidis liuoribus offam
atque oculum medico nil promittente relictum (16. 9–12).

Juvenal's death, the armies of the west and the east were both attacking the emperor Septimius Severus; in the terrible third century A.D. every single army of the provinces put up its own commander as emperor, and while the legions, like mad dogs, tore at one another and at the sheep they once protected, the wolves began to break in from the east and the north. The slightly comic figure of the centurion in Juvenal's poem, intimidating the civilians with his hobnails and his fists, was soon to change into the monstrous emperor Maximin, the Thracian herdsman who could push a loaded wagon and split a tree, and whose gigantic strength and brutal energy still glare at us from portraits sculptured in stone as hard as his will-power.

XXVII

SURVEY

SIXTEEN poems, the last incomplete. Five books. Less than 4,000 lines. A life's work.

Separately, the satires have shown us different stages of Juvenal's growth and different aspects of his technique. Taken all together, what rank do they give him as an artist?

Let us consider him first as a satirist. There are three questions we can ask about any satirical writer: does he tell the truth? does he deal with important subjects? and is his work effective?

With regard to Juvenal, the first of these questions has been hotly debated, and the debate has often issued in misunderstandings and misjudgements. Other satirists obviously do not tell the truth. It would be pointless to ask whether Gulliver really visited the flying island of Laputa and described it accurately—although there was once a clergyman who read the whole of *Gulliver's Travels* and angrily declared, 'I don't believe a word of it!' No one attempts to verify the adventures of Pantagruel in search of the Holy Bottle, the ascent of George III to heaven, or the descent of the emperor Claudius to hell. Juvenal's own predecessors are so whimsical and so strongly individual that, seeing the twinkle in their eyes and hearing them chuckle, we know we need not believe them. But Juvenal conceals his own personality, and avoids whimsy. Most of the time he appears to be deadly serious, an indignant but accurate reporter, telling, if not the whole truth, at least nothing but the truth. Some readers therefore have been led by the force of his conviction to believe everything he says, and to conclude that he gives an exactly true picture, the only true picture, of the Roman empire at the turn of the first century after Christ's birth. Others, pointing to his frequent use of rhetorical devices, his vehement utterance, the lack of discrimination he seems to show in denouncing mild misdemeanours and filthy crimes with the same energy, and the atrocious crudity of some of his descriptions, have depreciated him as a rancorous and prurient scandalmonger, or a cheap journalist, caring everything for the thrills and nothing for the facts.

There were some particularly violent attacks on him in France a few generations ago, where they sprang from the social, moral, and political disputes of the nineteenth century. Victor Hugo, a liberal, a passionate republican, and a hater of ortho-doxy, was never tired of praising Juvenal with that reckless enthusiasm which exhausts his readers and sometimes falsifies his subjects.* Meanwhile the conservatives, the professional scholars, and the orthodox united in criticizing Juvenal: on two main grounds—first, that he had a dirty and perverted mind so that he could not see the truth, and second, that he was so much of a rhetorician that he would not utter it.[1] The same two attacks have recurred with slight variations throughout the last 500 years of Juvenal's reputation, and have been met again and again by passionate defences and denials.

But surely both critics and partisans are misguided. To say that Juvenal had a warped mind is to ignore the fact that he was a satirist. To say that his rhetoric distorts the truth is both to misunderstand his method and to neglect the mass of confirmatory evidence from other observers of the Roman empire.

No writer holds the mirror up to nature. No writer shows us the whole of life. All writers select, and omit, and emphasize. No writer utters all the truth. Nearly every writer claims to do so. Satirists say they are 'telling the truth with a laugh', and Juvenal himself boasts:

> everything men do is the medley that makes my book—†

but immediately afterwards he goes on to ask:

> and when was there ever a richer crop of *vices*?‡

Like other writers, the satirist selects. Just as the lyric poet deals chiefly with love and exultation and grief, so the satirist deals mainly with stupidity, ugliness, vice, and crime. What gives him his special interest in these matters is hard to say, but it is

---

* See pp. 227–9.
† Quidquid agunt homines . . . nostri farrago libelli est (1. 85–86).
‡ Et quando uberior uitiorum copia? (1. 87).

not affection. Usually it is a fascinated or amused disgust in which attraction and repulsion are mingled, and it usually comes from the conflict between the satirist's own high ideals and his bitter experience of the world. Yet although he selects, he does not necessarily falsify.

In this connexion I often think of Swift. He was really fascinated by dirt, physical filth of all kinds. He constantly made his Gulliver fall into it, or make it, or have it thrust upon him, and he wrote several supremely disgusting poems about it. Yet he himself was a most fastidious man, who insisted on antiseptic cleanliness all around him. Did he therefore have a warped mind? No. It was his contemporaries that were dirty. Swift's friends and equals saw the dirt too, and tolerated or ignored it. Swift saw it and loathed it. Although he looked a little crazy then, and still does, he was right and they were wrong. That is one reason why he was a satirist.

Then again the satirist is a teacher. His purpose is to improve us by shocking us and to teach us by making us laugh. Therefore, as well as selecting what to show us, he will emphasize whatever is amusing and shocking in it. He will make the shadows darker, distort the outlines. The spectacle of ordinary life does not shock or even divert most of us. We accept it. But the satirist, who sees the faults we miss, must point them out and magnify them and twist them so as to achieve his purpose. So Swift's Yahoos are not men, but men deformed, retaining their worst qualities without their best. Juvenal's theme is not the Roman empire, but the single city which was its corrupt heart, and he points to the corruption because he judges it all-important—as the doctor points to the single spot on the X-ray photograph which will infect all the rest of the body.

To teach like that, to give the needed drive and heat to his accusations, Juvenal uses rhetoric. The doctor need only point, because his patient realizes he is ill; but the teacher has to convince as well as to diagnose.

Those who charge him with misusing rhetoric usually cite two different faults. Sometimes they say that he likes lambasting people so much that he loses his sense of fairness, and lines up silly eccentricities alongside grave crimes. For instance, in his denunciation of Nero, he says that Orestes (who like Nero

murdered his mother) was better than the emperor, since he at
least did not

> stain his hands with butchering his sister or with the blood
> of his Spartan wife, he mixed no cup of aconite
> for any kinsman, Orestes never sang on the stage,
> he wrote no epics!*

The answer to this criticism has already been given (pp. 78–79),
but can be amplified. It is that Juvenal is making a grim joke.
He says in fact that as well as being a criminal Nero was a fool
—which was worse. In Dio's description of the emperor's opera-
tic roles, precisely the same attitude appears, the same mixture
of indignation and amusement: see, for instance, the story of the
soldier who, when Nero was acting the part of Canace, asked
what he was doing and was told 'He's having a baby'.† Although
both Juvenal and Dio joke about it, their standards are perfectly
consistent. They do believe it is worse for an emperor to be a
buffoon than a murderer. For the Roman, dignity comes first.

Sometimes, however, Juvenal's critics charge him with being
completely insincere. He exaggerates everything, they say, and
without any real convictions of his own merely chooses subjects
which will sound dramatic and enable him to work up big
climaxes. Now, either this argument is guesswork about the
state of his mind, or it is capable of being tested by known facts.
If it is merely the arbitrary assertion that Juvenal does not
sound sincere, it can surely be met by the counter-assertion that
(as we shall see in the following chapters) there are thousands of
competent readers to whom he does. But if it is the charge that
he makes false statements for the sake of effect, then it is mistaken. There is not a single event or description in Juvenal's
satires which is known to be false. Nearly all his most shocking
stories are not only paralleled (and thus confirmed) but sur-
passed by tales in other authors of the early empire; and all of

---

* Par Agamemnonidae crimen, sed causa facit rem
  dissimilem. quippe ille deis auctoribus ultor
  patris erat caesi media inter pocula, sed nec
  Electrae iugulo se polluit aut Spartani
  sanguine coniugii, nullis aconita propinquis
  miscuit, in scaena numquam cantauit Orestes,
  Troica non scripsit! (8. 215–21).
† Dio 62. 9–10.

them are far outdone by well-authenticated historical incidents from the eighteenth, nineteenth, and twentieth centuries of the Christian era. The vilest sexual excesses he describes look innocuous beside those soberly related, as matters of fairly general knowledge, by the philosopher Seneca and the historian Suetonius. The uniformly gloomy picture of society which he draws can easily be supported by the tragically sombre history of his contemporary Tacitus, who like himself had lived through the tyranny of Domitian and felt ever after that the world was out of joint. Within the century after his death the emperors Commodus and Elagabalus were to outdo Nero both in vice and in folly. Nor can we moderns say that anything Juvenal reports is too base to be credible. The black Mass described in Huysmans' *Là-bas*, the tortures and 'scientific experiments' of the Nazi concentration-camps, the mass-murders (with sexual overtones) of Landru in Paris and Haarmann in Hanover, and many other atrocities of our own times would make Juvenal's worst monsters turn pale.[2] The only passages we cannot trust in his work are stereotypes from ancient history, where he unquestionably exaggerates a contrast for the sake of making a point, and descriptions of secret orgies which are undocumented elsewhere, and may be true, or may not.[3]

Careful critics sometimes charge him with a slightly different form of inaccuracy. They point out that he published all his extant work under the emperors Trajan and Hadrian, who were both enlightened rulers; but that he protests and denounces as though he were still living in Domitian's reign of terror. They complain that his First Satire shows Rome still irked by the presence of powerful informers, whereas the power of such men had vanished with Domitian's death; and that his Seventh describes the starveling poverty of literary men and others in terms and with illustrations which were appropriate for a period twenty-five years earlier. They conclude that he was so bitterly shocked by the reign of Domitian that he never recovered, and that he carried over his warped pessimism into later and happier times.*

Now, this charge is partly true. The reigns of Trajan and Hadrian were free from most of the abuses of Domitian's time.

* So Peter (*28*), 77–81, and H. M. Stephenson, 'Difficulties in Juvenal, *Sat.* I', *CR* 4 (1890), 229.

Most of the second century was sunny, after the intermittent glooms and thunderstorms of the first. Most of Juvenal's contemporaries forgot the past, or recalled it only as men in health remember a dangerous illness long ago. And indeed we have seen that he himself, in his later books, grew milder, more peacefully meditative, happier. Strictly, his work was an anachronism, and was false to its time.

But in a broader sense, it was true, because it was true of the whole Roman empire—not for an interval, but for all its life. The empire was not healthy, there at its centre: it was not a sound creature looking back on a past illness, but a sick organism which had temporarily rallied. What Juvenal did was to point to the telltale spot which showed that the disease was merely quiescent and could flare up again at any time. When he was still a young man, ambitious and idealistic, a member of an obscure Jewish sect had looked at the Roman empire, pointed to its diseases with the same accuracy, and foretold its downfall in terms more violent than any Juvenal ever dared to use. His most distinguished contemporary was a statesman who had lived through the Domitianic era in perhaps less actual danger than Juvenal but with more personal suffering and humiliation. Immediately after the tyrant's death he published a biography of a soldier he regarded as one of the tyrant's victims; and he spent the rest of his life writing the history of the first century of the empire, from the sinister Tiberius through the degenerate Nero to the sinister Domitian, in a tone of the darkest pessimism, unrelieved even by the bitter laughter which sometimes breaks out of Juvenal's satires. This was Tacitus. Like Juvenal, he saw that the empire by its very nature was corrupt. He could not, or would not, foretell its doom—although he did write a prescient study of the strong, virtuous, healthy barbarians across the frontier—but he reported the maladjustment and decay which he saw at its heart. The analytic historian and the anachronistic satirist were both true doctors and true teachers.[4]

What has been said about the truth of Juvenal's satires will help us in answering the second question, whether he deals with important subjects. For it is necessary to distinguish. Some books are topical, make a powerful impression on their age, and then are forgotten except as historical events. Other books come silently into the world. Although they deal with subjects of perennial interest, they are little regarded at the time of their birth. They seem, perhaps, so general as to have little impact on their special place and time. Yet generation after generation in a world of change finds something wise and memorable in them, and they speak to many different men with a universal voice. They deal with themes of permanent importance. There is a third and smaller group of books which speak both to their own age and to all time, which are welcomed as immediately valuable when they appear and which are still cherished in later ages, long after their authors and first readers have perished. Such are the greatest books of all: the dialogues of Plato, the novels of Tolstoy, the speeches of Cicero. In satire, such is the work of Rabelais, heartily welcomed and bitterly attacked as soon as it appeared, and continuously thereafter read and translated and echoed and censored, loved and hated, down to our own time.

But Juvenal's satires belong to the second group. Very few people read them when they were published: they were almost forgotten in the century after their author died. Yet they returned, they became known, and they have never since been lost or ignored. After the fall of Roman power, throughout the Middle Ages into the Renaissance, with still growing strength in the baroque era, and strongly still in the nineteenth and twentieth centuries, they were read, memorized, quoted, translated, adapted, imitated, and praised. Nor have they usually been praised as technical feats without substance. They have been praised for their power and wisdom.

This means that they deal with subjects of permanent importance. The testimony of the centuries cannot be dismissed. You and I may find this poem commonplace and that paradoxical, but if thousands of thoughtful men over hundreds of years have found them worth remembering, they must be valuable.

Yet they were ignored in their own time. Does that mean that they had no topical importance?

Not necessarily. Consider the themes as we have analysed them. Of the sixteen poems, twelve deal with the maladjustments of contemporary society, considered from different points of view: the relation of husbands and wives, of friends true and false, of parents and children, of civilians and soldiers, and so on.* Two (4 and 15) treat recent historical events. The other two, 10 and 13, are on moral topics: crime and punishment, and the true aim of human life. None of these problems was urgent, in the sense that if it were neglected Juvenal's world would instantly fall to pieces; but most were vital to its possible regeneration and its ultimate survival. A fair estimate might be that ten poems out of the whole collection concerned subjects important for Juvenal's own time.†

Nevertheless, they were not read, either then or immediately afterwards. For this there are two reasons. The first is that the truths they told were unpopular. Rome *was* losing its character in the flood of aliens—but neither Romans nor aliens liked to hear that said. The rich *were* greedy and snobbish and cruel—but they would not reward a poet who said so. The nobles *had* degenerated from the great standards of the early republic—but they could not relish a satire which mocked their degeneracy. Satirists always offend somebody in their own time; but Juvenal managed to offend almost everybody.

Then the other reason for his neglect is the anachronistic method he chose. In his First Satire, he announced that to protect himself against retaliation he would use only the names of dead men. To us this seems interesting enough nowadays. It transforms satire into something like history, and we enjoy reading about the fall of Sejanus or the extravagances of Nero at least as much as about the events of Juvenal's own lifetime. But for his contemporaries it must have been a little dreary, as though we were asked to listen to new satires in which the chief figures were Disraeli, General Grant, and Richard Wagner. There is a conflict here which he himself felt. His First Satire opens with a powerful tirade in which he says it is difficult for him *not* to write satire when faced with the crimes and follies of his own city and his own time. The subjects are *there, now*, crying for treatment. Nearly all his early satires carry this same sense of urgency. But an urgent problem which can only be illustrated by figures from the Rogues' Gallery of fifty or a hundred years back does not seem so urgent after all. Most satirists are

* These twelve are 1, 2, 3, 5, 6, 7, 8, 9, 11, 12, 14, and 16.
† They are 1, 2, 3, 4, 5, 6, 8, 10, 13, and 14.

really too topical: later readers have to look up the notes to find
who all their enemies were, and try to reconstruct their world.
Juvenal was not topical enough. Thus, by his anachronistic
technique, he lost the attention of his own contemporaries,
though he gained the interest of the succeeding centuries.[5]

The third question about Juvenal's work as a satirist has now
been answered by implication. In his own time he was not
effective. Not many satirists are, although they hope to be. He
was less effective than most. But as we shall see in the next
section of this book, he became a powerful moral teacher three
or four generations after his death, and since then he has been
known continuously as a voice of bitter protest and a source of
the deep wisdom that comes to replace lost illusions. He did not
expect this himself. He hoped to make an effect at once, to be
heard by the people among whom he lived.[6] But in one of his
finest later poems he tells us and himself that it is foolish to hope
for immediate rewards, since they are all illusory or dangerous:
courage and energy and the unbending mind are the true aims
of life.* It was right that such a man should be little thought of
in his lifetime, and should have his reward long after he and
his work had passed into the realm of the timeless.

A satirist is a kind of poet. An odd kind. His work is often
'closer to conversation';† but although it pretends, it is not
really prose. It is more compressed, swifter in movement, and
it rises now and then to that intensity of feeling and insistence
of rhythm which are the marks of all true poetry. As the word
drama covers not only tragedy but comedy, so the word poetry
covers not only epic and drama, but lyric and didactic; and
within the smaller area of didactic poetry there are two types—
the serious, positive, and noble type in which Lucretius and
Bridges, Pope and Vergil have all made masterpieces, and the
mocking, negative, seldom dignified type containing *Don Juan*
and *Hudibras* and *Absalom and Achitophel* and a hundred other
bold, energetic, devil-may-care demonstrations of protest, called
satire. Satire is a difficult kind of poetry to write, because of the
paradoxes involved in its nature: it is σπουδαιογέλοιον, 'serious
joking', talking flippantly about grave themes; and although
it uses some of the material of philosophy and some of the

---

* 10. 346–66.   † Sermoni propiora: Hor. *Serm.* 1. 4. 42.

structural methods of poetry it is apparently casual and improvised, not a lecture or a sustained poetic flight, but an excited
and interesting spur-of-the-moment talk which happens to fall
roughly into metre. For this reason several Greek and Roman
satires and most modern satires are in prose, where compression
is not so necessary, it is easier to seem casual, and digressions are
welcome. But the satirist who enters the field of poetry must be
judged by the higher standards of poetic art. Juvenal demands
such a judgement—since at the outset he declares his satire to
be the only type of contemporary poetry worth listening to,
and later he ventures to set his subjects up against those of epic
and drama.*

We have to ask, then, whether Juvenal is a good poet or not.
As soon as we ask, we hear a babel of voices confused and angry,
some denying that he is a poet at all, others extolling him as one
of the few great poets of the world, others more cautiously saying
that he combined considerable faults with unique merits, some
calling him a vulgar ranter and cheap copyist, others repeating
again and again those powerful lines which echo through the
centuries like avalanches through the Alps.[7] Now this difference of opinion may represent a fact about Juvenal, or a fact
about his critics. It may mean that he is an uneven writer, succeeding one moment and failing the next. Or it may mean that
most of his critics have not understood the right standards to
apply to satiric poetry, and have been trying him for breaking
laws to which he is not subject.

It would be nearly an endless and certainly a fruitless task to
weigh all their opinions against one another: let us look at
Juvenal for ourselves.

The first quality asked of a poet who writes long poems is
competence in structure. A lyricist need only utter a few musical
notes and then fall silent; but a dramatic or epic or satiric poet
must be able to control a large mass of material. (Also, the
satirist must do so without apparent effort.) In this Juvenal is
sometimes very good, and sometimes very bad. With the best
will in the world, none of his expositors has ever been able to
give a satisfying explanation of the plan of some of his poems: in
particular, the Sixth and the Fourteenth. Of course, we should
not expect a satirist to follow a strict logical sequence as though

* 1. 52–57; 6. 634–61; 15. 13–32: see p. 152.

he were a philosopher like Spinoza; or to cut out every step irrelevant to his argument, as though he were Alekhine playing chess; or to remain deadly serious all the time, as though he were a lawyer drawing a contract. Therefore he sometimes builds his poems irregularly because he wants them to look like improvisations.* Sometimes he goes off on digressions, to hold the interest of his audience by developing a striking point even if it breaks the sequence of the argument.[8] Sometimes, since every satirist is a humorist, he says the unexpected thing simply to shock his audience and befool them and make them laugh: Rabelais was the master of this trick, and would write whole pages about nothing at all, to see if anyone would be doltish enough to take them seriously. Surely a number of Juvenal's digressions are like that: there is one in the Twelfth Satire where he says that legacy-hunters, praying loudly for the recovery of a sick millionaire, will vow a sacrifice of 100 oxen— since elephants are not obtainable in Italy . . . and then goes off into a build-up of the elephant as large and clumsy as the animal itself or the vows of the hypocrites.†

And yet there are many important passages and several entire poems which can be explained on only two assumptions. One explanation is that the text of Juvenal's satires was mutilated in antiquity, so that important passages have been lost and the flow of thought has been distorted and broken.‡ And yet why should only a few of the poems be mutilated, while the rest remain clear? The other solution is that he was an erratic artist who sometimes succeeded and sometimes failed; that in satires like the Third, the Fifth, and the Tenth, where he hit on the right subject, stood apart from it, and saw it in perspective, he could create a poem with all its parts happily integrated; but that when he got excited he was unable to view his subject clearly enough to work out a well-balanced discussion of it, harmonizing part with part, but, instead of that, plunged into more or less incoherent denunciations and ill-judged outbursts of fury. Other artists have worked like that. We have already compared the Sixth Satire to certain paintings of Pieter Bruegel.§ And two modern novelists who have something of Juvenal's

* See p. 97.   † 12. 102–10.
‡ This theory was assisted by the discovery of the O fragment: see pp. 223–4.   § pp. 98–99.

spirit in them have both found the problem of structure painfully hard to solve. These are William Faulkner and Thomas
Wolfe. Faulkner succeeds more often than he fails; but Wolfe
could not construct a single novel. He poured out torrents of
reminiscence and evocative description and rhetorical energy,
but all in chaos—

> a universal hubbub wild
> Of stunning sounds and voices all confused—*

until his editor Maxwell Perkins reduced it to artistic form.
Much of Picasso's life-work gives observers the same impression.
That breathless facility, that excited interest in all shapes and all
colours, bar none, that constant hatred of discipline and repetition, that yearning for novelty have produced a vast number of
studies, and comparatively few mature and balanced works. It
is hard not to regret such a squandering of talents. In the same
way, though we admire Juvenal's successes, we must regret his
failures and blame them on his passionate nature and the ardour
of his conviction, which broke so many moulds.

Whether the structure of his poems is good or bad, a satiric
poet is scarcely worth listening to if he is not original: who wants
to listen to the thirty-seventh poem on the corruption of the
clergy? Is Juvenal original, or a copyist?

In our survey of the separate satires we have seen how many
of them are treatments of well-known themes. In fact, it is
almost impossible to discuss an important moral or social topic
without repeating something that has been said by one or more
predecessors. The Greek and Roman writers knew this, and
seldom hoped to produce new creations. Instead, their aim was
to build new syntheses. In all Vergil's works there are few lines,
incidents, conceptions, or ideas which could not be traced to
some other author, and yet, because he made a new blend and
use of all those borrowed elements, he is an unmistakably
original poet.

In the same sense Juvenal is original. There is no one like
him, and as far as we can see there never was. Yet he borrowed
freely.[9] The central ideas of his poems came ultimately from
the vast store of Greco-Roman philosophical arguments, worked

* Milton, *Paradise Lost*, 2. 951–2.

out by hundreds of students, debaters, and propagandists who had for centuries discussed whether high rank was a mark of merit, whether marriage was a help or a hindrance, and so forth. The applications of these ideas to contemporary Rome and their illustration from life were largely his own work, assisted by hints from the philosophical street-preachers, the earlier Roman satirists, and his friend Martial. So many of Juvenal's jokes and satiric ideas and proper names and turns of phrase are adapted from Martial that the epigrams of Martial were clearly one of the chief influences that trained him to be a satirist. What he did was to take Martial's keen perception, his disillusioned but witty sense of contrast, his trick of epigram, and his peculiar blend of suave poetry and vulgar colloquialism, to clean them up, to give them a moral purpose, and to build them into poems of major length. Further, he had had the normal middle-class school training in rhetoric, and had doubt-less listened to scores of display speeches on the bold rhetorical themes which served partly as a training-ground in elementary philosophical argument and partly as a substitute for the excite-ments of fiction. From this source too he drew a large number of general ideas and attitudes and methods of development and tricks of presentation. Finally, he knew many of his pre-decessors among the Latin poets well, and consciously or un-consciously or half-consciously he borrowed, parodied, and adapted their work: Vergil and Ovid were his favourites, with Horace and Persius close behind them, and of course Martial.

Yet most of his work was new, and the best of it was unique. To begin with, his purpose and his attitude were new, both within the field of satire and outside it. As far as we know and hear, he was the first pessimist to write poetic satire on a big scale. Other writers mocked or scolded, but they all expected to persuade, hoped for the betterment of their hearers. Juvenal, believing that the world had 'much less good than ill', pointed out its ills with remorseless loathing and harsh merriment. In this he was really closer to Lucretius than to any other Roman poet we know.[10] Like Lucretius too—but unlike other pessi-mists of antiquity, such as Palladas—he blended his pessimism with a strong sense of moral purpose, and was determined to lead a forlorn hope against the forts of folly and the guarded palaces of crime.

Second, he had a new idea of the scope and method of poetic satire. His predecessors conceived it as something close to comedy (so Lucilius and Horace) or philosophical discussion half-serious half-jocular (so Persius). But Juvenal set out to make it compete with oratory, with tragedy, and with epic. The huge Sixth Satire, though spoilt by its inferior planning, was something quite new in Greco-Roman writing, and rises to heights still unequalled in the satiric poetry of the world.

And finally, his style—though partly composed of adaptations from others—is boldly original. Very few pages of his poetry could be mistaken for the work of anyone else, and his best effects are unique, inimitable, unforgettable.[11]

Together with structural power and originality, style is the third quality by which a poet is estimated; and in style Juvenal's distinction is unquestioned. From what does it arise?

First, from vividness. Few poets can write well without seeing, far more clearly than ordinary men, every detail in their subject. Even the mystics have visions far brighter than ours: they see eternity as 'a great ring of pure and endless light';* and, where we only perceive a pale cloud, the symbolists can glimpse a swan. The satirist, reporting everyday life, must do so very clearly, for he has to show us the familiar in a brighter light. Here Juvenal outdoes nearly all other satiric writers. His work is full of brilliant and unfading pictures: the rich lady gossiping and examining her gold fringes while a slave is flogged near by;† the nobleman lying in a filthy tavern beside gangsters and eunuchs;‡ the decrepit old man gaping for his food like a young bird in the nest;§ the lion-tamer seized and carried off by his roaring pupil;‖ the perverts turning up their quivering eyes as they paint the underlashes;¶ the distant yell which shows all Rome is at the races;** the lovesick husband sipping his wife's bogus tears;†† the tyrant's statue hauled down, smashed, and cast into the furnace to be melted into cooking-pots; ‡‡ and the superb range in the First Satire, from the Egyptian officer waving his sweaty fingers in the air to the satirist burning in the arena as a living torch.§§

---

* Henry Vaughan, *The World.*   † 6. 481–5.   ‡ 8. 171–8.
§ 10. 228–32.   ‖ 14. 246–7.   ¶ 2. 93–95.   ** 11. 193–8.
†† 6. 276–7.   ‡‡ 10. 58–64.   §§ 1. 26–29 and 155–7.

Not only his descriptions but the sound-effects made by his words are vivid.* With alliteration or assonance, he echoes the tittering Greeks—

> rides, maiore *cach*inno
> *concutitur*†

the belching of an overfed courtier—

> *purpureu*s *m*agni *ru*cta*r*it sc*u*rra Palati‡

or the wailing of a defeated army:

> un*a* n*au*e, cruentis
> fluctibus *ac* tard*a* per dens*a* cad*au*era pror*a*.§

With unusual tricks in rhythm he can image a heavy helpless fall—

> et ruit ante aram summi Iouis ut uetulus *bos*‖

show pomp and make it seem foolish—

> Romanus Graiusque et barbarus *induperator*¶

or mock the importance of a distorted ideal—

> laudo meum ciuem nec comparo *testamento*
> mille rates.**

By halting the movement of a line at a gap between vowel-sounds he can punctuate after an important clause—

> mimus
> quis melior plorante gula?// ergo omnia fiunt . . .††

and mimic the first sob of a weeping woman—

> uberibus semper lacrimis semperque paratis
> in statione sua // atque exspectantibus illam‡‡

or echo the death-sigh of a proud general—

> bellorum pompa // animam exhalasset opimam§§

or sound a warning STOP—

> sed peccaturo // obstet tibi filius infans.‖‖

---

* For a fuller discussion see G. Highet, 'Sound-effects in Juvenal's Poetry', *StudPhil* 48 (1951), 697–706.

† 3. 100–1.　　‡ 4. 31.　　§ 10. 185–6.　　‖ 10. 268.
¶ 10. 138.　　** 12. 121–2.　　†† 5. 157–8.　　‡‡ 6. 273–4.
§§ 10. 281.　　‖‖ 14. 49.

Reversing this device, and eliding a vowel where we expect a pause, he can show a greedy gulp of food—

> pallida labra cibum accipiunt digitis alienis*
> optima siluarum interea pelagique uorabit.†

And by combining unusual monosyllabic and polysyllabic endings with odd successions of slow and fast rhythms within the line, he can show us the lurching dance of a gang of drunken Egyptian villagers—

> adde quod et facilis uictoria *de madidis et*
> blaesis atque mero *titubantibus.* inde uirorum
> saltatus nigro *tibicine, qualiacumque*
> unguenta . . .‡

But apart from sound-effects, Juvenal can make a phrase memorable simply by energy and concision. Some of his famous utterances are paradoxes: Messalina is 'the imperial whore';§ the reward of honesty in Rome is 'praise and starvation';‖ when an imperial government robs its subjects, still, 'victims have weapons'.¶ Other such effects are unexpected climaxes. The lady critic talks so much that

> neither a lawyer nor an auctioneer can speak—
> not even another woman!**

And he addresses the Egyptians (who think it sinful to eat certain types of vegetables) as

> holy nations, who can grow, in your own gardens,
> gods!††

The old man crushed by age and disease has

> a very little blood left in his body,
> which nothing warms but the fever.‡‡

More often Juvenal, the pessimist, prefers an anticlimax. The townsman who buys a tiny garden in a country place

---

* 10. 229.   † 1. 135.   ‡ 15. 47–50.
§ Meretrix Augusta (6. 118).   ‖ Probitas laudatur et alget (1. 74).
¶ Spoliatis arma supersunt (8. 124).
**   Nec causidicus nec praeco loquetur,
   altera nec mulier (6. 439–40).
††O sanctas gentes, quibus haec nascuntur in hortis
   numina! (15. 10–11).
‡‡   Minimus gelido iam in corpore sanguis
   febre calet sola (10. 217–18).

makes himself the master of a single lizard.*

Before leaving the city, he asks:

What can I do in Rome?—I cannot lie.†

And in an eloquent distortion of history, Juvenal says that the emperor Domitian

died when the horny-handed workers first began
to fear him, though he was long soaked with noble blood.‡

A number of his most effective anticlimaxes are arranged so that the unexpected drop comes in the last word of a well-built line, παρὰ προσδοκίαν. So, the superintendent of a rickety building puts in temporary props, and plasters up the cracks, and then

tells us to sleep sound inside the hanging *wreck*.§

However, some of Juvenal's finest phrases are straight statements, digested for years and summing up a situation briefly and permanently. They are not highly coloured. They are not distorted. They are the truth, seen in the cold clear light which falls upon the rakes and scoundrels of Hogarth, which pitilessly illumines Goya's *Disasters of War*. Thus, the Roman people, after giving up its power to vote

supreme command, police, army, everything, now
restrains itself and prays eagerly for only two things:
bread and races.||

The overbearing woman who orders her slave to be tortured shouts down her husband's opposition, and (in an often quoted line) screams:

This I will and command, my will can serve as a reason.¶

---

* Vnius sese dominum fecisse lacertae (3. 231).
† Quid Romae faciam? mentiri nescio (3. 41).
‡ Sed periit postquam cerdonibus esse timendus
   coeperat: hoc nocuit Lamiarum caede madenti (4. 153–4).
§ Securos pendente iubet dormire ruina (3. 196).
|| Nam qui dabat olim
   imperium, fasces, legiones, omnia, nunc se
   continet atque duas tantum res anxius optat—
   panem et circenses (10. 78–81).
Cf. Fronto on Trajan, *qui sciret populum Romanum duabus praecipue rebus, annona et spectaculis, teneri* (*Principia Historiae*, 17).
¶ Hoc uolo, sic iubeo, sit pro ratione uoluntas! (6. 223).

In a phrase of memorable simplicity Juvenal himself warns parents:

> You owe the utmost reverence to a child.*

In words which might be either good poetry or fine prose, he reflects:

> The harshest thing to bear in wretched poverty
> is that it makes a man ridiculous.†

And in his famous summary of the aims of life, he says that if we must ask heaven for anything

> we should pray for a sound mind in a sound body.‡

For 1,500 years men of many characters and professions, in many different nations and epochs, have been reading Juvenal. Some have known him well, all his words. Others have memorized a few favourite passages. Others again have found his most notable phrases in anthologies. But he has never been forgotten or despised during that long lapse of time. By some he has been loved, and by many respected. We may endeavour to analyse the verdict of fifty generations, but not to alter it. They have seen Juvenal's poetry as *memorable*, as *original*, and as *true*. They have listened understandingly as he stammers with eagerness or grows hoarse with rage; they have discounted the exaggerations thrown out in his excitement; when he becomes incoherent, mixing up mild misdemeanours with hideous crimes, they have realized that in a spoiled society a moralist cannot always distinguish; when they have seen him adapting an idea from another poet, they have enjoyed the new vitality he put into it; and although they recognize his moral and intellectual defects, they have admired the poetic gifts, the strength of will, and the unflinching conviction which, within the corrupt body of a rich, soft empire, enabled Juvenal to create a work of art and thought that endured like stone after the paint and the fat and the flesh disappeared.

* Maxima debetur puero reuerentia (14. 47).
† Nil habet infelix paupertas durius in se
quam quod ridiculos homines facit (3. 152–3).
‡ Orandum est ut sit mens sana in corpore sano (10. 356).

PART THREE

The Survival of Juvenal's Work

XXVIII

JUVENAL IN THE LATE EMPIRE

THE life of a good book is far longer than the life of a man. Its author dies, and his generation dies, and his successors are born and die; the world he knew disappears, and new orders which he could not foresee are established on its ruins; law, religion, science, commerce, society, all are transformed into shapes which would astound him; but his book continues to live. Long after he and his epoch are dead, the book speaks with his voice.

It is not possible to understand a good book fully without knowing the history of its survival. What the author said in it at the time he created it, what it meant to him and to his contemporaries—that is much of its meaning. But we cannot grasp *all* its significance if we look at it only in that narrow temporal and local frame. The essence of a good book is that it has many meanings: it is full of powers; it has depth and richness; it has the fertility and mutability of life itself; in different ages and places it manifests itself differently, yet it remains the same. Unless we know this, we shall underestimate the book. Not even its author, when he wrote it, could foresee all the meanings that it would have or imagine all the men and women who would draw strength and understanding from it. That is one of the marks of a great work of art: its creator can scarcely understand everything he puts into it; he knows only that he must give it intensity, and shapeliness, and power, and after he has made it he feels that he has made something greater than himself, something with a life derived from his own and yet independent of him, to aim at immortality in this world which he soon must leave.

It is not enough, therefore, to study the achievement of any great man without studying its power of survival. Thus we admire the architects of Notre Dame because they built a masterpiece which remained, and which remained beautiful, through many different ages. Although Shakespeare wrote plays for his own time and country, one essential sign of their genius is that they have been loved by millions, over more than half the world, in many languages, for centuries. A work of art need not succeed at first; and it may later be lost or destroyed by barbarism and ignorance; but, given the chance of preservation, if it survives and is constantly admired it is great.

This, then, is the assurance that Juvenal's satires compose a distinguished work of art. Over many centuries, through numerous difficulties and dangers, they have continued to live and be prized. In order to understand their value and meaning fully, we must now trace the history of their survival through 1,800 years.

The tale begins strangely. During Juvenal's own lifetime (as we have seen) his poetry was never mentioned by any-one known to us.* There is no sign that he had any influence at all. We have conjectured that the emperor Hadrian gave him a post at the newly refounded state college of literature, the Athenaeum, and that he ended his long life in quiet though disappointed comfort. This is only a hypothesis, but it does fit all the known facts. About A.D. 130, he died.

After his death, for a long time, his work was buried in absolute silence.[1] We have already seen why it was unpopular during his lifetime. It is easy to conjecture why it continued unpopular after his death. In the first place, it was pessimistic, sombrely critical of the empire and its ruling classes—but the generations that followed Juvenal's death were happy and optimistic under the benevolent emperors Antoninus Pius and Marcus Aurelius. In the second place, it was bitterly anti-Greek—but Hadrian himself became more and more strongly Greek in manner and outlook, while his two successors were as much Greek as Roman. Marcus Aurelius kept his spiritual diary in Greek, the language of philosophy. In such a reign, few were likely to relish a satirist who sneered at the Greeks and their tongue.† In the third place, the later emperors of the third century were fools and debauchees of the very types which Juvenal most savagely attacked. With utter contempt and loathing, he describes a nobleman who appeared in the arena, running about in a fancy shirt without even a helmet and

* See pp. 17–19.   † 3. 58–125, 6. 184–96, 11. 147–8.

a visor to conceal his face.* But in A.D. 180 Marcus Aurelius' son Commodus came to the throne, and spent most of his absurd career in showing off his gifts as a gladiator—defeating unarmed opponents, beheading 100 ostriches with 100 blade-ended arrows (very difficult!), and revelling in publicity far greater than that which attended the exploits of Nero's courtiers. He even dressed one of his mistresses as an Amazon — like Mevia at the beginning of Juvenal's First Satire.† Juvenal despised and mocked Oriental cults, Oriental vices, and Orientals generally. Commodus solemnly carried the image of the jackal-headed god Anubis through the streets of Rome.‡ Less than thirty years after Commodus' assassination, the little pervert Elagabalus became emperor: he brought to Rome a large retinue of Syrians; as the administrator of Rome's grain-supply he appointed a barber; he himself not only dressed in women's clothes but posed as a prostitute.§ It would have been unpopular to republish the satires of Juvenal under the benevolent Antonine emperors, and impossible under their corrupt successors.

There are other reasons too for his disappearance in the second century. Literary taste changed. Its arbiters were chiefly interested in the elaborate fine writing that Juvenal detested, and in the cultivation of old-fashioned authors and an archaistic vocabulary—both anathema to Juvenal. There is no mention of his work in Fronto (*fl.* A.D. 145), which is understandable, since Fronto was the tutor of Marcus Aurelius; nor in the satiric romancer Apuleius (*fl.* 160); nor in Apuleius' contemporary the antiquarian Aulus Gellius; nor in the other critics and grammarians of the second and third centuries—Julius Romanus (*fl.* 250), Nonius Marcellus (*fl.* 300), Festus, Charisius, and Diomedes—although they quote other Roman poets freely.[2]

The first readers to admire Juvenal after his death belonged to the opposition—although it was a group he himself would

* 8. 199–210.
† *Hist. Aug., Commodus,* 11. 9–12; Herodian, 1. 15. 5; Dio, 63. 19; Juv. 1. 22–23.
‡ *Hist. Aug., Pescennius Niger,* 6. 9; cf. Juv. 6. 511–41 and especially 532–4.
§ Dio, 73. 16–22 and 80. 11–16; *CAH* 12. 53–54; Juvenal on barbers and Syrians, 1. 24–25 and 3. 61–66.

have despised and rejected. They were Christian propagandists. At first their echoes of him are so faint as to be almost inaudible; but we know they are genuine echoes, partly because the Christians more than anyone else agreed with what he said, and partly because the echoes grew constantly stronger within the literature of the rising Church.[3]

The fiery Tertullian (*c.* 160–220), whose defence of Christianity always turns into a counter-attack, knew the pagan Latin writers well, including Juvenal's contemporaries Pliny, Tacitus, and Suetonius. He mentions them by name, but not Juvenal; nor does he quote Juvenal at length. Still, there are certain turns of phrase and thought which he shares with Juvenal and with no one else. The clearest is in a reference to the power of God:

> Who now will give us 'the power of treading upon snakes and scorpions'? the lord of all animals, or the god of not even a single lizard?

—evidently a memory of Juvenal 3. 231:

> to make oneself the landlord of a single lizard.*[4]

At the opening of Tertullian's work on chastity, he says:

> Chastity, the flower of morality, . . . will still linger a while in this generation, if nature makes it possible

—more hopefully than Juvenal, who thought the world was hopeless, and said:

> I think that Chastity lingered once, in the reign of Saturn, upon this earth.†[5]

A thorough search of Tertullian's writings might disclose further echoes; these are enough to show that he knew something of Juvenal.

After Tertullian there is another long silence, through the third century, terrible with wars, epidemics, and revolutions.[6] But Juvenal is not forgotten, and early in the fourth century he is quoted by name for the first time. The Christian Cicero, Lactantius (*fl.* A.D. 315), wrote an ambitious book designed to be a

---

* Vnius sese dominum fecisse lacertae (3. 231).
† Credo Pudicitiam Saturno rege moratam
  in terris . . . (6. 1–2).

manual of Christian education, in which he praised the satirist, saying:

Men have invented the name of Fortune, which is meaningless; how far removed from wisdom this is, Juvenal shows in the following lines:

> with wisdom, no divinity is needed; it is we
> who make you a goddess, Fortune, and set you in heaven.*[7]

So Juvenal appears for the first time in the guise which he was to keep for a thousand years or more—as a thinker with standards higher than most pagans, and as a coiner of pithy and memorable epigrams.

Two generations later we meet his first imitator in poetry. This was Ausonius of Bordeaux (A.D. 310–94), who combined cultivated Christian sentiment with a graceful turn for conventional poetry, with wide reading, and with a retentive memory. Juvenal was not by any means his chief love, but he was one of his models, and Ausonius thought well enough of him to name him and to borrow several of his best phrases.[8]

So did Ausonius' pupil and correspondent Paulinus of Nola, who imitated Juvenal's cartoon of a loftily coiffured lady, 'built into a turreted head', and other neat epigrams—some of which he may have got through Ausonius. More important was the fact that Paulinus was the first of a long line of poets who turned Juvenal's phrases to the service of Christianity. Thus Juvenal had called a selfish patron 'rich for himself, poor for his friends'. The antithesis reminded Paulinus of the paradoxes of his religion, so he wrote that a good man was 'a pauper for himself, rich for his friends', and 'rich in the wealth of Christ, poor for himself'.[9]

Greater than he was Prudentius (340–410), the chief poet of the early church. Born in Spain and well schooled both in pagan poetry and in Christian doctrine, he wrote at least one permanently interesting poem, *The Battle in the Soul*, which brought together the exciting struggles and adventures of Greco-Roman epic with the consciousness of guilt, insecurity, and conflict which Christianity had discovered in many souls of the later empire. He admired Juvenal chiefly for his ability to coin phrases, and adapted many of the best.[10]

---

* Nullum numen habes si sit prudentia: nos te,
 nos facimus, Fortuna, deam caeloque locamus (10. 365–6).

But Juvenal's return to light was slow. St. Jerome (340–420) thrice adapts one of his most famous lines, but never mentions his name. And in a famous treatise on marriage he apparently draws from Juvenal's misogynistic Sixth Satire and even echoes some of its most biting sentences, still without naming the satirist.[11] His colleague and friend St. Augustine (354–430) once quotes a fine passage on the decay of Roman morality from Juvenal, calling him simply 'their satirist'.[12] It looks as though Jerome and Augustine knew something of Juvenal's work, but had not read his poems continuously and had not really come to know his character and his thought.

St. Jerome and St. Augustine were writing about A.D. 400. But meanwhile, and for some decades before them, Juvenal had also been interesting the pagans. His poems had been somehow rescued from oblivion. Notes on their meaning had been written. Attempts were being made to establish their text in the form which would be most intelligible and closest to that which Juvenal himself wrote. Variations in text and interpretation were being noted down. Editions of his work were produced, with text and notes arranged so as to be handy for interested readers. And he was becoming an important author, whose books were read not as curiosities but as works of permanent importance.

This is one of the darkest periods in the story of Juvenal's survival. Although the devoted researches of Knoche and Vianello on the manuscripts and Wessner on the commentaries have done much to clear it up, it is still full of doubt and shadows.* But its outlines are these.

Having been forgotten for decades (we have seen why†) Juvenal's poems began to interest a few readers in the third and early fourth centuries. These men jotted down notes on the persons he mentioned, on the meaning of his brisk compressed phrases, and on the sense of obscure words; and at some time a few notes on the tradition of his exile were inserted. Then, roughly between A.D. 350 and 420, a well-trained pagan scholar

---

* See in particular Knoche (*45*) and Wessner (*53*); also N. Vianello's 'Il testo delle satire di Giovenale', *Atti della Società ligustica di scienze e lettere*, N.S. 12 (1933), 81–123.

† pp. 181–2.

living in Rome put the notes all together, and with his own very considerable additions made them into a complete running commentary on Juvenal's satires.[13] Whoever he was, he had been trained in such work by studying the older Latin authors— Vergil in particular, whom he quotes about eighty times, nearly as often as all other writers taken together.[14]

Now, we are told by the historian Ammian that about 390, in the reign of Theodosius I, some noblemen of the time who cared nothing for literature in general were reading Juvenal with enthusiasm.* And we have seen that up-to-date poets like Ausonius were imitating his poems. At this very time, the eminent scholar Servius, teaching in Rome, was writing a great commentary on Vergil. In it he quoted Juvenal more than seventy times, although all his predecessors in scholarship had ignored the satires. He did not think Juvenal a 'classical' author suitable for schools, but placed him with the 'modernists' like Lucan and Statius.[15] Still, he did consider Juvenal an important writer, whose use of language although unorthodox was interesting. And from the time of Servius onwards, words and phrases from Juvenal were constantly quoted by grammarians and literary critics: soon he actually became a school-author.[16] It seems likely, therefore, that the commentary on Juvenal was compiled by a pupil of Servius trained in his methods and on his favourite authors, and that it was intended to gratify the public interest in Juvenal's work which grew up during the fourth century. Perhaps we know the editor's name. In two of the manuscripts of Juvenal there is a note, 'I, Nicaeus, read and corrected [this work] at Rome in the house of the teacher Servius.'† This may merely be a note handed down from a man who went over one manuscript and made corrections in it for his own personal use; but it may well give us the name of the first editor of Juvenal.

Whoever the editor was, he produced not only a commentary but a readable text of the satires.[17] His commentary was the basis of the abbreviated and shortened sets of explanatory notes which have survived to our own time. Other editions of the text came out in antiquity, often with different readings here and

* Amm. Marc. 28. 4. 14; see p. 2.
† 'Legi ego Niceus apud M. Serbium Rome et emendaui': at the beginning of Satire 6 in Laur. 34, 42, and in the scholiast's handwriting at 7. 4 in Leid. 82.

there. But they all shared one very significant feature: they all stopped at the sixtieth line of Satire Sixteen. This can mean only one thing. It means that, when Nicaeus (if it was he) rediscovered and edited Juvenal's poems, most of the last satire had already been lost; and that there must have been *only one copy* of Juvenal's poems which was even partially complete, when they emerged from the long silence that enveloped them after the poet's death.[18]

It is even possible to guess at the history of this long-lost manuscript. If our conjecture that Juvenal was given a post in the Athenaeum be accepted,* is it not likely that he left a copy of his works to the library of the Athenaeum? that a copy was preserved there when his work went out of circulation elsewhere? that it was mutilated by age in a very common way, losing the final pages of the volume? that this one defective copy was naturally utilized as the master-copy from which others were made and on which the commentary was written? and thus that Juvenal owed both the comfort of his declining years, the preservation of his work, and his ultimate fame to Hadrian's foundation, the Athenaeum, which he himself greeted at the opening of Satire Seven?[19]

However that may be, the text of Juvenal as we know it dates from the edition put out in 400 or so. The worst corruptions and mutilations in it apparently go back beyond that date. But at some early time, perhaps in the same generation as this first edition, someone with more industry than brains produced another edition of Juvenal, which on the whole contained a far inferior text. Again and again its editor introduced changes which he thought would make Juvenal more intelligible and orderly, and usually made him much stupider. It is a common fault of strong-willed editors to assume that their author had no more imagination and less sense of style than they themselves.[20] The unfortunate thing is that this text, and not the other, the sensible one, was the text which became most widely known and copied.[21] The result is that, of the 500-odd manuscripts of Juvenal which exist, only one stands close to what Juvenal actually wrote. The others are all badly infected, in various degrees, with the diseases of the vulgate edition. But at least one danger had been avoided. Juvenal's satires might well

* For this conjecture see pp. 111–12.

have disappeared altogether. From 400 onwards he was a widely read and popular author.

The brilliant Egyptian poet Claudian, who served the half-barbarian marshal Stilicho (*fl.* A.D. 400), wrote two savage political satires against the chief ministers of the eastern empire. In these, and in some of his other poems, he imitated a number of Juvenal's bitterest, boldest pictures.[22] After the middle of the fifth century the smart Gallic poet Sidonius Apollinaris (who became bishop of Clermont) also knew the satires well; although Juvenal was not one of his favourite poets, he adapted some expressions from him in his own prose letters and his poems. In fact, it is in a poem by Sidonius on literary history that we find the first independent mention of Juvenal's banishment.[23] The Christian, or rather the more intensely Christian, Sedulius (*fl.* 470) introduced reminiscences of the Sixth and Fifteenth Satires into his poetical version of the New Testament; Bishop Ennodius of Pavia (d. 521) echoed Juvenal several times, and so did his contemporary, Alcimus Avitus, the bishop of Vienne (d. 521).[24]

Roman Africa had long been a cultured province, and its learning survived even the inroads of the Vandals. The Carthaginian poet Dracontius, who wrote in the later fifth century, copied Juvenal several times, and apparently knew his work.[25] The poets of the Vandal kingdom sometimes imitated lines from the satires;[26] and even in the late sixth century such phrases appear in the work of Corippus, who wrote about Roman generals fighting the barbarians, and who himself was waging a losing battle against barbarism.[27]

These, in various degrees, were poets. But Juvenal was now known not only as a coiner of poetic phrases but as a wise man. We have already seen his epigrams and his moralizings cited by St. Jerome and St. Augustine. Henceforward we find him quoted again and again in prose works of learning and of instruction, by teachers, philosophers, and princes of the church. Often such quotations were not the result of any deep study of Juvenal: parts of his work were entering the general storehouse of human wisdom. Probably the first, but certainly not the last, Pope to quote him was Gelasius I (492–6); but he does not name Juvenal and may not have known him directly.[28] Similarly

Saint Caesarius, bishop of Arles in a difficult time (503–43), when warning his flock against greed, backed up his warning by a line from Juvenal, and called it simply 'an age-old thought:

> Our hearts cannot contain two different interests.'*[29]

Often, again, a wise man who had read Juvenal would quote an epigram or a passage from the satires. Then those who read his book would remember the lines and cite them again, and so diffuse these immortal words and imperishable thoughts.[30] The most famous example of this in Juvenal's history is one which bridges the darkest gulf in the Dark Ages. The thinker and statesman Boethius (d. 524), imprisoned by the Ostrogoth monarch Theodoric and awaiting execution, wrote a *Consolation of Philosophy* in which he meditated on some of the deepest problems of life, especially the relation between virtue and suffering. In it he incorporated an adaptation of Juvenal's epigram,

> The traveller with empty pockets sings as he passes the thief.†

Nearly eight hundred years after Boethius' execution, the finest mind in Italy, Dante Alighieri, found Juvenal's thought in his work, meditated upon it, and used it in a dialogue which is one of the first philosophical discussions in modern European prose.[31]

Thoughts, and the books which carry them, have strange adventures. Juvenal's poetry (as we have seen) was all but forgotten and extinguished in the century after his death. Then it was resurrected. One copy was discovered, read, discussed, explained, edited, publicized, copied, and disseminated. From that one copy his work spread far over the civilized world and acquired strength to live through an almost equally difficult future, surviving an era when the men of power were not perverts and gladiators but simple-minded and bloody-handed savages. It is strange to watch how, within a few generations after the rediscovery of his poems, Juvenal not only became a school author in the west but actually was read, translated, and studied in the proud east—where few Roman writers ever penetrated. The famous professor Priscian (who taught Latin in Constantinople about A.D. 500) quoted the satires over a

---

* Pectora nostra duas non admittentia curas (~ 7. 65).

† Cantabit uacuus coram latrone uiator (10. 22). See Boethius, *Cons. Phil.* 2, Prosa 5. 22.

hundred times in his extant works.* The Byzantine savant John the Lydian, whom the great emperor Justinian favoured, knew something of Juvenal's work and his life-story.† The Byzantine historian John Malalas recorded the tale of Juvenal's exile in a confused but vivid version.‡ Just as the darkness closes in again for a time over much of civilization, we see Juvenal's work spreading wider and wider. One of the most unexpected discoveries made by the searchers for buried books in Egypt was a parchment page which carried fifty lines of the Seventh Satire, with explanatory notes both in Latin and in Greek and with critical signs which showed that Juvenal was not only read for amusement but studied with professional attention.[32] He had become part of the fast-dwindling culture of his world.

Surely it is a satirist's purgatory, bitter but ludicrous, that Juvenal, who despised the Greeks and detested Egypt, should have been partly brought down to us by a leaf of parchment from a Greek-speaking school in Egypt. If he had seen these pedantic marginal notes, these careful translations between the lines, these neat professorial symbols, what savage epigram would he have uttered?

* Knoche (45) 39.
† Jo. Lyd. *De magistratibus*, 1. 20~Juv. 5. 110–11; 1. 41 mentions Juvenal together with Turnus and Petronius.
‡ Jo. Mal. *Chron.* 10. 341 (see p. 239 n. 9).

XXIX

JUVENAL IN THE DARK AGES

BUT now the Dark Ages were beginning. The western empire and the eastern empire split apart. The west crumbled into barbarian kingdoms and the anarchies of repeated invasion. Roads and bridges and harbours and aqueducts were ruined; cities shrank to towns, and towns to villages huddled round a fortress; schools and libraries and museums were looted, burnt, abandoned; the mass of the people forgot how to read and write, and soon the spoken Latin language itself melted into a dozen rude dialects or was swamped by the languages of the conquering hosts.[1] Harsh new names marched across the field of history: Receswinth, Gunthamund, Ratchis, Godigisel, Hengest, Eormanric.

Those were bad times in the west. The river of culture sank underground, wandered hopelessly into swamps, 'forgetting that bright speed it had', or was lost in the waste land. Only a few thin currents ran on, through a few channels which wise men dug to keep the precious stream alive. These currents carried the Bible, and the church fathers, and Vergil, and a number of essential grammars and encyclopaedias, and a few edifying works. Vergil is the only pagan poet who never sank out of sight. Juvenal, with the others, was submerged for a time, but, never buried in the sands like some others, he was kept alive by being transmitted, however imperfectly, from scholar to scholar. His pungent epigrams and his vivid phrases were never forgotten.

The Irish Saint Columban (543–615) was one of the many missionaries who set out from the British islands to evangelize the Continent and save it from paganism and barbarism. In France he founded the monastery of Luxeuil, and in Italy the still more illustrious monastery of Bobbio, as centres of both devotion and scholarship. He knew something of Juvenal, although indirectly, and quoted him now and then in his poems.[2] (Long afterwards, in the tenth century, the first catalogue of Bobbio library showed that it had over 600 manuscripts, including at least two of Juvenal's satires.)[3] A generation later the bishop of Seville, Isidore (*c.* 540–630), wrote an ambitious work in twenty books which he intended to contain, and to preserve through the doubtful future, the essentials of learning. Learned as he was, he did not know Juvenal directly or understand him fully. He quotes lines from the satires often enough, but he explains that (together with Horace and Persius) Juvenal represented 'a new type of comedy'—for now men were forgetting the true meaning of drama and the essential nature of the genres of poetry.[4] Then in Eugenius, bishop of Toledo (d. 657) —who edited Dracontius, an earlier admirer of Juvenal—two or three tags from the satires appear.[5] Probably they were acquired through some poetic thesaurus or phrase-book; and similarly, when his successor St. Julian (680–90) cited one line of Juvenal in his *Commentary on Donatus*, he merely took it from some earlier grammarian.[6]

In Britain the first eminent scholar to emerge after the Anglo-Saxon invaders were civilized and Christianized was Aldhelm (*c.* 640–709). Well read, devoted to Latin poetry, and one of the few men of his time who understood such subjects as metre and grammar and the techniques of language, he quoted Juvenal about a dozen times; he knew who Juvenal was and how his poems were divided into books; but it seems that he took all his quotations from the master grammarian Priscian.[7] In the voluminous and wonderful works of his successor the Venerable Bede a few fragments of Juvenal's satires appear, but Bede had no real knowledge of the poems themselves.[8]

Now, for the second time in his history, the traces of Juvenal's influence in European culture were becoming faint indeed. Yet within the next hundred years he was once again to be studied, and copied, and known as a distinguished poet. Towards the end of the eighth century, the Dark Ages were lightened. Charlemagne, crowned 'emperor of the Romans' in 800, gathered round him a lively group of scholars from several countries, headed by the brilliant Alcuin of York. These men and their successors made the first Renaissance. They sought for manuscripts of Latin books long forgotten, and had them carefully copied and multiplied. They wrote good Latin themselves, and from them went out a radiation of learning and intellectual energy over many areas of western Europe. It was

in this burst of energy that Juvenal's works were again discovered and copied. The odd thing is that these Carolingian
savants and poets do not themselves seem to have known Juvenal.[9] No doubt that is because he sometimes deals with repellent
subjects and is frequently sarcastic about the Caesars, whereas
they were concerned with asserting spiritual nobility, and they
were in the service of a new Caesar. Still, it was their stimulus
which set others to work finding and recopying the satires.
Scholars and scribes began to dig out manuscripts of Juvenal
written several centuries earlier, to recopy them from the
OLDUNDIVIDEDCAPITALS into the newly perfected minuscule letters (in which this page is printed),[10] to lend them to one another,
to edit and emend them, to make extracts from them for anthologies, and to study and explain them as far as they could.

The laborious researches and acute analyses of Ulrich Knoche
have shown that this activity, to begin with, took place almost
entirely in France, and that the new stimulus to Juvenalian
study originated from French monasteries. He has deduced the
existence of five master copies of Juvenal's satires which were
written in the Carolingian age. All these have now vanished; but
we have copies made directly or indirectly from them. One of
the masters was transcribed in France before A.D. 815—and
from this our best manuscript, P, is descended. Another, full of
barbarisms, was perhaps made even earlier than 800; and there
were two more in the early ninth century. About the same time
a fifth was written in the famous monastery of Lorsch in the
Rhineland.[11] Then, between 820 and 825, at the Benedictine
abbey of Reichenau on Lake Constance, a monk compiled an
anthology in which he inserted a number of quotations from
Juvenal—evidently taking them directly from a copy of the
satires and not through grammarians. Soon afterwards, about
825, little Mico of St. Riquier in northern France did what most
anthologists do, and borrowed from his predecessor to make
another anthology. Mico's collection we still possess: it has many
citations from Juvenal, copied from a manuscript of the good
tradition.[12] Within the same period, in Spain, St. Eulogius
(who was martyred in 859) procured a copy of Juvenal's satires
on a tour of the monasteries in the foot-hills of the Pyrenees,
and took it back to Cordova 'not privately for himself, but for
all earnest students in common'.[13]

There must of course have been many more manuscripts in this period, which have since disappeared.[14] But the sad thing is that Juvenal was still haunted by the cheap and facile editor who had disfigured his text in order to produce a popular edition in the fourth or fifth century.* Although manuscripts derived from the better edition managed to survive to the time of Charlemagne and to get themselves copied, still most of the transcripts made at this time were handed down directly or indirectly from the inferior text. We shall see that this tradition predominated well into the Renaissance. It is miserable: as though most of the world knew Milton only through Bentley's degraded version.

After the lapse of several centuries and the second disappearance of Juvenal, the first scholar we know to have specialized in the study of the satires was Heiric of Auxerre, who was born in 841. We hear that he lectured on Juvenal, as well as on the satirists Horace and Persius and Petronius. In his most important poem, *The Life of St. German*, he used a number of really intelligent imitations and adaptations of Juvenal which show first-hand knowledge.[15] And in some of the extant commentaries to Juvenal, at the line 9. 37 (which is almost wholly Greek, being a parody of Homer), there is a pathetic note saying, 'In the Greek line there is one foot lacking, which Professor Heiric could not fill in.'[16] Evidently, then, it was Heiric who revived the study of Juvenal in the west, and who (using some ancient commentary now lost) wrote the medieval explanatory notes which have come down to us in various forms. Usually they bear the name of 'Cornutus'—simply because that was the name of the tutor and editor of the kindred satirist Persius; but they were either composed by Heiric or based on notes taken at his lectures. Although his work helped students at the time and was valuable for reintroducing the world to Juvenal, it is necessary to say that his explanations of problems in the satires were often outrageously silly and ignorant.[17] Poor Juvenal, so long saddled with an inferior text, was now bent under the burden of an idiotic commentary.

Heiric's chief pupil was Remy of Auxerre (841–c. 908), who also studied with the brilliant Irishman Dunchad. Teaching in Paris about the year 900, Remy is known to have lectured on

* See p. 187 and notes.

Juvenal; we hear that his commentary on the satires existed both at Glastonbury and somewhere in Germany; and his notes on other classical authors are full of explanations drawn from Juvenal and from Heiric's Juvenalian lectures.[18]

Interest in Juvenal almost immediately spread from France to northern Italy. Poets began to admire him again and to borrow his best effects, with or without acknowledgement. There are several such loans in *The Exploits of Berengar*, a quantitative Latin poem on the life of a tough Lombard prince, written apparently in Verona about 924.[19] And there are far more in the work of Liutprand, bishop of Cremona (*c.* 920–72), who copied Juvenal oftener than all other pagan authors and yet never mentioned his name—apparently because he wanted his readers to think his borrowings were original creations.[20] Several generations later the enigmatic social critic calling himself Sextus Amarcius Gallus Piosistratus, who wrote four books of satires about 1050, used some of the hardest passages of Juvenal's poetry in his work and mentioned Juvenal himself with respect.[21]

At Verona the austere and resolute reformer, Bishop Rather (890–974), knew Juvenal and quoted him, with particular interest in the most emphatically moral satires.[22] There must have been a real passion for Juvenal in northern Italy. Soon it became the mark of a learned man anywhere to know his poems. Shortly after the middle of the tenth century Gunzo, a priest from Novara near Milan, wrote a long and angry letter to the monks of Reichenau (a stronghold of Juvenalian learning): he was embittered because, during a visit to the Swiss monastery of St. Gall, he had been mocked by a young student for using the accusative case instead of the ablative in conversation. In his letter—which is very amusing, and still worth reading—he quotes the satirist several times, sharply to the point.[23] Early in the eleventh century Walter of Speyer, in Bavaria, was learning Juvenal's poems in school, and they were being taught under Abbot Gozbert in Tegernsee monastery.[24] At Verona a monk lamented the labour imposed upon students by the lack of explanatory notes covering the later books of Juvenal—apparently he had only a mutilated copy of the scholia.[25] In 1086 the scholar Aimeric wrote an *Art of Reading*, dividing literature into golden books, silver books, and so on.[26]

Juvenal was one of the nine golden authors; and so, as he entered the Middle Ages, his position was secure.

One of the odd things about him, though, is that (like many eminent writers) he is ambivalent. He is both attractive and repulsive. He is both disturbing and consoling. He is both a preserver and a destroyer, both positive and negative. As such, he appeals both to upholders of the established order in religion and politics and society and education, and to rebels. We have already seen him attracting both Christians and pagans. Later we shall see this ambivalence again. And now, towards the end of the Dark Ages, it is strange to see him beloved both by a heretic and by a Pope.

That prodigy of learning, the admirable Gerbert of Aurillac, scholar, scientist, musician, statesman—who lectured at Rheims before becoming Pope Silvester II—taught his pupils the satires of Juvenal as an essential part of their literary education.* And about the same time a scholar in Ravenna called Vilgard had been studying the classical writers so intensely that they led him into heresy. In a dream he saw Vergil, Horace, and Juvenal. They spoke to him. They promised to make him famous in return for expounding their work. And he began—the story is a little obscure, but we can guess what happened—he began to teach ideas which were derived from Greco-Roman standards and not from the code of the church. He was condemned by the archbishop of Ravenna as a heretic. It appears from the report that the same heresy was emerging elsewhere through Italy, had entered Sardinia, and was invading Spain.[27] Apparently Vilgard and those who shared his ideas were predecessors of some of the 'new pagans' who appeared during the Renaissance of the fifteenth and sixteenth centuries, some of them even among the clergy. We know nothing of this movement. We can scarcely guess what its principles were. We know only that it was exterminated 'by fire and sword'. But at least we know that it was another evidence of the lasting power of the poems of Juvenal, who had now become a companion of his predecessor Horace and his master Vergil, and was haunting the minds of men more intensely than he did during his short temporal life.

* Richer, *Historiae* (ed. and tr. R. Latouche, Paris, 1930, 1937), 3. 47 (v. 2, p. 56).

XXX

JUVENAL IN MEDIEVAL CULTURE

AFTER the renaissance of Charlemagne's time, there was a pause, and in some parts of Europe a retrogression. But with the twelfth century came a second and far more glorious renaissance. Cathedrals and epic poems, universities and systems of philosophy, grand castles and chivalrous histories thrust their way upwards in a springlike burst of energy.

Together with the work of greater men than he, Juvenal's books fed the hungry enthusiasms and nourished the growing minds of the medieval thinkers, students, and poets. There is scarcely one of any eminence who does not know him or cite his satires. There were four chief ways in which Juvenal's poems entered medieval culture.[1] They became material and stimulus for poets. They provided philosophers and historians with pithy epigrams and memorable illustrations. Often anonymously, they supplied 'winged words'—phrases that left their context and their creator to fly from mind to mind and become part of the general movement of thought. And they were an element in the curriculum of higher education, studied, expounded, copied, and annotated.

Poetry was bilingual in the Middle Ages: it spoke Latin, but it also sang in the vernacular languages which were now growing to maturity. Some poets, like Dante, wrote both in Latin and in the 'vulgar tongue'. It would be a great mistake to think that the Latin poems of the Middle Ages were stuffy and imitative and conventional, or that they were written in an unreal language artificially kept alive by pedants. One glance at the naughty songs of the wandering scholars, ten minutes with a Latin hymnal, a single page of the powerful Latin satires of the twelfth century, a single medieval Latin love-lyric, would make that amply clear. True, the vernacular languages had sentiment, and charm, and primitive energy, and a new melodiousness;

while Latin was the language of the mind. But Latin also carried strong emotion, ardent love and hatred, the records of heroism and the dreams of mystics. It was spoken, by a huge international community, far more widely than any single national language: men thought in it and taught in it, and suffered and rejoiced and disputed and prayed in it. Without Latin, the culture of the Middle Ages and the growth of civilization in the west would have been impossible, and Europe would have been a cage full of fighting savages.

Most of the poetry of the Middle Ages was therefore written in Latin, and in nearly all of it, from epic to satire, Juvenal's influence is easy to see. Two distinguished heroic writers— Joseph of Exeter (*fl.* 1190), who composed a famous poem on the fall of Troy and was a favourite of Richard Lionheart, and his contemporary William the Breton, author of an epic on the conqueror Philip Augustus of France—both drew from the satires.[2] The boldest medieval satirist, Bernard of Morval, (*fl.* 1150), worked phrases from Juvenal into his staggeringly clever *Contempt of the World*.[3] The brilliant Walter Map (*fl.* 1180) is believed to be the author of many sharp but nameless satiric poems, which again and again rival and echo Juvenal.[4] In Belgium a monk called Gilbert attacked the luxury and misrule of the great ecclesiastical foundations in a poem which converts several passages from Juvenal's thundering hexameters into almost equally skilful but much jauntier quatrains.[5] The Anglo-Norman satirist Jean of Auville, although he never mentions Juvenal in his poem *The Super-Sorrower*, begins it with a tag lifted from the Tenth Satire and scatters others taken from Juvenal here and there in his work.[6] At the same time Walter of Châtillon was adapting Juvenal in his lesser poems, jaunty and satirical in style, but profoundly sad;[7] several bitter political and social satires and lampoons on the corruptions of nobles and intellectuals use Juvenal's epigrams;[8] echoes from the satires sound here and there in the cheerful and sometimes scurrilous songs of the Goliards, the rootless scholars who were the intellectual and moral anarchs of the twelfth and thirteenth centuries.[9] And the old tradition of misogyny was taken up in a very funny dog-Latin poem on the troubles of marriage, written in Boulogne in 1298 and called *The Lamentations of Matthew*: it is just as confused and angry as Juvenal's Sixth, but more amusing, for the frankness with which its elderly author bewails his difficulties with his young and energetic wife. He uses quite a number of lines from Juvenal, though he borrows few or no sustained chains of ideas.[10] However, not all the satirists were on Juvenal's side: one of them actually denounced the neo-pagans who

> trust in Juvenal more
> than in the prophets' lore.[11]

In other types of Latin poetry, too, his impress is marked. Alfanus, archbishop of Salerno (*fl.* 1080), converted one of his most famous phrases into a stanza of Horatian lyrics.[12] Abbot Thiofrid of Echternach used some of his words in a metrical life of the British missionary saint Willibrord written in 1105.[13] In those odd productions, the Latin 'comedies' of the twelfth century—written for reading rather than performance, and based chiefly on Ovid—we meet an occasional neat Juvenalian epigram.[14]

Among vernacular poets in the Middle Ages, Juvenal was best known to Jean de Meun (*fl.* 1270), the second author of the *Romance of the Rose*, a vast medley of philosophy and satire and allegory in which several cruel attacks on the vanity and duplicity of women have derived from or passed through the Sixth Satire.[15] Other poets knew and used only part of Juvenal's work. For instance, the Italian Antonio Pucci (*fl.* 1375) when writing a sour lyric *On Old Age* began it with an adaptation of Juvenal 10; Wernher von Elmendorf turned one of Juvenal's best epigrams into part of a meditative German lyric; and Louis XII's doctor, in a morality play written against over-eating, praised Juvenal for his wisdom in connecting big banquets and sudden death.[16] It is common enough in the Middle Ages to find poets listing Juvenal among the important writers whose work is to be admired, even when they have no real knowledge of his poems.[17] The strangest of all his medieval reincarnations comes in a French play, *The Mystery of the Vengeance of Our Lord Jesus Christ*, by Jehan Michel (d. 1447). In the second act of this drama the emperor Tiberius is shown holding a council to discuss a dispatch just received from Pontius Pilate. It concerns the life and miracles of Jesus. Among Tiberius' councillors are Horace, Terence, Claudian, Porphyry, Maximian, and Juvenal: in fact, Juvenal is the first to speak—with a vague allusion to Vergil's prophecy of the miraculous baby in Bucolics 4. In such a context Juvenal has lost all his character as teacher and poet, and (as one of his admirers was to write) has merely left a name 'to point a moral, or adorn a tale'.*[18]

Satire is a blend of poetry and prose. Therefore it enters prose quite as easily as it enters poetry. And in prose it partakes both of rhetoric (formal and informal) and of philosophy. Thus both as a stylist and as a thinker Juvenal appealed to the prose-writers of the Middle Ages. A book could be filled with passages which medieval philosophers and historians and teachers based on Juvenal's satires, and a chapter with the names of such writers. It will be simpler to mention only those who were of special distinction or owed him a special debt.

Among philosophers the most eminent are Bernard Silvestris of Tours (fl. 1150), who recalls him in his strange speculations *On the Universe*;[19] Abelard's English pupil, John of Salisbury (fl. 1155), a learned man indeed, who knew Juvenal thoroughly;[20] the master of theology at Notre Dame, Peter Cantor (fl. 1165);[21] the brilliant Breton, Peter of Blois (fl. 1175);[22] the Benedictine scholar who wrought all medieval learning into his vast *Mirror*, Vincent of Beauvais (d. 1264); and that universal mind, Roger Bacon (c. 1214–94).[23] In an anonymous collection of excerpts from classical thinkers called *The Doctrine of Moral Philosophers* —which became one of the most influential ethical manuals of the Middle Ages—many passages from Juvenal appear side by side with thoughts from Seneca and 'sentences from Tully'.[24] Such books spread his fame widely.

Medieval historians also liked Juvenal for his strong sense of historical process and for his gift of political satire. Several of his crispest epigrams appear in the work of the first historian of the Czechs, Cosmas of Prague (fl. 1100).[25] The wise and elegant Polish historian, St. Vincent of Cracow (fl. 1210), gracefully adapts others.[26] Although the founder of English history, William of Malmesbury, did not really know the satires as complete poems, he borrowed some phrases from them; and there are more borrowings in his successor, Matthew Paris.[27]

Besides these, many who had scarcely heard Juvenal's name and had never read one of his satires were familiar with some of

* Johnson, *Vanity of Human Wishes*, 222~Juv. 10. 167.

those sentences which look so simple and yet remain so long in the memory. The formidable Pope Innocent III (1198–1216) used Juvenal's warning about avarice—

> your lust for money grows as fast as your bank-account—*

in his address to the great Lateran Council; and three times he reminded his hearers that sin was especially dangerous for the clergy, 'because, according to the satirist Juvenal,

> every moral fault carries more conspicuous
> guilt when its author is thought to be a greater man'.†28

In 1189, when news of the fall of Jerusalem to Saladin reached Denmark, a royal council was held. Esbjorn, brother of the great statesman archbishop Absalon, made a fiery speech calling on the Danes to join the Third Crusade. Reminding them of their ancient reputation for bravery, he spoke bitterly of the decline of morals in his own day, when princes were too often controlled by flatterers, and quoted 'the scoffer's poetic proverb—

> what nobles do not give, a stage-player will give you'.‡

Again, on his deathbed, Robert Grosseteste, chancellor of Oxford University (d. 1253), praised the friars' rule of voluntary poverty because it enabled them to keep free of vice, and added:

> the traveller with empty pockets will sing as he passes the thief.§

In the letters of Adam Marsh (d. 1258), the first Franciscan to lecture at Oxford, almost the sole reminiscence of the classics is an adaptation of a phrase from Juvenal's Eighth Satire, 'What is more glorious than to make an end of life in order to obtain life?'‖ Of all these echoes, the quaintest occurs in an earnest

* Crescit amor nummi quantum ipsa pecunia creuit (14. 139).
† Omne animi uitium tanto conspectius in se
  crimen habet quanto maior qui peccat habetur (8. 140–1).
‡ Anonymus, *De Profectione Danorum in Terram Sanctam*, c. 5, in J. Langebek, *Script. Rer. Danic.* 5 (Copenhagen, 1783), p. 347∼Juv. 7. 90:
    Quod non dant proceres dabit histrio.
§ Matt. Paris., *Chron. Mai.*, in *Rer. Brit. Med. Aevi Script.* 57, part 5, p. 401∼Juv. 10. 22:
    Cantabit uacuus coram latrone uiator.
‖ 'Quid umquam aestimabitur . . . gloriosius . . . quam propter causam vivendi, vivendi finem facere?' (*Rer. Brit. Med. Aevi Script.* 4. 1, p. 274∼ Juv. 8. 84).

preachment by the monk Helinand, who died early in the thirteenth century. Towards the end of his satire on the secret society of homosexuals, Juvenal says: 'Of course not even children nowadays believe in the underworld. But imagine it were real—then what do you think the great Romans of the past would feel when the ghost of one of these degenerates came down among them?' This is merely a rhetorical fiction, a prosopopoeia. But Helinand takes it seriously. When marshalling arguments to prove that hell really exists, he cites this passage, and piously mistranslates it: 'Juvenal the satirist, opposing the common opinion of the pagans, declares that we must give it credence: he says:

> Not even the children believe it, except the very smallest,
> but you must consider it true!'*[29]

All this widening knowledge of Juvenal's satires was helped by the work of many faithful students. Again and again they mention him in their books on education and on the art of writing. During the Middle Ages some classical authors were almost entirely forgotten; some were kept for amusement only (like Martial) or preserved because of a local connexion (like Catullus); but Juvenal was on almost every list of good reading. The Benedictine Conrad of Hirsau, early in the twelfth century, calls him 'best of the satirists'.[30] In a list of recommended books for the Paris colleges, that naïve character Alexander Neckam says that, because of his moral power, Juvenal ought to be read even by young students; and about the same time Thomas de Marleberge took a manuscript of Juvenal with him to Oxford, doubtless for use in teaching.[31] In the thirteenth century Everard the German not only lists him as a valued author but imitates and adapts his poems.[32] Towards the end of the same century the schoolmaster Hugo of Trimberg, in a critical survey of the authors of the early empire, gives a good brief description of the satirist:

> Now first in order comes the biting Juvenal,
> Strong of will and truthful, flattering no criminal.[33]

Even in remote Byzantium, the scholarly Maximos Planudes (*fl.*

---

* Nec pueri credunt, nisi qui nondum aere lauantur:
  sed tu uera puta (2. 152–3).

1300) found several lines of Juvenal quoted in Boethius, turned them into Greek verse, and identified their author.[34]

Students always need digests. To assist them, many dictionaries of hard words and anthologies of fine sayings were made in the Middle Ages. There is one German collection, dating from the twelfth century, which reflects the taste of the time: it has fourteen books of fine quotations altogether, and of these, five come from Christian literature, five from Ovid, and one each from Vergil, Horace, Lucan, and Juvenal.[35] In his lexicon of difficult words, *Derivations*, the English monk Osbern of Gloucester quotes Juvenal about 130 times.[36] In proportion to the extent of his work, it has been estimated that Juvenal was, during the Middle Ages, the most popular author for anthologies.[37] A number of the medieval commentaries on his satires have never been printed. There was one by the distinguished English scholar Nicolas Trivet, which is lost; others exist only in single library copies; but they were much used.[38] In fact, nearly all the important manuscripts of Juvenal's poems which now exist, and which have carried over our knowledge of the satires to the present day, were written in the Middle Ages—together with others, mentioned in the catalogues of abbey libraries and in similar lists, but now, alas, almost untraceable. One of the strangest of such survivals is this. There are a few medieval manuscripts in which famous pieces of Latin poetry are written out with musical notes (called *neumata*) attached, so that they may be sung: some of Horace's odes, well-known passages from Vergil, and so forth. In one or two of these we find a musical setting for the noble ethical exhortation which begins at Juvenal 8. 78; and it is tempting to believe that the music may go back to the first enthusiasts for Juvenal who chanted his majestic lines in the Romanesque cloisters of western Europe.[39]

The sign of a universal genius is that he appeals to many different men in many different ways. During the Middle Ages we have seen how broadly Juvenal's thoughts and words spread, from the wildest rebels to the sternest of the Popes. Now finally let us look at four authors who, although they lived in the Middle Ages, prepared the third and richest Renaissance. They are Dante and three of Dante's pupils.

For Petrarch, Juvenal was a classic, and therefore an authority

—since one of Petrarch's chief motives was the quest for certainty and authority. But even more, Juvenal was a wise man. Perhaps the cruelty and pessimism of the satires did not appeal to Petrarch, but he admired Juvenal's technique, and he respected him deeply for what he called 'wide experience and profound knowledge of humanity'. Of course he possessed a manuscript copy of the satires. It has been estimated that Juvenal stood fifth in the list of his favourite poets. Petrarch quoted him by name at least twenty times, and oftener than that with some general description such as 'the satirist'. Phrases from Juvenal's poems appear in Petrarch's most public works as well as his most private: now in a letter to an emperor, now in the margin of his own manuscript of Vergil, now in his autobiographical *Secret*.[40]

Boccaccio knew Juvenal as a master of satire. Several times he mentions him with respect for his courage and his conviction. But more, he imitates him. In his forties, Boccaccio fell in love with a handsome and unprincipled woman, who led him on and then made a fool of him. In order to cure himself—and also to take his revenge—he wrote a memorable but horrible satire on the woman, and indeed on all women. He made her dead husband return from the grave to describe her shallowness, perfidy, vanity, and lust, as a warning to Boccaccio—and, worse, to detail her secret ugliness and nastiness with a precision which outdoes Juvenal and rivals Swift. This disagreeable book, a sort of Consolation in reverse, is called *The Labyrinth of Love*, or *The Pigeon-Basket* (evidently two variants of the idea that love is a trap). It is in prose, not verse. It is based on Boccaccio's own personal experience. The idea of having the husband return from the grave to warn his wife's next suitor is apparently Boccaccio's own—or was it suggested by the name of Juvenal's consultant, Postumus? But certainly the attitude of the entire work and many passages throughout its bitter analysis are taken over from the Sixth Satire. Even in its violence, even in its occasional inconsistency and incoherence, it reminds us of Juvenal, and helps to convince us that he too, like Boccaccio, had suffered from a bad woman who made him love her and then hate her.[41]

Chaucer knew Juvenal as a man of wisdom. 'O Master Juvenal,' he makes one of his characters exclaim, 'you truly said that people scarcely know what they should pray for, without repenting what they have desired: a cloud of ignorance keeps them from seeing what is the best.' This is the theme of the Tenth Satire. He had never really read the satires. Yet, with that divination for which he is so remarkable, and with that impish wit which we love in him, he takes a quotation from the same poem:

> Juvenal seith of povert myrily,
> 'The povre man, whan he goth by the weye,
> Bifore the theves he may synge and pleye',

and then he puts it in the mouth of that bold, sexy, domineering woman, the Wife of Bath, who tore three pages out of her husband's book because it was full of misogynistic stories and examples in the vein of Satire Six.[42]

Dante himself knew little of Juvenal's poems. There are other paradoxes like this in the history of literature; still, it is strange. For Dante often wrote with Juvenal's bitterness and rancour. Like Juvenal, he was an exile. Like Juvenal, he was an Italian who loved his country and was embittered by its corruption. Like Juvenal—no, he was not, like Juvenal, a pessimist. There they differed. Juvenal had no love, and no God. But even although Dante did not know the satires, he quoted a number of the wisest aphorisms from them. He made Juvenal, after death, carry a message from his sweet-voiced contemporary Statius to his revered predecessor Vergil. And he placed Juvenal among the immortal minds of the pagan world, in Limbo, where he suffers desire without hope—which was his nature and his torture while he lived on earth.[43]

XXXI

JUVENAL IN AND AFTER THE RENAISSANCE

PRINTING was introduced into western Europe about 1440. It began tentatively, but multiplied its energies every year, both answering and stimulating a constantly increasing demand for books, learning, wisdom. The first important book to be printed was the Bible in Latin, and it was soon followed by the other books which men thought of as permanent, and which men most wished to possess: the real classics.

Juvenal's satires were first printed by Ulrich Han, probably in Rome between 1467 and 1469.[1] Thenceforward new editions of Juvenal appeared in rapid succession, year after year. A complete collection of them would cost a fortune and would be a bibliophile's delight. First came plain-text versions, and then, soon afterwards, annotated editions. The first two printed commentaries on Juvenal were published in 1474 and 1475: by Angelo Sabino and by his rival, the Apostolic Secretary Domizio Calderini.[2] The earliest book containing a printed erratalist was George Merula's commentary on the satires, issued at Venice by Gabriel Pierre in 1478—for previously all printer's errors had been corrected by the pen.* In 1486 George Valla brought out a valuable commentary containing precious extracts from a very old commentator, whose work would have been entirely lost (as Valla's manuscript of it is lost) if we did not have this printed version.[3] By the end of the fifteenth century bigger and bigger editions and commentaries were pouring off the presses of several countries, usually combining the notes of two or three predecessors into thick masses of print in which dross and diamonds are almost inextricably confused.[4] In Italy alone, something like seventy editions of Juvenal (with and without Persius) were published before 1500—more than of any other classical author except Cicero, Vergil, and Ovid.[5]

* So H. B. Wheatley, *Literary Blunders* (London, 1893), 78. On Merula's book see Sanford (*80*), 105–6.

The sad thing, however, is that although so many editions of Juvenal came out, they were all based on the inferior and corrupt text which had been created by a 'popularizing' editor over a thousand years earlier.* As we have seen, almost all the manuscripts copied in the Middle Ages were versions—sometimes with, and sometimes without, improvements borrowed from the better textual tradition—of the cheap 'vulgate' text.† Therefore when the first publishers began to print copies of the satires they had to use both a degraded text and the largely useless scholia dating from the Dark Ages. Much of the real Juvenal is still there, of course. But his best points are often blunted, often he sounds downright silly, and the early medieval explanations positively obscure his meaning.‡ In addition to this handicap, the true character of satire (which had been forgotten in the Middle Ages) was imperfectly understood for many years of the Renaissance: people thought it had something to do with satyrs, and with Greek satyric comedy. These two difficulties were only cleared up at the end of the sixteenth century.[6]

In 1605 Isaac Casaubon published an essay which really explained the name and nature of satire.§ And, more important for us, about 1573 the French scholar François Pithou got hold of *the only complete manuscript* which contains something close to what Juvenal actually wrote. (This is putting it very bluntly, but it is the fundamental truth.[7]) The manuscript had been written early in the ninth century at the Benedictine Abbey of St. Nazarius in Lorsch, not far from Mainz; and there it had stayed for seven hundred years. At the Reformation, the splendid library of the Abbey was carried off to Heidelberg by the Count Palatine; and apparently this manuscript went with it. How Pithou acquired it, no one knows; but in times of upheaval valuable books have a habit of wandering into the hands of keen collectors. Anyhow, he gave it to his brother Pierre Pithou, who in 1585 used it to publish the first decent text of Juvenal which had met the public eye for many centuries.[8]

The manuscript itself has now survived the chances and changes of eleven centuries. When Pierre died, he left it to his brother. His brother in turn left it, with the rest of his library and his house, to found a school at Troyes in northern France.

---

* See p. 187.　　　† See p. 194.　　　‡ See p. 306, n. 17.

§ I. Casaubon, *De satyrica Graecorum poesi et Romanorum satira.*

There it rested for the next 250 years or so. The French Revolution, taking over the whole library and the school, sent the manuscript to the Central School at Troyes. In 1804 Napoleon commanded that the best manuscripts available should be rounded up from all over France, apparently to strengthen the National Library in Paris. The commission which was appointed to make the selection from local libraries contained a professor from the university of Montpellier, that charming little southern spot where Rabelais once taught. Pithou's manuscript now made another of its mysterious jumps, from Troyes to Montpellier, where it entered the library of the medical school, and reposed there forgotten until an Italian scholar found and described it in 1842.[9] Since then it has been used by every intelligent editor. It is a thick leather-bound book of eighty tough yellow vellum sheets, filled with good handwriting, very nearly as legible now as when it was first written. There are a number of random scribbles on it, many annotations used in teaching, and some meaningful notes—in particular the name of its birthplace *Laureſheim* and the name of its godfather *P PITHOV*. Strange to handle it, and reflect that this single book bridges more than half the gap between ourselves and Juvenal.

But the Renaissance did not start from the introduction of printing. It was an intellectual exploration of the world; of the past; of the best. Largely it was an educational movement, in which every participant was both a teacher and a student. From its very outset Juvenal was an active element in it, keenly discussed.

He is rather a difficult author to use in education: for he is so vivid and energetic that he always interests students, and yet he describes such disgraceful acts in a tone of such convinced pessimism that he may corrupt the young—who are nearly always (he tells us) corruptible.* Even in the Middle Ages scholars had argued about his suitability for study. As more schools of the modern type were founded and as the standard of scholarship rose, the debate grew hotter. That admirable teacher Vittorino da Feltre, whose Jollity House produced many of the most distinguished men of the Italian Renaissance, and his successor Ognibene Leoniceno both thought that Juvenal

* See 14 *passim*.

could be used in the last year of school, when the boys were becoming men.[10] Aeneas Sylvius, scholar, writer, and diplomat, said in his *Education of Children* that although Juvenal's language was sometimes too daring, yet 'in certain satires he showed himself a man of such deeply religious feeling that he appears inferior to none of the teachers of our own [Christian] faith'.[11] Aeneas Sylvius wrote this in 1450, and eight years later he became Pope, under the style of Pius II: so that his opinion has some weight. His contemporary Ugolino Pisani leant over to the cautious side, saying, 'Juvenal, Persius, Martial, and others should not be publicly read and taught, but kept for private study—so that knowledge can be increased without contaminating inexperienced young men.'* A few generations later Martin Luther went much farther, saying that Juvenal's satires, together with other classical poems, ought to be absolutely banned and abolished.[12] However, the eminent humanist Guarino of Verona (who lectured at Ferrara from 1436 to 1460) specialized in Juvenal's satires, and held that without knowing them it was impossible to appreciate the full powers of the Latin tongue. Apparently he spread his enthusiasm, for we hear that in his time a man's learning was gauged by the number of lines from Juvenal he could recite from memory.[13] In the winter of 1485–6 the brilliant Politian lectured on two classical authors: Juvenal in Latin and Homer in Greek.

The Renaissance soon brought a fresh knowledge of Juvenal to countries outside Italy. Gregory of Sanok, one of the first Polish humanists, was studying and explaining him in Cracow about 1435.[14] The astronomer Georg Peurbach (teaching in Vienna about 1450) was the earliest German scholar to lecture on him; a survey of the rules and models of eloquence called *The Poetic Pearl*, compiled in 1472 by Albrecht von Eyb, contains a number of memorable epigrams from the satires; and early in the sixteenth century the Münster schoolmaster Johannes Murmellius produced an edition of three satires for the use of schools.[15]

In Spain about 1488, when Peter Martyr visited Salamanca for the first time, he volunteered to lecture on Juvenal, and selected the dangerous Second Satire. There was such a crowd to hear him that his path had to be cleared by senior members

* So R. Sabbadini, *Le scoperte dei codici latini e greci* (Florence, 1905), 201.

of the university with sticks and clubs, several people were taken out half-suffocated, and he was carried home in triumph after lecturing for well over an hour.[16] Juan Latino, the Negro slave who became an eminent Spanish scholar, was called (in an amusing adaptation of Juvenal's line on the phenomenally perfect woman)

> a rare bird on this earth, most like a black crow.*[17]

The poor but brilliant Francisco Sanchez, whom the Spaniards call El Brocense, used to apply to himself Juvenal's sad line:

> slow rises worth, by poverty depress'd.†

And in 1595, when he was over 70, he was taken into custody by the Inquisition and put under house arrest (where he died) for having remarked, during a lecture on Juvenal, that Jesus was born not in December but in September.[18] One of his own students reported him: which shows how dangerous it is to put in irrelevant bits of information when one is lecturing.

Juvenal's satires are really very hard to translate. Not many writers tried to make vernacular renderings of them during the Renaissance.[19] But original poets, challenged by his violence and ruthlessness and fascinated by his gift for epigram, imitated and adapted his work with increasing enthusiasm. The famous collection of droll character-sketches by the Alsatian scholar Sebastian Brant, *The Ship of Fools* (1494), was more like a string of epigrams than a book of satires; but he tried to build at least one poem on a Juvenalian plan, for the section 'Useless Wishes' takes over the scheme as well as the subject of the Tenth Satire.[20] The irrepressible John Skelton (c. 1460–1529) said his attack on Cardinal Wolsey, *Why Come ye not to Court?*, was inspired by his predecessor:

> Blame Juvenal, and blame not me.[21]

In France the first regular verse-satirist, Mathurin Régnier (1573–1613), boasted of following both Horace and Juvenal; and though his character was really more Horatian, his successors believed his shocking bluntness was inspired by Juvenal's

---

* Rara auis in terris, nigroque simillima corbo (~Juv. 6. 165).
† Johnson's version of Juv. 3. 164–5.

frankness.[22] Several of the early satirists of the Renaissance in Italy read Juvenal, and Alessandro Vinciguerra evoked him as a model; but on the whole their work was too solemn and elegiac to be really Juvenalian, or else, like Ariosto's, too nonchalant and happy.[23] In Spain, Bartolomé Leonardo de Argensola knew Juvenal well and sympathized with many of his convictions, particularly his distrust of women and his hatred for the busy intriguing life of courtiers.[24] The Spanish Juvenal was, in spirit at least, Francisco Quevedo (1580–1645), who suffered more bitterly than Juvenal from a suspicious monarch. In form his work was usually quite unlike Juvenal's, but there are many coincidences of theme, and occasional adaptations of famous passages from the satires. And there is a striking series of *Moral Sonnets* in which he digests, into fourteen pithy and meaningful lines each, the subjects of several of Juvenal's finest poems: strange metamorphosis, satire into sonnet.[25]

Towards the end of the sixteenth century a group of young English poets set out to rival the Roman satirists. They were the first English writers to achieve the blend of rhetorical vigour with colloquial negligence which Horace and Persius and Juvenal had cultivated. In varying degrees, they borrowed names, and themes, and developments from their Roman predecessors. The most original, who borrowed least, was John Donne; the most vigorous, careless, and nasty was John Marston; the most learned and classical, and at the same time the most versatile, was Joseph Hall.[26] (Later he became bishop of Norwich and was bitterly attacked by Milton for writing these very satires.) His knowledge of Juvenal was so thorough that he may be called the first Juvenalian poet in English literature. But the violence of this group had the effect which Juvenal himself expected: in 1599 their work was banned by the express order of the archbishop of Canterbury, who forbade the publication of any satires and epigrams thereafter.

During the Renaissance, prose satirists made little use of Juvenal. In his *Praise of Folly* Erasmus boasted that he did not 'imitate Juvenal in stirring up the secret pool of crime, and chose to describe what was laughable rather than what was disgusting'.* Still, he chose over fifty of Juvenal's finest epigrams for his collection of *Adages*. By a paradox we have seen elsewhere,

* Preface, *ad fin.*

Rabelais, though a great satirist, seems never to have read Juvenal. (He quotes him thrice, but apparently took his quotations from Erasmus' anthology and similar collections.)[27] Still, directly or indirectly, almost every educated man in the Renaissance knew something of Juvenal's work. The Spanish philosopher Juan Huarte de San Juan twice cited a famous line of Juvenal in discussing the psychology of passionate excitement; the Spanish mystic Pedro Malón de Chaide introduced a poetic paraphrase of Juvenal's couplet on remorse into his *Book of the Conversion of the Magdalen*.[28] John Calvin wrote only one poem in his whole life, a triumphal ode in praise of Christ, for New Year's Day 1541; and in it, remembering how Juvenal spoke of his own inexperience, he cried:

> What nature may refuse, my burning zeal will do.*

These are only a few chosen out of many echoes of the satires.

In the same way, it would be a pleasant but almost endless task to trace adaptations of Juvenal in drama.[29] The Renaissance playwrights liked three things in particular about his work: the wisdom of his 'commonplaces', his vivid character-sketches, and the sardonic pessimism with which he (like their own melancholiacs) surveyed a world out of joint. When satire was banned in England, the satiric spirit was simply diverted into other channels, one of which was drama.[30] Ben Jonson, who knew Juvenal well and loved him, never wrote a formal satire; yet in his sour comedies there is a good deal of Juvenalian spirit. The gloomy critic who often appears in them to pierce illusions and shams is a blend of Jonson and Juvenal, so much so that it is impossible to tell whose voice we hear in a speech like this:

> . . . one that dares
> Do deeds worthy the hurdle and the wheel
> To be thought somebody; and is in sooth
> Such as the satirist points truly forth
> That only to his crimes owes all his worth.

Jonson's tragedy *Sejanus* begins with courtiers quoting Juvenal's epigrams and reaches one of its climaxes in a transcription of the fall of the favourite from Juvenal's Tenth; and one of his strangest comedies, *Cynthia's Revels*, is largely based on the theme

---

* *Epinicion Christo cantatum, Works*, 5 (Brunswick, 1866), 423–7 *ad fin.* ~ Juv. 1. 79.

of Satire Eight, that true nobility is virtue.[31] Both Molière and Corneille later adapted passages from that same poem, each in a scene where a father discovers the degeneracy of his son.[32] Finally, the most famous playwright of all, in his most famous play, introduced a hero almost maddened by disillusionment, walking back and forward, back and forward (like Juvenal in the unfriendly streets of Rome) and made him read a book.

'What do you read, my lord?'
'Words, words, words.'
'What is the matter, my lord?'
'Between who?'
'I mean the matter that you read, my lord.'
'Slanders, sir: for the satirical rogue says here that old men have grey beards, that their faces are wrinkled, their eyes purging thick amber and plum-tree gum, and that they have a plentiful lack of wit, together with most weak hams; all which, sir, though I most powerfully and potently believe, yet I hold it not honesty to have it thus set down.'

Like other melancholy men, Prince Hamlet was reading Juvenal: the Tenth Satire, which tells of the weakness, folly, and ugliness of old age.[33]

The men of the Renaissance liked Juvenal well. But the times were not quite right for him. He could scarcely feel at ease in that bold and stirring epoch, when many a career was open to the talents and for some years at least hope rewarded those who trusted her. He spoke of an age of absolute monarchy, vast wealth unevenly divided, fat cities swelling like tumours, pomp, circumstance, and sham, rich perfumes mingling with the smell of decay. Something much more like that age was born in the seventeenth century and lasted until revolutions destroyed it. Something like Juvenal's Rome then appeared, in Venice and Paris and Madrid and London; men and women very like his courtiers and courtesans swaggered through Versailles and Blenheim and scores of petty palaces; men like Juvenal himself were flogged by the duke's footmen, or, after waiting in the earl's vestibule, were repulsed from his door.[34] Much of what Juvenal says is permanently true and has been admired through many changing centuries. But when his poems are read in an age like that which produced them they acquire a double energy, an intenser truth. So throughout the seventeenth and eighteenth centuries he was one of the most important, most widely read, most influential, best understood classical poets.[35]

He was really much better understood after Scaliger called him the best of the satirists (1561), after Pithou printed a proper text in 1585, after Casaubon's essay explained satire (1605), and after a succession of clear, efficient editions came out at intervals in the seventeenth century.[36]

Good translations of Juvenal now began to appear. The first complete version in a modern tongue (apart from Summaripa's early Italian one) was André Du Chesne's French rendering of 1607. It was followed by many more.[37] In English the first was a vigorous but occasionally clumsy rendering by Sir Robert Stapylton (1–6, 1644; complete, 1647). When it appeared, another translation had long been in the making. This was the work of Barten Holyday, archdeacon of Oxford—a proud and disappointed man like Juvenal himself. His version of the satires, heavily annotated, was not issued until 1673, after his death; but he used to say that Sir Robert had borrowed it in manuscript and had taken hints from it. If so, the hints were in the field of interpretation, since a comparison of the two shows that Holyday's rendering is far less imaginative and poetic.[38] However, both were soon supplanted by what is still the best verse translation of Juvenal in English, produced by John Dryden with a group of relatives and friends in 1693, and often republished.[39] An elaborate Spanish paraphrase in prose came out in 1642, a spirited Dutch prose rendering in 1682, followed in 1709 by a brisk verse translation from various hands, and an admirable Italian verse rendering by Count Camillo Silvestri in 1711.[40]

Still, after Juvenal's meaning had been explained, his atmosphere established, and his satires translated, one big difficulty remained. This will scarcely affect us today, when our novels are full of words and phrases which were unprintable twenty years ago, but it worried the men of the baroque age. It is that Juvenal is quite often guilty of Bad Taste. He never uses the most obscene words. But he describes carnal acts in terms of the most drastic vividness. For example, to tell us that the hateful emperor committed incest with his niece Julia and then forced her to procure abortion, he says she 'poured out lumps that looked like her uncle'.* There is really no one like him for creating a phrase that can turn your stomach in three words. And apart from that, he knew it was his duty as a satirist to be realistic, to mention common things and use working-class words and describe real life as perceived by all the senses: so his poems are full of terms which were eschewed by the loftier poets of his own time and considered Low by the baroque critics: swine-pox, spittle, sewers, boils, sow-belly.† His characters belch, vomit, scratch, smear their faces, and burst their livers.‡ This was repellent to most critics and poets in an age when Dr. Johnson reproved Shakespeare for making Lady Macbeth call her dagger a 'knife'—'an instrument used by butchers and cooks in the meanest employments'.[41] Also, most of those who read the classics with attention were educators, or guardians of public morality, or public men who believed in monarchy and the aristocratic structure of society. The Jesuit teacher, the Italian bishop, the English statesman were not likely to give unrestricted approval to an author who deals with subjects which may attract and horrify and distort young minds, who incites to violence of expression, and who voices, in memorable terms, the hatred of the ordinary man for the rich and the powerful. As Byron put it,

> I can't help thinking Juvenal was wrong,
>   Although no doubt his real intent was good,
> For speaking out so plainly in his song,
>   So much indeed as to be downright rude.§

Or as Boileau said, just after talking of Juvenal and Régnier,

> Le latin dans les mots brave l'honnêteté,
> Mais le lecteur français veut être respecté.‖

Therefore the men of the baroque age had a double attitude towards Juvenal's work. They often deplored its brutal realism;

---

* . . . cum tot abortiuis fecundam Iulia uoluam
    solueret, et patruo similes effunderet offas (2. 32–33).
† Porrigine (2. 80); longa saliua (6. 623); torrente cloaca (5. 105); uomicae putres (13. 95); uolua (11. 81).
‡ Ructauit (3. 107); bibit et uomit (6. 432); digito scalpunt uno caput (with a sinister double meaning, 9. 133); faciem linit (6. 481); rumpe miser tensum iecur (7. 117).
§ *Don Juan*, 1. 43.   ‖ *Art Poétique*, 2. 175–6.

they rarely ventured to emulate its full frankness, and toned it down even in translation; they claimed to prefer the politer, suaver Horace; but in practice they found Juvenal hard to forget and impossible to ignore.[42] His influence on satire in the seventeenth and eighteenth centuries is at least as strong as Horace's. All in all, the majestic Tenth Satire was the favourite. Next came the megalopolitan First and Third; the enormous but ill-planned Sixth was often cited, though not fully accepted; the grave Seventh, Eighth, Thirteenth, and Fourteenth were also popular; phrases were quoted from all the others.

Juvenal's most distinguished followers in the baroque age make a splendid list. Nicolas Boileau (1636–1711) began his career by publishing a set of satires closely modelled on Juvenal's matter and manner: it was only in later life that he partially mellowed down into a Horatian literary critic and letter-writer.[43] (It is worth noting that English writers got nearly as much Juvenal indirectly through Boileau as they drew directly from the satires.) John Dryden (1631–1700) at first bowed to convention by admiring Horace,* although he himself was temperamentally and artistically far closer to Juvenal: his famous character-sketch of the Duke of Buckingham surely owes much to Juvenal's picture of the versatile Greek immigrant:

> A man so various, that he seemed to be
> Not one, but all mankind's epitome:
> Stiff in opinions, always in the wrong;
> Was everything by starts, and nothing long;
> But, in the course of one revolving moon,
> Was chymist, fiddler, statesman, and buffoon. . . .†

But after he began to translate the satires, he realized Juvenal's mastery and declared that he preferred the 'vigorous and masculine wit' of Juvenal to the 'insipid salt' of Horace: 'Horace is always on the amble,' he said horsily, 'Juvenal on the gallop.'[44] Oldham, hater of the Jesuits (1653–83), was the most Juvenalian of English baroque poets, but his misfortunes overwhelmed him early.[45] Two books of *The Love of Fame* by Edward Young (1683–1765) are modelled on the Sixth Satire, although they are far lighter and less memorable.[46] Mr. Pope (1688–1744) was

---

* Dryden, Preface to *Sylvæ*.
† *Absalom and Achitophel*, 1. 545–50～Juv. 3. 74–78.

described by a daring friend, in a parody of a Juvenalian phrase, as 'a crooked mind in a crooked body'. He himself occasionally mentions and adapts Juvenal, but he is much more indebted to Horace and to his own spleen for his satiric ideas.[47] Samuel Johnson not only wrote dignified modernizations of Juvenal's Third and Tenth but knew all the satires well, cited them often, and felt them deeply. Once, when reading the passage about the poverty and mistreatment of scholars, he burst into tears; and for all their differences, I imagine that the great ungainly old Tory, so cruel and rude and yet so softhearted, so combative towards the strong and so gentle to the weak, so deeply devoted to literature and such a keen observer of life, so widely wandered, from slums to palaces, who suffered so grimly in youth and could never forget it in his later comfort and dignity, must have been very like Juvenal himself.[48]

In other countries too Juvenal's epigrams were heard and his sardonic smile was seen. The first regular verse satirist in German, Joachim Rachel (1618–69), built two complete satires on Juvenal's poems and adapted passages from Juvenal's work elsewhere.[49] In Italy the astonishing artist-adventurer Salvator Rosa (1615–73) echoed Juvenal in his satire on Poetry; and the brilliant Venetian nobleman Sergardi (1660–1726) published a series of *Latin* satires against an enemy, which were wholly within the tradition of Horace and Juvenal. (He even signed himself Quintus Sectanus, Quintus, the Fifth after Lucilius, Horace, Persius, and Juvenal.)[50]

But besides satiric poets, other eminent men admired Juvenal —and a vast cloud of triflers. Consider two thoughtful priests. Abraham a Sancta Clara (1644–1709), preacher to the Imperial Court in Vienna, was a gay and unpredictable talker and writer, a true satirist, 'telling the truth in a joke'. He cites Juvenal again and again.[51] Baltasar Gracián (1601–58), a Jesuit who saw deeply into the human heart, quoted a trenchant phrase of Juvenal to strengthen his own acute observation.[52] Consider two essayists. Addison (1672–1719), although far from sharing Juvenal's bitterness, knew the poems well and often used them as points of departure for his essays. Diderot (1713–84), always brilliantly original, modelled *Le Neveu de Rameau* partly on the hideous Ninth Satire, though he cleaned up the subject, changing it from physical perversion to intellectual vagabondage.[53] John Locke began *Some Thoughts concerning Education* with Juvenal's famous epigram—'A Sound Mind in a sound Body, is a short, but full Description of a happy State in this world'*—and proceeded to treat that ideal as the aim of every proper education. Later, warning parents against ruining their children by setting them bad examples, he cited Juvenal again.[54] Almost every wit of the age of periwigs and politeness knew Juvenal and used him: Butler, Churchill, Marvell, Prior, Rochester, Wycherley. . . .[55] The brilliant eunuch, Metastasio, translated the Third Satire at Vienna in 1739. Swift prided himself on not copying other writers: yet he knew and occasionally used Juvenal, and for his tomb he devised an epitaph saying that the chief torment of Juvenal had been his also, for now he lay

> where cruel indignation could not longer tear his heart.[56]

Gibbon read the satires carefully in his twenties, writing methodical comments on them, which still read well and are full of sound critical sense.[57] Virtue and vice both knew Juvenal. Clarissa Harlowe quoted him with approval.[58] And once, when Casanova asked his host for a lock on his door and was met with a disdainful protest, he reflected, 'I could have answered, with Juvenal,

> the traveller with empty pockets will sing as he passes the thief,†

but I should have embarrassed him.' Juvenal was now being quoted by one of his own characters.[59]

---

* Mens sana in corpore sano (10. 356).
† Cantabit uacuus coram latrone uiator (10. 22).

XXXII

JUVENAL IN MODERN TIMES

By the middle of the eighteenth century, the aristocracies of Europe and America were becoming quite as proud, quite as degenerate, and quite as irresponsible as those whom Juvenal had hated and despised in Rome. An age of revolution such as he never foresaw was approaching.

Its herald, Jean-Jacques Rousseau, 'used to read Juvenal because he attacked corruption'—doubtless the satires on social snobbery and on the life of the court. Upon the title-page of his *Letters from the Mountain* he placed Juvenal's 'Stake your life on the truth'.* The same phrase became the motto of Marat's revolutionary paper, *The Friend of the People*, and appeared on the front page of every issue. Not only that. In a number published during the worst days of 1791, Marat denounced the French people themselves, crying: 'We are not made for liberty!' and comparing the light ladies, the helpless littérateurs, the proud ex-nobles, and the universal money-grubbers of Paris to the Romans described in Juvenal's Sixth, Seventh, Eighth, and Thirteenth Satires. And then, with even more energy, he went on to liken the newly formed National Guard to the spoilt, pompous, brutal praetorian guards mocked by Juvenal in his Sixteenth Satire; and he translated several passages from the poem to prove his point.[1] This was published at a crisis, just after the escape and recapture of Louis XVI and just before the adoption of the short-lived Constitution. The old hater of monarchs had his wish at last.

In England too the revolutionaries of the mind were devoted to Juvenal. The rebellious Wordsworth, soon after his visit to republican France, planned to produce a modern version of the Eighth Satire (on true and false nobility) with the Duke of York and the Prince of Wales as the horrible examples. He knew the original poem well; he had Holyday's and Dryden's versions; and he actually wrote nearly 200 lines of his adaptation.[2]

* M. Reichenberg, *Essai sur les lectures de J.-J. Rousseau* (Philadelphia, 1939), quoting 'Vitam impendere uero' from Juv. 4. 91.

Nor would he have been alone: many social critics before and after 1795 composed similar modernizations of Juvenal, though none, perhaps, so outspoken.[3] But he was wise to abandon the idea. To write satire one needs more than indignation. One needs style: that, for such purposes, Wordsworth could probably have acquired. But one also needs close and cool observation of society—and that Wordsworth scarcely even wished to possess. He could observe the fields, but not the Haymarket; he could contemplate the lonely Lakes, but not Brooks's Club.

His friend Coleridge was chiefly impressed by Juvenal as a thinker: in particular, he admired the epigram:

> From heaven descended the commandment *Know Thyself.**

He said once that this was a fit description of the relation between the heaven-inspired Wordsworth and himself; he based part of a philosophical discourse on it; and in the last three years of his life he wrote one of his final poems on the same theme, saying that man could not know himself ('vain sister of the worm') and ought rather to try to know God.[4]

Revolutionaries of the mind were much encouraged in England by William Gifford's able translation of Juvenal, which appeared in 1802 and stimulated many imitators. The first American version, John Duer's rendering of the Third Satire (New York, 1806), is largely modelled on Gifford.[5]

The most Juvenalian of the revolutionaries was Lord Byron. He began his career as a literary rebel in 1809, with *English Bards and Scotch Reviewers*, a counter-attack on the Edinburgh critics who had tried to snub him. It opens:

> Still must I hear? Must hoarse Fitzgerald bawl
> His creaking couplets in a tavern hall,
> And I not speak?

—which is a close copy of the first lines of Juvenal's First Satire. The poem contains other such loans. It is still lively. Dead minds make dead copies; but lively writers make living works of art from what they read, works which—like children—are both new individuals and the transmitters of their parents' nature. Byron hated the classics as far as they were dead idols; but he admired Juvenal and others because they were permanently alive.

* E caelo descendit γνῶθι σεαυτόν (11. 27).

In his letters he quoted Juvenal; in his tragedy *Sardanapalus* he modelled a big scene on the Second Satire; and just before leaving England for ever, he made a generous gesture, half-Byronic, half-Juvenalian, towards one of the few contemporary writers he admired. He sent Sir Walter Scott a large urn full of bones taken from old Athenian tombs; and on it he caused to be engraved the famous passage:

> Weigh out Hannibal: how many pounds in the mighty marshal?
> Death alone can show what trifles are men's bodies.*[6]

One critic has suggested that Byron's interest in Juvenal began at school. For, in 1806, Hatchards published an anonymous modernization of the First Satire, called *A Farrago Libelli*. Obviously by someone of considerable energy and talent, it has been supposed an early rendering by the young Byron, who was just leaving school in 1805. But the weight of fact and opinion is against the attribution.[7] Apparently it was at Cambridge that Byron first read Juvenal. In 1809 his friend Hobhouse issued an agreeable adaptation of the genial Satire Eleven, and introduced Byron himself into it.[8]

In other countries too Juvenal was being read. Byron's Russian incarnation, Eugene Onegin, concentrated even more on belles and even less on books than Byron, but, although his knowledge of the Latin language was slight,

> Of Juvenal he could make mention,
> Decipher epigraphs at sight.†

In Germany, the brilliant and charming Lessing knew Juvenal well. He brought many of the ladies from the Sixth Satire into his comedy, *The Misogynist*; he cited occasional epigrams in his critical pieces; and he struck out a new line by discussing Juvenal as an authority for certain aspects of Greco-Roman art.[9] Lessing's friend Herder not only thought highly of Juvenal's moral standards but put him above Horace as an artist.[10] Schiller too emphasized the fact that Juvenal's passion flows from and expresses the agony of a true idealist who sees

---

* Expende Hannibalem: quot libras in duce summo
   inuenies? . . . mors sola fatetur
   quantula sint hominum corpuscula (10. 147–8, 172–3).

† Pushkin, *Eugene Onegin*, 1. 6, tr. Babette Deutsch (*Works*, ed. A. Yarmolinsky, New York, 1936, p. 114).

hypocrisy and corruption all around him. Goethe read the First Satire at Carlsbad in 1808;[11] he copied a pessimistic epigram about sexual continence in his commonplace-book; and elsewhere he cited a little-known passage from the Eighth Satire to show how the Romans plundered their subject provinces.[12]

None of these men, however, saw Juvenal primarily as a revolutionary. And indeed revolution is apt to end in tyranny. In Europe those who attempted to forestall revolution and those who overthrew the French tyrant often quoted Juvenal. Thus, in 1775 Edmund Burke was addressing the House of Commons on the proposal to strengthen English control over the American colonists by blockading them and cutting off their supplies. He warned Parliament that this, so far from removing their grievances, would increase them; and he ended—not by predicting armed rebellion in so many words, but by citing Juvenal's warning to a Roman governor against tyrannizing over the provincials:

Beggared, they still have weapons.*

In the same House, a generation later, Canning rose to discourage the belief that Napoleon could not be conquered, and that Napoleon's fortune was like a woman, subservient to his will. Fortune, said Canning, was no more than Chance: and he reminded members that

it is we,
we, Fortune, who make you a god and place you in heaven.†[13]

As scholarship improved and extended during the nineteenth century, far more intense work was done on Juvenal than at any time since the Renaissance. In 1801 Ruperti produced a detailed commentary in Latin which is still useful; in 1810 Achaintre issued what the French call a 'well-nourished' edition; others followed every five years or so. Of course, the curiosity of the century was Otto Ribbeck's announcement that about one-third of the Satires were forgeries, and his issue of an edition which threw large passages out and excised entire

---

* Burke, *On Conciliation with the Colonies*, 22 Mar. 1775, quoting Juv. 8. 124: 'Spoliatis arma supersunt'.

†   Nos te,
   nos facimus, Fortuna, deam caeloque locamus (10. 365–6).

poems because they did not fit his ideas of what 'the real Juvenal' should have written.[14] It was the fashion in those days to dissect books of the Bible, to rewrite Homer, and to re-arrange the classics generally on 'internal' evidence which was usually based much more on pseudo-scientific logic than on poetic imagination, so that Juvenal could scarcely escape. Ribbeck's theory was never accepted; but it elicited many rejoinders, whose net result was to make scholars examine Juvenal's style much more closely and demonstrate its homogeneity through 'true' and 'false' satires alike.[15]

But the first step in establishing a classical author's text is to find out what his manuscripts say and how they reached us. This had been partly forgotten, and the essential Pithou manuscript ('P') was lost. However, it was rediscovered during the forties at Montpellier, and used in 1851 by Otto Jahn as the basis of the first good modern text of Juvenal's satires. Ever since then, critics have been working on the chief textual problem of the satires—which is to cut away the interpolations made in anti-quity, to point out gaps where lines or whole passages have dropped away, and to survey the innumerable variants where one set of manuscripts presents one word or phrase, and another set produces another, both intelligible, but probably not both by Juvenal.[16]

For about fifty years after Jahn's edition, editors tended to accept the readings of the P manuscript almost without ques-tion.[17] But in 1905 A. E. Housman brought out a text which he called (with typical arrogance) an 'edition for the use of editors'. In this he explained forcefully that P was not the sole transmitter of the truth, that other manuscripts were often right when P was wrong, that no manuscript was either perfectly good or per-fectly bad, and that the text of the satires might well be hope-lessly corrupt or mutilated in some quite unsuspected area. This contention gained great support from an accidental discovery which had been made in 1899. A young Oxford man, examining an eleventh-century manuscript of Juvenal in the Bodleian Library, found that it contained one couplet and a passage of thirty-four continuous lines in the Sixth Satire which existed in no other known text, which were not quoted by any ancient authority (except for two lines which appear in the good scholia), which seemed from their energy and vividness to be by Juvenal, but whose absence had never been and could never have been suspected.[18] Scholars divided at once. Some said the new passages were forgeries. Others thought them genuine. The debate continues today. Genuine or not, these pieces are vitally important: for, if they are interpolated, we must ask where they came from, and expect similar interpolations elsewhere; and if they are genuine, we must ask why and when and how they fell out of about 500 manuscripts, and how they survived in only one fairly ordinary copy made as late as the eleventh century. Several fine papers have been written on this problem.[19] The latest big advance in the study of Juvenal's text has been made by Ulrich Knoche, a scholar whose acumen is exceeded only by his industry. In 1940 he published a detailed analysis of the textual tradition of Juvenal (45), for which he had examined nearly every important manuscript of the satires; and in 1950 he produced a text (58) based on that survey, with the fullest critical apparatus Juvenal has ever had. These are essential books.

There have also been valuable editions explaining the meaning of the satires, analysing their structure, clearing up difficult allusions, and creating something like the frame of reference Juvenal expected his readers to possess. In 1853 J. E. B. Mayor of Cambridge issued a very learned one (60), filled with illustrative passages from his enormous reading though not very useful in analysing interpretative problems. In 1895 Ludwig Friedländer of Königsberg, who had written an exhaustive survey of Roman life and manners partly based on Juvenal, published a large and helpful edition (55) which has not yet been superseded. In English the handiest are 'the unpretending school edition of Mr. J. D. Duff' (54),* produced in 1898 and often reprinted, and a good complement to it by H. L. Wilson of Johns Hopkins (64).

Books about Juvenal have been numerous in the last 150 years; but they have nearly all suffered from one of three defects. Either they have closely concentrated on a very few aspects of the satires; or they have been so brief and general as to raise more problems than they answered; or they have been trying to prove one very special theory. In English there is nothing but a little volume in a series of 'Ancient Classics for English

* So Housman (56), Introd. xxix.

Readers', published in 1872 by Edward Walford of Balliol; in German there are many editions, essays, and theses, but no single comprehensive study; in French there is Auguste Widal's *Juvénal et ses Satires* (Paris, 1870²), which is enthusiastic but not very scholarly, and Pierre de Labriolle's charming but too brief study (4); in Italian there are a number of brief general introductions and a set of *Studies in Juvenal* by Pietro Ercole (3), carelessly edited after his death in 1935; and there is little else except special papers.

Throughout the nineteenth century educated men continued to study Juvenal, to quote him, sometimes to imitate him. Tennyson read the satires to his wife during the evenings in 1857–8, when he was approaching 50: his copy (Nichols's edition of 1753), copiously annotated, is in Yale Library.* Emerson too read them, using Gifford's translation and a hack literal version by Lewis Evans, in 1864.† Thackeray, though he hated the classics, made a joke out of the Messalina passage, when he described Lady O'Dowd dancing down several partners at Government House, and finally retiring to the supper-room, 'tired but not yet satisfied'.‡ Browning too made something quaint, inventive, and humorous out of his knowledge of Juvenal. Speaking of the Sixth Satire, he produced a gay little Latin couplet of his own, and even found a rhyme for the satirist's name:

—the Fair Sex. . . .
What's their frailty beside our own falsehood?
Of their charms—how are most frank, how few venal!
While as for those charges of Juvenal—
Quae nemo dixisset in toto
Nisi (aedepol) ore illoto—
He dismissed every charge with an *Apage!*[20]

Speaking to the Congress of the United States in 1872, Charles Sumner delivered one of the longest and most effective rebukes ever administered in public to an American President. Among other things, he reproached Grant for his propensity to engage

* C. Tennyson, *Alfred Tennyson* (New York, 1949), 307; G. L. Hendrickson, 'The Marston Juvenals', *Yale Univ. Library Gazette*, 12 (1938), 86.
† K. W. Cameron, *R. W. Emerson's Reading* (Raleigh, N. Carolina, 1941), 35.
‡ *Vanity Fair*, c. 43 init.∼Juv. 6. 130.

in private disputes. He said that the Eleventh Commandment was 'A President of the United States shall never quarrel', and then went on to recall how Grant had attacked Sumner himself, like the bully in Juvenal's Third Satire:

> Poor me he fights, if that be fighting, where
> He only cudgels, and I only bear. . . .
> Answer, or answer not, 'tis all the same:
> He lays me on, and makes me bear the blame.*

Several more recent Presidents have forgotten this rule, without meeting such a pointed exposure of their errors.

In 1853, while working on *Madame Bovary*, Flaubert developed what he called a 'craze' for Juvenal, and—from him the highest of compliments—admired the *style* of the satires above all else.[21] A generation or so later, the Parnassian poet José-Maria de Heredia took the theme of one of his immortal sonnets and the final effect of another from the Tenth Satire.[22] One of the gloomiest reflections of the melancholy Swiss philosopher Amiel was illustrated with an epigram from the satires. 'Civilization', he wrote, 'tends to rot men away, just as great cities corrupt the air.

> We are suffering the disease of long peace.'†

That very passage, some years before, had been made the subject of a celebrated painting by Thomas Couture. Called *The Romans of the Decadence*, it showed a rich and drunken banquet, with expensively dressed and undressed men and women lolling about helplessly and crazily in a luxurious dining-room. By an apt invention Couture expressed the true depth of their degradation. Around the hall stand the statues of the great Romans of the past, gazing gravely down on their degenerate children. A drunken joker has climbed one of the pedestals, and with a laugh (like Don Juan inviting the Commander) offers a

---

*   Miserae cognosce prooemia rixae—
si rixa est ubi tu pulsas, ego uapulo tantum. . . .
dicere si temptes aliquid tacitusue recedas,
tantundem est: feriunt pariter, uadimonia deinde
irati faciunt.

The lines are Juv. 3. 288–9, 297–9, in Dryden's translation; Sumner added another version of 3. 290. For the speech see *The Congressional Globe*, 31 May 1872, p. 4120.

† Nunc patimur longae pacis mala (6. 292); Amiel, *Journal*, 20 Mar. 1880.

cup of wine to the cold lips of a statue. With motionless gravity
the statue seems to frown and reject it. The epigraph of the
picture is:

> We are suffering the disease of long peace: crueller than war,
> luxury invades us now to avenge the conquered world.*[23]

The most recent incarnation of Juvenal was the heir of the
Revolution, Victor Hugo (1802–85). He himself felt that he was
part Vergil and part Juvenal.[24] For, although he admired
Vergil's pastoral charm, his epic grandeur, and his subtle style,
he despised him for tolerating and even supporting a monarch.
And though he saw that Juvenal was rarely lyrical and only
negatively heroic, he prized the poet who could live in imperial
Rome and yet speak out against corrupt nobles and absolute
rulers. He himself wished to rival not one or two poets but all
geniuses. He was insatiable of greatness. So he became a bold
lyricist; a sombre elegist; a violent dramatist; a panoramic
novelist. But in his emulation of Juvenal he became something
else, something stranger. He became a lyric satirist, adding to
his seven strings a string of bronze.[25]

And Juvenal was always one of his main admirations. At
school, when he was 14, he translated part of the Eighth Satire,
on nobility; later in life, he knew some of the satires by heart;
most of all he loved the majestic Tenth.[26] Nowadays some of us
find it hard to understand how any modern poet can identify
himself with an earlier writer, Greek or Roman or medieval
or Renaissance, endeavour to rival him, work along his lines,
learn constantly from him as Dante learnt from Vergil. Yet
that is how much of the greatest poetry is written. Everyone
needs a teacher; it is best to have a great teacher. The Roman
poets thought of themselves as reincarnating their Greek predecessors: Horace was the Roman Alcaeus, Ennius and Vergil
strove to be Homer. So, too, many modern writers have consciously or unconsciously determined to follow a great precursor:
Milton following Vergil and many more, Shakespeare following
Seneca and a myriad others, Shelley emulating Aeschylus and
the other noble Greeks. That is how Hugo and his contemporaries Tennyson and Arnold and Carducci worked. So when

* Nunc patimur longae pacis mala: saeuior armis
  luxuria incubuit uictumque ulciscitur orbem (6. 292–3).

a young classical professor, Désiré Nisard, produced a book called *The Roman Poets of the Decadence* (27), which coldly and bitterly criticized the work of the post-classical poets like Lucan, Seneca, and Juvenal, the young 'romantics' at once saw it as an attack on their own principles and prototypes. Nisard's book, which came out in 1834 when Hugo, after passing one of the heights of his success, was just tasting failure again, represents one strong wave in the anti-romantic current which moved through the whole nineteenth century. Hugo detested it. It explains many of his savage attacks on short-sighted pedants, and probably also some of the uncritical enthusiasm with which he defends Juvenal.

Hugo admired him first of all as a political rebel like himself, exiled to a lonely desert by a powerful and suspicious emperor. His tremendous tirades against Napoleon III, *Les Châtiments*, were partly inspired by Juvenal's work; and at their opening he called on the Muse Indignation, Juvenal's patroness, to give him strength.[27] One entire poem in that series is addressed to Juvenal as to a guide and friend, 'the old free soul of dead republics'.[28] And there is one poem which is either very silly or very charming, or perhaps both, in which Hugo tells how his little grandson Charles was punished for misusing his Latin book by drawing doodles in it—patterns and trees and animals, including

a donkey, which resembled Monsieur Nisard, braying.

As the boy sat dolefully copying out 1,000 lines, Juvenal himself (whose text it was) appeared, looked over the disfigured book with a sympathetic smile, and said that he himself had once been punished by a powerful master for making caricatures.[29]

Then Hugo respected Juvenal as a thinker: a man who walked alone, brooding on great issues, life, death, happiness, failure, youth, and age. So Hugo's meditations on the dust of Napoleon are partly inspired by Juvenal's 'commonplaces' on the transitoriness of glory. The same ideas recur in the monologue of Don Carlos in the tomb of Charlemagne:

> Grasp at the empire, then, and contemplate the dust
> left by an emperor!*

---

* *Les Chants du Crépuscule*, II, v, 'A la Colonne'; *Hernani*, 4. 2 (in which 'Quelques lettres à faire épeler des enfants' comes from Juv. 10. 167).

When Paris was besieged, Hugo sent out (by balloon) a letter comparing the women of Paris, gallant in their trials, to the women of Rome with Hannibal at the gates, and quoting the Sixth Satire.* After one of his sons died, he wrote a powerful paraphrase of the passage on old age bereaved:

> This is the penalty of those who live too long. . . .†

Juvenal's skill as a stylist naturally appealed to Hugo. Phrases from the satires keep recurring in his work, now embedded in a poem, now as a chapter-heading.[30] One of Juvenal's most powerful effects, the heaping up of outrageous facts into a big indictment, one after another, 'when . . . when . . . when . . .', forming a continuous tirade, is rehandled by Hugo in the famous poem on the political corruption of contemporary Europe.‡

But most of all Hugo saw Juvenal as a great man. Greatness, he repeats again and again, is a quality of the soul. It can appear in prophets like Isaiah, in sculptors like Michelangelo, in dramatists like Shakespeare and Aeschylus; it flourishes on difficulty; it naturally draws abuse and misunderstanding; but it is unmistakable and inalienable. Hugo's longest meditation on greatness is *William Shakespeare*. There he places Juvenal among a group of the eternal souls whom he calls 'ocean men'; ranges him with the world's mighty exiles, with Dante, Thucydides, d'Aubigné, and St. John; and defends him ardently against the calumnies which are the involuntary tribute of littleness to nobility. 'Few poets have ever been more insulted', he writes. 'The calumnies against Juvenal have been so durable that they still continue today. They are handed down from one hack writer to another. These great haters of evil are hated by all those who like to flatter power and success . . . a crowd croaking around the eagles.'[31] Hugo regarded Juvenal as a friend (like himself, rough and combative but with a soft spot for children; like himself, a lonely exile). He knew him as a fellow artist in style and thought. But most of all he saw him as a model of that greatness which, to such eager and passionate souls, comes in its fullness only after their death.

---

* *L'Année Terrible*, 'Janvier 1871', ii, 'Lettre à une Femme'~Juv. 6. 287 f.

† *Toute la Lyre*, v, xl, headed 'omnia vidit / eversa'~Juv. 10. 258–70; also adapted in *Les Burgraves*, 2. 4.

‡ *Feuilles d'Automne*, xl, the last poem~Juv. 1. 22–68.

Let us look back over the centuries since Juvenal died. His after-life as an immortal author has been even stranger than his physical life as a mortal Roman. Fame, fame and admiration far greater than he ever hoped for, careful study by many generations of scholars, multiplication of his satires into hundreds of thousands of copies, translation by amateurs and professionals, hacks and geniuses, imitation and emulation by writers in many languages—all these have been his. His thoughts have helped to mould the characters of great men. His epigrams, with their concentrated meatiness, have nourished many an active mind, and with their cool bitterness have sobered several intoxicated idealists. 'There is', says Solomon, 'there is that speaketh like the piercings of a sword: but the tongue of the wise is health.'* Juvenal's sayings have both these powers. Some of them have long since left his book, and are now part of the general wisdom of the world.

His main influence has been on thinkers. Although he was not a trained philosopher or even a deep reasoner, he saw things so clearly and said things so forcibly that, once read, his utterances can scarcely be forgotten. In particular, no one has ever stated with more crushing conviction and more trenchant example two important truths which mankind constantly forgets and constantly must relearn: the fact that wealth without responsibility brings softness and decay, and the fact that uncontrolled power brings cruelty and madness. Moralists and political philosophers, essayists and historians, preachers and teachers, have been quoting his poetry ever since the fourth century after Christ.

Next, he has powerfully moulded much of the formal verse satire of subsequent ages. There are, of course, many other types of satire—prose, which his work affects but little; the milder, more versatile and conversational, Horatian verse satire; the Menippean, blending verse and prose; and others. But in the vein which Lucilius first struck and which Juvenal first worked deeply and refined through white heat, the vein of indignant protest, he has been the master workman and all others his followers: Claudian, Bernard of Morval, Jean de Meun, Régnier, Quevedo, Hall, Dryden, Boileau, many more. One remarkable thing, however, is that Juvenal is *not* well known to a number of

* Prov. xii. 18.

men whose character and outlook would seem to make them sympathetic to his work: Dante, Rabelais, Swift. . . . Apparently they felt his power to be too strong, liable to make them imitators rather than originals. But by now, no doubt, they have all met him, and heard him speak his poems.

Third, we should remember that he was a skilful technician. Therefore he has always appealed to certain poets, even if they were not satirists. Many a miniaturist has made one of Juvenal's phrases into the point of an apparently original epigram—thus reversing the process by which Juvenal expanded Martial's epigrams into passages of satire. Dramatists have used some of his boldest scenes and strongest soliloquies. Poets of many other types have borrowed his pungent phrasing and his vivid pictures. The last to do so on a big scale was Victor Hugo.

Since Hugo's time, satiric poetry in the sustained, quasi-formal manner has seldom been written—one can point to only a few poets like Ventura Ruiz Aguilera and Roy Campbell[32]— so that Juvenal has not recently exerted so much influence on literature as he has done at other times, for instance in the twelfth or the seventeenth century. But his name is not forgotten. It appears again and again in the strangest company. The French politician Léon Blum, during a debate in the Chamber of Deputies, once staked the fate of his Cabinet on his ability to identify a line of Juvenal quoted by one of his opponents. (He lost.)[33] And recently one of his central problems has been raised again by a Russian historian. This is R. Wipper, who has been attempting to revise the judgement of history on Tsar Ivan the Terrible, a subject fully worthy of Juvenal's boldest satire. He rebukes the nineteenth-century historians for their short-sightedness, saying:

To some extent these judges of Ivan Grozny resemble Seneca, Tacitus, and Juvenal, who, in their sharp attacks on the Roman despots, concentrated their attention on court and metropolitan affairs and remained indifferent to the vastness, the borderlands, the external security and the glory of the celebrated empire.*

To begin with, this remark is not true, either of Juvenal or of Tacitus. Apart from that, it is evidence of a reverence for

---

* R. Wipper, *Ivan Grozny* (Moscow, 1944), 149: quoted and trans. by E. Crankshaw, *Cracks in the Kremlin Wall* (New York, 1951), 122.

power which is both very new and very old: it implies that, however brutal and lustful and maniacally suspicious a monarch may be, his moral character is unimportant provided he holds his realm together. And that is precisely what Juvenal knew to be false. He understood that the strongest empire in the world can be wrecked, and will be wrecked, if its rulers start to make their own moral standards—which invariably means yielding to the corruptions of wealth and the madnesses of power.

It is a proof of Juvenal's eminence that one of his central themes is still debated by an apologist for the most powerful empire in the world. But what of his future influence? It seems to me that he has merely suffered, like so many other classical poets, from the extreme specialization which scholars have inflicted on him. What he needs most is one or two good modern verse translations and adaptations—made without pedantry, eliminating or modernizing obsolete allusions, and putting the violence which characterizes so much contemporary literature into Juvenal's own more economical and more effective form. We do not live, as yet, in an age like that which he described. Those who believe that it is approaching—men like Aldous Huxley, Arthur Koestler, and George Orwell—are the heirs of Juvenal today. They are looking into a future which is still not inevitable. But if it should ever descend on us, we must hope that rebels and satirists will arise among us to attack it; and we can be sure that, when they do, they will draw strength from the harsh and powerful voice which has sounded among men for eighteen centuries and is still not silent.

NOTES ON CHAPTER I

1. Juvenal is not mentioned or quoted by Charisius, Diomedes, Donatus, Festus, or Nonius: see Knoche (*45*) 35 n. 5 and 37. Servius, however, quotes him seventy-four times (Knoche 37). Lactantius cites 10. 365–6, giving Juvenal's name, in *Diu. Inst.* 3. 29 (*PL* 6. 443). For a fuller discussion of this subject see pp. 181–8.

2. Amm. Marc. 28. 4. 6: 'Et primo nobilitatis . . . digeremus errata . . . (28. 4. 14) : Quidam detestantes ut uenena doctrinas Iuuenalem et Marium Maximum curatiore studio legunt, nulla uolumina praeter haec in profundo otio contrectantes: quam ob causam non iudicioli est nostri.' (Marius Maximus was a historian who lived at the turn of the second and third centuries: his work is lost.)

3. For Vergil's letter of despair see Macrob. *Sat.* 1. 24. 11, and for his wish to destroy the *Aeneid*, Suet. *De poetis* (restored by A. Rostagni, Turin, 1944), p. 99. The melancholy of the poem can be seen most clearly when it is contrasted with its chief models, the Homeric epics. Thus, in *Iliad* 10 Odysseus and Diomede make a night reconnaissance into the enemy's lines: they are successful; after catching and killing a Trojan spy they return driving the horses of Rhesus and are welcomed by their comrades 'with the hand of friendship and kind words'. In *Aeneid* 9 Nisus and Euryalus make a night reconnaissance into the enemy's lines: they are successful; but they are both caught and slaughtered on the way back. In *Odyssey* 11 Odysseus visits the world of the dead: he sees his mother and many famous heroes and heroines, and at last leaves the underworld with his interest satisfied. In *Aeneid* 6 Aeneas visits the world of the dead: he sees his father and many souls who are to become famous Roman heroes; but the glorious pageant ends in the sad vision of the emperor's adopted son, who was to die with all his promise unfulfilled. In both these episodes, and in many others, Vergil emphasized the labour, waste, and sadness which are part of every great achievement; evidently he felt that both Aeneas' and his own tasks were almost too heavy to be borne.

NOTES ON CHAPTER II

1. *Grauis iuueni mihi barba sonabat*, 1. 25; old age, 10. 188–288; elderly friends, 11. 203, 13. 16–17. A Roman ceased to be a *iuuenis* at 45, according to Varro (Censorinus, *De die natali*, 14. 2).

2. Free-born, because he hates and despises foreigners (1. 26, 1. 103–5, 1. 129–31, 3. 58–125, 4. 23–24, 6. 16–17, 7. 13–16, &c.) and freed slaves (1. 102–11, 5. 28, 7. 13–16, &c.). See F. I. Merchant, 'The Parentage of Juvenal', *AJP* 22 (1901), 51–62—who, however, goes beyond the evidence in calling Crispinus a freedman on p. 58—and C. Strack, *De Juvenalis exilio* (Frankfurt a/M, 1880), 8–9. Juvenal's attitude to freedmen is quite unlike that of Horace, who was the son of a former slave. I cannot think why the ancient biographers say Juvenal was 'the son or foster-son of a freedman' unless either they misunderstood 1. 20 or they wanted to make him more like Horace. Weise (*39*) 5–6 suggests that they misunderstood 1. 102 and thought Juvenal was there speaking in his own person: which is plausible.

3. Here is Baedeker, pointing out the sights on the way from Rome to Naples:

'78 M. Aquino (374 ft.), the ancient Aquinum, a small town picturesquely situated to the left on the hillside and on a mountain-stream, is celebrated as the birthplace of the satirist Juvenal . . . and of Thomas Aquinas. . . . By the side of the Via Latina may be distinguished the relics of the ancient Roman town: . . . remains of temples of Ceres (San Pietro) and Diana (Santa Maria Maddalena), and a triumphal arch.' (*Southern Italy and Sicily*, Leipzig, 1903¹⁴, 4.)

Those are the temples Juvenal himself knew and made his friend name as characterizing Aquinum: *Heluinam Cererem uestramque Dianam* (3. 320). He also made his friend say to him 'whenever you hurry back from Rome to your Aquinum' (3. 318–19), which seems to be intended to imply that Aquinum was his birthplace and his first home. E. v. Mészáros, 'Decimus Junius Juvenalis életehéz', in *Egyetemes Philologiai Közlöny*, 61 (1937), 219–27, suggests that 'your Aquinum' means no more than 'your favourite holiday resort', and supports this by a number of similar phrases in Pliny's letters. Some of these are not quite relevant: e.g. in *Ep.* 1. 4. 1–2, 1. 9. 4, 1. 22. 11, 2. 17. 1, 3. 7. 1, and 4. 6. 1, Pliny is clearly speaking of country houses situated in various districts and described by the appropriate geographical adjective (*in Laurentino meo*), not by a noun like *Aquinum*. On the other hand, *Tuscos meos* in 5. 6. 1 and *Campania tua* in 5. 14. 9 would help to prove Mr. Mészáros's point. But there is *uestram Dianam*, which quite clearly means that Juvenal is one of the townspeople of Aquinum: it could scarcely be said of a summer visitor. The evidence of the ancient lives, for what it is worth, and a note in the scholia also make him a native of Aquinum; and an inscription bearing his family name was found there (see c. 4). His affection for the small towns of Italy also helps to show that he was not, like Umbricius (see 3. 84–85), a son of the metropolis. Read 3. 1–9, 3. 164–84, 3. 190–8, 3. 223–31, 10. 99–102, 14. 179–88; and contrast his defiantly proud *municipalis eques* in 8. 238 with Tacitus' contemptuous *municipalis adulter* in *Ann.* 4. 3. E. Grossi, *Aquinum* (*Biblioteca di Geografia Storica*, 3, Rome, 1907), 159–60, n. 1, says that the town is hot in the summer but well watered, and suggests that *gelidos agros* in 3. 322 means 'cool irrigated fields'. He adds (172–3) that there still exists a *fontana Luina* which apparently goes back to the Helvii, and some *Case Tiane* which may recall the cult of Diana.

4. In 1. 15–17, he says he went to school and wrote the historical speeches which were the parallel to school essays nowadays. Line 15 means studying with the *grammaticus*, lines 16–17 with the *rhetor*. He describes these two parts of the school routine again with vivid detail in 7. 150–243; and it is clear from his constant naïve use of historical clichés that this part of his education made a strong impression on him. (For instance, Hannibal as a school topic, 7. 160–4; Hannibal as a cliché in Juvenal's poetry, 10. 147–67, ending with a reference to schoolboy speech-making. See L. Halkin, 'Hannibal ad portas!' *EtCl* 3 (1934), 437–40.) However, he says himself that he has never read any philosophers (13. 120–3); indeed, it is clear from the unevenness of his logic and the shallowness of his abstract thinking that he has never been trained in the difficult philosophical arguments which were the regular study of young college men, and which give a certain weight to the satires of his predecessors. (On this, see Highet (*22*)). When Horace went to Athens, he attended lectures on philosophy (the phrase is *audire philosophum*, Sen. *Ep.* 76. 1, Petr. *Sat.* 71. 12) which he remembered all his life afterwards. Persius was too delicate, but being rich he had his own philosophy tutor (*Vita Probi Valeri*, 15–17).

5. The only other references to his youth are 1. 25 (mentioned in n. 1) and *tempestate mea* in 4. 140. In this latter sentence Juvenal says that a courtier who was one of Nero's boon companions and had become plump and elderly in 82 (see pp. 80–81) was the most experienced gourmet of his, Juvenal's, time. This suits the conjecture that Juvenal was born about 60 and shows that he felt himself elderly by the time he began to publish his satires, in the era of the 'good emperors'.

6. This is Satire 4. The council described in it took place in 82 or 83, when Juvenal was in his early twenties: see p. 257, n. 5. Of course this is not to imply that he wrote the satire then, still less that he dared to publish it; but rather, that that was the time when he received the impressions which he later remembered and worked into Satire 4. Its vividness consists not only in such details as *nec melior uoltu* (4. 104), *Montani uenter abdomine tardus* (4. 107), *tempestate mea* (4. 140), but in the liveliness with which the ministers pass before us one by one (4. 75–118), in their habit as they lived.

7. Hor. *Serm.* 1. 9. 48–52. *Serm.* 1. 5 is an example of his humorous silence about the diplomatic negotiations of his patron, referred to again in 2. 6. 38–58. Augustus tried to get him to leave Maecenas' 'parasitic table' and enter the palace as private secretary, but he wisely refused (Suet. *De Poetis*, restored by A. Rostagni, Turin, 1944, pp. 113–14).

8. See Hor. *Serm.* 2. 6 and *Ep.* 1. 7—which has an appropriate story about a poor man who was once the dependant of a nobleman, and then through his bounty became an independent yeoman.

9. Although the word *sportula* means 'basket' and implies a gift of food, Hug in *RE*, 2nd series, 3, 1884–6, points out that there is no evidence that private persons ever distributed food in this way to their callers and dependants: only money. (*Sportula* in 3. 249–53 means a picnic to which each guest brings his own contribution of food, and so it is not relevant here.) Juvenal says the dole was distributed in the morning (1. 128) and Martial in the evening (*Ep.* 10. 70. 13–14). This inconsistency led H. M. Stephenson, 'Difficulties in Juvenal, *Sat.* I', *CR* 1 (1887), 243, to suggest that Juvenal may have lived very much later than Martial; but the difference is not important. As Hug suggests, the practice may have varied from house to house; or, more probably, it may have changed in the few years between the end of Martial's working career and Juvenal's appearance as an author.

10. Juv. 1. 147–71. Notice the frequent allusions in this poem to Lucilius as the predecessor whom Juvenal most admires: 19–20; *animo flagrante* in 152 = *Lucilius ardens* in 165; Mucius in 154; and the comparison of Lucilius armed (165) to Juvenal arming (169).

11. A certain amount of confusion has been introduced into discussions of

Juvenal's career by scholars who assume that large poems like his satires must necessarily have been composed in one continuous effort and published immediately after the latest date mentioned in them: see, for instance, the arguments of Ercole (*3*) 91 and Friedländer (*55*) 7. But in fact some of his satires must have been 'twenty years a-growing' before they were ready for final publication. When they are looked at as products of a slow but powerful mind, they lose many of their difficulties.

12. For Pliny's account of the case—which he and Tacitus doubtless felt to be a parallel to Cicero's prosecution of Verres and an assertion of the independent integrity of the senate even under the imperial régime—see *Ep.* 2. 11 and 2. 12.

13. There is a good discussion of this by A. Gercke, *Seneca-Studien* (Leipzig, 1895), 189–90. On the dating of the *Histories* see J. Asbach, *Römisches Kaisertum und Verfassung bis auf Traian* (Cologne, 1896), 151–2. Asbach places the *Annals* before 115, but he is corrected and they are put after 116 by Schanz–Hosius, *Geschichte der römischen Literatur* (Munich, 1935[4]), 2. 672. In any case, it seems likely that Tacitus began work on the *Annals* soon after the *Histories* was finished; and word of the new project, if not its precise scope, would soon get about in literary circles. Hence Juvenal's joke would be valid at any time after 109 or 110.

14. The dates of these comets were worked out by L. Friedländer with the help of two Königsberg astronomers, from the records kept by Chinese astronomers. See his edition (*55*) 7–10, repeating data from his earlier pamphlet, *De cometa a Juvenale in satira sexta commemorato* (Königsberg, 1872).

15. F. A. Lepper, *Trajan's Parthian War* (Oxford, 1948), 95–96, places the earthquake in December 115 and the main Parthian campaign in 116.

16. Nettleship (*6*) thought so, 132–4. But really it is impossible to believe that Book III, containing Satire 7, was published before Domitian died; and that Book I and Book II were issued after his death.

17. References and a few details on the Athenaeum in S. B. Platner and T. Ashby, *A Topographical Dictionary of Ancient Rome* (Oxford, 1929), 56, and in two articles called 'Das Athenaeum in Rom' by F. Schemmel, *WKP* 36 (1919), 91–95, and *BPW* 41 (1921), 982–4. No one says anything precise about the date of the foundation of the Athenaeum. The closest indication we have is in Aurelius Victor (*Caes.* 14. 1–3), who, after describing the adoption of Hadrian and the death of Trajan, begins his life of Hadrian thus:

Igitur Aelius Hadrianus eloquio togaeque studiis accommodatior pace ad Orientem composita Romam regreditur. ibi Graecorum more seu Pompilii Numae caerimonias leges gymnasia doctoresque curare occepit, adeo quidem ut etiam ludum ingenuarum artium, quod Athenaeum uocant, constitueret.

This has been taken by Schemmel (cited above) and by H. Bardon, *Les Empereurs et les lettres latines d'Auguste à Hadrien* (Paris, 1940), 426 f., to mean that Hadrian founded the institute after the Jewish rebellion, which would put it in 136 or so. But the first sentence appears to me to describe Hadrian's return to Rome to enter it for the first time as emperor; *pace ad Orientem composita* would describe his settlement of the eastern problems which confronted him on his accession (see W. Weber in *CAH* 11, 301, who, in very similar phraseology, says 'in Palestine, Egypt, Cyrenaica, calm was restored'). Furthermore, Aurelius Victor says *occepit*, which only makes sense if it refers to the beginning of Hadrian's reign; and he mentions the death of Antinous (130) *after* the foundation of the Athenaeum. Finally, it seems more likely that such a munificent gesture was part of Hadrian's policy on entering Rome for the first time as emperor, when he was anxious to placate public opinion and took many extraordinary measures to relieve deserving classes from financial burdens. I am happy to see that the same timing for Book III, namely, Hadrian's first sojourn in Rome from 118 to 121, has been suggested by A. P. Genovese in his valuable *Giovenale* (Florence, 1933), 205–6.

18. *Hist. Aug., Hadr.* 14. 2. The meaning of Hadrian's order, and its later modification, are discussed by E. Schürer, *Geschichte des jüdischen Volkes im Zeitalter Jesu Christi* (Leipzig, 1901³⁻⁴), i. 674–9.

19. Juv. 1. 1: *semper ego auditor tantum?* In 1. 15–18 he says he might as well write poetry *too*, but adds that this is because he has been to school like everyone else—not because he has already written some. This could scarcely have been uttered before an audience which already knew him as a poet.

20. The farm is at Tibur (11. 65). Its staff includes a foreman and his wife (11. 69), a shepherd who has a flock of sheep and goats (11. 151, 66, 153), and a cowherd (11. 151), all living on the farm (11. 152–3). The sons of these two hands are working in Juvenal's town house (11. 151)—along with at least one more (*cunctis*, 11. 149, usually of more than two). He speaks of the youngsters in a tone of affection (11. 152–5) quite unlike his earlier bitterness about the cost of filling slaves' bellies (3. 167). Notice also that in Book I he goes all the way to Aquinum for comfort when Rome grows too hot (3. 319–22), which he might not have done if at that time (like Horace) he had owned a country retreat as near the city as Tibur. By the way, the phrase *agello cedo paterno* in 6. 57 has often been taken to mean 'if some girl can live virtuously in a small town, then I shall leave the farm I inherited from my father'—presumably as having lost a bet. But I find it very hard to believe that Juvenal could use *rure paterno* to mean 'on *her* father's estate' in 55 and *agello paterno* only two lines later to mean 'from *my* father's farm'. Also, the implied wager is ridiculous, and virtually unheard-of in ancient literature. The argument is clearer and more Juvenalian if we take it thus: 'there are many stories about a [supposedly virtuous] woman living on her father's estate; well, let her live chastely in a small town, and *then* I grant that she can live chastely on her father's farm; but even then. . . .' This is a typical pattern of satire in Juvenal: a cynical remark followed by another equally cynical but pointing in the direction. The interpretation offered here is supported by the scholiast and accepted by Després, Ruperti, and Kiaer (*25*) 125. The difficulty in it is taking *cedo* to mean *concedo*: there are a few examples in *TLL* 3. 278. 39–58, the best being Tac. *Ann.* 12. 41. I should suggest that it is a case of 'The use of the simple for the compound verb in Juvenal', on which H. L. Wilson has a good paper in *TAPA* 31 (1900), 202–22, and that it should be compared with Juvenal's use of *stillo* for *instillo* in 3. 122 and *scribo* for *inscribo* in 6. 205.

21. Mart. 7. 91. 1. Martial uses *facundus* very freely (as a modern writer might say 'my literary acquaintance'), applying it not only to Cicero, Vergil, and Seneca, but to the city of Corduba, Catullus the farce-writer, Restitutus the lawyer, his patrons M. Antonius Primus and L. Arruntius Stella, and others. Therefore it does not mean that the person to whom it is applied must be a professional rhetorician (so Strack, cited in n. 2, 23), but merely that he has a sense of style and is interested in literature.

22. It is just possible that Juvenal was a pupil of Quintilian's, or at least an admirer: see Kappelmacher (*24*). It is possible also that Quintilian's remark about contemporary satirists is an allusion to Juvenal: having described Lucilius, Horace, and Persius—Juvenal's self-chosen predecessors——he goes on (10. 1. 94): 'sunt clari hodieque et qui olim nominabuntur'. Now, if Juvenal had published nothing but had shown Quintilian some of his sketches, it would be a wise and civil gesture for Quintilian to call him 'distinguished' and to foretell his future fame. But if the sentence must refer to satirists who had actually published, then Juvenal cannot be meant, and probably Quintilian is thinking of Juvenal's immediate predecessor Turnus.

NOTES ON CHAPTER III

1. Discussions of the biographies will be found in Dürr (*12*); Ercole (*3*); Highet (*14*): G. Koertge, 'In Suetonii de uiris illustribus inquisitionum capita III', *Dissertationes philologicae Halenses*, 14 (1900), 243–51; D. Naguiewski, *De Juvenalis vita observationes* (Riga, 1883); L. Rittweger, *Die Verbannung Juvenals und die Abfassungszeit seiner siebenten Satire* (Berlin, 1886); C. Strack, *De Juvenalis exilio* (Frankfurt a/M, 1880); C. Synnerberg, *De temporibus vitae carminumque Juvenalis rite constituendis* (Helsingfors, 1866); Vahlen (*16*); and Wessner (*53*), § 7.

2. A good example of the regular biography of an author is Probus's life of Persius, which appears at the opening of Persius' works: yet even there the last paragraph of the life comes in the wrong place and looks very odd. For a discussion of the shape of classical biographies see F. Leo, *Die griechisch-römische Biographie* (Berlin, 1901) and W. Steidle, *Sueton und die antike Biographie* (Munich, 1951).

3. For instance, one biography says he was exiled by 'Claudius Nero', which is impossible for a man who was still writing in A.D. 127. (This is IIb in the collection of lives printed by Dürr, *12*.) Another (Dürr III*c*) explains his death by saying that in Egypt 'cum careret consuetis spectaculis et ludis qui Romae fiebant angore et taedio periit'—which is obviously a gross misinterpretation of Juv. 11. 52–53.

4. In the P manuscript the two biographies are written on a page stitched on at the back of the book, in a hand much later than that of the copyist who wrote the text of the satires and scholia—probably the hand of the corrector or interpolator. See Beer (*41*) 11–12.

5. The relevant notes are those on 1. 1 (which took the place of a biography in the P scholia), 4. 38, 7. 92, and 15. 27. The notes on 4. 38 and 7. 92 are shown by internal evidence to be partly false, but contain shreds of the truth.

6. A determined critic of the lives, C. Strack (cited in n. 1), who was one of the first to point out that they were connected only with the inferior tradition of the text, was still unable to suggest how and why the statement could have been invented, although he was sure it had been. 'Difficile autem videtur iudicare,' he says sadly on p. 9, 'unde exilium eiusque caussam grammaticus excogitaverit. Atque ego non eum me fingam, qui demum veram et solidam narratiunculae originem invenerim.'

7. Sid. Ap. *Carm.* 9. 271–3:

> et qui consimili deinde casu
> ad uolgi tenuem strepentis auram
> irati fuit histrionis exul.

8. For instance, in *Carm.* 23. 160–1 he boldly identifies Ovid's Corinna with Augustus' daughter Julia.

9. Jo. Malalas, *Chronographia*, 10. 341 (*PG* 97. 400): ὁ δὲ αὐτὸς βασιλεὺς Δομετιανὸς ἐφίλει τὸν ὀρχηστὴν τοῦ πρασίνου μέρους τῆς Ῥώμης τὸν λεγόμενον Πάριδα, περὶ οὗ καὶ ἐλοιδορεῖτο ἀπὸ τῆς συγκλήτου Ῥώμης καὶ Ἰουβεναλίου τοῦ ποιητοῦ τοῦ Ῥωμαίου ὡς χαίρων εἰς τὸ πράσινον. ὅστις βασιλεὺς ἐξώρισε τὸν αὐτὸν Ἰουβενάλιον τὸν ποιητὴν ἐν Πενταπόλει ἐπὶ τὴν Λιβύην, τὸν δε ὀρχηστὴν πλουτίσας ἔπεμψεν ἐν Ἀντιοχείᾳ τῇ μεγάλῃ ἐπὶ τὸ ἐκεῖ αὐτὸν οἰκεῖν ἔξω τῆς πόλεως. ὅστις Πάρις ὀρχηστὴς ἐκεῖ ἀπελθὼν ᾤκει ἔξω τῆς αὐτῆς πόλεως, κτίσας ἑαυτῷ οἶκον προάστειον καὶ λουτρόν, ὅπερ ἐστὶν ἕως τῆς νῦν, τὸ λεγόμενον Παράδεισος καὶ ὁ Οἶκος. κἀκεῖ τελευτήσας κεῖται ἐν σορῷ ὄπισθεν τοῦ οἴκου ἐν τοῖς κήποις αὐτοῦ. Suidas transcribes the gist of this in the entry Ἰουβενάλιος (Suidas, 2, ed. A. Adler, Leipzig, 1931, 640–1).

10. The younger Helvidius Priscus, L. Junius Arulenus Rusticus, Herennius Senecio, and others (Suet. *Dom.* 10). See J. Asbach, *Römisches Kaisertum und Verfassung bis auf Traian* (Cologne, 1896), c. 9. 'Feindliche Strömungen', and M. P. Charlesworth in *CAH* 12. 30–32.

11. This is well argued by Naguiewski (cited in n. 1), 37–38.

12. So, for instance, Rittweger (cited in n. 1) 6: 'Jener histrio Paris wurde im Jahre 83 n. Chr. . . . getötet. Juvenal muß also zwischen den Jahren 81 und 83 n. Chr. jene Verse auf den Paris verfaßt haben.' Teuffel (*38*) 536 reasons in the same way, without thinking of Juvenal's methods and of Domitian's peculiar character.

13. The fact that the lampoon (or a fragment of it) *now* appears in Satire 7 has nothing to do with the date of that poem. We are never told that Juvenal was banished for writing Satire 7; and indeed, if it had been possible for the scholiasts to point to any of the existing satires as having caused his exile, they would have done so quite clearly. On the contrary, some of the biographers are dimly aware that the lampoon was written earlier, and later inserted into its present context: 'ut ea quoque quae prima fecerat inferciret nouis scriptis,' says the P life. The most reasonable explanation of its present position is that Juvenal recalled the lines many years after his exile, and inserted them into his poem complimenting a kinder emperor. Even at that, they do not fit well into the context. Juvenal has been saying (7. 53–87) that it is hard to be a poet when you are in danger of starving. He continues that argument in 7. 93–104. But the lines associated with the lampoon, 88–92, do not say that Paris merely feeds poets. They say that he gets them honorary commissions in the army, with the privileges these entail. If we look closely at the passage, we can see traces of the insertion. In 82–87 Juvenal is talking of Statius. He ends:

> esurit, intactam Paridi nisi uendat Agauen.

Line 93 runs on with the same thought:

> haut tamen inuideas uati quem pulpita *pascunt*.

But the intervening lines have nothing to do with one poet who is starving: they describe several favoured poets getting gold rings. That would indicate that they were not originally composed for this context, nor indeed for the Seventh Satire, which is obsessed with dire poverty: see *esuriens Clio* (7), *parua cella* (28), *imagine macra* (29), *nuda senectus* (35), *maesta paupertas* . . . *corpus eget* (60–62), *intestina poetae* (78). Vahlen (*16*) 3–4 saw that lines 88–92 hung closely together, but failed to explain their connexion with the context, calling them a 'digression' and a 'contrast'.

14. It is far more likely that Juvenal was sentenced to *deportatio*, which involved loss of civil rights and confiscation of property and which meant that the victim was kept in a fixed spot, often under military guard, than that he was given the milder sentence of *relegatio*, like Ovid. Domitian was 'non solum magnae sed etiam callidae inopinataeque saeuitiae' (Suet. *Dom.* 11. 1). On *deportatio* see T. Mommsen, *Römisches Strafrecht* (Leipzig, 1899), 974 f., and Kleinfeller s.v. *deportatio in insulam* in *RE* 5. 231–3.

15. Juv. 1. 147–71. He may not have known that Tigellinus (155) procured the death of the satirist Petronius, but he certainly knew that Tigellinus was *praefectus praetorio* under Nero. Since he calls Domitian a 'bald Nero' (4. 38), he means 'Tigellinus' to be interpreted as Domitian's *praefectus praetorio*, once more Crispinus.

16. Trajan's titles appear in 6. 205. Hadrian is *Caesar* and *dux* in 7. 1 and 7. 21 (see pp. 17–18). The view taken in this book, that Domitian banished Juvenal, has been held with slight variations by Borghesi (*Œuvres complètes*, 5. 512), Friedländer (*55*), C. F. Hermann, *De Iuvenalis satirae septimae temporibus* (Göttingen, 1843), Naguiewski (cited in n. 1), and Wilson (*64*). Rittweger (cited in n. 1) is one of the few who believe Trajan responsible. Dürr (*12*), Ercole (*3*), Teuffel (*38*), and Weidner (*63*) with some others think the emperor in question was Hadrian; Hild (*15*), Strack (cited in n. 1), and Vahlen (*16*) deny the whole tradition. As we have seen in n. 6, it is hard to tell why and how the tradition could have been invented, so that it is dangerous to dismiss it altogether. Trajan or Hadrian? It is possible that either of them ordered the poet's banishment. Trajan was fond of a ballet-dancer called Pylades; Hadrian was in love with the handsome youth Antinous: either might have taken a gibe at an influential dancer to be an attack on his own favourite. But it is almost impossible to explain how Juvenal could have written and published a number of further satires, if he had been exiled immediately after issuing Satire 7. Those who think Trajan or Hadrian banished him for writing Satire 7 can scarcely explain how Satires 8, 9, 10, 11, 12, 13, 14, 15, and 16 can ever have been allowed to appear, or how they (unlike Satires 1–5) betray no signs of shock or recent injustice. Any explanation of the exile which puts it in the *middle* of Juvenal's career as a writer is hideously involved and improbable. Any explanation which puts it at the *end* of his life makes it hard to account for the calm tone and innocuous contents of Books IV and V. Only by placing the exile *before* the publication of the satires in their present form (though of course not before the conception of some of them) can we produce a satisfactory explanation of the tone of Juvenal's poetry regarded as a whole, violent and rancorous at the beginning, gloomy but resigned in the middle, cynical but idealistic towards the end. A similar fate befell Juvenal's contemporary Dio Cocceianus (called Chrysostom). At first wealthy and brilliant, something of a dilettante, he was exiled and impoverished by Domitian and returned under Nerva: during his exile he underwent a profound conversion, and emerged as an ethical teacher.

17. The note in 10. 193–5 is not found in any other author, and looks like personal reminiscence. Hyperboles about Britain in 2. 159–61 and Spain in 3. 54–55.

18. See G. Highet, 'A fight in the desert', *CJ* 45 (1949–50), 94–96, for a parallel story told by Norman Douglas.

19. Juv. 15. 43–46. The savages, *barbara turba*, are the fellaheen of the villages and countryside. The disgraceful city is the luxurious and polyglot Canopus, which only Rome excelled in vice (Juv. 6. 83–84).

20. See Juv. 6. 527–8 (n. 28), 10. 193–5, and 13. 163 (p. 31). The name *attegiae* for the huts of the Moors (14. 196) appears nowhere else in Latin literature, and is known only from an inscription, *CIL* 13. 6054.

21. The first scholar to accuse Juvenal of ignorance on this point was apparently Milton's opponent Claude Saumaise (Salmasius), in his *Plinianae Exercitationes* (1689), 317 G–321 E.

22. The identification of Ombi with the site called Nubi or Nubt had been suggested by an earlier excavator of Dendera, J. Dümichen, in his *Geschichte des alten Aegyptens* (Berlin, 1879), 125–6; and Mommsen had pointed out that the two towns Ombi and Tentyra are mentioned together in the list of the Ravenna geographer: see *Ravennatis anonymi geographiae libri quinque* in A. Gronovius's edition of Mela (Leyden, 1722), book 3, para. 2, p. 764: 'item ad aliam partem sunt ciuitates ex regione Thebaidae, id est, Corton, Laton, Tentyra, Ombos, Hiera Sicamina.' For an account of the discovery and the identification of Ombi and Nubt see W. M. F. Petrie and J. E. Quibell, *Naqada and Ballas. 1895* (London, 1896), 65–70; and, more generally, P. H. Boussac, 'L'Exil de Juvénal et l'Ombos [*sic*] de la XVᵉ satire', *RevPhil* 41 (1917), 169–84, and E. Meyer, *Geschichte des Altertums* (Stuttgart, 1926⁵), 1. 2, § 181. Petrie and his party actually found traces of cannibalism, human bones gnawed and broken; but these were prehistoric (pp. 30–33). There are descriptions of elaborate feasts at Tentyra (like the festival in Juv. 15. 38–50) in Petrie's later work *Dendereh* (London, 1900), 57 f. On Set, the god of the night sky, one of whose incarnations was the crocodile, see E. A. W. Budge, *The Gods of the Egyptians*, ii (Chicago and London, 1904), c. 14; and on Hathor, goddess of jollity and happiness and beauty, see vol. i, p. 435.

23. Juv. 1. 129–31. The officer was Vespasian's general Tiberius Julius Alexander, who was Jewish by origin; but what Juvenal hated in him was his connexion with Egypt. M. Rostowzew, 'Ἀποστόλιον', *RM* 12 (1897), 76–77, shows that *Arabarches* means the governor of that part of Egypt which was known as 'Arabia'.

24. Schol. 1. 1. The suggestion that Crispinus was responsible for the banishment of Juvenal comes from B. Borghesi, 'Annotazione alle satire di Giovenale', *Œuvres complètes*, 5 (Paris, 1869), 513–16. J. Earle, 'On Juvenal, Sat. 1. 155–157', *Trans. Ox.Phil.Soc.* 1887–8, 6–9, proposed that 1. 155–7 was a concealed autobiographical reference to Juvenal's own banishment.

25. On Pentapolis see Broholm in *RE* 12. 1. 164, s.v. Kyrene, and Kees in *RE* 19. 1. 509–10, s.v. Pentapolis. John Malalas also gets the end of Paris wrong, saying that Domitian enriched and banished him, whereas he had him murdered out of hand.

26. Ulpian, *Dig.* 48. 22. 7. 5. See T. Mommsen, *Römisches Strafrecht* (Leipzig, 1899), 973 and 975, n. 2. There is a learned but confusing and ultimately useless discussion of this particular sentence in J. V. Francke, *Ueber ein Einschiebsel Tribonians beim Ulpian, die Verbannung nach der großen Oase betreffend* (Kiel, 1819): accepting the story that Juvenal was sent away on a half-farcical military appointment, Francke believes that this must disprove the tradition of his exile to the Oasis; but the story is not convincing. Augustus sent the pet philosopher of Antony and Cleopatra, Philostratus, to Ostrakiné in the desert of Sinai (Crinagoras, *AP* 7. 645, and C. Cichorius, *Römische Studien*, Leipzig, 1922, 314–18). There is a rather Dostoievskian prostitute banished to the Oasis in B. P. Grenfell and A. S. Hunt, *Greek Papyri*, ser. ii (Oxford, 1897), no. 73; although it is possible that Πολιτική means her name and not her profession, and that she was a victim of Diocletian's persecution of the Christians (see J. G. Winter, *Life and Letters in the Papyri*, Ann Arbor, 1933, 147–8 and 147, n. 3). In 397 the eunuch Eutropius had Theodosius' general Timasius exiled to the same spot (Gibbon, *Decline and Fall*, c. 32, Everyman ed. 3. 293).

27. Martial 1. 86. For Syene as an ivory market see Juv. 11. 124 and W. Schwarz, 'Aethiopien', *RhM* 49 (1894), 358–9; on its military importance see Kees, s.v. Syene, in *RE*, 2nd series, 4. 1021–3; for the three cohorts at the post in 99, see J. Lesquier, 'L'Armée romaine d'Égypte', *Mémoires de l'Institut français d'Archéologie orientale du Caire*, 41 (1918), 88. 90. 94. L. Herrmann, 'Juvenaliana', *REA* 42 (1940), 450–2, accepting the dubious tradition that Juvenal's exile was disguised as a military posting, points to Martial's friend Varus, who was reading poems in Rome in 93 and died as an N.C.O. in Egypt two years later (Mart. 8. 20 and 10. 26).

28. Juv. 13. 163 and Mayor ad loc. Meroe is mentioned again in 6. 526–9, where Juvenal says that the superstitious woman will, if ordered, go as far as hot Meroe for lustral water to sprinkle in the temple of Isis at Rome. Friedländer in his 1895 edition (55) suggested that this was not to be taken literally. But fifteen years later an expedition to Meroe discovered a large temple of Isis which contained lustral utensils and Greco-Roman cult-objects, showing clearly that some devotees did actually make the pilgrimage from Greece and Rome: see Garstang, Sayce, and Griffith, *Meroe* (London, 1911).

Juvenal's accuracy is further confirmed by *CIL* 3. 83, an inscription giving the name of a Roman who went all the way to Meroe to see the Lady Queen (Isis, Juv. 6. 530). See J. de Decker, 'Le Culte d'Isis à Méroé en Éthiopie', *RIPB* 54 (1911), 293–310.

NOTES ON CHAPTER IV

1. Here is the fragmentary text of the second inscription (*CIL* 10. 5426):
. . . IVVABERIT / HVIC VNIVERSVS POPVLVS / AQVINATIVM TABVLAM / AENEAM PATRONATVS TRA/DITAM SED ET STATVAM / PERPETVABILEM CVM PIC/TVRAM SIMILITVDINIS / EIVS HOC IN LOCO AD PEREN/NEM TESTIMONIVM CENSVER / CONSTITVENDAM. Similar tributes to friends of Aquinum appear in *CIL* 10. 5395 and 5398. Note also the appearance of a Trebius (the name of Juvenal's acquaintance in Satire 5) at Aquinum in *CIL* 10. 5528 and 5529. As for Juvenal's own name: in Martial and later writers, in the P manuscript, and in the shorter of the biographies attached to it, he appears simply as Iuuenalis. In the longer P life and in several manuscripts, two names—Iunius Iuuenalis—are given. The forename D., or Decimus, is added in a fair number of manuscripts and discussed in some of the medieval commentaries.

2. Jupiter, 6. 59; Mars, 6. 59 and 14. 261–2; but Ceres is the guardian of chastity, 6. 50, and it is shameful that her temple should be used for love-affairs, 9. 24; she demands purity and kindness, 15. 140–1. A mild joke on the myth of Proserpina in 10. 112. There are brief introductions to Juvenal's view of religion by E. E. Burriss, 'The religious element in the satires of Juvenal', *CW* 20 (1926), 19–21; J. D. Jefferis, 'Juvenal and religion', *CJ* 34 (1939), 229–33; and M. Morlais, *Études philosophiques et religieuses sur les écrivains latins* (Paris, 1896), c. 10.

3. There is a good discussion of the stone by De Chaufepié (*11*), though it is marred by uncritical acceptance of the biographies of Juvenal. His main point is that, since Juvenal the poet was poor while Juvenal the dedicator of the stone was rich, they cannot have been identical. But this objection has been answered by J. A. Hild, 'L'Inscription d'Aquinum et la biographie de Juvénal', *Bulletin de la Faculté des lettres de Poitiers*, 7 (1889), 335–49, and more fully on pp. 36–39 of this book.

4. Mommsen added the figure I 'because the first cohort is most frequently mentioned and the figure I could fall out most easily' (*CIL* 10, 531); but neither of these reasons is compelling. We hear of 2nd, 3rd, 4th, and 5th Dalmatian units in various parts of the empire (see C. Cichorius, s.v. *cohors Delmatarum*, in *RE* 4. 283–4), and this could have been any of them. See De Chaufepié (*11*) 17–18.

5. This is the sum of 400,000 sesterces. On the qualifications for knighthood see T. Mommsen, *Römisches Staatsrecht* (Leipzig, 1887), 3. 1. 496–509, and A. Stein, *Der römische Ritterstand* (Munich, 1927), 21 f. and 70 f. Until the reign of Trajan an officer who holds *only* the *praefectura cohortis* is at the beginning of his career, so that this Juvenal must have been a young man:

see A. von Domaszewski, 'Die Rangordnung des römischen Heeres', *BonnJbb* 117 (1908), 129, who cites many inscriptions to prove it. Other officers from Aquinum appear in *CIL* 10. 5393, 5399, and 5401.

6. See Mommsen (cited in n. 5), 3. 1. 495 and 552–65; and J. Marquardt, *Römische Staatsverwaltung* (Leipzig, 1876), 2. 366–8.

7. On the duumvirate see Kübler in *RE* 4. 2. 2328, s.v. *decurio*; Last in *CAH* 11. 460–2; Liebenam in *RE* 5. 2. 1804–41, s.v. *duoviri*; and F. Spehr, *De summis magistratibus coloniarum atque municipiorum* (Halle, 1881). Aquinum was a *colonia*.

8. De Chaufepié (*11*) 65 opposes this suggestion, on the ground that we do not know whether the cult of Titus was ever established at Aquinum. But surely it is unlikely that a town so near Rome would omit to honour the beloved emperor. Juvenal's more successful contemporary, the younger Pliny, similarly served for a short time in the army (as tribune in the 3rd Gallic Legion) and then became priest of the deified Titus (*Ep.* 3. 11. 5, *CIL* 5. 5667). Hild (*15*) suggests that an ex-officer became priest of the emperor under whom he had served.

9. So De Chaufepié (*11*), L. Rittweger, *Die Verbannung Juvenals und die Abfassungszeit seiner siebenten Satire* (Berlin, 1886), C. Strack, *De Juvenalis exilio* (Frankfurt a/M, 1880), and others.

10. In spite of his poverty Juvenal knows little or nothing about the lives of the ordinary men and women who work for a living; he is not a Zola, not even an Orwell. In 3. 172–9 we see only the small-town officials, with the public in the background. Codrus in 3. 203–11 is a bohemian intellectual. In 4. 153 working men are credited with Domitian's murder, which they did not commit. On the other hand, Juvenal knows a good deal about the usages, the personalities, and the scandals of high society. He is not an angry proletarian, but a middle-class intellectual who has had some experience of aristocratic life and has been *déclassé*.

11. Juv. 1. 106, *quadringenta*, possessed by an ex-slave from the East. (M. Bonnet, 'Juvénal I, 105', *RevPhil* 30 (1906), 58–60, shows that it means capital, and not income, which would be *quadringena*.) See also 14. 322–4, where the *quadringenta* are the summit of normal human desire, and 5. 132–3, where they might be bestowed as a gift by God, or by some manikin like God only kinder (= the emperor!). In general, see T. Mommsen, *Römisches Staatsrecht* (Leipzig, 1887), 3. 1. 499–500, and A. Stein, *Der römische Ritterstand* (Munich, 1927), 27 f.

12. Juv. 3. 153–9. (On *pinnirapus* see M. Rostowzew, 'Pinnirapus iuvenum', *RM* 15 (1900), 223–8, who shows that it means 'champion gladiator'.) Juvenal also jeers at men who contrive to keep up their rank as knights through pretence and show, and at others who lose their knighthood through irresponsibility: 1. 58–61, 11. 42–43.

13. On *suffragia* see O. Hirschfeld, *Röm. Verwaltungsgeschichte* (Berlin, 1877), 266, n. 7. Letters of recommendation can be seen in Cicero, *Ad fam.* 13 (the whole book except for 13. 68 is composed of such letters); Pliny, *Ep.* 10. 12 and 10. 87, cf. 10. 51; Fronto (ed. S. A. Naber, Leipzig, 1867), *Ad M. Caes.* 5. 37. 52 (p. 87) and *Ad L. Verum* 2. 7 (pp. 133–5). The practice is mentioned in Epictetus 3. 7. 31; Tac. *Ann.* 14. 50; Suet. *D. Vesp.* 23. 2;

Hist. Aug., Pescenn. Niger, 1. 5; *Elagab.* 6. 1–2; *Alex. Sev.* 35. 5–36; Dio 60.
17. 8 and 65. 14. 3. See also *CIL* 6. 2132, and an amusingly earnest letter
from a young sailor hoping for a transfer, who says he needs both *epistulas
commendaticias* and money to bring it off, *Michigan Papyri* (ed. H. C. Youtie
and J. G. Winter, Ann Arbor, 1951), 8. 468, p. 26.

14. We might even conjecture that he applied to a dignitary of the same
cognomen as his (though of a different *gens*): to C. Iulius Iuuenalis, who was
consul just at the time when our Juvenal might expect promotion, in 81.
(See W. Liebenam, *Fasti Consulares*, Bonn, 1909, s.v. A.D. 81, and Groag in
RE 10. 1. 656, s.v. Iulius (304).)

NOTE ON CHAPTER VI

1. In the first Book, as it stands, there are about 987 lines: 171 in Satire 1,
170 in 2, 320 in 3, 154 in 4, and 172 in 5. The second Book contains about
693, of which over 30 were discovered as recently as 1899 (see p. 223); we
cannot be sure of the original length of the poem. Book III has 662 lines:
242 in 7, 271 in 8, 149 in 9. There are 698 lines in Book IV, with 366 in 10,
202 in 11, and 130 in 12. In the fifth Book we find 811 lines (249 in 13, 330 in
14, and 172 in 15, with a fragment of 60 lines in 16); but, as we shall see,
the 16th probably ran to 300 lines or more (pp. 288–9): so that the old man
finished his career with a giant book of over a thousand lines, bigger than
any of the others, even the ambitious first. Of course, these figures are only
provisional. They omit the most obviously interpolated lines (like 3. 281)
but not lines which, although questioned, have not been clearly shown to be
forged. And there is no way of estimating how much of Juvenal's work we
have lost through the accidental dropping or deliberate excision of passages
from the interior of the satires. (See pp. 223–4, 336.)

NOTES ON CHAPTER VII

1. *Sources, analogues, and adaptations.* Apparently this satire is largely new
and original. Other verse-satirists wrote poems discussing their mission and
their method (Lucilius 26, frg. 588–96 Marx; Hor. *Serm.* 1. 4, 1. 10, 2. 1;
Persius 1), but none of them seems to have adopted Juvenal's point of view
or limited his motives so closely to indignation and his subject so deter-
minedly to vice. For a discussion see M. P. Piwonka, *Lucilius und Kalli-
machos* (Frankfurt a/M, 1949), 104–14. The satire has been less often imitated
as a whole than most of Juvenal's poems. The gloomy general view of Rome
reappears, probably without connexion, in Lucian's *Nigrinus* 17–23. The
whole poem was modernized by Anthony à Wood's nephew Thomas as
Juvenalis Redivivus (London, 1683); it helped to inspire Boileau's ninth satire
(where 250–66 ∼ Juv. 1. 52–57) and *Le Dix-huitième Siècle* of N. L. J. Gilbert
(1751–80); and its opening was imitated by Salvator Rosa in *La Poesia* and
Byron in *English Bards and Scotch Reviewers*.

2. The four parts of the poem are these:

(a) *motive in general* 1–18: why I write poetry;

(b) *motive in particular* 19–80: why I choose satire;

(c) *subjects* 81–146: the main themes of my satire are greed and extravagance;

(d) *illustrations* 147–71: but the dangers of writing contemporary satire limit my choice of illustrations and confine me to the past.

This division is the same in principle as that accepted by Gylling (*20*) 7–13, Stegemann (*34*) 9–18, Duff (*54*) 115–32, de Labriolle (*4*) 24–26 and (*59*) 3–5, J. Elmore, 'The plan of Juvenal's first satire', *CW* 18 (1924–5), 166–7, and W. C. Helmbold, 'The structure of Juvenal I', *Univ. of Cal. Publications in Classical Philology*, 14 (1951), 47–60. J. E. Church, 'The construction of Juvenal, Satire I', *TAPA* 35 (1904), lxxi–lxxiv, divides the poem into an *exordium* (1–21), a *confirmatio* (22–146), and a *peroratio* (147–71), which is irregular because it contains no *propositio* (though surely 19–21 might deserve that name), and unconvincing because the last part of the poem does not perform the rhetorical functions of a peroration, but adds an entirely new train of ideas. Gauger (*19*) 3 makes the same mistake in calling 147–71 an 'epilogue'. Hartmann (*21*) 21–28 and Friedländer (*55*) 128 hold that all or most of 97–146 is a 'digression', which seems unlikely. Sydow (*37*) 19–21 realizes that 127–31 are not 'irrelevant', but scarcely sees that the whole of the section 94–146 deals with the relationship of patron and client. C. Knapp, 'A brief review of Juvenal satire 1', *CW* 19 (1925–6), 19–21, agrees with the division given at the beginning of this note, but would mark only two paragraphs in the poem, 1–80 and 81–171.

3. This was a new departure for satire. Gauger (*19*) 13 points out that Horace also had drawn a distinction between verse-satire and the higher forms of poetry (*Serm.* 1. 4. 39–44), which was recalled by Persius in his prologue (1–7); but he scarcely realizes the novelty of Juvenal's scorn for conventional poetry and the loftiness of the claims he was to make for satire. G. Hirst, *Collected Classical Papers* (Oxford, 1938), 65–66, indicates the real truth: Juvenal has remembered a passage where Vergil (one of his chief models) says that Greek mythological themes are outworn and that he intends to write on a contemporary subject (introduction to *Georg.* 3). Juvenal here says the same, but he cannot, like Vergil, write of the heroic deeds of Caesar, only of vice and crime.

4. See, for instance, G. Hirst (cited in n. 3), 66–67, who points to the threefold repetition of the theme of the rich man's litter in 30–33, 63–67, and 158–9. Gauger (*19*) 3–8 gives an extremely complicated, and to me rather unconvincing, scheme—arranging the passage into two groups of four and four groups of two 'Skandalfälle'. Hartmann (*21*) 10–19 and Stegemann (*34*) 11–15 see two chief topics treated: perversions of nature or of sex, 22–29, and the maladjustments of Roman society, 30–80.

5. The word *tener* shows that this character was a genuine eunuch, and not still potent like the fakes in Juv. 6. 368–78. (I have read somewhere that the powerful eunuchs of the Chinese imperial court used to marry for the same reason—to prove that they were really men, or as good as men; but I have been unable to verify it.) Certainly Eutropius, the wrinkled old eunuch of the emperor Arcadius, had a wife: Claudian, *In Eutrop.* 2. 88–90. L. Valmaggi, 'Note a Giovenale', *BFC* 1 (1894–5), 257–9, and F. Eusebio, ' "Spadone" marito', *BFC* 2 (1895–6), 19–21, suggest that Juvenal's main objection to such a marriage is that no children could be born of it. Even granting Juvenal's affection for children, this is surely rather naïve?

6. Friedländer (*55*) 134 and others say the lady is only hunting; but that will not explain Juvenal's indignation at her costume, nor indeed will it explain the costume itself. She would not put on fancy dress to hunt in a lonely forest, nor would Juvenal object if she did. Statius (*Silu.* 1. 6. 55–56) also says that women in the arena looked like Amazons; and Juvenal's line contains an echo of Vergil's description of the Amazon princess Penthesilea, 'aurea subnectens exsertae cingula mammae', *Aen.* 1. 492.

7. The hairdresser was probably Cinnamus, at whom Martial sneers in 7. 64. If he was, then part of Juvenal's hatred of him is based on the fact that he had reached the coveted rank of knighthood—which Juvenal himself had lost (pp. 37–38).

8. Similar eccentricities are related of the English dandies. Lord Petersham had a different snuffbox for every day in the year; and once, when his fine Sèvres box was admired, he observed that it was 'a nice summer box, but it would not do for winter wear' (E. Sitwell, *The English Eccentrics*, Boston, 1933, 137). The young Disraeli carried different walking-sticks in the morning and afternoon, changing punctually at midday (A. Maurois, *Vie de Disraéli*, Paris, 1927, 53).

9. The relation between Juvenal and Lucilius has never been fully explored (despite Highet, *23*, and Kappelmacher, *24*), because it is impossible to draw firm deductions from such a miserable set of fragments as remains to us from Lucilius' satires. But a few points are worth making. (1) Lucilius was extremely popular in Juvenal's day, preferred by some not only to all other satirists but to all other poets. (Quint. 10. 1. 93). (2) He came from a small town, Suessa Aurunca, which lay only a score of miles from Juvenal's home of Aquinum; and he was a knight, as Juvenal had been: so that he would naturally suggest himself as a model. (3) What Juvenal admired most in him was his combativeness—imaged in the picture of Lucilius as a furious swordsman running berserk (Juv. 1. 165–6)—his sweeping energy (Lucilius as a charioteer, 1. 20), and his outspoken candour (1. 151–4). Piwonka (cited in n. 1), 104–14, has an interesting comparison of the two poets, taking Lucilius and Horace as representatives of a gentler, more sociable, far more humorous, chattier, more discursive, more playful, and ultimately more positive type of satire than that created by Juvenal. This may well be true, but is it not likely that, if we had three or four hundred consecutive lines of Lucilius, we should find them far more like Juvenal than like Horace, particularly in their energy and their love of giving pain? As for the other satirists, Juvenal mentions Horace once, with a compliment to his graceful style (1. 51, *lucerna = lucubratio = limae labor*), and borrowed a few themes from him, but could not respect his mild outlook or his evasive manner. He copied one satire of Persius (Pers. 2 ∼ Juv. 10), but never speaks of him.

10. Juv. 1. 81–87. The four cardinal passions, the four emotions that move mankind, are hope, fear, pain, and pleasure: pleasure and pain being felt about present experiences, fear and hope about the future. They were so defined by Zeno in his book Περὶ παθῶν (Diog. Laert. 7. 110, and see Clement, *Paed.*, ed. Stählin, 1. 3. 21–25). They appear in a famous passage of Vergil (*Aen.* 6. 733) and a neat line of Horace (*Ep.* 1. 6. 12). It is interesting and characteristic that Juvenal should have altered one of them. He keeps hope and fear, and he keeps pleasure; but he has changed grief to anger, and so it appears again in 6. 189. *Gaudia* and *discursus* are a pair of less emotional opposites, 'business and pleasure', which Juvenal adds to fill out the list: they are the outward activities of human beings, while the four πάθη are inward states.

11. e.g. de Labriolle (*59*) 4 says that 81–86 are 'a rather clumsy interruption'; Sydow (*37*) 19–21 declares that the whole passage 81–131 is rambling and disconnected.

12. Juv. 1. 88: *auaritia*) (*alea*; 1. 140, *luxuriae sordes*; the double madness of losing £1,000 at dice and grudging to buy one's slave a shirt, 92–93. The only commentator who seems to have clearly recognized that these are the two special vices described in this section is Gauger (*19*) 9–10. A modern parallel to 92–93 is provided by Mr. Williams Hope, who, although he had inherited £40,000 a year, 'would one day spend thousands of pounds on a ball or supper, and then keep his servants on cold meat and stale bread' (Gronow, *Last Recollections*, London, 1866[2], 124). J. De Decker, 'Juvénal, Sat. I, vers 81–86', *RIPB* 55 (1912), 178–85, suggests on the basis of 84 that Juvenal is here proposing to take sexual lust as his only subject; but this distorts the meaning and is false to the facts.

13. The composition of this third section, 87–146, has been much criticized, usually because the leading theme, Money, and its context, the patron–client relationship, have been misunderstood. But it is clear enough, although occasionally distorted by an overdeveloped detail. After a brief introduction on the waste of money in gambling (88–93), Juvenal turns to the millionaire who spends his money not on his household and his friends and clients but on country houses which he enjoys alone and on sumptuous dinners to which he invites no guests. From the mention of the dinner Juvenal passes naturally to the *sportula*, which is a token-share of dinner. From line 95 to line 126 he talks of the *sportula* and its abuses. Then he speaks briefly of the middle of the day, during which the clients accompanied their patron to the forum (128–31, and there may well be a lacuna after 131, as suggested by Housman, *56*). Finally, he talks of the different dinners enjoyed by the clients (132–4) and the patron (135–46), ending with a death-wish for the greedy millionaire, killed by the combination of his own meanness and extravagance. (He tried to digest a whole peacock, alone; and then to prepare for a second dinner. He dropped dead. Good.) Thus, 87–146 is a survey of the client's day, distorted by the new attitude to money which has appeared to corrupt Rome. G. Hirst (cited in n. 3), 66–67, well emphasizes that the whole passage is symmetrically constructed, on a chiastic pattern.

14. In this connexion I sometimes think of the piercing high E which breaks into the last movement of Smetana's quartet, *From My Life*: it was intended by the composer to image the unbearable sounds that rang through his head before the onset of the deafness in which his life closed.

15. At most, Roman satire sometimes made fun of some well-known eccentric who had just died and who was still remembered as living: Tigellius in Hor. *Serm.* 1. 2, Claudius in Seneca's *Apocolocyntosis*. And yet Juvenal's predecessor Turnus had written something about Nero and Locusta (see the scholion on Juv. 1. 71).

16. This point, that Juvenal chooses dead people as the symbols of *permanent* spiritual facts, is well made by A. T. Christ, *Ueber die Art und Tendenz der Juvenalischen Personenkritik* (Landskron, 1881).

17. So E. Epkema, *Prosopographiae Juvenalis pars prima* (Amsterdam, 1884); Ercole (*3*) 109–13; L. Friedländer, *De nominibus personarum in Juvenalis satiris* (Königsberg, 1872), and (*55*) 25 and 99–106; Peter (*28*); F. Strauch, *De personis Iuvenalianis* (Göttingen, 1869); and Teuffel (*38*).

NOTES ON CHAPTER VIII

1. *Sources and analogues.* I know of no extended treatment of the theme in Greek or Roman satire, strictly defined; but it was common enough for philosophers to mock and denounce pæderasty, and there are a number of ancient attacks on hypocrites who pretended to be strict moralists but secretly gave way to lust. See, for instance, Philo, *De specialibus legibus* 3. 37–42; Musonius in Stobaeus, *Anth.* (ed. Hense), 3, pp. 286–9; Lucian, *Fugitivi* 18, *Icaromenippus* 29, *Symposium* 15; the grave words of St. Paul in Romans i. 27; and an amusing attack on the Στύακες and παιδοπῖπαι by Hermeias of Curion in Athenaeus 13. 15. 563 d–e. The Cynics generally opposed pæderasty. On this there is a fine collection of material in G. A. Gerhard, *Phoinix von Kolophon* (Leipzig, 1909), 140–56; and on false Stoics see K. Praechter, *Hierokles der Stoiker* (Leipzig, 1901), 148–50. For all its repulsive subject, this satire is full of memorable epigrams, and was very often quoted by medieval poets and thinkers. For evidence of its wide popularity see S. Consoli, 'La satira II di Giovenale nella tradizione della cultura sino alla fine del medio evo', *RFIC* 42 (1914), 209–48. Modern imitations usually confine themselves to the theme of hypocrisy. It is sometimes said that Agrippa d'Aubigné drew from it when he wrote his pungent attacks on homosexuality at the court of the Valois: see *Les Tragiques* (ed. A. Garnier and J. Plattard, Paris, 1932), book 2, *Princes*. There are a few adaptations from Juvenal there, it is true: lines 23–24 are Juv. 1. 74; Bathyllus of 6. 63 appears in 934; the *double inceste* of 706 may be from *morbo utroque* of 2. 50; and probably the marriage contract of 825–6 owes something to the marriage ceremony in 2. 117 f.; but the most mordant descriptions, e.g. the portrait of Henri III in ball-dress, 773–96, and the account of the *mignons* in 1259–1318, are apparently based on d'Aubigné's personal observation and owe little or nothing to Juvenal, unless 1318 is a variation on Juv. 1. 38–39. The lines 1075–9 seem to have been drawn from the passage in Seneca quoted below in n. 5.

Date. As has been pointed out on pp. 10–11 and 235–6, Juvenal evidently worked slowly and thoughtfully, building up his poems piece by piece. The conception of the satire obviously came to him very early—probably with his first discovery that the Roman nobles who seemed so grand and who bore such proud names were really worthless. The wish to escape to the North Pole is so crude, and the tone of the work so violent, that he probably conceived it in his twenties. Agricola's campaigns (about A.D. 77–83) are fairly recent (see lines 159–61), and Domitian's censorship (taken in 85) is twice mentioned (63 and 121). One other sign which points to an early date for the conception of the poem is that here, and almost only here, Juvenal believes that Rome corrupts the outside world (2. 159–70). In other poems he believes that the outside world is corrupt and helps to corrupt Rome (3. 58–125, 6. 295–300, 14. 187–8, &c.). Of course, the *publication* of the satire in its present form, with its attack on Domitian, must be after 96, although not long after (*nuper* in 29). No doubt he recited it frequently before issuing Book I as a whole.

2. These four stages are:

(1) the hypocrites, 1–63
(2) the half-revealed homosexual, 64–81
(3) the secret society, 82–116
(4) Gracchus flaunting his shame, 117–48.

The fifth section, 149–70, is not an epilogue, but a climax. Though the main sections of this poem are clear enough, critics have not always seen that they form a climax. Both Gauger (*19*) 14 and Stegemann (*34*) 18–24 see only three parts: 1–63, 64–148, and 149–70. Friedländer (*55*) 162 and de Labriolle (*59*) 14 agree almost exactly in this scheme: (*a*) 1–35, (*b*) 36–63, (*c*) 64–82, (*d*) 83–116, (*e*) 117–42, (*f*) a 'Zusatz', 143–8, and (*g*) 149–70, Gylling (*20*) 14 f. finds four parts (1–35, 36–63, 64–142, and 149–70, cutting out 143–8 altogether). Ercole (*3*) 190–1 seems to make only three sections: 1–81, 82–116, and 117–70.

3. Juvenal knew very little about philosophy, especially at the rather early age when he conceived this satire: so he used Aristotle and Pittacus as impressive names, without really understanding whether they had any close relation to Stoicism or not. So also the phrase *Socratici cinaedi* (10) probably carries no difficult implications about the descent of Stoicism from the teachings of Socrates, but is merely a nasty allusion to the affection of Socrates for Alcibiades and others. However, Juvenal had learnt enough about Stoicism to use its own ideals to mock it: for instance, republicanism (*Curios*, 3; *Scauros*, 35), sternness (*tristibus*, 9; *atrocem animum*, 12; *rarus sermo*, 14), physical toughness (*hispida membra*, 11; *supercilio breuior coma*, 15; *hirsuto collo*, 41), and reverence for the heroic souls of the past (*uerbis Herculis*, 19–20; *tertius Cato*, 40). For a fuller treatment of this subject see Highet (*22*) 260–4.

4. Juv. 2. 82–116. The parodies of the *Aeneid* in 99–100 (from *Aen.* 3. 286 and 12. 94) emphasize the fact that Otho and his admirers were not heroes but heroines.

5. Juv. 2. 143–8. There is another peculiar transition from homosexuality to the arena, just like this, in Seneca, *N.Q.* 7. 31:

'id quod unum toto agimus animo nondum perfecimus—ut pessimi essemus. adhuc in processu uitia sunt . . . muliebres munditias antecessimus. colores mere-tricios matronis quidem non induendos uiri sumimus . . . cottidie comminiscimur per quae uirilitati fiat iniuria, ut traducatur quia non potest exui: alius genitalia excidit, alius in *obscenam partem ludi* fugit et locatus ad mortem *infame armaturae genus* in quo *morbum suum* exerceat legit.'

Juvenal was clearly very serious about the idea that the courage required to appear as a gladiator was negligible compared with the disgrace. In Satire 8, after describing different types of shameful behaviour indulged in by noble-men, he ends:

haec ultra quid erit nisi ludus?

and goes on to describe this same man, Gracchus, fighting as a *retiarius* (8. 199–210). Apparently a large part of the disgrace consists in the fact that Gracchus does not fight in armour which would partly or wholly conceal his identity. The light costume of the net-thrower shows him off to everybody unmistakably: so one of the atrocities of Commodus was that he took off his clothes before exhibiting himself as a gladiator and appeared 'wearing only a tunic and barefooted' (Dio 73. 17. 4). Further, it is implied that Gracchus chose to enter the arena as a net-thrower so that he could show off his pretty body partly undressed, and therefore that this was another part of his homosexual activity. It is clearly stated in the O fragment of Satire 6 (O 7–13) that the net-throwers were despised as *disgraceful* by the regular gladiators and were given the poorest quarters in the gladiatorial school. Housman saw this, in 'Tunica retiarii', *CR* 18 (1904), 395–8, but overstated his case, being partly answered by S. G. Owen, 'On the *tunica retiarii*', *CR* 19 (1905), 354–7.

6. Juv. 2. 149–59. The passage is very carefully worked. It begins with a parody of *Sunt aliquid manes* from Propertius 4. 7. 1, and goes on to a re-miniscence of the visit of Aeneas to the underworld (149–51 are inspired by Verg. *Aen.* 6. 296 and 302–3). Then the succeeding four lines are serious: *tot bellorum animae* is a fine phrase, of epic grandeur, and the roll-call of heroes echoes the pageant of Roman history in *Aen.* 6. 808–46.

7. Juv. 2. 159–70. This is the same kind of thought as appears in Tacitus' praise of the simple and uncorrupted people of the north in his *Germania* (see 18–20); but Juvenal has gone farther.

8. *Atrocem animum* in 2. 12 is a bitter parody of *atrocem animum Catonis* in Hor. *Carm.* 2. 1. 24. In general see G. Boissier, *L'Opposition sous les Césars* (Paris, *c.* 1921⁹), c. 2, § 4.

NOTES ON CHAPTER IX

1. *Sources, analogues, and adaptations.* The satire is mainly built on four sets of contrasts: city *v.* country, rich *v.* poor, Roman *v.* foreigner, and sincerity *v.* flattery. The first of these had already been treated by Horace (*Serm.* 2. 6, *Ep.* 2. 2. 65–80, and *Epod.* 2) and Martial (1. 49, 10. 70, 12. 18—addressed to Juvenal—and 12. 57), as well as by the rhetoricians (Seneca maior, *Controu.* 2. 1) and philosophers like Seneca (on whom see Schneider (*30*)

66–68). The contrast of rich and poor often appears in Horace, but Juvenal seems to owe most here to Martial (3. 38 and 4. 5). Similar feelings are expressed a generation later, not by a Roman but by a Greek, in Lucian's *Nigrinus*. It has been suggested that Lucian knew this satire and the Fifth, and, in his *De mercede conductis, Nigrinus*, and *Nekyomantia*, answered and supplemented them: so R. Helm, *Lucian und Menipp* (Leipzig, 1906), 218–22, and J. Mesk, 'Lucians Nigrinus und Juvenal', *WS* 34 (1912), 373–82 and 35 (1913), 1–32. But A. Hartmann, in 'Lucian und Juvenal', *Juvenes dum sumus* (Basel, 1907), 18–26, replies fairly convincingly that there is no connexion except community of experience and similarity of viewpoint. In his hatred of foreigners, particularly those from Greece and the East, Juvenal represents a long-standing tradition in Rome, and Cato is his chief ancestor. Flattery and parasitism were of course an old subject for comedians, psychologists, and satirists: they had already been treated in Latin by Ennius (*Poetae Romani ueteres*, ed. Diehl, Bonn, 1911, p. 47, fr. 379) and Horace (*Serm.* 2. 5). See O. Ribbeck's splendid study, 'Kolax', in *Abhandlungen der philologisch-historischen Claße der königlich sächsischen Gesellschaft der Wissenschaften*, 9 (1884), 1–113. The best-known *adaptations* of the poem are Wyatt, *Of the Courtier's Life*, Régnier 3 (*La Vie de la cour*), Boileau 1 (*Le Départ du poète*), Boileau 6 (*Les Embarras de Paris*), and Johnson's *London*.

2. Rev. xviii. 4–5 and 7–8. On the connexion between these denunciations and the fire of Rome in Nero's reign, with the ensuing persecution of the Christians, see L. Herrmann, 'Quels Chrétiens ont incendié Rome?', *RBP* 27 (1949), 633–51.

3. De Quincey, *Confessions of an English Opium-eater* (*Works*, ed. Masson, Edinburgh, 1890, vol. 3), 360 f. and especially 376; Cobbett, *Rural Rides*; Balzac, *Père Goriot* fin. Similar treatments of city life will be found in Dickens's *Bleak House*, Hugo's *Les Misérables*, France's *Thaïs*, Daudet's *Sapho* ('Oh! ce Paris! . . . ce qu'on lui donne et ce qu'il nous renvoie!'—c. 6 *fin.*), and Farrell's *Studs Lonigan*. Far more brutal and sordid city scenes than anything in Juvenal have recently been set down by two men who resemble him closely: George Orwell, in *Down and Out in Paris and London*, and Nelson Algren, in *The Man with the Golden Arm*. Algren lives in a sort of Subura in Chicago, and apparently both loves and loathes the city about which he writes. The quotation is from Eliot's *Waste Land* (61–65), embodying a quotation from Dante's *Inferno* (3. 56–57, lines describing the hopeless souls in Limbo).

4. When Florence was denounced by Savonarola she was very wealthy, ranked as a political power, and was aspiring to be a great city.

5. Rev. xviii. 4. See also the strange 'prophecy of Hystaspes': 'cum haec facta erunt, tum iusti et sectatores ueritatis segregabunt se a malis et fugient in solitudines' (Lactantius, *Diu. Inst.* 7. 17. 10), which is explained by H. Windisch, 'Die Orakel des Hystaspes', *Verhandelingen der koninklijke Akademie van Wetenschappen te Amsterdam, Afd. Letterkunde*, N.R. 28 (1929) 3; F. Cumont, 'La Fin du monde selon les mages occidentaux', *Revue de l'Histoire des Religions*, 103 (1931), 64 f.; and H. Fuchs, *Der geistige Widerstand gegen Rom* (Berlin, 1938), 31–35. Perhaps Mr. Fuchs goes too far in connecting the feeling of permanent loathing for city life with Jesus' prophecy of a single disaster to Jerusalem (Matt. xxix. 15 f., Mark xiii. 14 f., Luke xxi. 20 f.), Horace's desire to escape from war-torn Europe (*Epod.* 16), and Sertorius' wish to settle in the Canary Islands outside Roman dominion (Plut. *Sert.* 8–9; Sallust, *Hist.*, ed. Maurenbrecher, Leipzig, 1893, 1. 100–3). Still, these are interesting acts and utterances, and closely allied to this theme. W. L. Westermann, 'Concerning Urbanism and Anti-Urbanism in Antiquity', *Bulletin of the Faculty of Arts, Fouad I University*, 5 (Alexandria, 1949), 81–95, suggests that hatred of the great city is a comparatively late development and confined to Rome only, but perhaps he does not take full enough account of such negative evidence as pastoral poetry. There is something similar in the 'Potter's Prophecy', an Egyptian document which foretells that Alexandria, 'the City beside the sea, shall become a place where fishermen dry their nets' (E. Bevan, *A History of Egypt under the Ptolemaic Dynasty*, London, 1927, 240–1).

6. Martial left for Spain about 98, and his longest poem to Juvenal (12. 18), published about 101, is on the same theme as Juvenal 3—but seen from the other point of view, praising country life instead of denouncing the city. Of course Umbricius is not Martial: he was born in Rome (29 and 84–85) while Martial was born in Spain; he failed to make his way by *artes honestae* (21) while Martial was moderately successful through flattery and grossness and wit. But the basic situation is the same: farewell to an old friend leaving the city for a small country town. Umbricius also sounds like Alceste in the last act of Molière's *Misanthrope*:

> Je vais sortir d'un gouffre où triomphent les vices,
> Et chercher, sur la terre, un endroit écarté,
> Où d'être homme d'honneur on ait la liberté.

Indeed, Act 1, Scene 2 of the same comedy often reminds me of Juv. 3. 41 f. and 86 f.

7. The name Umbricius is common enough in inscriptions, one of which (*CIL* 10. 3142) comes from Puteoli, very near Cumae where Juvenal's friend is bound. It was also the name of a famous soothsayer of the previous generation or so (Pliny, *H.N.* 10. 6. 19, and see P. Wuilleumier's report of one of his inscriptions in *Bull. Soc. Nat. des Antiquaires de France*, 1929, 172–9), but that was not our Umbricius' vocation (see lines 42–45).

8. They live on the *sportula* (1. 119–20, 1. 132–4, 5. 2); they own slaves (3. 10 and 3. 167); when really starving, their horrid alternatives are either to beg in the streets (5. 6–11) or to go into speculative business (7. 4–12), since they are too old to join the army or become merchants or farmers (7. 32–33). But they never think of working day by day or adopting a profession, and they despise the Greeks who do (3. 76–78).

9. Juvenal at this time thought the Jews lived by begging (3. 16 means that the wood full of beggars has become a beggar itself; and see 3. 296 and 6. 543) together with the quackery of an absurd religion (6. 544–7, cf. 6. 159–60). It was only later that he saw them as a well-organized religious group with a long tradition (14. 96–106).

10. The quotations are from Coleridge's *Kubla Khan*. Juvenal has carefully worked out this passage in order that it may recall and contrast with a description of a beautiful natural cave beloved by another goddess, Ov. *Met.* 3. 157–62.

11. Compare 3. 21–28 with 1. 22–30, and note in particular the energy of the climaxes, each of them composed of four elements of increasing size and weight:

cum tener . . . spado	dum noua canities
Meuia . . . mamma	dum prima . . . senectus
patricios . . . sonabat	dum superest . . . torqueat
cum pars . . . gemmae	et pedibus . . . bacillo.

On the symmetry which balances the beginning of this poem against its end (and helps to justify *auditor* in 322) see G. Hirst, *Collected Classical Papers* (Oxford, 1938), 69–70.

12. It is Umbricius, not Juvenal, who was born in Rome (84–85) and is going to live in Cumae (321). Inferences about Juvenal's own birth drawn from lines 84–85 are therefore invalid. But the experiences of Umbricius coincide closely with those of Juvenal, even to the personal touches: the Subura (3. 5, cf. Mart. 12. 18. 1–2) and expulsion from the knights' seats (3. 153–9, cf. p. 57). G. Giri, 'Una satira di Giovenale e gli effetti delle letture pubbliche', *La Cultura*, 1 (1921–2), 539–5, points out that some of the elaborate descriptions are out of place in Umbricius' speech, and really show us Juvenal himself, addressing his audience.

13. The whole poem is beautifully balanced. Here is its structure:

Introduction 1–20.

Poverty 21–189:

   (*a*) honesty starves 21–57
   (*b*) foreigners oust Romans 58–125
   (*c*) poor men are helpless 126–89.

Discomfort and danger 190–314:

   (*a*) falling buildings and fires 190–231
   (*b*) crowds and traffic 232–67
   (*c*) accidents, fights, thefts, murders 268–314.

Epilogue 315–22.

There is a full and careful analysis of the structure of the poem in Hartmann (*21*) 31–64. Gauger (*19*) 20–25 suggests that the introduction goes down to 28, but in fact the break at 20 is unmistakable. Sydow (*37*) 14 points out that the two main parts of the poem are outlined by Juvenal in 6–9 and by Umbricius in 21–24.

14. Juv. 3. 33. *Praebere* is used by Juvenal only of offering part of one's own body: see 5. 172 and 10. 269–70. Mayor (*60*) 185 quotes Prop. 3. 20. 28 and Lucan 8. 614–15 for a similar use of *praebere caput*. The phrase apparently cannot mean 'sell slaves', and although that was a degrading task about which Martial often jokes, Juvenal never refers to it, his nearest allusion being to furniture auctioneers in 7. 9–12. These men therefore sell *themselves* as slaves. Why? Either because they have gone into a fraudulent bankruptcy and, after stowing away the profits, are sold up (so G. F. Schömann, 'Zu

Juvenalis 3, 33', *NJbb* 99 (1869), 765–7), or, more probably in my view, because they intend to take the money paid as their purchase-price, invest it on a sure thing, make a profit, and buy back their freedom again. The equivalent thing nowadays is the woman in James Jones's *From Here to Eternity* who became a prostitute in order to save money, retire early, and live as an independent lady. Juvenal's grudge against unworthy knights shows up once again in *munera nunc edunt* (3. 36), for only knights could give games: see J. W. Spaeth, 'Martial's equestrian cobbler', *CW* 37 (1943–4), 171–2.

15. Juv. 3. 41–57. This part of the speech is weakened by its assumption that a career means dependency, leaning on someone rich and powerful whom you must flatter or deceive (41–45) or assist in his vices and crimes (45–57).

16. Juv. 3. 58–125. Juvenal is here developing the stock character of the Flatterer (see n. 1), but he adds the personal touch that these Greek and Oriental flatterers are dangerous competitors for Roman clients.

17. We cannot tell whether Terence was a Negro or a Berber; but since his owner set him free *ob ingenium et formam*, and since Romans did not think Negro features handsome, we might infer that he was one of the fine-boned, sensitive, frail Berber types. On xenophobia in antiquity there is a useful study by T. J. Haarhoff, *The Stranger at the Gate* (Oxford, 1948[2]).

18. Cato's partial acceptance of Greek culture is shown by his use of Greek rhetorical figures in his speeches (E. Norden, *Die antike Kunstprosa*, Leipzig, 1898, 1. 165–8, queried, but unconvincingly, by R. Till, *Die Sprache Catos*, Phil Suppl. 28, 1935, 22), and his study of Greek literature late in life. Juvenal is here very like Cato: for although he detests the Greeks for their unscrupulousness, he still uses a lot of Greek words, and perforce recognizes the achievement of Greek artists and savants. On this see M. Bodendorff, *Persius Martialis Juvenalis quo modo de Graecis iudicent* (Königsberg, 1892).

19. See pp. 35–36. The names of the small towns mentioned in this poem show where Juvenal's heart lay: Praeneste, Gabii, and Tibur (190, 192) are in Latium, not far north of his own country, while Sora, Fabrateria, and Frusino (223–4) are Volscian towns only a few miles from Aquinum. Only Volsinii (191) in Etruria takes us a little farther away from his home.

20. G. Hirst (cited in n. 11) 81–82 suggests that the line about the pigeons (3. 202) is meant to add still another detail to the misery of the poor city-dweller—namely, the maddening noise of the birds. It is true that their cooing is echoed in

a pluuia, molles ubi reddunt oua columbae;

but both the echo and the adjective *molles* seem rather sympathetic. Perhaps, then, the detail is meant to emphasize the man's isolation, all alone at the top of the house without human company: instead of human conversation he has the rain on the roof and the birds' voices, while the fact that they at least have a family life increases his loneliness. But he does not hate them, any more than Codrus hates the 'philistine' mice which eat his books: 3. 207 is really quite a pleasant little joke. It is *men* who mistreat the city-dweller: see the climax in 209–11. When Umbricius moves to the country he will not (like Horace in *Serm.* 2. 6. 65 f.) enjoy talking to his neighbours, but he will have another sympathetic animal as his tenant (231).

21. Juv. 3. 190–231. Most of this theme, developed with such vigour and skill (a fine parody of Vergil in 198–9), is Juvenal's own; previous satirists do not mention it, and rhetoricians do not treat it with such vivid detail (De Decker (*18*) 36–38).

22. Small hours, 232–8; morning, 239–48; luncheon, 249–53; afternoon traffic, 254–61; bath and dinner, 261–7; after-dinner hours, 268–301; night, 302 f. Notice also that both the day section and the night section reach a climax in the threat of violent and unnatural death, the worst of the dangers of the city (257–67 and 305).

23. Juv. 3. 315–22. *Auditor* is the only sensible reading. When a villager has a friend who writes poetry, he may well promise to come 'as a listener' to the poems 'wearing country boots', but not 'as a junior officer in military uniform'. The former phrasing explains *ni pudet illas*: the satires are products of urban culture and might despise a countryman.

NOTES ON CHAPTER X

1. *Sources, analogues, and adaptations.* The chief source of Satire 4 is probably a heroic poem by Statius on Domitian's German wars (which Juvenal is parodying: see n. 12)—hence the numerous references to warfare (111–12, 124–8, 135, 146–9). Extended parody of epic is not very common in Greek and Roman satire. The best-known examples in Greek are *The Battle of Frogs and Mice* and the *Silloi* of Timon (ed. O. Wachsmuth, *Corpusculum poesis epicae graecae ludibundae*, 2, Leipzig, 1885²); and in Latin the first book of Lucilius, the *Council of the Gods*. O. Weinreich, 'Juvenals IV. Satire und Martial', in his *Studien zu Martial* (Stuttgart, 1928), 166–70, points out that Juvenal is also mocking the poems which flattered Domitian as a miracle-working god who possessed superhuman power over animals (65–71): see, for instance, Martial 4. 30, which tells how a poacher who hooked one of Domitian's pet fish was instantly struck blind. There is more on this theme in c. 17 of F. Sauter's *Der römische Kaiserkult bei Martial und Statius* (*Tübinger Beiträge*, 21, Stuttgart, 1934); and see cc. 6–14 of K. Scott's *The Imperial Cult under the Flavians* (Stuttgart, 1936). Further, the satire contains themes drawn from the literature of gourmandise, of which poetic examples remain in Archestratus' *Hedypatheia* (ed. P. Brandt, in vol. 1 of the *Corpusculum* mentioned above), in a fragment of its adaptation, the *Hedyphagetica* of Ennius, and in Hor. *Serm.* 2. 4. Martial has a couplet (13. 81) on the central theme, a turbot too big for its dish; and another (14. 97) on a gold platter for a surmullet. Lastly, the story about the fisherman who catches a phenomenal fish and takes it to his monarch appears in Herodotus 3. 42. As for modern adaptations, I have met with none of any importance, doubtless because the satire is on such an odd subject.

2. Introduction, 1–36 (anecdotes of Crispinus, 1–27; transition, 28–36); story, 37–154 (narrative, 37–149; conclusion, 150–4). Some critics have found it impossible to see any connexion between the two parts of this poem. Ribbeck (*49*) 76–83 rejects the whole introduction. Gylling (*20*) 38–45 suggests that an editor took a genuine fragment of Juvenal (1–27), attached it to the main body of the satire after Juvenal's death, and then forged 28–33 to make a bridge; but who could have written 28–33 except Juvenal himself? C. F. Nägelsbach, 'Ueber die composition der vierten und sechsten satire Juvenals', *Phil* 3 (1848), 469–82, was the first to point out that the two sections of the poem were linked because they both dealt with extravagant behaviour at Domitian's court and were both fish-stories. T. Birt, 'Der Aufbau der 6ten und 4ten Satire Juvenals', *RhM* 70 (1915), 524–50, added that Juvenal would feel quite justified in making such a loose transition as this because he was writing satire, which ought to sound like improvisation and casual conversation. Friedländer (*55*) 233–4 and Weidner (*63*) 63 both think that 1–27 are an early effort of Juvenal's, tacked on by himself. Ercole (*3*) 161–8 and de Labriolle (*59*) 37 both point out that the connexion between the two parts of the satire is no thinner than that between the elements of other satires, such as 2 and 11. Stegemann (*34*) 30–34 has an elaborate defence of the unity of the poem, pointing out that Juvenal begins with the crimes of Crispinus and goes on to his follies, then describes the folly of Domitian but ends with his crimes.

3. *Mullus* is the red mullet or surmullet (the *sur* is from the same root as 'sorrel' and means 'red'). See E. Préchac, 'De quelques animaux dans la littérature et dans l'art', *REL* 14 (1936), 102–5, and his note in *REL* 17 (1939), 279 explaining *mullorum iubis* in 6. 40; E. de Saint-Denis, 'Quelques noms de poissons en latin classique', *EtCl* 12 (1943–4), 129–51; and D'Arcy Thompson, *A Glossary of Greek Fishes* (*St. Andrews University Publications*, 45, London, 1947), 264–8. There are a number of references to the high prices paid for the fish and the passion for serving it fresh—indeed, bringing it in alive and watching it die: see A. C. Andrews, 'The Roman craze for surmullets', *CW* 42 (1948–9), 186–8.

4. The immortal gourmet Anthelme Brillat-Savarin was once confronted with exactly the same problem, a giant turbot too big for any available pot. He solved it by improvising a steamer out of the laundry-boiler: see his *Physiologie du Goût* (Paris, 1865), 330–4, and note how strikingly the protest of Montanus in 4. 131 (*absit ab illo / dedecus hoc!*) corresponds to the cry of the hostess to her husband when he proposed to chop up the fish: 'Oserais-tu bien déshonorer ainsi cette pauvre créature?'

5. Because of the reference to the Chatti as dangerous and to the general atmosphere of war on the northern frontiers (146–9), the incident described in the poem is dated to 82–83 by J. Asbach, 'Die Consularfasten der Jahre 68–96 n. Chr.', *BonnJbb* 79 (1885), 135 f.; and see his 'Die Kaiser Domitian und Traian am Rhein' (*Westdeutsche Zeitschrift*, 3, 1884, 5) and his review of K. H. Zwanziger's *Der Chattenkrieg des Kaisers Domitian* in *Westdeutsche Zeitschrift*, 5 (1886), 369–70, giving the date 83 for the war with the Chatti— apparently accepted by R. Syme in *CAH* 11. 162–4, and by S. Gsell, *Essai sur le Règne de l'empereur Domitien* (*Bibliothèque des Écoles Françaises d'Athènes et de Rome*, 65), 184–7. Now this council took place in the autumn verging towards winter (lines 56–57), and the Chatti were threatening, not defeated (146–9). Therefore it took place in the autumn of 82. By a curious chance

we have a record of a council which Domitian held in his Alban palace on 22 July 82: the subject was a small legal dispute, and the meeting was attended both by senators and (as here) by knights, *adhibitis utriusque ordinis splendidis uiris*: CIL 9. 5420. It is very possible that Juvenal was at this time waiting about the place in hope of promotion (see p. 39) and during these months conceived the first idea of his poem, which was later to be strengthened by the despised triumphs of Domitian and the appearance of Statius' poem. (Statius won a prize for it at Domitian's Alban contest, and felt this as one of the peaks of his career: see *Silu.* 5. 2. 65–67.)

6. See E. Fraenkel, *Plautinisches im Plautus* (*Philologische Untersuchungen*, 28, Berlin, 1922), 248 on Plautus, *Captiui*, 901–8; Petr. 69. 6–70. 3, cf. 49; pork as the regular food of old Rome in Juv. 11. 83–84, as the food of the vulgar in his own time, 11. 81.

7. Sen. *N.Q.* 3. 18. 2: 'mirabamur tantum illis inesse fastidium ut nollent adtingere nisi eodem die captum, qui (ut aiunt) saperet ipsum mare: ideo cursu aduehebatur', &c.

8. Juvenal begins by saying *Ecce iterum Crispinus!* in a half-conscious reminiscence of Hor. *Serm.* 1. 4. 13–14. Editors have used a good deal of space in discussing whether *iterum* can possibly mean 'for the second time' after the first appearance of Crispinus in 1. 26–29. Several of them (e.g. Ercole (*3*) 162) point out that Satire 4 was probably conceived and written before Satire 1, and infer that these words must allude to some other attack on Crispinus, now lost. But they forget that Juvenal published his first five satires as a Book, and that he therefore intended Satire 1 and Satire 4 to be read in their present order—so that *iterum* can look back to nothing except the short, emphatic beginning of Satire 1. There is another difficulty in the sentence, which is that Juvenal adds that he intends to write more satirical poetry about Crispinus. If he ever did so, he did not publish it in any form transmitted to us: doubtless because his public grew tired of hearing about Domitian and Domitian's court.

9. The loincloth, 4. 24; the catfish, 4. 32–33. *Silurus* is apparently the 'shall', a cousin of the genuine silurus, and a foul feeder whose coarse flesh is eaten only by the very poor in Egypt. The great silurus does not live in the Nile, but other types of catfish do (D'A. W. Thompson, cited in n. 3, pp. 236 and 47). The contempt in Juvenal's *municipes* (= 'dirty Egyptian') I could render only by bringing in mud.

10. Gsell (cited in n. 5), 61, n. 6 observes that the Romans were fond of curiosities and that Domitian might well have shown the phenomenal fish to his 'friends', without making the council ridiculous. The story in Juvenal may therefore be based on a real incident, which he has interpreted in his own way.

11. Epic cadences 39, 44, 62–64, 68, 108; lofty phraseology 29, 40, 45, 60–61, 65–66, 68–69, 81, 107 (a parody of epic periphrasis), 112, 123–4, 130–5, 144–5. All this is well developed by Scott (*32*). Juvenal tells Calliope to sit down and talk normally (34–35) because epic poets always tell her to stand up and sing—Verg. *Aen.* 9. 525–8 and Stat. *Theb.* 4. 34–38.

12. Valla's note on 4. 94 in his edition is apparently taken from the scholia which he was using, and which are now lost:

Acilius Glabrionis filius consul sub Domitiano fuit, Papirii Statii carmine de bello Germanico, quod Domitianus egit, probatus:

> lumina, Nestorei mitis prudentia Crispi,
> et Fabius Veiento—potentem signat utrumque
> purpura, ter memores implerunt nomine fastos—
> et prope Caesareae confinis Acilius aulae.

Compare line 1 with Juv. 4. 81, *Crispi iucunda senectus*: both the epic periphrasis and the characterization are the same. F. Buecheler, 'Coniectanea', *RhM* 39 (1884), 283–5, suggested that *lumina* could have been part of a phrase referring to the blind Catullus (*orbatus lumina*, for instance; cf. Juv. 4. 113–18). Veiento occurs in Juv. 4. 113; and Acilius, close to Crispus, in 4. 94. Later, the phrase *dux magnus* (4. 145) is one which Statius in an extant poem uses with reverent seriousness of Domitian (*Silu.* 3. 1. 62): see c. 11 of Sauter (cited in n. 1) on its significance.

13. This interpretation is due to O. Weinreich, cited in n. 1. However, Mr. Weinreich perhaps goes too far in suggesting that *facili cardine* in 63 means the door opened miraculously: it simply means that the imperial household was ready and willing to receive the gift, and that anything which flattered Domitian would get in at once, while Roman senators had to stand and wait: 'exclusi spectant admissa obsonia patres' (64).

14. This is one of the earliest documents on the Roman imperial Cabinet. For a full discussion see E. Cuq, 'Mémoire sur le *Consilium principis* d'Auguste à Dioclétien', in *Mémoires présentés . . . à l'Académie des Inscriptions*, 1ᵉ série, 9 (1884), 2. 311–504, especially 217–322; and J. B. Mispoulet, 'Le Turbot', *RevPhil* 13 (1889), 32–44. Prosopographical discussions of the chief personages in the satire will be found in B. Borghesi, 'Annotazioni alle satire di Giovenale', *Œuvres complètes*, 5 (Paris, 1869), 509–34, S. Gsell (cited in n. 5), and *PIR*. Here is a summary of the essentials:

(1) PEGASUS (4. 77); *consul suffectus* under Vespasian (Gaius 1. 31 and 2. 254; *Inst.* 2. 23. 5); governor of many provinces (schol. Juv. ad loc.) and *praefectus urbi* under Vespasian (Pomponius, *Dig.* 1. 2. 2. 53); a distinguished legal authority, who succeeded Proculus as the head of his law school. His strange name, the scholiast says, came from the device on the ensign of his father's pinnace; his others are unknown.

(2) Q. VIBIUS CRISPUS (4. 81): *consul suffectus* under Nero in 61 (Borghesi 520) and consul three times (so says Statius in the fragment cited in n. 12); boon companion of Vitellius (Dio 64. 2. 3); governor of Africa about 71 (Pliny *N.H.* 19, prooem. 4); Borghesi 434; *pecunia, potentia, ingenio inter claros magis quam inter bonos*, says Tacitus austerely (*Hist.* 2. 10). J. Asbach, 'Die Consularfasten der Jahre 68–96 n. Chr.', *BonnJbb* 79 (1885), 118, suggests he was consul together with Veiento in March 83.

(3) ACILIUS GLABRIO senior (4. 94): now about 80 years old (92–94), he is possibly the M'. Acilius Aviola who was consul in 54, and changed his name (so Groag in *PIR*, s.v.).

(4) M'. ACILIUS GLABRIO (4. 95), son of (3), was to become consul along with Trajan in 91 (*CIL* 6. 1988, Dio 67. 12. 1, Fronto *Ad Marc.* 5. 22 and 23), and was probably a praetor or ex-praetor at this time. Domitian, apparently suspecting him but having nothing concrete against him, tried to

kill him by ordering him to fight bears and/or a huge lion (Dio 67. 14. 3), which he did with success. But then he was exiled as a revolutionary (Suet. *Dom.* 10. 2) and in 95 executed on the additional charge of 'atheism and . . . Jewish customs' (Dio. 67. 14. 2–3). This might be a periphrasis for a conversion either to Judaism or to Christianity; and since in the catacomb of Priscilla a funeral chamber has been found, dating to the second century, with inscriptions near by bearing the names of Acilius Glabrio, it is known that his descendants became Christians and it is likely that he himself was one. It is strangely moving to think of this gallant man fighting with beasts under the eye of Domitian and conquering them, only to die in exile later. Juvenal speaks of him with as much sympathy as he can muster for any aristocrat. On the funeral chamber see P. Styger, *Die römischen Katakomben* (Berlin, 1933), 100–12. The suggestion that Acilius was a Christian convert is questioned by K. Friedmann, 'Ancora sulla persecuzione di Domiziano', *Atene e Roma*, n.s. 12 (1931), 69–83, on grounds which do not seem very compelling.

(5) RUBRIUS GALLUS (4. 105) was an experienced general who commanded for Nero against Galba (Dio 63. 27. 1), and then for Otho against Vitellius, apparently leading the praetorian guard (Tac. *Hist.* 2. 51); finally he took up the cause of Vespasian (ibid. 99), who made him governor of Moesia and used him against the Sarmatians (Josephus, *Bell. Iud.* 7. 92). The scholiast on this line says he seduced Domitia (apparently meaning Domitia Longina, the empress) when she was a girl.

(6) MONTANUS (4. 107, 130–43). In 66 a certain Curtius Montanus was expelled from the senate for lampooning Nero, but because of his father's pleading he escaped exile or death (Tac. *Ann.* 16. 33). Since the old gourmet here is described as a friend of Nero's (137), he was probably the father. After the Flavian victory, the son appeared in the senate again, making violently anti-monarchic speeches (Tac. *Hist.* 4. 40, 42–43). It is a familiar combination, the soft, self-indulgent father and the excitable, high-principled, revolutionary son. A T. Iunius Montanus was *consul suffectus* in 81 (*CIL* 6. 328)—perhaps this man.

(7) CRISPINUS (4. 108), *princeps equitum* in 4. 32 and therefore apparently *praefectus praetorio* together with Fuscus (9). Juvenal says he was an Egyptian and rose from poverty. But it should be emphasized that there is little external evidence for his rank or his existence—no inscription bearing his name, and only two epigrams by Martial. One of these (7. 99), dating to A.D. 92, flatters him as a confidant of the god-emperor; the other (8. 48) says that someone stole his purple cloak (cf. Juv. 1. 27). Both treat him rather more familiarly than one would expect if he were commander of the household troops; and O. Hirschfeld, *Untersuchungen auf dem Gebiete der römischen Verwaltungsgeschichte*, 1 (Berlin, 1877), 223, felt sure that he was only an imperial secretary. I have sometimes wondered also whether Crispinus might not be a false name given him by Juvenal, on the model of the praetorian prefect who served under Claudius (Tac. *Ann.* 11. 1. 3, 11. 4. 5).

(8) POMPEIUS (4. 110). Almost wholly unknown. A Cn. Pompeius Ferox Licinianus was consul in an unknown year (*CIL* 6. 468); Borghesi (524–6) suggests he may be this man.

(9) FUSCUS (4. 112): Cornelius Fuscus left the senatorial for the equestrian order at the beginning of his career; supported Galba and became governor of Pannonia, then backed Vespasian (Tac. *Hist.* 2. 86). He was made *praefectus praetorio* by Domitian (Joannes Lydus, *de magistratibus* 2. 19, 3. 22), and commanded in the second Dacian war of 86–87, during which he was killed in a tremendous disaster (Suet. *Dom.* 6. 1, Dio 67. 6 and 68. 9; his epitaph in Mart. 6. 76). See Gsell 209–15.

(10) VEIENTO (4. 113): A. Didius Gallus Fabricius Veiento was praetor early in Nero's reign (Dio 61. 6. 2) and was expelled from Italy in 62 for writing a mock will full of libels against senators and priests (Tac. *Ann.* 14. 50). Under Domitian he was a well-known informer (Aur. Victor, *Epitome* 12. 5), but survived his reign and was found dining cheek by jowl with Nerva, to the rage of more honourable guests (Pliny, *Ep.* 4. 22. 4) and speaking in a prominent position in the senate (ibid. 9. 13. 13, 9. 13. 19–20). In his third consulship he set up a bronze inscription to Nemetona, a local deity of Mainz, which he was perhaps visiting on business connected with Domitian's German war (*ILS* 1010; Mommsen in *Westdeutsche Zeitschrift, Korrespondenzblatt,* 3 (1884), cols. 86–88, and 12 (1893), cols. 124–5). Statius, in the fragment cited in n. 12, says he was consul for the third time together with Crispus, apparently in 83. Statius calls him Fabius, doubtless as a polite allusion to his political skill (*prudens*, says Juvenal). A man of the same name is mentioned as rich and haughty in Juv. 3. 185. In 6. 82–113 Juvenal tells the story of a senator's wife called Eppia who ran away with a gladiator, and brings in the name Veiento at the end. Either he means that Veiento was notably ugly or he implies that he was her rejected husband. The inscription gives his wife's name as Attica; but Juvenal could easily have used Eppia as a metrical substitute (see p. 291).

(11) CATULLUS (4. 113): L. Valerius Catullus Messallinus, consul in 79 with Domitian (see *PIR*, s.v.); a notorious delator (Aur. Vict. *Epit.* 12. 5), who did not outlive Domitian (Pliny, *Ep.* 4. 22. 5–6, Tac. *Agr.* 45).

The Cabinet is therefore composed of twelve men: Domitian; the two praetorian prefects, Crispinus and Fuscus; and nine senators, all but one (Acilius junior) apparently of consular rank. Three of these—Catullus, Pompeius, Veiento—are strong supporters of Domitian; three more are skilful and accommodating administrators—Crispus, Montanus, Pegasus; and three are endangered by the emperor's suspicions—Rubrius Gallus and the two Acilii, who were later to suffer death and bereavement.

15. M. P. Charlesworth in *CAH* 11. 26–27 implies that Domitian was used by the *delatores* instead of using them, and that he began to listen to them only after the conspiracy of Saturninus in 88. This may be, but it is a kindly interpretation of Suet. 10. 5 and Dio 67. 11. 2.

16. There is an even more bizarre story about a party Domitian gave to the foremost senators and knights, frightening them almost literally to death, in Dio 67. 9. For the pallor of his friends see lines 74–75 and 104 in this satire; their haste, 75–76 and 94; their courtesy appears in the elaborate periphrasis which Montanus substitutes for a blunt 'No' in 130–1; and note the flattery of Domitian's generalship in 124–8, even in *castra*, 135.

17. 4. 153–4. Tillemont and others believed that *cerdones* meant the

Christians, as humble folk, and that Juvenal was describing God's vengeance on Domitian as a persecutor; but F. Görres, 'Zur kritik einiger quellen- schriftsteller der römischen kaiserzeit', *Phil* 41 (1882), 719–31, shows this to be absurd.

NOTES ON CHAPTER XI

1. *Sources, analogues, and adaptations.* The theme of dinner and hospitality (humble, vulgar, luxurious, or mean) was a favourite with satirists: see L. R. Shero, 'The *Cena* in Roman satire', *CP* 18 (1923), 126–43 and Hartmann (*21*) 65–67. Here Juvenal may be following Lucilius book 30, frg. 1060 f. But his friend Martial had been subjected to similar humiliations and had written epigrams on them (3. 49, 3. 60, 4. 68. 4. 85, 6. 11). The younger Pliny also comments on the topic in *Ep.* 2. 6. After Juvenal, Lucian treated the same theme in *Cronosolon* 17–18, *Epistulae Saturnales* 3, *Nigrinus* 22, and with particular emphasis in *De Mercede Conductis* 26. (On the possible connexion of Lucian's and Juvenal's work see p. 296.) There is a very funny variation on the subject by Régnier, 'Le Souper ridicule', his 10th satire; a politer one by Boileau, his 3rd; an adaptation by Joseph Hall, the 2nd in his 5th book of satires; a translation by Chapman published in 1629; a powerful expan- sion by Oldham; and an amusing little piece by Addison in *The Tatler* (255, 23–25 November 1710) on a domestic chaplain who was discharged for pre- suming to stay at table and share dessert with My Lord and My Lady.

2. The name Virro is extremely rare. We know of only two or three men who possessed it, the most eminent being Vibidius Virro, a spendthrift wastrel whom Tiberius expelled from the Senate in A.D. 17 (Tac. *Ann.* 2. 48. 3). R. Syme, 'Personal names in *Annals* I–VI', *JRS* 39 (1949), 17, dis- cusses the name and suggests that the ex-senator was a Paelignian: if so, he lived only forty miles or so from Juvenal's birthplace Aquinum. Juvenal uses it again in 9 for a revolting pervert; but there too one of the main themes is the relation between patron and client. As for the poor dependant in this satire, his name is Trebius; and the same name occurs several times in Aquinum (*CIL* 10. 5528 and 5529).

3. Here is an analysis of the poem:

(1) Introduction, 1–11;
(2) Invitation and place at table, 12–23;
(3) Drinks, dishes, and service, 24–65 (line 66 is spurious);
(4) Bread, 67–79;
(5) Fish, 80–106;
(6) A pause, and a parenthesis, 108–13;
(7) Game and truffles (but none for the clients, who are shown still *hoping* in 166–9), 114–24;
(8) Conversation and sociability, 125–45;
(9) Dessert, 146–55;
(10) Conclusion, 156–73.

Gylling (*20*) 50–51 is surely wrong in describing 1–23 as a 'double prologue', of which 1–11 treat of 'the vileness of parasites' and 12–23 explain 'why they are eventually invited to dine'. *Primo fige loco* in 12 indicates very clearly that Juvenal is not prologuizing but beginning a point-by-point description. For a more detailed analysis of the satire see Hartmann (*21*) 65–92. One of Juvenal's best jokes is his studied omission of the main course from the clients' dinner, with the long hungry wait, *interea*, from 114 to 169. Yet this has been misunderstood by some editors, who think there must be a gap in the manuscripts (so Ribbeck, 49, 141, corrected by H. Wirz, *Zur Kritik der fünften Satire Juvenal's*, Aarau, 1868, 4–5). There is indeed a lacuna; but it is in the clients' bellies.

4. The poem is a *suasoria*—or, more exactly, a λόγος ἀποτρεπτικός. The point Juvenal is urging (*propositio*) is made in lines 1–11; the reasons why his hearer should accept it (*tractatio*) occupy 12–155; and 156–73 serve as a final clinching reason, equivalent to a *conclusio*. Thus, *quis enim tam nudus?* (163) recalls lines 6–11, and *pulsandum . . . flagra pati* (171–3) takes up the theme of lines 3–4.

5. Juv. 5. 8. *Crepido* is a sidewalk, a stretch of pavement in a main street (Petr. 9), where a beggar can establish himself more permanently and accost more passers-by than in a little side-street: in the Middle Ages this would be the church steps, and nowadays a street-corner.

6. Hartmann (*21*) 70–71 points that, if the patron handed out the dole regularly, he was under no obligation to invite his clients to dinner *also*; and that Juvenal, by such touches as *duos post menses* and *tertia ne cessaret culcita* (5. 15–17), has distorted the gratuitous invitation into a duty ungraciously performed. Still, Juvenal hated the *sportula*, and never thought of it as an adequate substitute for the dinner which, in the old days, client and patron used to share as friends.

7. *Vertice raso* in 5. 171 is the mark of the *stupidus* in the mimes, the idiotic *morio* of private dinner-parties (Pliny, *Ep.* 9. 17; Lucian, *Convivium* 18; Tert. *De Spectaculis* 23); and *pulsandum* refers to the *alapae* of Juv. 8. 192 and Mart. 2. 72. A clown act called 'The Three Stooges', which used to appear in short film farces during the 1940's, had a perfect *stupidus* in it, a burly man with a head clipped or shaven smooth, who was always being slapped on it by his quicker and cleverer fellow stooges.

8. See Juv. 5. 111–13. This little paragraph, 107–13, has often been called 'out of place', e.g. by Friedländer (*55*) 257; but it is Juvenal's method of reproaching the host, placed here to balance his final reproach to the guest (156–73). Many critics have objected to it because it interrupts the sequence of courses in the dinner—which is exactly why Juvenal put it in, as a relief to an otherwise rather too regular and predictable sequence. Also, it marks a pregnant pause in the banquet, just before the appearance of the main dishes. And lastly, it prepares the idea of the host's deliberate cruelty, which reappears in 120, which is enhanced by the contrast in 125–45, and which is finally worked out in 156–60.

NOTES ON CHAPTER XIII

1. Poor wives, 6. 72 and 582–91; the extravagant wife, 6. 352–65; social prominence, 6. 80–81, 82 f., 161–83, 385–8, 602–9. Unmarried girls are not mentioned. Neither are the demi-mondaines who fill the pages of the elegiac poets—because it does not matter how CloClo and FrouFrou and the other girls from Maxim's behave, whereas Eppia (82) and Manilia (243) and the others are ladies who owe a duty to society.

2. *Sources, analogues, and adaptations.* Quintilian says (*Inst. Or.* 3. 5. 8) that there were two ways of discussing marriage, general and particular: *an uxor ducenda?* and *an Catoni ducenda?* That is, it could be debated whether marriage was a good thing for anyone, and also whether it was a good thing for the wise man. Therefore there are two main currents of thought in this controversy during antiquity, one popular and the other philosophical. (The third, the rhetorical current, takes arguments from both the other two.) Juvenal 6 naturally uses the popular ideas most, but some of the philosophers' arguments also appear.

The popular theme of the pride, greed, deceitfulness, and viciousness of women enters Greek literature (as noted on p. 92) with Hesiod (*Op.* 50–105). It recurs in bourgeois contexts in Semonides (E. Diehl, *Anth. Lyr. Graec.*, Leipzig, 1925, 1. 248–53), Aristophanes (esp. *Lysistrata, Thesmophoriazusae, Ecclesiazusae*), and Herodas (Mimes 5 and 6). Evidently there were many anthologies of hard sayings against women collected from the poets (Euripides and Menander were favourites) and some also in praise of marriage: see, for example, *Berliner Klassikertexte*, 5 (ed. W. Schubart and U. von Wilamowitz-Moellendorff, Berlin, 1907), no. 20; *Disticha Argentinensia*, ed. O. Plasberg, *ArchP* 2 (1903), 185–96; Clement of Alexandria, *Strom.* 2. 23. 137–43, and see *Protr.* 11. 11. 113. 1 f.; Stobaeus, *Anth.* (ed. C. Wachsmuth, Berlin, 1884), vol. 4, cc. 22–23. Centuries after Juvenal, the topic of woman as man's plague recurs in the bitter epigrams of Palladas (*AP* 9. 165–8). In Latin it appears in satire (Lucilius, frg. 279–83, 504–5, 678–86, and 990–1007; Varro, frg. 166–8; Petron. 111–12); comedy (e.g. Caecilius Statius from Menander, O. Ribbeck, *Scaen. Rom. Poes. Frag.* 2, Leipzig, 1898³, pp. 68–72); mime (Publilius Syrus, ibid., pp. 369–70); and romance (Apul. *Met.* 9. 5–7, 9. 14–31, 10. 2. 12).

In philosophy there were of course many general discussions of the state of marriage: see Xenophon, *Oec.* 7–10, and Plutarch, *Praecepta Coniugalia*, for examples. Theophrastus wrote a book, or part of a book, on it (περὶ γάμου or περὶ βίων), regarding it unfavourably, and some of his ideas were taken over by Seneca in the lost *De matrimonio*, which was copied by Juvenal and later by Jerome *Aduersus Iouinianum*. See F. Bock, *Aristoteles Theophrastus Seneca de matrimonio* (*Leipziger Studien*, 19, 1899, 1–70), and further parallels in J. Van Wageningen, 'Seneca et Iuuenalis', *Mnem* n.s. 45 (1917), 417–29. However, K. Praechter, *Hierokles der Stoiker* (Leipzig, 1901), Exkurs, ii, 121–50, and E. Bickel, *Diatribe in Senecae philosophi fragmenta*, i (Leipzig, 1915), have shown that the main current of thought in Seneca is Stoical in origin; and that on the whole the Stoics were the supporters of marriage among the philosophers. They also condemned pæderasty: so that Juvenal's remark in 6. 33–37 is the reverse of Stoic doctrine, putting him rather with the Cynics or the Epicureans. See Highet (*22*) 260–4 for a further discussion of his antipathy to Stoicism; and for other references to the theme, particularly in philosophical literature, Gauger (*19*) 41–50 and Schuetze (*31*), c. 8.

The wisdom or unwisdom of marriage is mentioned as a theme for rhetoric by Sulpicius Victor, *Inst. Or.* 3; Theon, *Progymnasmata*, 12; Hermogenes, *Prog.* 11; and fully discussed by Aphthonius, *Prog.* 13, who comes down heavily in favour of marriage. (Yet even so he scarcely praises women as such, confining himself mainly to eulogies of family life.) See also De Decker (*18*) 23–29.

On the truth or falsity of the poem there are discussions by E. Barthélemy, 'Juvénal et les femmes', *Mercure de France*, 144 (15 Dec. 1920); C. T. Harris, 'Juvenal's Sixth Satire' (Columbia University thesis, 1949, unpublished); F. Poulsen, *Glimpses of Roman Culture* (tr. J. Dahlmann-Hansen, Leyden, 1950), c: 6, with charming illustrations; M. Quartana, 'Giovenale, la sua satira e le donne', *Atene e Roma*, 22 (1919), 198–214; and N. Vianello, 'La sesta satira di Giovenale', *Historia*, 4 (1930), 747–75.

Adaptations of parts of the poem and quotations from it have always been numerous. The ferocious line 130 and the epigram 460 (which may not be Juvenal's own) were often cited. Imitations appear in *Le Roman de la Rose* (ed. E. Langlois, Paris, 1921)—for details see p. 311, n. 15; the *Corbaccio* of Boccaccio; Quevedo, *Riesgos del matrimonio*; d'Aubigné, *Les Tragiques* 2 (*Princes*), 1011–18; Boileau 10; E. Young, *Love of Fame*, 5 and 6; Fielding's modernization of 1–300 in Hudibrastic octosyllables, written before he was 20 as 'all the revenge taken by an injured lover' and his later letter *To a Friend on the Choice of a Wife*; and finally in the *Lettre à une Femme* sent out of besieged Paris by Victor Hugo through the balloon-post (*L'Année Terrible: Janvier*, ii), which compares the Parisian women to the women of Rome when Hannibal was at the gates.

P. Grenade has proposed that the last lines of the poem allude to the report that Trajan was poisoned by his wife Plotina (Dio 68. 33) and perhaps appeared in a posthumous edition for safety's sake (*REL* 28, 1951, 50). This seems to me wildly improbable, particularly since it spoils the point of the poem: poison is common in palaces, but now that Roman women are corrupt the horror has spread to every street.

3. So Ribbeck (*49*), followed by a few scholars such as X. Prinz, 'Quelques passages de Juvénal', *RIPB* 9 (1866), 1–9, 69–79, and 10 (1867), 1–20, 85–103. Ribbeck wrote a special paper attempting to justify his excisions and rearrangements in this particular satire: 'De Iuvenalis satira sexta', in *Symbola philologorum Bonnensium in honorem F. Ritschelii collecta* (Leipzig, 1864–7), 1–30. His work called out a flood of rejoinders, which (although now largely obsolete) benefited the study of Juvenal because they were based on careful analysis of Juvenal's style. Such were M. J. Hofmann, *Zur Kritik und Erklärung einiger Satiren des Juvenal* (Amberg, 1878); *Vindiciae Juvenalianae* by B. Lupus (Bonn, 1864) and O. Meinertz (Königsberg, 1866) together with Meinertz's *Zur Kritik und Erklärung der Satiren des Juvenal* (Konitz, 1871); W. Schulz, *Quaestionum Juvenalianarum caput primum* (Leipzig,

1885) and his 'Quaestiones Iuvenalianae' (part of the same work) in *Hermes*, 21 (1886), 179–92; and Weise (*39*), who is still useful.

4. This is the suggestion of Teuffel (*38*) and Leo (*46*). It has been controverted by R. Clauss, *Quaestiones criticae Juvenalianae* (Leipzig, 1912); G. Mosengel, *Vindiciae Juvenalianae* (Leipzig, 1887); G. Schoenaich, *Quaestiones Iuvenalianae* (Halle, 1883), which also answers Ribbeck on Satire 6 (see n. 3); Sydow (*37*); and Vahlen (*51*). Of course this theory is not the same as the well-based hypothesis that two different editions of Juvenal's work were published when he was rediscovered in late antiquity, long after his death: on this, see pp. 185–8.

5. Thus, de Labriolle (*4*) 125 says that 6 is 'une suite de morceaux'; Friedländer (*55*) 278 declares that most of it is composed of '26 Abschnitte ... die nicht bloß roh, äußerlich oder gar nicht verbunden sind, sondern auch großthentheils eines innern durch Zusammenstellung des Gleichartigen oder Verwandten herzustellenden Zusammenhanges entbehren'; and Gauger (*19*) 41 complains that 'eine feste Disposition kann ja auch gar nicht in J.s Absicht gelegen haben'.

6. This is the chief point made by De Decker (*18*) and Gauger (*19*). J. Bergmueller, *Quaestiones Iuvenalianae* (Erlangen, 1886), shows that many formulae of transition and development in the satires come from the practice of orators. N. Salanitro, *Introduzione a Giovenale* (Naples, 1944), opposes the general thesis that Juvenal is a rhetorician, by pointing out that rhetoric is artificial and unrealistic while satire is sincere and lifelike, so that Juvenal is not 'rhetorical': an argument which looks painfully like begging the question. The undeniable truth that Juvenal had some rhetorical training and practice has often been exaggerated and mis-stated by those who did not realize that practically every educated man of his time had the same training (the work of the elder Seneca has several fascinating reminiscences of Ovid as a 'declaimer'). For instance, Alejandro Vicuña, *Juvenal* (Santiago, 1940), 221, asserts without a shadow of evidence that Juvenal actually became a professor of rhetoric, 'y desde allí dictamina profesorialmente'—which of course proves that he had no sincere convictions, but makes it difficult to understand how he could have had any pupils if he suffered from *incapacidad de análisis* and *ausencia de talento descriptivo* (p. 223).

7. Some of the satires move to a climax, crescendo (2, 3, and 6) or diminuendo (7 and 14), and the movement is always felt beneath the countercurrents that run through each poem. In smaller passages Juvenal often contrives to cover a theme completely by what at first sight seems to be a random selection of details. For instance, in 3. 232–314 he describes a complete twenty-four hours in the city (see pp. 74–75, and n. 22 on p. 256).

In 3. 69–70, throwing out names of places in Greece with apparent carelessness, he mentions six localities which sum up the whole Greek world—the peninsula, the islands, and the Asiatic coast. In 6. 306–13 he shows the women's scorn of chastity by describing first their expression, then their words, and last their actions. Stegemann (*34*), from whom this last example is taken, is good on the theme in general, though perhaps too much in love with easeful regularity. G. Hirst, *Collected Classical Papers* (Oxford, 1938), 65–73, points out some subtle and hitherto unremarked examples of the careful structure which underlies many of Juvenal's poems.

8. The chief sections of the poem, and the themes with which they deal, are:

(*a*) 1–132*: *women's unchastity makes marriage absurd.*

(*b*) 136–285: *married love is an illusion.* Here Juvenal makes the transition to a new topic quite clear by the violent contrast between the vile wife of Claudius (*turpis* and *foeda*, 131–2) and the superlative *optima*, as well as by the question (136), the first which Postumus has asked. But even here it is impossible to fit in two sections, 184–99 and 242–67, which seem to belong to section (*c*), all the more so because there is a very natural transition from 231–41 to 268 f.

(*c*) 286–351: *Roman women have been ruined by luxury.* The important question in 286 shows the opening of this section, and its close is indicated by the resumption of the theme of the virtuous past, from 288 (*quondam*, an emphatic initial spondee) to 342 f. (*tunc . . . sed nunc . . . iam*).

(*d*) 352–661: *the follies and crimes of women make marriage impossible.* Juvenal first gives nine types of foolish and offensive behaviour (352–591), showing in almost every case that it is the husband who suffers (*uir, tu,* or *maritus* in 360, O14, 377, 389, 400, 432, 456, 463, and 509). Then he moves on to four types of crime committed by wives (abortion and substitution of children, 592–609; drugging, 610–26 and 133–5; child-murder, 627–52; husband-murder, 652–61) The skeleton of the poem is therefore this:—

Juvenal says that it is ridiculous to marry; he answers the objection that marriage is sometimes made by love; he explains that women's nature makes marriage impossible; and he ends by saying that it is painful and may well be lethal. This is a good bold simple structure, ending in a powerful climax, and so resembling Satires 2, 3, and 5. But the chief difficulty in it is to find some reason for the arrangement of the various types of married women's folly, in 352–591, and here the manuscripts appear to have been badly disturbed.

There have been many other attempts to set out a scheme for this poem. Here are a few of the most plausible:

Birt (cited on p. 97):

(*a*) 1–132: *the disappearance of chastity.*
(*b*) 136–345: *the mistreatment of husbands.*
(*c*) 346–591: *the misbehaviour of wives to persons outside the family.*
(*d*) 592–661: *wives who commit crimes.*

Vianello (cited in n. 2, p. 265):

(*a*) 1–285: *the dishonour of women.*
(*b*) 286–378: *the causes of Roman degeneracy.*
(*c*) 379–473: *types of married women.*
(*d*) 474–591: *daily occupations of married women.*
(*e*) 592–661: *criminal and unnatural wives.*

* 133–5 are obviously misplaced, and must follow 626.

C. F. Nägelsbach, 'Ueber die composition der vierten und sechsten satire Juvenals', *Phil* 3 (1848), 469–82:

(*a*) 1–285: *marriage is impossible.*
(*b*) 286–300: *wealth has spoilt the Roman women.*
(*c*) 300–661 : *women are now hopelessly corrupt.*

(Naegelsbach points out that the movement is the same within the first and the third parts. Juvenal begins with the vices of women, then goes on to describe their defects and weaknesses, and finishes with the worst outrage possible—open adultery in 279–85, husband-murder in 652–61.) This is fundamentally the scheme adopted by Stegemann (*34*) 36–66, whose entire dissection of the poem is well worth studying. Gauger (*19*), Gylling (*20*), and others merely chop the poem into little pieces, which is a confession of failure.

9. Juv. 6. 1–132, the general theme being the most powerful objection possible against marriage—that one's wife will inevitably be unfaithful. P. Menière, *Études médicales sur les poètes latins* (Paris, 1858), c. 15, diagnoses Messalina as a nymphomaniac, and mentions pathetic modern parallels.

10. Juv. 6. 136–285. The guiding theme in this section is that it is impossible to find happiness in marriage even through loving one's wife. This is shown by the key-words: *optima . . . teste marito*, 136; *desiderio*, 142; *digna*, 161; *deditus*, 181; *si . . . non es amaturus, ducendi nulla . . . causa*, 201–2; *simplicitas uxoria*, 206; *amantis*, 209; *concordia*, 231; and finally a sloppy love-scene with expressive alliteration on *s, fletumque labellis exsorbes*, 276–7.

11. Juv. 6. 1–10. Notice the implied identification of the noble, simple Golden Age of myth with the great days of the Roman republic. Is there a scornful allusion to the childless Cynthia's figure (*necdum inclinatae mammae*, Prop. 2. 15. 21) in the cave-woman's *ubera magna*?

12. Juv. 6. 300–51. The leading theme here is the degeneration of what were once the religious cults of chastity and wifehood into perverse orgies: *Pudicitiae aram*, 308; *effigiem deae*, 310; *Bonae secreta Deae*, 314; *ritus ueteres et publica sacra*, 335–6; *quas aras?*, 345. It is fair to say, however, that ceremonies of secret societies are usually made out worse than they really are: e.g. the adventures of Hell-Fire Francis at Medmenham Abbey.

13. This section is 6. 352–661, which breaks up into complaints against offences which are (*a*) domestic, 352–78; (*b*) social, 379–456; (*c*) personal, 457–507; (*d*) religious or superstitious, 508–91; and (*e*) criminal, 592–661.

14. 6. 413–23, 475–95. In or near Juvenal's own time, Hadrian exiled a woman called Umbricia for five years, 'quod ex leuissimis causis ancillas atrocissime tractasset' (Ulpian, in *Dig.* 1. 6. 2). In the early years of the nineteenth century there were cases of extreme savagery among women who owned serfs in Russia; at the same period the infamous Delphine Lalaurie was hunted out of New Orleans for flogging and torturing her house-slaves (H. Martineau, *Retrospect of Western Travel*, New York, 1838, 2. 136–43), and more recently we have seen Irma Greese, the female warder of Belsen concentration camp.

15. De Labriolle (*4*) 126 says the theme of the whole poem is that *impotentia muliebris* which is denounced in Livy 34. 2, Sen. *Const. Sap.* 14. 1, and Tac.

Ann. 1. 4 and 12. 57. As the Goncourt brothers said, 'L'excès en tout est la vertu de la femme' (Sainte-Beuve, *Nouveaux Lundis*, 10, Paris, 1880³, 398).

16. Censennia, 6. 136–7; Bibula, 6. 149–60; emeralds, &c., 6. 457–60; big sacrifices, 6. 518–19; vivid passages which sound like personal experience, 6. 432–3, 451–6 in spite of its borrowing from Martial 11. 19, 6. 507; a middle-class woman aping the rich, 6. 352–65.

17. What was Juvenal's own attitude to sex? Surely it should be considered in any estimate of this remarkable poem. We notice, then, that he never speaks of women in a sexual context without contempt or repulsion. He never praises the beauty of women. Unlike Martial, he never says that making love to women is pleasant. On the other hand, he once says—in an emphatic place at the beginning of Satire 6 (33–37)—that it is easier to be an active homosexual. (Horace, discussing a similar problem, had said 'slave-girl *or* boy', *Serm.* 1. 2. 116–18; but Juvenal, like Lucian, *Symp.* 39, speaks only of the boy.) In two or three other passages there are noticeably tender references to boys as objects of affection or love: 5. 56–62, 11. 145–58, 15. 135–7. And then there is Martial's emphatic sentence, in his letter to Juvenal about the delights of life in the Spanish country-side (12. 18. 22–23):

> uenator sequitur, sed ille quem *tu*
> secreta cupias habere silua.

It looks then as though Juvenal had begun his life with normal instincts, and had then been so disgusted by women that he turned to active homosexuality. The passives, the *pathici*, the *molles*, the women-men, he despised and hated. A professional active, like Naevolus in 9, was disgusting to him; but far less disgusting than Naevolus' passive employer. The combination of activity and passivity he describes (in a very early poem) as *morbus uterque* (2. 50); but nowhere else does he satirize the actives, whom—from disappointment or disgust—he himself had joined.

NOTES ON CHAPTER XV

1. This is one of the more clearly constructed satires. Here is an outline:

(*a*) *Dedication*, 1–35:
 —praise of the emperor's generosity, 1–21
 —dismissal of the stingy rich, 22–35.
(*b*) *Theme*, 36–243: the miseries of literary men
 —poets, 36–97
 —historians, 98–104
 —lawyers (regarded as orators), 105–49
 —high-school teachers, 150–214
 —elementary-school teachers, 215–43.

The only problem which has caused much discussion in the structure of the poem is Friedländer's objection (see his edition 55, 11–13) that the connexion between the dedication, or introduction, and the main body of the poem is weak, since the introduction says that better times are here, whereas throughout the rest of the satire Juvenal complains that literary men live in misery; also that the introduction deals only with poets, whereas Juvenal later discusses several other types of bookmen. Friedländer suggests that 1–21 were written for Hadrian's return to Rome, and attached rather flimsily to an earlier satire. Dürr (*13*) 19–21 agrees with this and suggests that the original introduction of the satire was simply lines 22–35. These objections are answered by A. Hartmann in a closely argued paper, *Aufbau und Erfindung der siebenten Satire Juvenals* (Basel, 1912). He points out that the satirist's job is not to describe happy futures but grim presents, and that the gloom of the main body of the poem is well summed up in line 1:

> et spes et ratio studiorum *in Caesare tantum.*

As for the mention of poets in the introduction, Juvenal is quite justified in taking the most distinguished type of literary activity as an *a fortiori* instance of the misery of all. Stegemann (*34*) 66–71 has a good analysis, pointing out that Juvenal begins by describing 'inactive' littérateurs like poets and historians, and goes on to the lives of more energetic people like lawyers and teachers. Stegemann also shows that, as we approach the end of the satire, the work of each class described grows harder, their dignity smaller, and their pay more miserable. I have sometimes wondered whether a few lines were not missing from the end: something to round off the poem as powerfully as 5. 170–3 or 6. 655–61; but the explanation is probably that this satire was meant to end on an anticlimax, fading away into squalor like 8 and 9.

2. *Sources, analogues, and adaptations.* Philosophers and teachers as well as poets preceded and followed Juvenal in complaining about their poverty. See, for instance, Crates the Cynic (Diog. Laert. 6. 86, with a marked resemblance to Juv. 7. 184–8); Theocritus 16; Orbilius (in Suet. *De gramm.* 9), who, like many of us, 'docuit maiore fama quam emolumento'; Petronius 83, where Juvenal seems to have found a model for his 7. 35 in 'sola pruinosis horret facundia pannis'; and many poems in Martial, such as 1. 76, 3. 38, 4. 46 (∼Juv. 7. 117–21), 5. 56, 8. 55, 10. 76, 11. 3, 12. 6. Lucian also discussed the theme in *De Mercede Conductis*. A grammarian who was a contemporary of Juvenal addressed a similar plea to Hadrian and got a cold reply (*AP* 9. 137–8); and some centuries later Palladas outdid all but Juvenal in bitterness: see *AP* 9. 169–75 and note the resemblance between 9. 174 and Juv. 7. 216–18. Modern adaptations appear in Régnier, *Sat.* 4; Joseph Hall 6. 1; and Boileau, *Art Poétique*, 4. 179–86.

3. Contrast the boring epics of 1. 2 and 52–54 with the sublime epics of 7. 27–28 and 66–68; contrast the compliments to the *Thebaid* in 7. 82–86 with the parody of Statius in 4 (see p. 258, n. 12). Composing a ballet-scenario for Paris (7. 87) is like writing a story expressly for Hollywood sales nowadays: Juvenal's metaphor *intactam uendit* connotes high-level pandering.

4. L. Radermacher, 'Zur siebenten Satire Juvenals', *RhM* 59 (1904), 525–31, points out the disproportionately short space given to the historians, and suggests that Juvenal has to put them in because he is following a conventional pattern of the genres of literature. But there is a better explanation in T. Birt's *Antike Buchwesen* (Berlin, 1882), 517—that historians were not as a rule poor men and needed no patronage. (The fact that Tacitus was so popular and successful would keep Juvenal from making much of the misery of the contemporary history-writers.) Hartmann (cited in n. 1), 8, adds that Juvenal is not bound by any scheme, but is merely trying, as in other satires, to make his picture as comprehensive as possible.

5. This is emphasized several times: *celebres notique poetae*, 7. 3; *tantum admirari, tantum laudare disertos*, 7. 31; *fregit subsellia uersu*, 7. 86. R. Pichon, *De sermone amatorio apud Romanos elegiarum scriptores* (Paris, 1902), 6, suggests that the section on Statius (7. 82–87) is a skilful parody of lovers' language: look at such fond expressions as *iucundae, amicae, laetum, promisit diem* (for the usual *promisit noctem), dulcedine, captos, libidine.*

6. So Juv. 7. 216–21, 157, 168, 228–9, and 119–21. *Maurorum epimenia* means that the onions were poor enough to be the rations issued to the roughest slaves, those who appear forbiddingly in 5. 52–55 and whose kinsmen are revolting in 14. 196.

7. Juv. 7. 36–47. In 40 the reading is surely Heinrich's conjecture *maculosas*, which was read by the scholiast, and explained in two different ways: 'alii: sordibus dixit; alii: pictas' (see Wessner (53) ad loc.). In 42, the scholiast gives two different explanations of *sollicitas portas*, one referring to mourning in a household, the other to a besieged city. The first is wrong, because Juvenal uses *portae* only of city-gates, not of house-doors; and the second is far too obscure to be understood as it stands. The probable reading is Jessen's conjecture *porcas*, made in his 'Witz und Humor im Juvenal', *Phil* 1 (1889), 320–7, and backed up in his 'Zu Juvenal', *Phil* 13 (1900), 505 f. The corruption to *portas* was suggested by *ianua*; the substitution of z for c is easy; and the type of joke which produces a vulgar word last in the line παρὰ προσδοκίαν is one of Juvenal's favourites: see 8. 158, 10. 156, 10. 158, 12. 73, and 14. 14. Like a number of slightly puzzling passages in Juvenal, this can be elucidated by reference to the lines of Ovid which were at the back of his mind when he wrote it:

> nec uoce silentia rumpunt
> sollicitiue canes canibusue sagacior anser (*Met.* 11. 598–9).

G. Wörpel, 'Einige Bemerkungen zu Juvenal VII 40 ff.', in *Beiträge . . . A. Schöne dargebracht* (Kiel, 1903), 11–23, proposes that Maculo is a Jewish name meaning something to do with sickness, and that the recital-hall was therefore a slaves' hospital taken over for a kosher butchery; but this is far too ingenious for the average reader to pick up, and I am informed that Wörpel's Hebrew derivations are quite untenable.

8. Juv. 7. 178–88. L. Herrmann, 'Juvenaliana', *REA* 42 (1940), 448 f., suggests that this rich man was the elder Pliny. The house described by Juvenal resembles the younger Pliny's Laurentinum with its swimming-pool (Pliny, *Ep.* 3. 5. 14), sunlit dining-room and colonnade (*Ep.* 2. 17), which the elder Pliny built and left almost finished to his adopted son; and young Pliny was a pupil of Quintilian (*Ep.* 2. 14, 6. 6). This sounds convincing. If true, it will be another example of Juvenal's not too carefully concealed dislike for Pliny and his circle (see pp. 292–4).

9. Juv. 7. 229–43, cf. 7. 113–14. P. Stumpf, 'Juvenal VII. 112–114', *Blätter* *für das Bayerische Gymnasial- und Schulwesen*, 16 (1880), 446–9, supports the reading *Lacernae*, and proposes that Juvenal has added a good point by naming a *bad* driver in an *unpopular* team—the Reds being far less admired than the Blues and the Greens.

10. Juv. 7. 105–49. Matho, going bankrupt here in 129, was seen at an earlier stage of his career, bloated with success, in 1. 32–33. Martial also reports on him, at first in a friendly tone (4. 79 and 6. 33), and then with hostility in 7. 10, 7. 90, 8. 42, 10. 46, and 11. 68. Juvenal mentions him briefly again in 11. 34. The name is a cognomen of the Pomponii.

11. This was done, for instance, by Victor Hugo (see p. 228). J. Dürr, 'Juvenal und Hadrian', in *Festschrift zu Otto Hirschfelds sechzigsten Geburtstage* (Berlin, 1903), 447–51, points out the various reflections of Hadrian's administrative reforms which appear in the satires.

NOTES ON CHAPTER XVI

1. *Sources, analogues, and adaptations.* The idea that nobility of birth was meaningless or misleading and that true nobility consisted in virtue was popular with Stoic philosophers, and even more so with Cynics. Bion of Borysthenes applied it to himself (Diog. Laert. 4. 46–47) and his admirer Horace, more deviously, to his own refusal to stand for office (*Serm.* 1. 6). See also Philo, *De Nobilitate*; Sen. *Ep.* 44; and Dio Chrysostom, *Or.* 3, 4, and 15. The topic was also treated by rhetoricians: see the examples in Val. Max. 3. 4–5 and a good development by Julius Bassus in the elder Seneca, *Contr.* 1. 6. Persius handled it briefly and unsatisfactorily in *Sat.* 4. In the Middle Ages it was much discussed: see E. Curtius, *Europäische Literatur und lateinisches Mittelalter* (Berne, 1948), 186–7. In modern times there were adaptations by Joseph Hall (4. 3); Boileau (*Sat.* 5), who in turn was copied by Oldham; Wordsworth thought of making a modern version (see pp. 219-20), and several were actually published in the revolutionary age. The famous line 8. 20 was borrowed by many thinkers in the age of aristocracy: for instance, Baltasar Gracián; the main idea of the poem was taken up by Corneille and Molière in two father-and-son dialogues; and finally, it has been suggested that Dryden built the preface of *All for Love*, a counterattack on the degenerate nobleman Rochester, on this poem: see F. L. Huntley, 'Dryden, Rochester, and the Eighth Satire of Juvenal', *PQ* 18 (1939), 269–84.

2. The only man of this name in *PIR* 3 is Valerius Ponticus, exiled in Nero's reign for legal chicanery (Tac. *Ann.* 14. 41). It was actually Lucullus who conquered Pontus and triumphed over it. Martial uses the cognomen fairly often, notably for a rich and mean patron very like Juvenal's Virro in 3. 60, 4. 85, and 9. 19. Gauger (*19*) 57 points out that Juvenal brings in nearly every distinguished family in Rome somewhere in this satire: the gens Aemilia in 3 and 9, Curia in 4, Sulpicia in 5, Valeria in 5, Fabia in 14, Cornelia in 21 and 105 and 231, Claudia in 21, Iunia in 27, Antonia in 38 and 105, Sergia in 231, Iulia in 242. (Again a concealed enumeration: see n. 7 on p. 266 of the notes.)

3. The structure of the poem is fairly clear:

(*a*) 1–70: *exordium* and general statement of the theme.

(*b*) 71–145: *propositio* and particular application.

(*c*) 146–268: *confirmatio* and examples—note that the bad examples form a climax of infamy, from Rubellius Blandus, who is noble but useless, through Lateranus, who is noble but degraded, to Damasippus, who is still worse degraded, and Gracchus, worse yet, and then to Nero, murderer and fool, ending with Catiline and Cethegus, murderers and traitors. Since this is a satire with a positive purpose, the good examples now follow.

(*d*) 269–75: *conclusio*.

This division is accepted by Gylling (*20*) and with a small variation by Gauger (*19*), who divides at 38 instead of 70.

4. Plautius Lateranus, *animi ualidus et corpore ingens*, appears in Tac. *Ann.* 11. 36, 13. 11, 15. 49, 15. 53, 15. 60, and Arrian, *Epict.* 1. 1. 19. Epona was a Gallic nature-deity. See P. Lambrechts, 'La colonne du dieu-cavalier au géant', *Latomus*, 8 (1949), 150–3, and É. Thévenot, 'Les monuments et le culte d'Épona chez les Éduens', *AntCl* 18 (1949), 385–400, both of whom give pictures.

5. Juv. 8. 171–6. The habit of slumming was popular with Nero himself for a time (Tac. *Ann.* 13. 25, Suet. *Nero* 26, Dio 61. 8. 1, 61. 9. 1–4), and it is possible that Petronius wrote his *Satirica* to divert the young prince with vicarious enjoyment of the same kind of adventure (G. Highet, 'Petronius the Moralist', *TAPA* 72, 1941, 176–94).

6. Juv. 8. 269–75. The 'thing he will not name' is a thief, one of the two groups which, according to legend, joined to become the earliest citizens of Rome. The pointed avoidance of the word emphasizes one of the chief lessons of Satire 8—that a Roman noble ought not, as governor of a province, to be a thief: see 8. 89–134.

7. We have already seen Juvenal correcting Tacitus, in 2. 102 f.: see p. 15. The description of Lateranus in 8. 146–82 is markedly different from Tacitus' picture of him. And the characterization of Rubellius Blandus in Juv. 8. 39–72 is so emphatically unlike the sketch of Rubellius Plautus given by Tacitus (*Ann.* 13. 19–22, 14, 22, 14. 57–59, 16. 10, 16. 30) that many have doubted whether the same man could be meant by the slightly different names. F. Wolffgramm, *Rubellius Plautus und seine Beurtheilung bei Tacitus und Juvenal* (Prenzlau, 1871), believes them identical, and suggests that the difference in their portrayal is caused by the difference between Tacitus' and Juvenal's views of virtue and defeat: Tacitus thinking that such men were essentially good, so that their cruel fate was caused by the cruelty of the gods, while Juvenal held that virtue meant activity, energy, and determination. L. Niessen, *Quaestiones Juvenalianae* (Münster, 1889), 20–24, believes it impossible for Juvenal to contradict Tacitus, and solves the problem by making Juvenal's R. Blandus the brother of the R. Plautus who appears in Tacitus.

NOTES ON CHAPTER XVII

1. *Sources, analogues, and adaptations.* No treatment of the subject of Satire 9 on the same scale has survived, although no doubt the character of the active pervert was discussed by philosophers and portrayed by dramatists. (Studies of the κίναιδος, the pathic—not Naevolus, but his employer Virro—were frequent; but that is a different theme.) The only thing like it in Roman satire is the character of Encolpius in the *Satirica* of Petronius; and there he is portrayed as genuinely in love with his male consort Giton (see 94, for instance), not as a male prostitute like the hero of Satire 9. But the same topic is touched on briefly in Petronius, *Sat.* 92. 7–10 ∼ Juv. 9. 34–37.

The form of the poem is unique in Juvenal, for it is the only time he writes an entire satire in dialogue, like his predecessors, Hor. *Serm.* 2. 3, 2. 5, 2. 7, and Persius, 3 and 4. R. Hirzel, *Der Dialog* (Leipzig, 1895), 2. 62–63, points out that in this dialogue-satire Juvenal is working in one of the main traditions of the satiric pattern. This particular satire is especially interesting because it does not so much discuss a theme for argument or describe an odd event as expose the character of Naevolus. Here satire merges into the tradition of drama. The shameless parasite Phormio boasts of his own shamelessness in the same way in Terence, *Phormio* 326–45, and Donatus says the speech was copied from another author, conjectured to be Ennius in his satires (see P. Wessner's edition of Donatus (Leipzig, 1905), 2. 432 and appendix). In Hor. *Serm.* 1. 9, an almost equally unpleasant character talks to Horace and reveals one of his faults after another. But it seems likely that Juvenal here is thinking rather of the mime. This piece closely resembles Herodas 2 (see Headlam's note on 2. 74); we know that a similar figure to Naevolus, the *cultus adulter*, was a stock character in the mime (see H. Reich, *Der Mimus* 1 (Berlin, 1903), 116–17 and 563 f., and compare Juv. 9. 22–25); and we know, too, that homosexuality had been treated in mimes, though not from this precise point of view, by Cleomachus of Magnesia (Strabo, *Geog.* 14. 1. 41). Conceivably the satire is also intended as a parody of the theme of the *exclusus amator* (on which see E. Wüst, 'Mimus', *RE* 15. 1746.)

Because of its repulsive theme, the satire has been little imitated as a whole. Boileau borrowed its opening for his third satire, and Diderot apparently took hints from it for *Le Neveu de Rameau*—which, like 9, is in dialogue, reports the conversation of a calm and cynical observer with a social vagabond, and allows the vagabond to boast of his own licentiousness: 'Puisque je puis faire mon bonheur par des vices qui me sont naturels, que j'ai acquis sans travail, que je conserve sans effort, qui cadrent avec les mœurs de ma nation. . . .' (In the same context, the nephew of Rameau quotes Juv. 1. 74.) However, the style of the poem is so brilliant that it has been frequently quoted: medieval citations are assembled by S. Consoli in 'La satira IX di Giovenale nella tradizione della cultura sino alla fine del medio evo', *RFIC* 49 (1921), 79–97. The beautiful poetry of 9. 126–9 is worthy of a better setting, and once more shows the peculiar character of Juvenal, who, like Swift, had a soft heart inside his armour of cynicism.

2. Juv. 9. 1–26. The structure of the poem is clear. It does not move on like a discussion, it simply describes Naevolus' despair (with its causes and effects), at the same time deploying the full baseness of his character and revealing that of Virro. It falls into three main sections:

(a) 1–91: Naevolus, his appearance, character, and career.

(b) 91–123: Virro, his cruelty and his vain attempt to keep his vices hidden.

(c) 124–50: Naevolus should still hope, since Rome is corrupt.

The name Naevolus occurs in Martial 3. 71 and 3. 95 for a passive pervert; and in 1. 97, 2. 46, and 4. 83 for less repulsive types.

3. See A. Maurois, *A la recherche de Marcel Proust* (Paris, 1949), 22 ('Quel est, pour vous, le comble de la misère?' 'Être séparé de Maman') and 149–56. Albert Le Cuziat, disguised in Proust's novels as Albertine, was (says Maurois on 151) 'presque seul à connaître un Proust ténébreux et assez effrayant qui compensait, par un sadisme intermittent, son masochisme douloureux'. With this compare Juv. 9. 95–99.

4. Satire 1 ends with the partial defeat of the satirist himself; 2 with the spread of moral infection from Rome through the world; 3 with the exile of Umbricius from his native city; 4 with Domitian killed by the wrong people; 5 with the conversion of Trebius into a clown and a slave; 6 with the murder of Postumus (or anyone) by his wife; 7 with the least important of the professional men doing the most sordid job for the most bitterly stingy reward; and 8 with the assertion that the noblest Romans are descended from slaves and thieves.

5. So *exhausti . . . clientis*, 9. 59; *deditus . . . deuotusque cliens*, 9. 71–72. Compare 5. 14–15 and 9. 38–40; 3. 164–7 and 9. 63–69; 3. 124–5 and 9. 92; 1. 144–6 and 9. 59–62.

6. Jachmann (*43*) 197–205 shows that line 5 was meant to replace line 4, as a 'Dezenzinterpolation'. Weidner (*63*) explains: 'Als Ravola im Ehebruch mit Rhodope abgefaßt wurde, natürlich von dem Herrn des Hauses', which means that he does not know who Ravola was, who Rhodope was, or what they were doing. It is really impossible to understand the worst parts of Juvenal without knowing Martial.

NOTES ON CHAPTER XIX

1. *Sources, analogues, and adaptations.* The theme is prayer (see 6–8, 23, 54–55, 111, 115, 188–9, 289–91, 354–5). Juvenal considers it under two aspects: (1) what is the right relation of man to the gods? (7–8, 55, 346–62); and (2) what are the things which men ought to wish for? (1–6, 23 f., 54, 114 f., 133 f., 188 f., 289 f., 363–6). In both these aspects it had been much debated, by Cynics, Stoics, and Epicureans. As has been pointed out in the text, Juvenal's answer to the second question is on the whole Epicurean; but his comment on the first question is not—since the Epicureans believed the gods did not answer prayers or alter the course of human life; it is a mixture of Stoicism and enlightened traditionalism. The earliest complete discussion of the second question which we have is the Socratic dialogue *Alcibiades II*, not by Plato but perhaps by Xenophon: see 150 D, which

anticipates Juvenal's *erroris nebula* in 10. 4. Many other philosophical treatments are mentioned in Schuetze (*31*), c. 9, and remarks on it by Seneca are
listed in Schneider (*30*), c. 7. H. F. Rebert, in *Virgil and Those Others* (Amherst,
1930), proposes that the passage on old age (188–288) is a reply to Cicero's
Cato Maior; while H. C. Nutting, in 'Three Notes on Juvenal', *AJP* 49 (1928),
258–66, suggests that the end is based on Cicero's *Tusculan Discussions*—
357–8 covering book 1, 359 book 2, 360 books 2 and 4, and 363 book 5.
N. Terzaghi, *Per la Storia della Satira* (Turin, n.d.), 69–86 and 155–9, discusses the theme as it appears in fable and satire, and suggests that Juvenal's
point of view is ultimately Cynic; but his definition of the subject is a little
too wide to be useful.

In satire, Horace touched on the theme several times, especially in *Ep*. 1. 6
(and see *Ep*. 1. 16. 57 f.). Persius gave his entire second satire to it, which
Juvenal appears to have read and adapted and expanded. The parallels and
differences are interesting:

> Pers. 2. 31–40 ~ Juv. 10. 289–345 (beauty)
> Pers. 2. 41–43 ~ Juv. 10. 188–288 (long life)
> Pers. 2. 44–51 ~ Juv. 10. 23–53 (wealth)
> Pers. 2. 71–75 ~ Juv. 10. 346–66 (virtue).

Persius omits the prayers which his quiet heart could not conceive: glory in
war (Juv. 10. 133 f.), political power (Juv. 10. 36 f. and 56 f.), eloquence
(Juv. 10. 114 f.); his objection to the prayer for wealth is the unrealistic one
that men waste their money in expensive sacrifices (2. 44 f.) while Juvenal's
is the realistic one that rich men are more likely to be poisoned or executed
(10. 12 f.); and there are other small differences. The important distinction
is that Persius starts with wicked prayers and ends by saying that we should
have a virtuous heart when we do pray; while Juvenal speaks of foolish
prayers and ends by saying that we should pray for virtue and strive to
achieve it.

In rhetoric the topic of the change of fortune (56–187) was much handled,
with the examples of the great men of history who had risen from nothing or
fallen from the pinnacle. It is treated (with two of Juvenal's examples, Venti-
dius and Marius) by Valerius Maximus 6. 9 and 7. 2, *ext*. 1; and by the
author of pseudo-Quintilian, *Declamationes* (ed. C. Ritter, Leipzig, 1884),
268, p. 96. See K. Alewell, *Über das rhetorische παράδειγμα* (Leipzig, 1913), 60–
61 and 117; and De Decker (*18*) 41–44.

In history, the fine description of the fall of Sejanus (58 f.) may have been
suggested by Tacitus' account, which we have lost, alas. (It appeared in
Annals 5; see the Furneaux edition, Oxford, 1896, Appendix IV.) But
clearly Juvenal was also thinking of Domitian, whose statues were melted
down after his death and whose name was chiselled out of nearly every
Roman inscription where it had once stood in a place of honour: see Pliny,
Pan. 52. 4–5; Suet. *Dom.* 23. 1; Dio. 68. 1; and S. Gsell, *Essai sur le règne de
l'Empereur Domitien* (*Bibliothèque des Écoles françaises d'Athènes et de Rome* 65,
1894), 330–1. Statues of Greek rulers melted down, even into chamber-pots
as in Juv. 10. 64, appear in Plut. *Political Precepts* 27. For a modern parallel
to the destruction of the statues see E. F. Henderson, *Symbol and Satire in the*

French Revolution (New York, 1912), 263, who gives newspaper illustrations of crews pulling down the statues of Louis XIV in the Place Vendôme and the Place des Victoires.

Juvenal's art has seldom been as well displayed as in 10. 56–64. Observe how he begins with a mild *quosdam*, which might include anybody; goes on to statues and triumphal chariots, which could belong to only the highest officials and the emperor; then moves to *adoratum populo caput*, which really sounds as though he meant the emperor himself—the phrase hangs in the air at the end of the line with *et crepat ingens* . . . and then comes the tremendous molossus *Seianus*; the description ends with a fine anticlimax, *matellae*. But see, in line 77 the word *Augustum* appears in exactly the same place as *Seianus* of 63, so exactly as to remind us that the melting statues of 61–63 might have belonged to the emperor instead of the general. Once more Juvenal has pointed out a fatal weakness in Rome, which was to increase after his death: the temptation and the power of ambitious soldiers to break their oath and seize the throne. E. Bertrand, 'Juvénal', *Annales de l'Université de Grenoble*, 7 (1895), 455, compares the fall of Sejanus to the last days of Robespierre; but it is impossible for us not to think of the corpse of Mussolini, with Italian bullet-holes in it, hanging head downwards from a butcher's hook.

There are many fine analogues for this poem. Long before Juvenal, Leonidas of Tarentum wrote a poem on a skeleton which summed up much of it (*AP* 7. 472), and a generation later Lucian touched it in *Icaromenippus* 25 and worked it out more fully, but far more lightly, in *The Ship*. The passage on old age—which Hamlet was reading when Polonius boarded him (see p. 213)—has inspired several modern poets: e.g. Victor Hugo (p. 229). Johnson adapted the entire poem in his *Vanity of Human Wishes*; and Byron said of it 'The Tenth Satᵉ has always been my favourite, as I suppose indeed of everybody's. It is the finest recipe for making one miserable with his life, and content to walk out of it, in any language. I should think it might be redde with great effect to a man dying without much pain, in preference to all the stuff that ever was sung or said in churches' (Byron, to F. Hodgson —who had translated Juvenal with Drury and Merivale—9 Sept. 1811: *Letters and Journals*, ed. R. E. Prothero, N.Y., 1898, 2. 32). Separate lines and phrases from this poem, such as 10. 22, 10. 81, 10. 111, 10. 153, 10. 172–3, and 10. 356–66, have been quoted countless times throughout the western world, and are still known.

2. The structure of Satire 10 is bold and simple:

(*a*) 1–53: Prologue: *Most wishes are mistaken*—the commonest and most oolish being for wealth (12–27) and social distinction (36–46).

(*b*) 54–55: General question: *What wishes then are wise?*

(*c*) 56–345: Negative answers—

> *not power* (56–113)
> *nor eloquence* (114–132)
> *nor military glory* (133–187)
> *nor long life* (188–288)
> *nor good looks* (289–345).

(d) 346–66: Positive answer and conclusion: *We should wish only for health and virtue, leaving the rest to the gods.*

The only important problems arising from this scheme are (a) the meaning and punctuation of 54–55, and (b) the meaning of 358. The second question is easy: *spatium uitae* is shown by 188 to mean *multi anni*; therefore *extremum* is predicative, and means *extremum inter munera naturae*. Juvenal is telling us that a brave heart considers long life to be the least important of the gifts of nature. As for 54–55, surely they are, as suggested above, a question preparing for the final question in 346. In 1–53 Juvenal has said generally that very few people know what to wish for, and has given examples of wishes which are dangerous (8–22) and foolish and ludicrous (28–53). In 54 he sums this all up, in a line which may be either a statement or a question (as in *TLL*, s.v. *ergo*, 769–70). Having observed that most wishes are dangerous or silly (= useless, *superuacua*), he asks, 'What then is it right to pray for?' The succeeding lines, to 345, survey and discard special prayers which are often made, and lead up to Juvenal's own answer in 346 f. F. Buecheler, 'Coniectanea', *RhM* 34 (1879), 355–6, proposed that both 54 and 55 were questions. Knoche (45) 31 cuts out both lines: but they are well defended by E. Bickel in 'Iuvenaliana', *RhM* 67 (1912), 142–6, and 'Zur Gebetsatire Iuvenals und dem Interpolationenproblem', *RhM* 92 (1944), 89–94, roughly on the grounds given above. In his first article Bickel proposed to keep *superuacua* and accept the hiatus, merely lengthening the final *-a*, which is surely intolerable; in his second, to read *superuacuo*. But the simplest and clearest emendation is Doederlein's *uel*, meaning 'even', as in 3. 5 and 11. 128: the monosyllable naturally fell out after *aut* when some scribe decided it was merely a variant.

3. Juv. 10. 189: *hoc recto uoltu, solum hoc et pallidus optas*, briefly and clearly explained by the scholiast (ed. Wessner, *53*, 173): *laetus et tristis uitam longam optas*, and confirmed by W. S. Fox, 'Note on Juvenal x. 188–89', *CP* 9 (1914), 193–6. J. Elmore, '*Recto vultu* and *recta facie* in Juvenal', *AJP* 46 (1925), 268–70, proposes that the former phrase means 'with set anxious face', but supports this by quotations which prove the opposite. The variant found in the Oxford MS. and elsewhere, *altus caelumque tuens*, looks like an attempt to rewrite *recto uoltu* and make it easier.

NOTES ON CHAPTER XX

1. *Sources, analogues, and adaptations.* For some remarks on the general theme of dinner as a subject for satire see n. 1 on c. 11. This particular variation is the Modest Dinner, contrasted with vulgar or vicious luxury. It had been treated by Lucilius in Satire 13 (frg. 438–45), 14 (frg. 453–75), and perhaps 20 (frg. 568–77); by Varro in his *Manius, Modius*—which contains Epicurean preachments (see E. Norden, *In Varronis Saturas Menippeas observationes selectae*, Leipzig, 1891, 273), Περὶ ἐδεσμάτων (see O. Hense, 'Eine Menippea des Varro', *RhM* 61, 1912, 8–17), and possibly in his Ταφὴ Μενίππου; and by Horace (*Serm.* 2. 2 and 2.6; *Ep.* 1. 5). Even closer to Juvenal are a few poems by Martial: 5. 78 covers many of the same motives that are used in this satire, and see also 10. 48 and 11. 52. Schuetze (*31*), c. 6 gives scattered quotations from philosophers talking on the same theme. With the end, 11. 193–204, cf. Pliny, *Ep.* 9. 6. Although the poem has been quite often quoted, it has seldom been imitated as a whole.

2. Gauger (*19*) 74–76 assumes that the dinner is to take place on Juvenal's farm, and that the poem directly illustrates the ideals of country life. This is contradicted by 152–3 and by the whole description of the setting in 193–206. Gylling (*20*) 63 makes the same odd mistake.

3. The *structure* of the poem is simple and clear, and closely parallel to that of Satire 5:

(*a*) 1–55: introductory chat.

(*b*) 56–63: the invitation.

(*c*) 64–89; the food (with reflections on old Roman manners).

(*d*) 90–135: the furniture and dishes (with reflections on manners old and new).

(*e*) 136–61: the servants and the wine.

(*f*) 162–82: the entertainment.

(*g*) 183–208: conclusion, the preliminary relaxation and comfortable bath. This scheme is not really obscured by the comparisons Juvenal draws between his own manners and those of Republican Rome, and between those of the unspoilt ancestors and the degenerate rich of his own day. Gylling (*20*) gains nothing by breaking the satire into fourteen small paragraphs.

4. The entertainment, 11. 162–82. The suggestion by S. Reinach ('Juvénal et Stace', *RevPhil* 31, 1907, 45–50) that 11. 180–1 means the poetry of Statius has been competently answered by P. de Labriolle in 'Juvénal, Satire XI, 179–182', *RevPhil* 5 (1931), 343–7.

5. For these three indications of the degeneracy of the rich see lines 120–9, 162–8, 175. The interpolations in 165–70 are expelled and the sense of the passage restored by Jachmann (*43*) 216–28.

6. Juvenal in 11. 198 says that the roar shows the Green team has won. The Greens were the favourite team of the common people, the Blues of the aristocracy: see R. Goossens, 'Note sur les factions du cirque à Rome', *Byzantion*, 14 (1939), 205–9.

NOTES ON CHAPTER XXI

1. *Sources, analogues, and adaptations.* The subject is topical; but it is described in the manner of epic, like the storms in Homer, *Od.* 12. 403–23, and Vergil, *Aen.* 1. 81–123; and it is therefore another example of epic parody in satire—see lines 22–24, 62–66, 70–74, note the comic comparisons in 34–36 and the laugh at religious pictures in 27–29 and 81–82. There is a similar storm, with mock-heroic speeches, in Petronius 114. As a topical subject treated in terms borrowed or distorted from epic, the poem is therefore descended from Lucilius 1 and Hor. *Serm.* 1. 9; and its closest ancestor is a poem which also discusses legacy-hunting in mock-epic style, Hor. *Serm.* 2. 5 (carrying on the dialogue of Homer, *Od.* 11. 90–149). Juvenal uses epic terms for topical or nearly topical themes again in Satires 4 and 15.

The general theme, the corruption of friendship into flattery through money, and its narrower application to the hunting of legacies, was treated by a number of philosophers and satirists: e.g. Hor. *Serm.* 2. 5; Plut. *How to tell a Flatterer from a Friend* (*Moralia* 48–74); Lucian, *Dialogues of the Dead* 5–9 and *Timon*; and often in Martial. Juvenal had already handled it in 3. 58–125. See O. Ribbeck, 'Kolax', in *Abhandlungen der philologisch-historischen Claße der königlich sächsischen Gesellschaft der Wissenschaften*, 9 (1884), 1–113.

The philosophical attitude that a merchant facing bankruptcy in a big speculation and a ship facing destruction in a storm are both amusing examples of human folly (cf. 12. 57–61) is Epicurean: see Lucr. 2. 1–6. The danger of seafaring was also a well-known rhetorical theme: see Seneca the elder, *Contr.* 7. 1, *Suas.* 1.

Structure. The pattern of the poem is clear:

(a) 1–16: *Ceremony*: Juvenal is offering public sacrifice for the safe return of a friend—

(b) 17–82: *Occasion*:—who survived a disaster at sea (storm, 17–29; cargo jettisoned, 30–51; gear and mast overboard, 52–61; landfall, 62–82).

(c) 83–92: *Ceremony completed*: Juvenal also offers sacrifice at home.

(d) 93–130: *Reflection*: this is genuine friendship, not toadying.

Gylling (*20*) makes nine main sections, which boil down to the above plan.

Authenticity. Ribbeck (*49*) suggested that the poem was a forgery, written by the 'declaimer' who added so many bad poems to Juvenal's real works. O. Haenicke, *Kritische Untersuchung über die Echtheit der 12. Satire von J.* (Putbus 1877), defends the satire, although he treats it rather unsympathetically. His best point is the familiar one, that what Ribbeck called the mannerisms of the 'declaimer' who forged this and other satires are demonstrably characteristic of Juvenal's style all through his poems; and, roughly, his position is that Satire 12 is bad, but authentic.

2. Juv. 12. 37–47. The fact that Catullus was running into Ostia (12. 75 f.) and importing wool from Baetica (12. 40 f.) shows that he had been in Spain; the silver plate in 43–47 with its Greek associations might have been bought in Greece or might have been acquired from Spanish connoisseurs.

3. Juv. 12. 93–130. The closest modern parallel is probably the swarm of beggars who beset the Golden Dustman: see Dickens, *Our Mutual Friend*, book 1, c. 17.

4. Juv. 12. 129–30, modelled on Cic. *Laelius* 52 (so J. E. B. Mayor, 'Note on Juvenal XII 129 130', *JP* 12, 1883, 269).

NOTES ON CHAPTER XXIII

1. *Sources, analogues, and adaptations.* On the pattern of the *consolatio* see n. 4. The content of this particular consolation is the two main arguments outlined on pp. 141–3 and in n. 4. The first of these is based on the theme often discussed by philosophers, poets, and rhetoricians—the degeneracy of the present (*De saeculo*: see De Decker, *18*, 22 f.). The second, in particular the idea that a criminal's guilty conscience and fear of discovery were his own punishment, was treated by many writers of distinction, whose ideas coincide with Juvenal's in whole or in part: Lucr. 3. 1011–23; Sen. *Ep.* 97. 12–16 and 105. 7–8; Plut. *On the Slow Vengeance of the Divine Power*, 10. 11, and *One Cannot Live Pleasantly by following Epicurus*, 6. 1.

2. Pliny, *Ep. ad Trai.* 96. 7, *ne depositum adpellati abnegarent.* This is discussed by C. C. Coulter, 'Further notes on the ritual of the Bithynian Christians', *CP* 35 (1940), 60–62, who points to 'Defraud not' in the words of Jesus to the man with great possessions in Mark x. 19, to *Digest*, 16. 3, and to the discussion in H. J. Roby, *Roman Private Law* (Cambridge, 1902), 2. 94–97.

3. 13. 16–17. In an early paper, *De Juvenalis vitae temporibus* (Königsberg, 1875), Friedländer suggested that *qui . . . reliquit* meant Juvenal himself, because Calvinus is always addressed in the second person, not in the third. But this would destroy the argument of the poem: Juvenal himself has never been surprised at the degeneracy of his times, but his friend might be, and it is part of the consolation to explain to him that, with his age and experience, Calvinus ought not to wonder at another expression of this degeneracy. Friedländer was set right by L. Schwabe, 'Iuvenal's Geburtsjahr', *RhM* 40 (1885), 25–27, and dropped the idea in his big edition (*55*) 526.

4. *Structure.* The arrangement of the consolatory arguments is:

(*a*) 1–12: introduction.
(*b*) 13–173: *de crimine*—
    (i) *usitatum*, 13–70
    (ii) *necessarium*, 71–119
    (iii) *leue*, 120–73.
(*c*) 174–249: *de ultione*—
    (i) *neglegenda*, 174–192
    (ii) *certa ex conscientia*, 192–239
    (iii) *certa ex natura*, 239–49.

Gylling (*20*) divides the satire into the same sections, but has not grasped the general scheme. G. Mosengel, *Vindiciae Juvenalianae* (Leipzig, 1887), 20–21, observes that 38–70 and 70–120 (he means 71–119) seem to repeat each other, but refuses to take this as evidence for a 'double recension'; but in fact the two passages are developments of two slightly different topics. Sydow (*37*) 18–19 says the satire is messily arranged but coherent. On the *consolatio*, or λόγος παραμυθητικός, see R. Volkmann, *Die Rhetorik der Griechen und Römer* (Leipzig, 1885), 358–60; C. Favez in *OCD*; K. Buresch, *Consolationum . . . historia critica, Leipziger Studien*, 9 (1886), 1–169; and Sister M. E. Fern, *The Latin Consolatio as a Literary Type* (St. Louis, 1941), which, however, does not mention this poem, or indeed go quite far enough into the structure of the *consolatio*. I have not been able to see the introduction to J. D. Duff's edition of Sen. *Dialogues*, 10, 11, 12, which is said to discuss the question.

NOTES ON CHAPTER XXIV

1. *Sources, analogues, and adaptations.* There are two main themes in this poem—education and greed. Both were often studied by moralists, poets, and satirists. The *Eryxias*, attributed to Plato but clearly written after his day, is an early discussion of greed, which ends with the same conclusion as 14. 139, that desire grows with possession. Theophrastus gives, in *Characters*, 30, a description of the stingy man which looks quite like Juv. 14. 126–34. The topic was often treated by popular preachers like Bion of Borysthenes and the Cynics: see H. Herter, 'Zur ersten Satire des Horaz', *RhM* 94 (1951), 9 f., for many quotations. From them it passed over into Latin satire, and appears in Lucilius, book 19 (frg. 557 f.), book 29 (frg. 806 f.), and perhaps elsewhere (e.g. frg. 501–2). Perhaps lines 208–9 are quoted from Lucilius: see E. Baehrens, 'Zu Ennius, Lucilius, Juvenalis', *NJbb* 135, 1887, 482–4, and Wessner, *53*, 285. Varro handled avarice in his Ἀλλ᾿ οὐ μένει σε and also in his *Eumenides*, on which see E. Norden, *In Varronis saturas Menippeas observationes selectae* (Leipzig, 1891), 329 f. Horace thought a great deal about the subject, and discussed it in *Serm.* 1. 1 and 2. 6 in particular. There is a close tie between *Serm.* 1. 1 and Juvenal 14 in several things, even in the fact that both poems apparently begin with one topic and pass to another which illustrates it (see Herter's article cited above for a discussion of this as it affects Horace). Hor. 1. 1. 64–67 reminds us of Juv. 14. 152–5 and Hor. 4–12 of Juvenal 191–205. Phrases from other poems of Horace appear here too: e.g. Hor. *Ep.* 1. 1. 102–3 recurs in Juv. 14. 112 and 288. Persius likewise touched on greed, and seems to be imitated in two passages: Pers. 5. 132–48 ∼ Juv. 14. 190–209, Pers. 6. 75–80 ∼ Juv. 14. 322–31. Discussions of greed also appear in the work of the rhetoricians (see Seneca the elder, *Controu.* 2. 1 (9) and 5. 2) and in the philosophers (see Seneca the younger, *Ep.* 115). Further citations are found in Schuetze (*31*) 9–16. There is an odd echo from Juvenal himself: 14. 315–16 = 10. 365–6. The commentators (e.g. Duff, *54*, and Weidner, *63*) say this is awkward, and Knoche (*58*), following Leo (*57*), cuts out the couplet in 10. Yet it may well be a joke. In Satire 10 the sentence was a grave judgement on the unreal power of the goddess Fortune, meaning the Destiny which makes us happy or miserable by raising us high or dashing us down. Here the remark is transferred to Fortune, meaning Wealth; and, since no one does formally worship Wealth in a temple (Juv. 1. 113–14), the transference is surely meant to raise a wry smile.

On education there are innumerable discussions: from Juvenal's own time see Sen. *De ira*, 2. 21; Quint. *Inst. Or.* 1. 2. 6; Tac. *Dial.* 28–29; and Plut. *On Educating Children*, esp. para. 20. Petronius, frg. 37, appears to be making a point about Jewish proselytes similar to that in Juv. 14. 96–106.

2. If a satirist never mentions sloth but talks a great deal about anger and pride, the inference is obvious. So by surveying the relative space Juvenal allots to different topics and the energy with which he treats them, we can see that he was most urgently concerned with (1) problems of the family: marriage, education of children, sexual morality. Then (2) he thought persistently also about wealth and poverty, extravagance and greed—a theme which appears at the opening of the first and is still prominent in the last page of the last satire. Next in importance came (3) crime; then (4) gluttony; and then (5) topics which occupied him less often or less intensely, such as ambition, nobility, city life, and Oriental fanaticism.

3. Juv. 14. 86–106. Juvenal may here have been mixing up Christian converts with Jewish proselytes, for the early Christians also observed the sabbath, kept themselves apart from the world, and respected the law of Moses. To a Roman eye there would not be much difference (see p. 260); and indeed the Christians claimed to be the heirs of the Jews—see M. Simon, *Verus Israel* (Paris, 1948). Still, Juvenal knew quite a lot about the Jews and their faith—more than any of his contemporaries and predecessors in Roman literature except possibly Tacitus. J. Bernays, 'Die Gottesfürchtigen bei Juvenal', in *Gesammelte Abhandlungen* (ed. H. Usener, Berlin, 1885), 2. 71–80, points out that Juvenal seems to be using the right expressions here: in 97, *caeli numen* is equivalent to *shamayim*, one of the Hebrew periphrases for 'God'. Bernays also thought that in 96 and 101 *metuo* was intended to recall the Hebrew phrase 'God-fearing' and that the expression specifically meant 'Jewish proselytes'. However, L. H. Feldman, 'Jewish "sympathizers" in classical literature and inscriptions', *TAPA* 81 (1950), 200–8, shows that the words have no such precisely limited meaning; yet they still seem to be an intentional echo of the Hebrew. Furthermore, in 96–106 Juvenal has carefully distinguished the two recognized stages of conversion to Judaism: the father, who observed some Jewish rules but not all, was a Proselyte of the Gate, *ger ha-sha'ar* (from 'the stranger within the gate', Deut. v. 14, xv. 21); the son, who had himself circumcised and joined the Jewish community, was a Proselyte of Righteousness, *ger ha-zedek* or *ger ha-berit*. (See E. G. Hirsch, s.v. 'Proselyte', in *The Jewish Encyclopaedia*, New York and London, 1905, vol. 10.) On Jewish exclusiveness, H. J. Rose, 'Juvenal XIV. 103–104', *CR* 45 (1931), 127, cites Ps. cxlvi. 9, Prov. v. 16–17, and John iv. 9. Juvenal in 3. 14 and 6. 542 says the Jews have hay and a basket as their 'furniture'. H. Rönsch, 'Zu Juvenalis', in *Collectanea Philologa* (Bremen, 1891), 249–54, shows conclusively that pre-cooked food was kept warm for the sabbath in a basket of hay (Exodus xxxv. 3 with Mishnah 12)—not, as some have suggested, cooked slowly in hot damp hay (since such cooking would technically be a violation of the sabbath), but simply kept warm. Further references are cited by A. Cameron, 'Notes on Juvenal', *CR* 40 (1926), 62–63. H. Lewy, 'Philologisches aus dem Talmud', *Phil* 38 (1929), 390–1, takes up the description of the sabbath as 'barefooted' in 6. 159, and suggests that it is Yom Kippur, the Day of Atonement, on which the Jewish law commands fasting and forbids the putting on of shoes. Doubtless Juvenal had seen something of the Jewish community who were his neighbours in the Subura: see Mart. 12. 91. 1–2 and Juv. 3. 5, and the *Corpus Inscriptionum Iudaicarum*, ed. J. B. Frey (Rome, 1936), vol. 1, lxxiii–lxxiv.

4. *Structure.* The plan suggested in the text is this:

(*a*) 1–106: *Introduction*: parents teach vice by example.
(*b*) 107–255: *Particular instance*: they teach greed as a virtue

    (i) yet greed is miserable (107–37)

     (ii) leads on to crime and the breakdown of traditional standards of
          morality (138–88)
     (iii) and is actually dangerous for the parent himself (189–255).
  (c) 256–331: *General discussion*: greed means both folly and vice
     (i) it is ridiculous (256–302)
     (ii) and uncomfortable (303–31).

In *Serm.* 1. 1 Horace passes rather in the same way from the general introduction about μεμψιμοιρία to the particular examination of greed. V. D'Ago-
stino, 'La satira XIV di Giovenale', *Convivium*, 4 (1932), 227–44, divides the
poem into four sections:

  (a) 1–106, a general introduction.
  (b) 107–331 a particular instance
     (i) 107–255, riches bring misery
     (ii) 256–302, the effects of wealth
     (iii) 303–31, the insatiability of greed.

But surely we need a stronger punctuation for the long section about the
foolish father, 189–255. Gylling (*20*) breaks the poem into two at 107, and
subdivides into these sections: (*a*) 1–37, 38–58, 59–85, 86–106; (*b*) 107–34,
135–55, 156–209, 210–55, 256–316, 316–31 (which he calls an epilogue,
although it is surely another and final argument).

NOTES ON CHAPTER XXV

  1. *Sources, analogues, and adaptations.* There are sufficient parallels for the
facts described by Juvenal. Plut. *On Isis and Osiris*, 72, reports a similar religious feud in his own time. The crocodile-cult of the Ombites is described by
Aelian, *On the Nature of Animals*, 10. 21, and the hatred of the Tentyrites for
crocodiles, ibid. 10. 24. An Egyptian who would eat raw flesh was shown to
Nero, who characteristically considered giving him a live man to eat (Suet.
Nero 37. 2); human flesh was ritually eaten in an Egyptian revolt not long
after the events of Satire 15 (Dio 71. 4); and it has even been suggested that
the atrocity related by Juvenal was a case of ritual cannibalism—so J.
Moreau, 'Une Scène d'anthropophagie en Égypte', *Chronique d'Égypte*, 15
(1940), 279–85—although there is little to support that interpretation. As
for modern times, E. W. Lane, writing in 1836, declared:

'Cases of blood-revenge are very common among the peasantry of Egypt. . . . The
relations of a person who has been killed . . . generally retaliate with their own
hands rather than apply to the government, and often do so with disgusting cruelty,
and even mangle and insult the corpse of their victim. . . . Often a case of blood-
revenge involves the inhabitants of two or more villages in hostilities, which are
renewed, at intervals, during the period of several generations'—

which is Juvenal's *uetus atque antiqua simultas*, 15. 33. This is from c. 3 of
Lane's *Manners and Customs of the Modern Egyptians* (Everyman ed. pp. 108–9,
and see pp. 201–2 on the *barbara turba*). A similar outrage was reported from
Tunisia in 1907, closely paralleling the course of the fight in Satire 15: see

G. Highet, 'A fight in the desert', *CJ* 45 (1949), 94–96. As this is written, the ferocious Cairo riots of 1952 have just been announced.

The theme of fanaticism—really an extension of the general topic of superstition—was often discussed (particularly with reference to the Egyptians). See, for instance, Cic. *Tusc.* 5. 27. 78; Philo, *De uita contemplatiua* 1. 8; Plut., *On Isis and Osiris*; and Maximus of Tyre (ed. H. Hobein, Leipzig, 1910), 2. 5. 22–23. The other theme, of cruelty and human sympathy, was even more popular, appearing in philosophy (e.g. Philo, op. cit. 5. 40–44—which looks quite like Juv. 15. 16–60; Sen. *Ep.* 95. 51–53; Lucian, *Demonax* 10); in rhetoric (e.g. Seneca maior, *Contr.* 2. 1 (9), 10–13, and pseudo-Quintilian, *Decl. Magn.* 12); and in poetry (Ter. *Haut.* 77 and Lucr. 5. 951–9, 1009–19, 1107–15).

2. *Structure.* The pattern is clear and simple:

    (*a*) 1–32: general introduction: *this story is incredible but true.*
    (*b*) 33–92: story: *an Egyptian mob killed and ate a man.*
    (*c*) 93–131: comparison: *this was brutality, not necessity.*
    (*d*) 131–72: moral: *men are now worse than animals.*

The shape of the poem is rather like Satire 12, therefore: introduction, story, comment on the story, and moral.

3. The games are popular, but trashy: 3. 34–37, 6. 352–4, 7. 243, 9. 143–4, 10. 36–46, 11. 193–202. The gladiators are the lowest of the low, 3. 155–8, 6. 82–113, 6. 216, 8. 199–210. In the O fragment, 6. O7–13, the point is that there are moral distinctions *even* in that sink of baseness, the gladiatorial school. Ladies and gentlemen as gladiators and beast-fighters, 1. 22–23, 2. 143–8, 4. 99–101, 6. 246–67, 8. 199–210, 11. 3–20. In an early poem Juvenal seems to protest against being kept out of the knights' seats at the games, 3. 153–9; but later he refuses to go at all, 11. 193–204.

4. Juvenal repeats that the *nation* is guilty in 15. 29, 31, 126, 129–31, and 169–70. Lines 129–30 appear to me to imply a death-wish for all Egyptians.

5. Juv. 15. 1–13, 126–8. Herodotus' description of Egypt in his second book brings out a similar set of paradoxes. When westerners go east, for whatever reason, it is common enough to find them developing this same fascinated hatred of a country in which they have spent some considerable time: they cannot ignore it or forget it, but must keep remembering its charm mixed with queerness and squalor and cruelty. See, for instance, L. C. Arlington's *Through the Dragon's Eyes* (London, 1931): Mr. Arlington knows China very well and likes its art, but he is disgusted by the cruelty and callousness of the Chinese; he illustrates his book with pictures, and embellishes it with vivid descriptions, of atrocious Chinese tortures.

6. Juv. 15. 140–2 contains a religious sanction, with an appeal to the Eleusinian mysteries (see Mayor, *60,* ad loc.) and to the only goddess whom Juvenal reveres (cf. 3. 320, 6. 50, and the obverse in 9. 24 and 14. 219). It also alludes to the Stoic doctrine of the brotherhood of man, well epitomized in Ter. *Haut.* 77. The following lines, 15. 142–7, on the distinction of men and animals, come from Ov. *Met.* 1. 84–86, and express a favourite philosophical idea (see Mayor, *60,* on line 147). Lines 149–58 are reminiscent of Lucretius 5. 951–9, 1009–19, 1107–15.

7. Juv. 1. 147–9; 13. 28–30; 15. 31–32, *nostro aeuo*, contrasted with the heroic age—as again in 15. 65–71; 15. 165–71, the smiths of the Bronze Age making instruments of peace for agriculture, contrasted with contemporary eaters of human flesh. Hence also the comparisons with past history (15. 93–115). In a similar spirit, Gulliver was told by the king of Brobdingnag that the majority of the British were 'the most pernicious race of little odious vermin that Nature ever suffered to crawl upon the surface of the earth' (*Gulliver's Travels, A Voyage to Brobdingnag*, c. 6: Everyman ed. p. 120). And compare c. 7, 'nature . . . could now produce only small abortive births' (Everyman ed. p. 125) with Juv. 15. 65–71.

8. See pp. 68–70; Juv. 1. 1–13, 1. 52–54; 4. 34–36; 6. 634–61; and in 15, lines 13–26 (epic), 29–32 (tragedy), 65–71 (epic), 115–19 (tragedy). For the animals see 15. 159–64: a note in Mayor (*60*) gives other examples of this slightly inaccurate common-place. R. Reitzenstein, *Hellenistische Wundererzählungen* (Leipzig, 1906), 27–29, suggests that this poem is a parody of a type of wonder-tale with a moral (much used by the Stoics) called 'aretalogy'; and that it belongs to the same group as Hor. *Serm.* 1. 8. This may be, but the poem sounds too deadly serious to be easily classified as parody of any genus whatever.

9. G. J. Vossius declared the Fifteenth Satire spurious in 1647: see his *Poeticarum Institutionum libri tres* (Amsterdam, 1647), book 3, c. 9, para. 17; but he gave no reason, and perhaps he was thinking of the Sixteenth (see p. 287 of this book). More recently the poem was attacked as a forgery by C. Kempf, *De satira quinta decima quae sub Iuuenalis nomine circumfertur* (Berlin, 1843), who raised the following objections: (1) the subject is repulsive; (2) the story is irrelevant to a satirist working in Rome; (3) the 'digressions' in 13–26 and 62–72 are unlike Juvenal's style; (4) there are mistakes in facts, as when the author says no one worships Diana in Egypt—although there was a cult of Bubastis, who is Diana—or puts Ombi and Tentyra close together; (5) the style is weak and the thought rambling and inept. Kempf was followed by Ribbeck (*49*) 13–15, who added several precise stylistic arguments. These objections were answered and the satire was defended by K. F. Hermann, in a slashing review of Kempf, *Zeitschrift für die Alterthumswissenschaft*, 2 (1844), 74–79, which is still well worth reading for its penetration and sympathy; W. S. Teuffel, 'Bibliographische Berichte über Juvenalis', *NJbb* 43 (1845), 118–20; A. L. Döllen, *Beiträge zur Kritik und Erklärung der Satiren des Juvenalis* (Kiev, 1846), 217–51, 252–422; and finally G. Palm, *De Juvenalis satira quinta decima* (Halle, 1882), who pointed out that: (1) Juvenal likes repulsive subjects; (2) the aim of the story is to denounce cruelty and fanaticism, which a Roman could well do; (3) Juvenal often 'digresses'; (4) the factual errors could be scribes' mistakes; and (5) the weaknesses of the writing do not make the poem a forgery. Hermann (p. 75) added that the poem was an attack on the Egyptomania which spread over Italy under Hadrian. We now know that there is a better answer for the fourth objection, but the other replies dispose of the thesis of forgery and justify the poem as authentic.

NOTES ON CHAPTER XXVI

1. *Sources, analogues, and adaptations.* The subject of this seems to be very largely Juvenal's own idea. No doubt the basic criticism of the rough arbitrary manners of professional soldiers goes back to the New Comedy and entered Latin with the *Miles Gloriosus* of Plautus. Persius has several digs at coarse materialistic centurions: 3. 77–85 and 5. 189–91: and after Juvenal Apuleius described a far worse assault case involving a soldier, *Met.* 9. 39–42. Juvenal has borrowed the name Coranus (16. 54) from Horace's satire on legacy-hunting (*Serm.* 2. 5. 57), which he also used in Satire 12. But the sharp division between the professional army and the citizens, and between the praetorian guards and the civilians of Rome, was comparatively new, and must have provided valuable material for a satirist. In addition, the poem seems to reflect Hadrian's own new measures to keep the army contented. The first episode, the story of the beaten civilian who cannot get his case tried inside Rome, is the obverse of Hadrian's order that soldiers may not leave their units to engage in legal business (16. 7–34 and *Dig.* 22. 5. 3. 6); no doubt the second (16. 35–50) is another result of the same order. The third (16. 51–60+), on the soldier's power to dispose of his property in his father's lifetime, also results from Hadrian's activity. See B. d'Orgeval, *L'Empereur Hadrien: œuvre législative et administrative* (Paris, 1950), 87 and 348–51.

2. Coleridge's note implies that, in his dream, he had actually finished the poem: for 'on awaking he appeared to himself to have a distinct recollection of the *whole*', he remembered 'the *general purport* of the vision', and he compared it to 'the images on the surface of a stream'—which form a complete picture, although they are transient.

3. For a long time I thought that the sole surviving copy of Juvenal must have been in five papyrus rolls, and that it had lost the end of the fifth roll, but Mr. C. H. Roberts, of St. John's College, Oxford, has pointed out to me that papyrus rolls often lost their beginnings but seldom their ends (which were preserved inside); that parchment books were beginning to be used for collections of poems by the end of the first century A.D.; and that the final pages, or the last quire, of a parchment codex, is often lost. See two illuminating articles: F. G. Kenyon, 'Papyrus rolls and the ending of St. Mark', *Journal of Theological Studies*, 40 (1939), 56–57, and C. H. Roberts, 'The ancient book and the ending of St. Mark', ibid. 253–7, with references to Birt's work on the subject.

4. *Authenticity.* The scholiast, who has very few notes on this satire, observes: 'Ista a plerisque exploditur et dicitur non esse Iuuenalis.' But Servius and Priscian both believed it authentic, because they quote lines from it with Juvenal's name: see Priscian 8. 6. 31 and 8. 15. 82, Servius on *Aen.* 1. 16 and 2. 202. In some manuscripts the satire appears in the wrong place, before 15; and it was seldom or never quoted in the Middle Ages. It has been often challenged and often defended. For instance, Guarino's pupil Angelo Decembrio believed it was too short to be a real poem by Juvenal and thought its style unlike his. When Gibbon read it at Lausanne in his twenties, he thought it doubtful, but added: 'Il me semble que je reconnois la touche du maître au *Vers 55*' (*Journal à Lausanne*, ed. G. Bonnard, Lausanne, 1945, 37). But when he came to write *The Decline and Fall* he determined against it, and in a note on c. 5 (Everyman ed. v. 1, p. 120, n. 1) said: 'Upon the insolence and privileges of the soldiers, the 16th Satire, falsely ascribed to Juvenal, may be consulted; the style and circumstances of it would induce me to believe that it was composed under the reign of Severus, or that of his son.' In modern times the first large-scale attack on it was delivered by C. F. Heinrich in his edition (Bonn, 1839) 2. 514–45, his arguments being (*a*) that the scholiast doubted the authenticity of the poem, (*b*) that the style was unlike Juvenal's, and (*c*) that the structure made it a '*fetus abortivus*'. This was soon answered by W. E. Weber in a review, *NJbb* 32 (1841), 150–9, showing that most of the objections were flimsy. The question still remains open, but most modern scholars believe the satire genuine. Wessner (*53*) 288 remarks that the only real reason why the scholiast expressed any doubt was that the satire was imperfect when he began his work of commenting on it; and there are notably fewer notes even on the remaining sixty lines than there are proportionately on the rest of the satires. There is a good analysis of the whole problem in Ercole (*3*), c. 6, who concludes that the objections to the style of the satire are trivial and that its resemblances to Juvenal's other works are convincing. See also Knoche (*45*) 105–6, who points out that works of doubtful authenticity were always placed last in a collection and that therefore some scholars in antiquity may have assumed this, imperfect as it was, to be doubtful; he adds that one ancient editor placed 16 before 15, probably to save it from complete destruction.

5. In an excellent article, 'Juvénal et les prétoriens', *REL* 13 (1935), 95–106, M. Durry shows that although Juvenal says he is talking about the army in general, all the examples in the surviving part of the poem are taken from the praetorian guards. Now in 15 we saw that Juvenal had harked back to his early life, reviving the memories of his loathing for Egypt. Perhaps, therefore, in 16 he recalled another part of his youth, and—although more diplomatically—attacked the proud praetorians whose colonels he had so often loathed: Crispinus (1. 26–29 and 4. 1–33), Tigellinus (1. 155), Sejanus (10. 58–107), and even Fuscus (4. 111–12). To officers in other units of the British Army, it is said, members of the Guards Brigade sometimes appear rather lofty in manner, *laeti phaleris omnes et torquibus . . . .*

6. *Structure.* On the principle *ex pede Herculem*, we can guess at the size and scope of this satire:

    (*a*) 1–6: *Introduction*;

    (*b*) 7–250: *General advantages of all soldiers*

        (i) in legal affairs (7–60+);

        (ii) in social prestige and in financial matters (e.g. high pay, frequent largesses, good food and drink and lodging, admiration everywhere);

    (*c*) 251–500: *Special advantages of lucky soldiers*

        (i) rewards and plunder

        (ii) promotion and the path to power;

    (*d*) 501–550: *Conclusion.*

If Juvenal spent twenty-seven lines (8–34) on explaining only one of the ordinary advantages of military life over civilian life, in the comparatively uninteresting sphere of the law, he must, at the most cautious estimate, have spent 100 lines in all on the legal advantages of soldiers, and then at least as much on their ordinary advantages outside the law-courts—before turning to his main subject, *felicis praemia militiae* (16. 1–2), which would deserve more vivid and more detailed treatment.

NOTES ON CHAPTER XXVII

1. The first heavy attack on Juvenal in the early nineteenth century was delivered by Nisard (*27*). The discussion of Juvenal in this chapter of Nisard's book is rather curious—because, although Nisard clearly set out to depreciate Juvenal's work, and through it to attack certain tendencies he disliked in contemporary French literature, he was forced at the end to recognize Juvenal's powers of vision and of description, and to institute a parallel between ancient Rome and modern Paris which redounds to Juvenal's credit. This critique evoked a passionate defence by Hugo; and that in turn was followed by a quieter work, Martha (*26*), and a brilliant lecture, G. Boissier's 'Juvénal et son temps', *Revue des Cours littéraires*, 3 (1865), 249–65. Both of these stressed the unevenness of Juvenal's standards and the dangers of imagining him to be a staunch Stoic and a devoted republican. It is difficult to be sure about French politics, but I have the strong impression that both Martha and Boissier were intending to uphold the monarchy of Napoleon III against revolutionary propagandists such as Victor Hugo.

2. J. K. Huysmans, *Là-bas* (Paris, 1891), c. 19. On German concentration-camps see (among others) C. Burney, *The Dungeon Democracy* (London, 1945); E. Kogon, *The Theory and Practice of Hell* (tr. from *Der SS-Staat* by H. Norden, New York, c. 1950); A. Mitscherlich and F. Mielke, *Doctors of Infamy, the story of the Nazi medical crimes* (tr. H. Norden, New York, 1949); and O. Nansen, *From Day to Day* (New York, 1949). On Russian prison-camps see *The Dark Side of the Moon* (with introduction by T. S. Eliot, New York, 1947) and *El Campesino: Life and Death in Soviet Russia* (tr. I. Barea, New York, 1952). There are brilliant studies of Landru, Haarmann, and others by William Bolitho in *Murder for Profit* (New York, 1926).

3. Exaggerated contrasts: e.g. Demosthenes, whose father owned an armament factory, is described as 'bleared with the smoke of the glowing ingots' (10. 130). Secret orgies: 2. 82–116 and 6. 314–41. Towards the end of the eighteenth century Johnson's former friend Mrs. Thrale said (after reading Juvenal) that unnatural vice, particularly Lesbianism, was actually worse in her own time than in the Roman empire: see *Thraliana*, ed. K. C. Balderston (Oxford, 1951²), 2. 740 and 2. 949.

4. Anachronistic satires of the same type are now beginning to come out of Europe; though Hitler and Mussolini are both dead they haunt the memory and the imagination. A recent example is an Italian book not unlike Satire 4, on the lusts and corruptions of Mussolini's régime: Alberto Moravia's *The Fancy Dress Party* (New York, 1952).

5. *Juvenal's use of proper names* is a tricky problem. It has been stripped

to its essentials in the text, but deserves further analysis here. He says in
1. 150–71 that he will not attack powerful contemporaries *by name*: notice
nomen in 153, *Tigellinum*, obviously a cover-name drawn from the past, in
155, and the carefully anonymous phrases *qui dedit . . . aconita* (158) and
auditor cui frigida mens est criminibus (166–7). It seems to follow therefore that,
if he does use the name of a living person, the individual must either be
powerless to injure him (like Marius Priscus in 1. 49) or be unimportant
(like Codrus in 3. 203–11) or be mentioned in a friendly manner (like Caesar
in 7. 1). So Teuffel (*38*) 541, Friedländer (*55*) 99–106, and Peter (*28*) 78 n. 2,
and before them F. Strauch, *De personis Iuvenalianis* (Göttingen, 1869).
E. Epkema's *Prosopographiae Juvenalis pars prima* (Amsterdam, 1884) is not very
illuminating.

And yet this may leave two classes of names unaccounted for. The
first is best typified by Cluvienus. At the end of the long and splendidly
vigorous tirade 1. 22–80 Juvenal reaches a climax and cries that, even if he
has not the gifts of a poet, his resentment at the crimes of Rome will turn
into a creative force and will make poetry—

> any old type
> of verses, such as I can write, or Cluvienus.

Now, who was Cluvienus? It would be utterly pointless to end a strong
passage like this with an utterly unknown and meaningless name:

> any old type
> of verses, such as I can write, or Henry Sturges.

Therefore the name must have meant *somebody* at some time. Nor is it merely
a type-name meaning 'anybody at all', like John Doe, Joe Doaks, Mr.
Whosis. The Latin for that is Titius or Seius (Juv. 4. 13 and Mayor, *60*, ad
loc.). But Cluvienus is an uncommon name, and seems never to occur before
Juvenal's time. (There is no evidence to warrant us in accepting the guess by
Schneidewin that the name ought to be substituted for Calvinus in Mart. 7.
90. 3: 'Miscellen', *Phil* 3, 1848, 131.) The scholiast did not know who Cluvienus was, and simply gathered from the context—as we do—that he was
meant to be a less-than-average good poet. The note is *delerus poeta uel indoctus*,
echoed in glosses elsewhere (O. Ribbeck, 'Glossa', *RhM* 39, 1884, 315,
quotes one equating *Cludidenus* and *imperitus*) and in Ennodius, where he
appears in an altered shape in conjunction with a not unskilful adaptation
of Juv. 1. 18 (*Carm.* 1. 7, *praef.* 9–12):

> ad Camenalem tamen ignominiam—quibus numquam Gluuidenus deest—
> uersus adieci, et periturae (ut dictum est) cartae non peperci.

Accordingly, Cluvienus must be the name of a poet who had, just before
Juvenal recited Satire 1, achieved some notoriety by issuing an emphatically
mediocre poem. In that case, Juvenal made an unfortunate choice in
selecting and in emphasizing a name which so soon became meaningless,
and also in failing to express the poor man's mediocrity more pointedly.
(Vergil is much more effective about Bavius and Maevius in *Buc.* 3. 90–91,
and so is Horace about Crispinus in *Serm.* 1. 1. 120–1.)

However, it is also possible that Cluvienus is not the poet's real name at all, but a cover-name. There are plenty of instances of this trick in Latin satire. The woman Horace hated was called Gratidia. When he wrote about her he changed her name, inserted a slighting allusion to her grey hair, and called her Canidia (Porphyrio on *Epod*. 3. 7). And we might guess that, when he recited the poem to his friends, he actually said 'Gratidia', reserving the safer name only for written publication of his work. (The practice is familiar from love-poetry also: Catullus could name his mistress Clodia when he read her his poems, but he called her Lesbia when they were published.) Sometimes both names have got into the tradition—either because the real name was known, written in the margin by a reader, and in a later copy substituted for the cover-name; or because the author himself, in a later edition, when he grew bolder, withdrew the pseudonym and put in the real name. (Knoche (*45*) 303–4 suggests that editors might alter names for fun, *spielerisch*, but that is surely a little illogical.) G. Pasquali, *Storia della tradizione* (Florence, 1934), 425–6, cites several such variants in Martial. A good example is 1. 10. The title of the poem in the A^A edition was DE GEMELLO; in B^A and C^A it was DE VENUSTO. In the poem itself the man is called Gemellus by A^A and B^A; he is called Venustus by C^A. Clearly one was the real and one the cover-name. In Hor. *Serm*. 1. 2. 27, a man with unpleasant breath is called Rufillus. But Seneca, quoting the line (*Ep*. 86. 13), calls him Buccillus, which looks much more appropriate as a cover-name. In Juvenal there are a few doublets which seem to have appeared in this way: Gallus and Cossus in 7. 144, perhaps Tutor and Numitor in 8. 93, Lateranus and Damasippus in 8. 167, Ponticus and Regulus in 8. 179: on these see Knoche (*45*) 303 f. I have wondered whether Pollitta in 2. 68 (whose name varies in the manuscripts) may not have been Gallitta of Pliny, *Ep*. 6. 31. 4–6.

Now, imagine that Juvenal, when publishing his poems, inserted the more or less meaningless cover-name Cluvienus at 1. 80; but, when reciting them, used the real name of a contemporary poet who was known to his audience. In that case, it would be pointless for us to search for a Cluvienus. We should do far better to look for a known poet whose name would fit into this metrical position in the line. And in fact there are several. The man might be Decianus of Mart. 1. 61. 10; or he might well be Julius Cerialis, who wrote poems of the type Juvenal detested—bucolics in emulation of Vergil, and a Gigantomachy (Mart. 11. 52).

It is suggested, therefore, that some of the names in Juvenal's topical references are cover-names only, which have merely a metrical correspondence (and perhaps also a faint similarity in sound) to the name of the real person known to Juvenal and his audience.

But is it true that Juvenal never uses the name of an influential living contemporary except in a compliment? There are some examples which might make us doubt this. In Satire 2 there is a vile degenerate despised even by a debauched woman (2. 50):

> Hispo subit iuuenes et morbo pallet utroque.

Now, this poem was published in the first part of Trajan's reign (p. 12); and an eminent statesman of Trajan's time was called Hispo. His full magnificent name appears to have been Galeo Tettienus Severus M. Eppuleius Proculus Ti. Caepio Hispo (*PIR*² E 83). Pliny describes his powerful intervention in a senatorial investigation (*Ep.* 4. 9. 16–20); and he was consul in 101 (*Dig.* 40. 5. 26. 7, and see *AJA* 43, 1939, 283). His colleague in the consulship, by the way, was Rubrius Gallus—at whose father and lineage Juvenal sneers bitterly in 4. 104–6. The cognomen Hispo is uncommon, as R. Syme points out in a valuable discussion, 'Personal names in *Annals* I–VI', *JRS* 39 (1949), 14–15; it would be perfectly well known to Juvenal's audience as that of a senator. Therefore, either Hispo had died just before Juvenal published his first book—in which case the name would still shock the public and bitterly offend Hispo's family; or else Juvenal was here using the name of a real, living, powerful contemporary, but sheltering himself under his own preliminary declaration (1. 170–1), rather as modern authors try to protect themselves against libel-suits by adding a caution: 'The characters in this work are wholly imaginary, and any resemblance to living persons is purely coincidental.' Weidner (*63*) suggests in para. 10 of his preface that Hispo must have been dead when the poem appeared; and yet we know that an Eppuleius Proculus was proconsul of Asia (*CIL* 11. 14 and 5. 5813) and that Tettienus Severus was proconsul of Asia in 117–18 (*Ann. Epigr.* 1930, n. 77): surely the same man.

No doubt the name Hispo appealed to Juvenal because it recalled the *hispida membra* of the homosexuals he had already castigated (2. 11). Still, it seems very daring. A further complication in this problem appears when we look at the manuscripts. In the inferior groups the name reads Hispo. In one (Vind. 107) it is Hispp. In the good scholia it is Hippo. In P it cannot quite be read. Did Juvenal actually publish Hippo to safeguard himself, and was Hispo inserted later by someone who either knew the allusion to the real pervert, or merely thought of *hispida membra*?

Let us look at another example. Juvenal uses the name Hispulla in 6. 74 for a rich lady who is having a love-affair with an actor; in 12. 11 he adds that a prize bull would be 'fatter than Hispulla'. Now Calpurnia Hispulla was the aunt of Pliny's wife (*Ep.* 4. 19 and 8. 11); and there were two other ladies called Hispulla, both friends of Pliny—one the widow and the other the daughter of Corellius Rufus, a man of consular rank (*Ep.* 1. 12. 9 and 3. 3). The name is rare, and as Syme suggests (*JRS* 39, 1949, 14–15) it even has a local habitation in northern Italy. Would it be possible for Juvenal to use it, in such contexts, without mortally offending Pliny and his friends?

It is notable that Pliny, although he knew Martial and wrote a letter about him (*Ep.* 3. 21), never mentions Juvenal; nor does Juvenal name Pliny. A. Guillemin, *Pline et la vie littéraire de son temps* (Paris, 1929), 23, suggests that this is because they belonged to different literary groups. Yet when we recollect that Juvenal says Pliny's great case, the impeachment of Marius Priscus, was a waste of time (1. 47–50), and when we add to that his use of a name from Pliny's own immediate circle, we may conclude rather that the two men were antipathetic, and that Juvenal revenged himself by side-hits like these while Pliny maintained a lofty silence.

Another such side-hit has been divined by L. Herrmann, 'Juvenaliana', *REA* 42 (1940), 448 f. Pointing to the description in Juv. 7. 178–88 of the villa built by a rich man who grudges to pay fees to Quintilian for his son's education, he suggests that its features reflect the layout of the villa of which Pliny was so proud (*Ep.* 2. 17). Since we know that Pliny was a pupil of Quintilian (*Ep.* 2. 14. 9), the passages would then be a veiled sneer at his adoptive father and at himself. If Juvenal was also a pupil of Quintilian, as has been suggested by Kappelmacher (*24*), then the enmity between Juvenal and Pliny might go very far back. Both men came from country towns. One succeeded—although it meant enduring the rule of Domitian. The other failed—and was ruined by Domitian. Juvenal could not admire Pliny, and it seems likely that he expressed his scorn of him by half-covert allusions in his satires.

There are other possible digs at Pliny's friends. In 3. 133 Calvina is a woman who will sleep with a rich man's slave for money. The name is that of a gay lady of Nero's time (Sen. *Apoc.* 8. 2, Tac. *Ann.* 12. 4, Suet. *Vesp.* 23. 4), but also of a kinswoman of Pliny, who gave her 100,000 sesterces as a wedding-present and wrote her a letter about money (*Ep.* 2. 4). In 1. 40 Gillo is a gigolo who will sleep with a rich old lady for money. But Q. Fulvius Gillo Bittius Proculus was Pliny's stepfather-in-law and had been consul in 97 (*Ep.* 9. 13. 13): he was highly distinguished, having been proconsul of Asia and an Arval Brother. When the satire was published, he was surely alive. In 3. 203 Procula is an odd-looking woman, either a giantess or a dwarf; but she was also a lady from Padua whom Pliny knew and admired (*Ep.* 1. 14. 6).

Then, apart from names which resemble those of Pliny's friends, Juvenal throws mud at a number of others which were borne by distinguished contemporaries. For example, Creticus, used to stigmatize an effeminate lawyer in 2. 67, was a real cognomen in the family of the Caecilii Metelli (as some of the scholia point out)—so that the gibe must have indirectly wounded some persons who were alive, powerful, and proud. (This has been observed by R. L. Dunbabin, 'Notes on Latin authors', *CR* 39, 1925, 112.)

Again, a legacy-hunter in 5. 98 is called Laenas. But Laenas was a cognomen of the Popilii; and at the time when Juvenal published his first book there was a rising young statesman called Sergius Octavius Laenas Pontianus, who was to become consul in 131 (*CIL* 14. 2610). His grandmother, by the way, was Rubellia Bassa, daughter of Rubellius Blandus, whom Juvenal rebuked later, in 8. 39–72.

The family of the Lamiae cannot have been overjoyed to hear themselves described (in 4. 154) as the impotent victims of Domitian; nor to learn (in 6. 385–92) that one of their kinswomen prayed passionately for the success of a musician. When Juvenal published Satire 6, at least one Lamia was prominent in public life: L. (Aelius) Lamia Aelianus, consul in 116 (*PIR*² A 204).

Then in 8. 96 there is a quick reference to Pansa as a Roman official who is expected to despoil the provinces. Within a year or two of the publication of the Third Book, containing Satire 8, Corellius Pansa was consul (in A.D. 122: *PIR*² C 1293 and *CIL* 6. 10048). He might well have been the son of Pliny's friend Hispulla (*Ep.* 3. 3), whom Juvenal had already insulted. Also, a P. Licinius Pansa was on his way up in the senatorial career, for he was to become consul in 134 (*PIR* L 155 and *CIL* 3, p. 878).

This list could be much lengthened; and it could, I believe, be used to show that Juvenal took particular care to wound certain great families by using their own special names to typify certain kinds of vice and folly. Whether that is true or not, there seems to be enough evidence to prove that (a) Juvenal sometimes satirized real contemporaries under metrically correspondent cover-names, (b) he stigmatized real names belonging to influential persons—particularly within Pliny's circle—and to prominent families, (c) he shielded himself against possible retaliation by saying in his introduction that he would attack only the dead by name, and (d) this practice (which is most noticeable in his early books and dies away later) was largely responsible for his failure to achieve success in his own time.

6. The present moment appears in nearly every satire. See 1. 87–89; *nunc* and *iam* in 1. 95 and 1. 139; *nunc* in 2. 162; *debuerant olim* in 3. 163; *nondum* in 5. 1; *nostra tempestate* in 6. 25–26 and *nunc* in 6. 659; *iam* and *posthac* in 7. 3 and 7. 18; 8. 87–88 deals with the immediate future; while topical events are the basis of 11 (see lines 3–8), 12 (see *adhuc, nuper* in 15–16), 13 (*recenti* in 5), and 15 (*nuper* in 27).

7. For instance, quite recently, Mr. E. V. Marmorale in *Giovenale* (Naples, 1938, 2nd edition with polemical preface, 1950) has asserted bluntly that Juvenal is not a poet. But such an assertion is not of much critical value. Either it means that Mr. Marmorale does not consider verse satire to be poetry—in which case he rules out Parini and Pope and Horace and Boileau from the rank of poets, a proceeding in which few will follow him; or else it means that he thinks Juvenal is inferior to them in poetic gifts, which is an arbitrary personal opinion rather than a scholarly judgement. Croce, while praising the first edition of Mr. Marmorale's work, said that he had decided that Juvenal did not wish to write 'lirica e poesia', but that poetry kept creeping in among his rhetoric. (See *Poesia antica e moderna: interpretazioni*, Bari, 1943[2], 101–7.) The mistake here is the assumption that lyrics are poetry and that rhetoric in verse is not, whereas they are simply different types of poetry. Competent answers to Mr. Marmorale have been given by E. Aguglia, 'Giovenale e la critica recente', *Atene e Roma*, 7 (1939), 135–51, and M. R. Posani, 'Precisazioni critiche sulla poesia di Giovenale', *Atene e Roma*, 11 (1943), 103–20. At the other extreme, Victor Hugo places Juvenal with Homer and Tacitus and ten others in 'la région supérieure de la poésie et de la pensée' (*William Shakespeare*, i, ii, v, p. 100).

8. These digressions and expansions were analysed by J. Vahlen in 'Quaestiones Iuvenalianae', *Opuscula Academica* (Leipzig, 1907), 223–53, with a subtlety later overdone by W. Schulz, 'Quaestiones Iuvenalianae', *Hermes*, 21 (1886), 179–92. See also M. J. Hofmann, *Zur Kritik und Erklärung einiger Satiren des Juvenal* (Amberg, 1878) and Hartmann (*21*).

9. There is a fuller discussion of Juvenal's sources in Highet (*23*). On his borrowings from rhetoric and popular philosophy see J. Bergmueller, *Quaestiones Iuvenalianae* (Erlangen, 1886); De Decker (*18*); Gauger (*19*); Highet (*22*); and Schuetze (*31*). There has been no complete treatment of his knowledge of Cicero; but see H. C. Nutting, 'Three notes on Juvenal', *AJP* 49 (1928,) 253–66, and H. F. Rebert, 'The literary influence of Cicero upon Juvenal', *TAPA* 57 (1926), 181–94. For Horace there is an uncritical survey by P. Schwartz, *De Juvenale Horatii imitatore* (Halle, 1882). For Lucan see para. 55 of W. E. Heitland's introduction to C. E. Haskins's edition of Lucan (London, 1887). On Martial and Juvenal there is quite a lot: I. Amato, *Rapporto spirituale tra due poeti di Roma imperiale* (Palermo, 1940); G. Boissier, 'Relations de Juvénal et de Martial', *Revue des Cours et Conférences*, 7. 2 (1899), 443–51; Colton (*17*), which is thorough although unpublished as yet; J. Cousin, 'Nature et mission du poète dans la poésie latine :16: Martial et Juvénal', *Revue des Cours et Conférences*, 40. 2 (1938–9), 548 f.; Nettleship (*6*); N. Salanitro, *Gli Epigrammi di Marziale a Giovenale* (Naples, 1948); and Wilson (*40*), with a shorter version in *TAPA* 29 (1898), xxviii–xxxii. On Seneca there is an industrious but impercipient thesis by Schneider (*30*), as well as discussions of the sources of Sat. 6, E. Bickel, *Diatribe in Senecae philosophi fragmenta*, i (Leipzig, 1915), 10–11; F. Bock, *Aristoteles Theophrastus Seneca de matrimonio (Leipziger Studien*, 19, 1899, 47 f.); and J. Van Wageningen, 'Seneca et Iuvenalis', *Mnem.*, n.s. 45 (1917), 417–29. On Vergil there is a not very penetrating collection by J. Gehlen, *De Juvenale Vergilii imitatore* (Göttingen, 1896). On the whole topic of Juvenal's sources see also A. Gercke, *Seneca-Studien* (Leipzig, 1895), 186–91; Kappelmacher (*24*); Scott (*32*); Strube (*36*); C. Weyman's review of Friedländer (*55*) in *Blätter für das Gymnasial-Schulwesen*, 33 (1897), 270–7, and his 'Zu lateinischen Dichtern II', *Neophilologus*, 7 (1922), 283.

    10. On Lucretius and Juvenal, I know only B. Lavagnini, 'Motivi diatribici in Lucrezio e in Giovenale', *Athenaeum*, 25 (1947), 83–88, which does not set out to be complete.

    11. Juvenal's style has not yet been given the close analysis that it deserves. For all its care, Kiær's book (*25*) is not fully satisfactory because it does not compare Juvenal's style with that of other writers. It appears to me that in his choice and use of words, as in his manner and material, Juvenal was endeavouring, usually with success, to raise satire to a higher plane. Thus, his vocabulary is full of colloquial expressions: *basium*, the 'vulgar' kiss-word; *lassus* nine times, the loftier *fessus* never; *iumentum*, never used by poets except Lucretius 5. 1331 and Horace *Ep*. 1. 18. 46; *nemo* thirty-five times (a pronoun never used in Horace's lyrics and only four times in the whole *Aeneid*); *erga* and *industrius*, words never used in all the rest of non-dramatic poetry before Juvenal; the prosy word *negotium*; and so forth. (For these and other illuminating data see B. Axelson, *Unpoetische Wörter*, Lund, 1945.)

    On the other hand, he is not nearly so colloquial as Horace. There are fewer conversations in his satires; fewer diminutives; fewer tricks of ordinary speech such as syncope; his adverbs are more vivid but less everyday (A. Bagby, *Adverbs in Horace and Juvenal*, Baltimore, 1891); he has remarkably few interjections (F. Rohde, *De interiectionum usu apud aetatis argenteae scriptores Latinos*, Königsberg, 1911). And Juvenal never uses the obscene words which are common in Catullus and Martial and occur too often in Horace: *pedo, caco, futuo, paedico*, and so on; *mingo* and *meio* are the farthest he will go. Instead, he uses drastic, vivid words: *anhelo, palpito, ructo*.

    And poetic words are much commoner than one would expect in his style. He uses *ingens* nearly as often as Lucretius (see K. E. Ingvarson, 'Ingens dans la poésie', *Eranos*, 48, 1950, 66–70); he will call a ship's mast *arbor* like an epic poet; and of course poetic expressions are common in his parodic passages (see Scott, *32*). His periphrases also, sometimes funny, are sometimes a serious device to raise his satire to the level of thoughtful poetry (see J. De Decker, 'De l'originalité de la périphrase dans les satires de Juvénal', *RIPB* 50, 1907, 84–99). Horace likes proverbs, which are unpretentious and folksy, like Sancho Panza; Juvenal, like Don Quixote, prefers *sententiae*, which belong to a higher realm of thought.

NOTES ON CHAPTER XXVIII

1. Did Lucian the Greek satirist (*fl.* A.D. 160) know Juvenal's work and use it? Helm and Mesk have suggested that *Nigrinus* and *De Mercede Conductis* in particular were answers to Satires 3 and 5. (For references, and for Hartmann's answer, see the first note on c. 9, p. 252.) A. Gercke, in his review of Friedländer (*55*) in *GGA* 158 (1896), 971–2, added that the opening of *Nigrinus* resembles the opening of Satire 9. Still, all the resemblances look like the coincidences between the work of two observers viewing similar worlds from different points of view. And although Lucian knew some Latin (Helm 60, n. 3), it is unlikely that he would choose to read and answer a Roman writer without making clearer and more pointed allusions to his predecessor and his opponent.

2. See the discussion in which Wessner (*81*) answered the arguments of H. J. Thomson, 'Lucan, Statius, and Juvenal in the early centuries', *CQ* 22 (1928), 24–27. The only conceivable hint that Juvenal might have been known in the middle of the second century comes from a long poem inscribed on a monument in Africa and dated not later than the Antonine period (*CIL* 8. 213). The third line begins:

> Ecce Secundus adest iterum. . . .

T. Kleberg, 'Juvenalis in the Carmina Latina Epigraphica', *Eranos*, 44 (1946), 421–5, thinks that this might be a reminiscence of Juv. 4. 1:

> Ecce iterum Crispinus. . . .

But the resemblance is scant, the words are commonplace, and the line in the inscription was much more probably suggested by the opening of the poem, *Huc iterum pietas*. . . .

3. It is very hard to tell whether Minucius Felix, earliest of the defenders of Christianity in classical Latin, had read Juvenal and was unconsciously imitating him, or was using phrases which Juvenal had also written but which belonged to the public domain. H. Boenig in his edition of Minucius (Leipzig, 1903) gives a number of apparent adaptations of Juvenal; but most of these are simply treatments of social and ethical commonplaces, where it is impossible to trace any close or exclusive kinship between Juvenal and Minucius in thought and expression. For instance, the assertion that temples were often used for arranging love-affairs appears in Minucius, *Oct.* 25. 11 and in Juvenal 6. 489 and 9. 22–24; but there is no verbal resemblance in their phrasing and the idea often occurs in other writers. I can see only three phrases in *Octavius* which might be echoes of Juvenal:

Oct. 4. 1, dolere nescio quid uoltu fatebatur ~Juv. 2. 17
Oct. 21. 11, nisi forte Iuppiter iam senuit ~Juv. 6. 59
Oct. 25. 9, Aegyptia illa non numina sed portenta ~Juv. 15. 2;

and all these could quite well be familiar clichés adapted by both authors.

4. Tert. *Adu. Marc.* 4. 24. 12–14 (*CSEL* 47. 502): 'Quis nunc dabit "potestatem calcandi super colubros et scorpios?" utrumne omnium animalium dominus, an nec unius lacertae deus?' (The echo was pointed out by C. Weyman, 'Zu lateinischen Dichtern II', *Neophilologus*, 7, 1922, 283.) The first edition of 1521, based on lost manuscripts, omits *lacertae*. Tertullian is recalling the words of Jesus in Luke x. 19.

5. Tert. *De Pudic.* 1 (*PL* 2. 1031–2): 'Pudicitia flos morum . . . tamen aliquatenus in saeculo morabitur, si natura praestruxerit' ~Juv. 6. 1–2. This was signalized by H. Hoppe, *De sermone Tertullianeo quaestiones selectae* (Marburg, 1897), 24–26, who adds that Tertullian's indignation frequently resembles Juvenal's. Perhaps also the Figaro list of professions in *De Pallio*, 6. 2 may have been inspired by Juv. 3. 75–78. But in the *Apologeticus* the parallels suggested by Z. K. Vysoký, *Příspěvky k Poznání Pramenů Spisů Tertullianových, Práce z Vědeckých Ústavů*, 44 (Prague, 1937), are far from convincing: *Apol.* 6. 3 ~ Juv. 6. 349 f., *Apol.* 6. 4 ~Juv. 6. 27, and *Apol.* 6. 6 ~Juv. 6. 457 f.

6. Arnobius has no trace of Juvenal—E. Rapisarda, *Arnobio* (Catania, 1946) 254, can point only to two obvious commonplaces; nor has St. Cyprian of Carthage; nor has Commodian, even in the satirical parts of his work—see P. L. Ciceri, 'Di alcune fonti dell' opera poetica di Commodiano', *Didaskaleion*, 2 (1913), 363–422. Juvencus (*fl.* 330) 4. 647 (*CSEL* 24. 139) has *regem dominumque salutant* like Juv. 8. 161, but it is a fairly obvious tag, occurring in Martial too (10. 10. 5) and in slightly different forms in Cyprianus Gallus, *Genesis* 1052 and 1136 (*CSEL* 23. 40 and 43).

7. Lactantius, *Diuinae Institutiones*, 3. 29 (*PL* 6. 443 B) ~Juv. 10. 365–6, with the inferior reading *abest*. The commentaries to St. Paul's epistles attributed to the converted Jew Isaac, who lived in the second half of the fourth century, contain the phrase *erroris nebula* (~Juv. 10. 4) five times, in *PL* 17. 60 B, 76 A, 182 C (*sublata erroris nebula*), 357 C, 437 D: see A. Souter, 'Notes on Juvenal', *CR* 14 (1900), 414. But it looks rather like an obvious philosophical image: in the same way a Middle English mystic wrote a treatise called *The Cloud of Unknowing* (ed. P. Hodgson, London, 1944).

8. Ausonius knew Juvenal's name, and mentions him with a quotation of 2. 3 in his *Cento* 8 *fin.* (H. G. E. White's Loeb edition, New York and London, 1919, vol. 1, p. 390). Since he had a remarkable memory, he retained and used a certain number of tags from the satires: for example—

Bk. 5 (*Commem. Prof.*) 1. 17 (White's edition 1. 98) ~Juv. 10. 9
Bk. 6 (*Epit. Heroum*) 15. 1 (White 1. 148) ~Juv. 5. 56
Bk. 7 (*Ecl.*) 2. 16 (White 1. 164) ~Juv. 8. 87+Juv.10. 111
Bk. 10 (*Mosella*) 270 (White 1. 244) ~Juv. 7. 241
Bk. 14 (*Caesares*) 2. 12 (White 1. 332) ~Juv. 4. 38
Bk. 18 (*Epist.*) 22. 46+57 (White 2. 76) ~Juv. 11. 180–1
Bk. 19 (*Epig.*) 34. 3 (White. 2. 176) ~Juv. 9. 129
Ibid. 104. 1 (White 2. 212) ~Juv. 6. 172.

Further suggestions will be found in C. Hosius, *De Iuuenalis codicum recensione interpolata* (Bonn, 1888), 14; H. A. Strong, 'Ausonius' debt to Juvenal', *CR* 25 (1911), 15; A. Zingerle, *Zu späteren lateinischen Dichtern* (Innsbruck, 1873 and 1879); and the index to Schenkl's edition, *MGH* 5. 2 (Berlin, 1883). Ausonius' pagan friend Symmachus knew Statius well, but not Martial, and he quotes Juvenal only once: in *Ep.* 4. 34. 3 he says 'mandari enim periturae chartae epistulas quereris' ∼ Juv. 1. 18. W. Kroll, *De Q. Aurelii Symmachi studiis* (*Breslauer phil. Abhandlungen*, 6, 1893, 2), 60, suggests that *Ep.* 1. 3. 2 and 3. 11. 2 show a knowledge of Juv. 7. 55, but there is really nothing in common except the fairly obvious metaphor *moneta.*

9. The works of Paulinus are in *CSEL* 29. See *Carm.* 25. 86, *turritum aedificata caput* ∼ Juv. 6. 502–3. *Carm.* 9. 3 has *memori . . . pectore,* which could conceivably be a reminiscence of Juv. 11. 28; *Appendix Carm.* 3. 214 begins *hoc natura negat* ∼ Juv. 1. 79; and there is a clear echo of the Tanaquil passage from Juv. 6. 566 in *Carm.* 10. 192—and also in Aus. *Ep.* 28. 31.

The antithesis of wealth and poverty is in *Carm.* 18. 232 (*CSEL* 30, 107) and *Ep.* 32. 3 (*CSEL* 29. 277) ∼ Juv. 5. 113. It is also found, in the form 'pauperibus locuples, sibi pauper', perhaps inspired by Juvenal, in a Christian inscription from the period 422–32: *Carmina Epigraphica* (*Anthologia Latina,* ed. F. Buecheler, Leipzig, 1895), 1. 312. Possibly the end of line 5 in that poem, *nutritus in aula,* is remembered from Juvenal 3. 117+4. 93.

10. Prudentius (ed. J. Bergman, *CSEL* 61), *Apoth.* 457 ∼ Juv. 10. 55; *Apoth.* 748 ∼ Juv. 3. 97; *Ham.* 763 ∼ Juv. 1. 85; *Psychom.* 116 ∼ Juv. 6. 238; *Psychom.* 183 ∼ Juv. 6. 502–3; *Contra Symm.* 1. 582 ∼ Juv. 6. 350; ibid. 2. 288–9 ∼ Juv. 6. 2–3; ibid. 2. 555–60 ∼ Juv. 8. 3–4 and 7. 125–6; ibid. 2. 866 ∼ Juv. 15. 9–11; *Perist.* 2. 514 ∼ Juv. 6. 343; and a touching echo in *Perist.* 10. 700, where a martyred child whose body contains 'more milk than blood' is described in the same phrase as the kidling of Juv. 11. 68. These are only a few examples; many more are given in E. B. Lease's *Syntactic, stylistic, and metrical study of Prudentius* (Baltimore, 1895), 71–72. I have been unable to see Schuster's *Studien zu Prudentius.*

11. Juv. 1. 15 is echoed in *Ep.* 50. 5 (*PL* 22. 516), *Ep.* 57. 12 (*PL* 22. 578), and *Adu. Rufinum,* 1. 17 (*PL* 23. 430). Perhaps *nosse mensuram suam* in *Ep.* 61. 3 (*PL* 22. 604) is an allusion to Juv. 11. 35. But the suggestion made by E. Luebeck, *Hieronymus quos nouerit scriptores* (Leipzig, 1872), 198–9, that *pauimenta uerrunt* in *Ep.* 56. 13 (*PL* 22. 646) and *pauimenta uerrerint* in *Adu. Heluidium,* 20 (*PL* 23. 214 B) is an adaptation of Juv. 14. 60 seems very unlikely, the words and the idea being so common. E. Dralle, *De fragmento Winstedtiano* (Marburg, 1922), 42, compares *Ep.* 22. 28 (*PL* 22. 413–15) and *Ep.* 79. 9 (*PL* 22. 730–1) with the O fragment of the Sixth Satire, and hints that they all derive from an interest in obscenity for its own sake. One odd coincidence is the remark of St. Hilarion, *nudus latrones non timet* (*Vita S. Hil.* 12, *PL* 23. 34), which is so convincing in its context that it cannot be inspired by Juv. 10. 22; perhaps both sentences come from a proverb. On the connexion between Jerome's work and the Sixth Satire see n. 2 on c. 13, p. 264.

12. Aug. *Ep.* 138 (*a*). 3. 16 (*PL* 33. 532): 'audiant satyricum suum garriendo uera dicentem: "Seruabat castas..."' (Hor. *Serm.* 1. 1. 24, Juv. 6. 287–95).

13. The original of the commentary which is partly reproduced in the P manuscript (and fragmentarily elsewhere) was compiled by a pagan in Rome at some time later than A.D. 352 and earlier than A.D. 399, because it mentions Cerealis, prefect of Rome in 352, on 10. 24 (Mommsen, 'Zeitalter des Scholiasten Juvenals', *Gesammelte Schriften*, 7, Berlin, 1909, 509–11) and on 8. 175 speaks of gladiators in the present tense, although the shows were abolished in 399 (U. Knoche, *Überlieferung Juvenals*, Berlin, 1926, 64–65). It was made by a single man, because he refers to himself in the singular (on 6. 117), and he was a trained scholar—as we see from his references back (e.g. on 13. 33), his citations of other authors, his interest in grammar, his professional expressions like *notandum* (on 3. 231, e.g.) and the care with which he quotes variants and balances different interpretations. For instance, on *uigilata proelia* (7. 27) he asks: 'utrum *quae tu pugnans cum animo scripseris*, an *ea quae de pugna conscribis?*' On *mitem animum* (14. 15) he comments: 'Interrogatiue pronuntiari potest, sed melius ironicos.' He had access to learned books (A. Gercke, 'Plinius in den Juvenalscholien', *Seneca-Studien*, Leipzig, 1895, 191–5): in fact, he produces some information, such as the life-story of Tigellinus on 1. 155, which is found nowhere else. However, he meant his commentary not for scholars but for the general public, since he does not name the critics whose work he uses, or insert their reasons for maintaining different interpretations (Matthias, *48*, 7–8). He was not really a very intelligent annotator, and sometimes copied his sources carelessly: e.g. the scholion on 14. 91 applies to Posides three different sets of distinctions granted to Posides and two other freedmen, because the scholiast has been hasty in copying out Suetonius, *D. Claudius* 28: see Wessner (*53*) xxxviii–xxxix and 284, and in general c. 6 of Knoche cited above.

14. S. Consoli, 'Studi intorno agli scolii di Giovenale e di Persio', *RFIC* 50 (1922), 38–54, lists and discusses the quotations. (They are also given on p. 290 by Wessner, *53*.) The scholiast's favourite authors are Vergil, Cicero, Horace, Lucan, Sallust, and Terence; but he (or his sources) also knew Tacitus and Suetonius.

15. Wessner (*81*) 331 points out that Servius groups Juvenal with the *neoterici*, not with the *idonei*. He observes on 299–300 that Macrobius quotes Juvenal (3. 10. 2 ∼ Juv. 1. 15) without mentioning his name, and that Martianus Capella does the same (2. 119 ∼ Juv. 3. 118, 5. 425. 6 ∼ Juv. 13. 39 and 13. 79)—as though they wanted to show their knowledge of a newly fashionable poet. There are also one or two echoes in the *Querolus*, an imitation of Plautus' *Aulularia* which looks like a student's adaptation dating from the fourth century: p. 32, l. 14 in Peiper's edition ∼ Juv. 8. 129–30, and a good adaptation of Juv. 13. 129–34 in p. 45, ll. 3–4: 'plus est hoc quam hominem perdidisse, damnum uere plangitur.'

16. e.g. he is constantly cited in Cledonius' *Commentum artis Donati*, which dates from the sixth century (*GL* 5. 42, 5. 47, 5. 64, &c.); he appears thrice in the Bembine scholia to Terence (J. F. Mountford, *The Scholia Bembina*, Liverpool, 1934, 116).

17. Knoche (*45*) 47–48, n. 1, suggests that the critical edition of the text was made first, and then the scholia. This would be logical; but we cannot really tell whether they were issued together or separately. Certainly the editor collated several manuscripts, noted variant readings, and inserted critical signs.

18. So Knoche (*45*) 46–47, n. 3, and 63–64; E. Lommatzsch, *Quaestiones Iuvenalianae* (Leipzig, 1895), 12 and 20: Wessner (*53*) 288; the same fact is hinted at by W. M. Lindsay, reviewing Housman (*56*) in *CR* 19 (1905), 463. It is quite hopeless to try to account for the loss of 16. 61 f. by the mutilation of P or any such comparatively recent manuscript. What we have to explain is a set of three distinct facts: (*a*) the mutilation of the text in all the manuscripts at exactly the same place; (*b*) the absence of scholia beyond 16. 45: (*c*) the absence of quotations from the latter parts of 16 in the grammarians and other late scholars. Only a very early mutilation of the master-copy will explain all three.

19. St. Jerome, who knew at least one line of Juvenal (see n. 11), studied at the Athenaeum with Donatus, and may well have heard the citation there. Knoche (*45*) 63–64, n. 2, suggests that the single copy which survived belonged to 'a public library in Rome'.

20. This officiously 'corrected' edition is usually called the 'vulgate' version of the satires. Knoche (*45*) 294 f. describes the types of change which the vulgate editor introduced. For example, he altered tenses and moods to ensure a schoolboyish correctness, making *dices* into *dicas* in 1. 150; changed cases to make the syntax simpler, converting *uolgo* into *uolgi* in 15. 36; harmonized numbers, substituting *nocentem* for *nocentes* in 6. 647, because of *sexum*; filled up gaps in the metre, whether they were intentionally made by Juvenal or not—changing *obstet* to *obsistat* in 14. 49; and abolished difficult names (*alti* for *Appi* in 6. 385) or else altered them to simple ones (*Galba* for *Gabba* in 5. 4). A variant in the text which goes back before this editor's time (since it was known to Servius) probably originated in the same way. In 1. 2 Juvenal mentions an epic poet who is hoarse with declaiming his own works, and calls him Cordus. Since the man is not mentioned elsewhere in Juvenal, some scholar cast around to see how he might make the allusion more intelligible. In 3. 203 f. he found a man of literary tastes called by the old Athenian name of Codrus (which Vergil had used for a poetic friend in *Buc.* 7. 22, and 26). The scholar therefore suggested Codrus as a variant for Cordus in 1. 2—in order to make Juvenal's poetry more 'consistent'; but he neglected the really essential facts, that Codrus is a sympathetic character and Cordus an unsympathetic one, and that Juvenal's attitude to the two men is utterly different. It is not even stated that poor Codrus is a poet: he may be only a student of literature (3. 206–7)—although C. Hosius, in 'Bibliotheksfeinde und -funde', *Von Büchern und Bibliotheken, Festschrift für E. Kuhnert* (Berlin, 1928), 150–1, ingeniously proposed that the odd line 'praetextam in cista mures rosere camilli' quoted in Quintilian 8. 3. 19 might have been by Codrus. Recently J. G. Griffith, 'Varia Iuvenaliana', *CR*, n.s. 1 (1951), 138–9, makes it quite clear that *Codri* is utterly wrong in 1. 2. See a good dissertation on the work of these 'improvers' and varnishers by Cremer (*42*).

21. The more authentic tradition of Juvenal's text, together with good scholia to explain it, is thought by Knoche (*45*) 53 to have descended from the original critical edition described above (p. 299) through another edition, which he calls *Π*, and in which he sees the ancestor of the P manuscript. I am not quite sure why it has to be postulated.

22. The chief debt which Claudian owes to Juvenal is in that strange blend of satire and epic, the *In Eutropium*, where the eunuch statesman is treated with the same contempt and loathing as several figures of Juvenal's such as Crispinus. In particular note these clear adaptations:

In Eutrop. 1. 110 f. ∽ Juv. 10. 191 f.
In Eutrop. 1. 279–80 ∽ Juv. 2. 115–16.
In Eutrop. 435–60 ∽ Juv. 2. 153–8.
In Eutrop. 2. 325 f. ∽ Juv. 4. 72 f.

And on the whole subject see T. Birt, *Zwei politische Satiren des alten Rom* (Marburg, 1888), 52–61. Apart from this Juvenal was not one of Claudian's favourite authors, since he was more interested in writing lofty heroic poetry, but small echoes of the satires occur here and there throughout his work: *Prob. et Olyb. Cons.* 54 ∽ Juv. 14. 299; *In Ruf.* 1. 79 ∽ Juv. 1. 27; *Bell. Gild.* 1. 83+86 ∽ Juv. 6. 290–1; *Bell. Gild.* 1. 99 ∽ Juv. 6. 292; *Bell. Gild.* 1. 192–3 ∽ Juv. 6. 600; *Bell. Gild.* 1. 323–4 ∽ Juv. 11. 76f.; *Poll.* 202 ∽ Juv. 10. 1.

23. The exile of the anonymous poet who looks like Juvenal is in *Carm.* 9. 271–3, just after Ovid and before Claudian, and close to Petronius and Martial. See p. 23. Sidonius' borrowings from Juvenal are simply peculiar words and interesting phrases. There is no certainty even that he took from Juvenal all the rare words which they both use, such as *archimagirus* (*Ep.* 2. 9. 6 ∽ Juv. 9. 109), *paropsis* (*Ep.* 2. 9. 6 ∽ Juv. 3. 142), *chironomunta* (*Ep.* 6. 7. 2 ∽ Juv. 5. 121), and *urtica* (*Ep.* 8. 8. 3 ∽ Juv. 2. 128). But in *Ep.* 5. 94 it is likely that he was consciously copying the image *pulsare* in Juv. 6. 193, for he adapts it again in *Carm.* 2. 416. And he borrows odd words from Martial in the same way. Echoes of phrases from Juvenal appear in *Ep.* 1. 2. 2 ∽ Juv. 9. 15; *Ep.* 7. 17. 2 (in a poem) ∽ Juv. 1. 104; *Carm.* 5. 323–4 ∽ Juv. 2. 99–100; *Carm.* 9. 342 ∽ Juv. 2. 40 (+Mart. 1. 3. 6); *Carm.* 22. 198–9 ∽ Juv. 2. 55. The famous Juv. 1. 15 appears in *Ep.* 2. 10. 1; and Juvenal is quoted as 'satiricus' in *Ep.* 8. 9. 1 (∽ Juv. 7. 62) and *Ep.* 8. 16. 1 (∽ Juv. 1. 6). The other parallels cited by Geisler in his index to Luetjohann's edition in *MGH* 8 are faint and unconvincing.

24. Sedulius' works are in *CSEL* 10: the echoes are *Pasch. Carm.* 1. 273–5 ∽ Juv. 15. 10–11; 3. 216 ∽ Juv. 6. 67. Ennodius (*CSEL* 6) *Carm.* 1. 7. praef. 9–12 ∽ Juv. 1. 18+1. 80; *Ep.* 1. 4. 17 ∽ Juv. 6. 43; *Dictio* 12. 5–6 ∽ Juv. 6. 10. Alcimus Avitus (*MGH* 6) 4. 13 ∽ Juv. 6. 223; 6. 35 ∽ Juv. 2. 85. But the echoes which have been pointed out in the fifth-century Gallic Christian poets Orientius and Claudius Marius Victor (*CSEL* 16) are too faint to prove any real knowledge of Juvenal, being merely tags like *omnibus in terris* (Orientius, *Commonitorium* 1. 485 ∽ Juv. 10. 1) and *exclamare libet* (ibid. 2. 75 ∽ Juv. 8. 29), though it is in a passage about drunkenness where Orientius might have used many reminiscences from Juvenal. Claud. Mar. Vict. *Alethia* 3. 194–5, *mendax Graecia* ∽ Juv. 10. 174. Cyprianus Gallus uses a tag from the Sixth Satire for Potiphar's wife: *uiresque a crimine sumit* (*Gen.* 1200 ∽ Juv. 6. 285).

25. Dracontius (*MGH* 14) *Laud. Dei* 2. 308 ∽ Juv. 10. 22; 2. 444 ∽ Juv.

12. 57; 3. 59–63 ~ Juv. 1. 28–29 (a clear imitation); 3. 87–89 = Juv. 8. 83 (direct quotation); 3. 473–4 and *Orestis tragoedia* 234 ~ Juv. 6. 284–5; *Laud. Dei* 3. 745 ~ Juv. 10. 356; *Satisfactio* 15 ~ Juv. 1. 85.

26. e.g. Luxorius (*PLM* 4. 405) 481. 6 ~ Juv. 10. 60; poeta incertus (*PLM* 4. 341) 400. 6 ~ Juv. 6. 334; and see the anonymous poems of the Codex Salmasianus (*Anthologia Latina*, ed. A. Riese, 1, Leipzig, 1884), where *Carm.* 358 (p. 280) is based on Juv. 2. 1–63 and 310 (p. 259) adapts Juv. 6. 503–7.

27. e.g. Corippus (*MGH* 4) *Johannis* 2. 393 ~ Juv. 1. 18, and 4. 622 ~ Juv. 2. 46; though *tua castra sequentur* in 8. 274 is probably too obvious to be borrowed from Juv. 4. 135. Venantius Fortunatus does not seem to have known Juvenal at all: see Manitius's index to the edition of Leo and Krusch in *MGH* 4, and S. Blomgren, 'De Venantio Fortunato Vergilii aliorumque poetarum priorum imitatore', *Eranos*, 42 (1944), 81 f. Therefore, when he writes *quo natura negat* (*Carm.* 3. 10. 10), he is probably not quoting Juv. 1. 79, but simply using a phrase which had become public property. We find it everywhere, sometimes in poets who knew Juvenal well (Claudian, *In Eutrop.* 1. 225, Corippus, *Joh.* eleg. introd. 33, Dracontius, *Laud. Dei*, 2. 289), sometimes in poets who knew only phrases from his work (Maximian, *PLM* 5. 342, 5. 54, and Arator, *Act. Apost.* 1. 528, *PL* 68. 139), and sometimes in poets who had clearly never read him at all. (A few tags from Juvenal, none important, are pointed out on pp. 79–80 of A. Ansorge's *De Aratore veterum poetarum Latinorum imitatore*, Breslau, 1914.) Cassiodorus, by the way, does not seem to have read and remembered Juvenal's poems.

28. In his letter condemning the Lupercalia (*PL* 59. 114 c), where Gelasius quotes the Scriptures often and profane writers very seldom, he says 'sicut ille dixit: iram atque animos a crimine sumunt' ~ Juv. 6. 285.

29. This appears in St. Caesarius's *Admonitio uel Suggestio humilis*, found and published by A. Malnory, *Saint Césaire, évêque d'Arles (Bibliothèque de l'École des Hautes Études*, 103, Paris, 1894), 297, and is a quotation of Juv. 7. 65, with an inferior reading, *nostra* for *uestra*.

30. The aphoristic hexameters called *Monosticha Catonis* (which of course are not by Cato but cannot be surely dated) contain two allusions to Juvenal's work: see *PLM* 3. 237:

> quemlibet ignauum facit indignatio fortem (23) ~ Juv. 1. 79
> diuitiae trepidant, paupertas libera res est (24) ~ Juv. 10. 22.

31. Dante, *Conv.* 4. 13. 12. J. H. Sacret, 'Dante's knowledge of Juvenal', *RR* 28 (1937), 307–10, and Adrianus a Forti Scuto in his edition of Boethius (London, 1925) ad loc., argue that Dante is quoting Juvenal directly here, whether or not Boethius directed his attention to the passage. On Dante's knowledge of Juvenal's satires see n. 43, p. 317. The same line was cited earlier in the same century by the compiler of *Les Faits des Romains*. He speaks (p. 155 *b–c*) of Deiotarus disguising himself as a slave, comments that poor men are safer than rich men, and then goes on: 'Dont puet l'en bien savoir que, qui verais povres est, il est plus seürs que cil as grans richeces. Dont li proverbes dist: *Li povres pelerins chante segurement devant le larron.*' Charming to see Juvenal's *uiator* turning into a medieval pilgrim.

32. The page contains Juv. 7. 149–98 in a good uncial hand. It was written about A.D. 500, and was found at Antinoe in 1914. At least two other scribes have added Greek and Latin notes in the margin and between the lines, and there are additions by others on a smaller scale. There are *diplai obelismenai* above and below 7. 192, which implies that some critics thought it spurious. Jahn had excised the line before the parchment was discovered, and now Knoche omits it from his text (*58*) largely because of the existence of these signs. The text in general is eclectic. For a facsimile and illuminating discussions see C. H. Roberts, 'A Latin parchment from Antinoe', *Aegyptus*, 15 (1935), 297–302, and 'The Antinoë fragment of Juvenal', *JEA* 21 (1935), 199–209. In the fifth century there was even a bishop of Jerusalem called Juvenal: he had just as hard and unhappy a life as his namesake. See E. Honigmann, 'Juvenal of Jerusalem', *DOPap* 5 (1951), 211–79.

NOTES ON CHAPTER XXIX

1. A dry but competent book on the subject is P. Courcelle's *Histoire littéraire des grandes invasions germaniques* (Paris, 1948). On the death of spoken Latin see G. Gröber, 'Sprachquellen und Wortquellen des lateinischen Wörterbuchs', *ALL* 1 (1884), 35–67, and F. Lot, 'A quelle époque a-t-on cessé de parler latin?', *ALMA* 6 (1931), 97–159.

2. Columban, *Versus ad Sethum* 38 (*MGH/E* 3. 184) ~ Juv. 14. 139, one of the favourite lines of the Middle Ages; and the tag *utile consilium* (~ Juv. 9. 124) in *Carm.* 2. 93 (*PL* 80. 289 B).

3. Muratori, *Antiquitates Italicae Medii Aevi*, 8 (Arezzo, 1775), 459 B. There are a few glosses from Juvenal in the Bobbio Grammarian (? 7th–8th century) on whom see Knoche (*45*) 43–44.

4. Isidore, *Etymologiae* (ed. W. M. Lindsay, Oxford, 1911), 8. 7. 7: noui comici, qui et satyrici; he seems to be confusing the difference of Old and New Greek comedy (Aristophanes and Menander) with the difference between genuine Roman comedy (Plautus) and satire (Juvenal). The quotations of Juvenal are these: *Etym.* 1. 36. 11 ~ Juv. 14. 139; 3. 22. 12 ~ Juv. 13. 93; 12. 2. 21 ~ Juv. 12. 34–36; 14. 8. 13 ~ Juv. 10. 153; 15. 5. 4 ~ Juv. 13. 83; 18. 7. 8 ~ Juv. 6. 590; 19. 31. 12 ~ Juv. 2. 124 and 6. 89. Isidore takes his Juvenalian references from Servius, according to Wessner (*81*). His friend St. Braulio of Saragossa (d. 651) uses Juv. 1. 15 in *Ep.* 11 (*PL* 80. 657 c), but he certainly got it through Jerome, as the context shows.

5. Eugen. Tol., *Carm. misc.* 40. 4 (*PL* 87. 393 A) ~ Juv. 8. 25 (*iustitiaeque tenax*), 77. 3 (*PL* 87. 397 D) ~ Juv. 9. 124 (*utile consilium*).

6. *GL* 5. 321 ~ Juv. 6. 70 (for the length of the final syllable of *subligar*).

7. Aldhelm, *De metris* (*MGH* 15), p. 79 ~ Juv. 13. 118 and 10. 133; 85 ~ Juv. 13. 19 and 13. 23; 164 ~ Juv. 9. 50; 167 ~ Juv. 14. 129–30; 183 ~ Juv. 11. 203; 184 ~ Juv. 3. 97 and 14. 280; *Laud. Virg.* 67 ~ Juv. 6. 382; 2058 ~ Juv. 6. 87. M. Manitius, 'Zu Aldhelm und Baeda', *SB Wien*, 112 (1886), 564–7, suggests that all Aldhelm's quotations are not taken directly from Juvenal but through Priscian (as is shown by his using Priscian's reading *combibet* for *nostra bibat* in 11. 203).

8. Bede quotes Juvenal only once in an admittedly authentic work: *In Marci ev. expositio* 1. 4 (*PL* 92. 169 D) ~Juv. 14. 139, where he says the author of the line was 'poetarum quidam'. In *Elem. philos.* (a doubtful work) he quotes Juv. 2. 8–9 and 2. 14–15, saying the author is 'satyricus' (*PL* 90. 1138 D); and in *Vit. S. Cuthb.* 23 (*PL* 94. 587 B) he uses the paradox *pauperibus qui diues, inops sibi*, which comes from Juv. 5. 113, but had been used by many Christian poets before Bede.

9. Alcuin cites one line from Juvenal in his grammar (*PL* 101. 861 ~Juv. 4. 98); but does not name him in the catalogue of authors in York library (*PL* 101. 843–4), although he does say there were some authors unnamed among the books. Manitius (*78*) 356 declares that Juvenal appears to be quite unknown as a poet to the Carolingian writers. Although *utile consilium* (~Juv. 9. 124) occurs in a poem in praise of King Pippin by Ermoldus Nigellus (*MGH/PL* 2. 83. 119), it was only a cliché by that time; and there is no sign that Alcuin's pupil Hrabanus Maurus knew any complete poem by Juvenal, although he cites short phrases (*PL* 111. 363 C, 500 A–B, and 581 D).

10. This act of transcription from the old copies, where the text was written continuously without spaces between the words and in capitals which were hard for the eighth and ninth-century copyists to read, was one of the most important events in the history of our classical books. If a work was not recopied from capitals into minuscule, it was almost certain to be lost; and yet the process of recopying was exceedingly difficult—as though today all our books had to be reprinted in a new alphabet with new word-arrangement and punctuation. The Carolingian scholars helped themselves out of some of their difficulties (and got into others) by borrowing and collating different manuscripts: there are traces of this activity in Juvenal's text (Knoche, *45*, 87–89).

11. On these five master-copies, see Knoche (*45*) 374–83. They are the heads of various classes of existing manuscripts. Knoche describes them as follows: (1) Ξ, in continental minuscules, written early in the ninth century probably in France, a transcription of a manuscript in rustic capitals which represented a special edition made within the vulgate tradition and marked by the inversion of Satires 15 and 16;

(2) Γ, in continental minuscules, written early in the ninth century probably in France, a transcription of a manuscript in rustic capitals which represented a mixed edition, partly the superior and partly the vulgate tradition, in a form allied to the progenitor of Ξ;

(3) Ψ, in continental minuscules, written early in the ninth century probably at Lorsch, a transcription of a manuscript in rustic capitals which represented an interpolated version of the vulgate tradition;

(4) Λ, in continental minuscules full of barbarisms, written late in the eighth or early in the ninth century perhaps at Lyons and certainly in France, a transcription of a manuscript in rustic capitals which represented a version of the good tradition contaminated with Ψ;

(5) Π, in continental minuscules, written before 815 probably in France, a transcription of a manuscript in rustic capitals which represented the good tradition far more purely than any of the others. A copy of Π (which Knoche

calls π^2) was made between 815 and 820 or so, and from that (at one remove) the Pithoeanus manuscript is descended.

12. Knoche (*45*) 44. The text of Mico is in *MGH/PL* 3. 2. 1. 279–94. (On p. 279 he calls himself 'Micon levita parvus'.) The anthology itself is an alphabetical series of lines each containing a metrically interesting word, arranged like this:

(L) LECTICA causidici nova cum veniat lectica Mathonis (∼Juv. 1. 32). But even before this we hear of an anthology which contains some lines from Juvenal, and which may have been put together in the seventh or eighth century: see A. Riese, 'Ein prosodisches Florilegium', *RhM* 26 (1871), 332–6.

13. St. Eulogius made his journey in 848. Here is Paul Albar's account of it:

'In Pampilonensium territoria ultro progrediens monasterium Sancti Zachariae ingressus, et aliorum coenobia ipsarum regionum gliscenti voto percurrens, multorum patrum est amicitia dulcoratus. . . . In quibus locis multa volumina librorum reperiens, abstrusa et paene a multis remota, huc remeans suo nobis in sacratissimo pectore conlocavit. . . . Inde secum librum Civitatis beatissimi Augustini, et Aeneidos Virgilii, sive Iuvenalis metricos itidem libros, atque Oratii Flacci saturata poemata, seu Porfirii depicta opuscula . . . non privatim sibi, sed communiter studiosissimis inquisitoribus reportavit.'

(Alvarus, *Vita S. Eulogii* 3. 9, *PL* 115. 712 C–713 A.) There is no trace of the manuscript in Cordova now, according to a recent report kindly sent to me by the Institut de Recherche et d'Histoire des Textes. See also Knoche (*45*) 42.

14. A few mentions are collected from library catalogues by Manitius (*79*). L. N. d'Olwer, 'Un Glossaire de Virgile et Juvénal', *ALMA* 4 (1928), 104–13, describes a tenth-century Spanish manuscript called *Agnicio multorum nominum vel verborum ignorancium* which contains thirty-seven glosses on hard words in Juvenal, taken from Satires 1, 2, 3, 6, and perhaps 7. Probably they were copied from the margin of a little school anthology. The text is of course of the inferior class. Francesco di Angelo Gaddi, who died in 1500 or so, possessed a manuscript of Juvenal written in 'Lombardic' script—but where is it now? (See Gabotto, *76*, 44.)

15. On Heiric and Juvenal, see Traube in *MGH/PL* 3. 2. 1. 424, n. 3, and M. Manitius, *Geschichte der lateinischen Litteratur des Mittelalters*, 1 (Munich, 1911), 502. I have not been able to see J. Liebl's *Die Disticha Cornuti* (Aug. Aciliae, 1888). The chief adaptations in Heiric's poem, *Vita S. Germani* (*MGH/PL* 3. 2. 1. 424 f.), are these: 1. 76 ∼Juv. 6. 165, altered; 1. 89∼Juv. 7. 237–8, skilfully adapted; 1. 127∼Juv. 15. 72; 1. 233∼Juv. 3. 122; 3. 171 ∼ Juv. 3. 198; 3. 449 ∼ Juv. 7. 148 altered; 5. 212 ∼ Juv. 10.153; and our old friend, *quod natura negat* (1. 79) in 6. 116.

16. Schol. ad 9. 37: 'unus pes deest versui Graeco, quem magister Heiricus scire non potuit.' Knoche (*45*), 58 and 255, points out that this means Heiric was using a manuscript of the inferior tradition. There is a good discussion of the connexion between these 'Cornutus' scholia and the school of Heiric in Wessner (*53*) xxiii–xxxi. Heiric's master Lupus of Ferrières does not seem to have been familiar with Juvenal, although he knew Martial.

17. These inferior scholia are of course not yet all published. There are some horrible examples in C. F. Hermann, *Schediasma de scholiorum ad Juvenalem genere deteriore* (Göttingen, 1849): e.g. on 5. 97:

'PROVINCIA adverbialiter dicit, id est celeriter: aliquando significat et providentiam; ergo habet tres sensus: provincia celeriter, provincia regio, id est patria, atque providentia: ergo ponitur et pro officio, velut ex provincia factum id est ex officio.'

On 6. 459:

'ELENCHUS proprie vocatur titulus libri, a Graeco quod est elcos, id est sol, quia sicut sol suo splendore mundum illuminat, ita titulus totam illuminat paginam.'

And a simple one on 6. 428:

'OREXIS dicitur vomitus, eo quod ex ore exeat vomitum [*sic*].'

This particular mistake became widespread and lasted into the Renaissance: Aeneas Sylvius, in *De Curialium Miseriis* (ed. Mustard, Baltimore, 1928), §19, p. 43, complains that courtiers' meals are irregularly served, and goes on 'hinc subitae mortes atque intestata senectus (∼ Juv. 1. 144), et orexis et uomitus et iliorum dolor'. The essence of these scholia is that they contain things which no Roman could ever have written down. So W. Hoehler, *Scholia Iuuenaliana inedita* (Leipzig, 1889), gives this on 1. 3:

'TOGATAS Romanos significat, quia illi omnes toga utebantur . . . togatae uero feminino genere eos uocauit propter luxuriam illius temporis.'

18. On Remigius of Auxerre, see Manitius (cited in n. 15) 1. 512–13, and P. Courcelle, 'La Culture antique de Remi d'Auxerre', *Latomus*, 7 (1948), esp. 252. It is hard to date the compilers of manuals of mythology called the Mythographi Vaticani, who also cite Juvenal, but their activity probably began with the revival of scholarship in the Carolingian age. For quotations see A. Mai, *Class. Auct.* 3 (Rome, 1831), p. 24, § 60 ∼ Juv. 8. 272–3; p. 45, § 125 ∼ Juv. 9. 2; p. 57, § 156 ∼ Juv. 6. 172–4.

19. *Gesta Berengarii* (*MGH/PL* 4. 1. 354 f.): 2. 202 ∼ Juv. 4. 67—an amusing loan, 'stomachum nitidis laxare saginis'; 4. 134 ∼ Juv. 6. 230; and others. The commentator on the poem also quotes Juvenal 1, 3, 5, and 7.

20. Liutprand's works are edited by E. Dümmler (Hanover, 1877²). An analysis of his relation to Juvenal is given by M. Maas, 'Liutprand und Juvenal', *Phil* 56 (1897), 525–34, who shows about eight verbal quotations, fourteen close adaptations, and a number of words apparently suggested by Juvenal. See also Manitius (*78*).

21. e.g. an adaptation of 2. 12 in *Serm.* 2. 358 (ed. M. Manitius, Leipzig, 1888, p. 34); and in 3. 268 (p. 54) he says

nunc age Nasoni, num Gallo, num Iuvenali
et Parce parcant et Gratia sit pia?

22. Rather's writings are in *PL* 136. According to Manitius (*78*) he quotes from Juvenal 1, 3, 7, 8, and 10.

23. *Gunzonis grammatici diaconi Novariensis epistula ad Augienses fratres* (*PL*

136). The story of the misplaced case is in 1286 B; but the whole letter is worth reading as an example of rare bad manners.

The citations from Juvenal are 1284 C ～Juv. 8. 140–1; 1286 A ～Juv. 2. 14; 1286 D ～Juv. 7. 66 (omitting the essential word *attonitae*); 1287 C ～Juv. 2. 56 (reading *Arachnae*, and explaining it as dative); 1290 D ～Juv. 6. 330; 1292 D ～Juv. 9. 5; 1295 C ～Juv. 4. 1–2; 1297 A ～Juv. 4. 1–2.

24. Walter's work is in *MGH/PL* 5. 1; and see W. Harster's *Walther von Speier* (Speyer, 1877). When describing his education, in the first book of his poetic life of St. Christopher (the book called *Scolasticus*), Walter says that along with 'Homer', Horace, and Persius, he read Juvenal—

> planxit Romanae Juvenalis signa coronae—

which apparently means that Juvenal deplored the character of the Roman crowd (1. 98, p. 19). Here and there in his poem there are reminiscences of the satires: e.g. in the third line of the preface (p. 12) *Veneris credenda marito* (～Juv. 7. 25), and in 4. 44 (p. 41) *totos pande sinus* (～Juv. 1. 150). Walter's master was Bishop Balderich of Speyer, trained at St. Gall. On Tegernsee, see E. Stemplinger, *Horaz im Urteil der Jahrhunderte* (Leipzig, 1921), 48.

25. This comes from a poem called *Verona* quoted in 'Vermischte Bemerkungen' by R. Peiper, *RhM* 32 (1877), 517–18. Perhaps the monk was using the scholia which George Valla later possessed—for they break off in the middle of Satire 8 (see n. 3 on p. 318). He speaks of :

> Iuuenal . . .
> cuius nempe duos extremos carpere libros
> egestas commentorum nos distulit egre.

26. Apud gentiles sunt libri authentici, hoc est aurei, artes VII, auctores IX: . . . Terentius, Virgilius, Oratius, Ovidius, Salustius, Lucanus, Statius, Juvenalis, Persius. (Codex Turon. 416, *Comptes Rendus de l'Académie des Inscriptions*, 6 (1870), 249 f).

27. Rodulphus Glaber 2. 12 (*Recueil des histoires des Gaules et de la France*, Paris, 1874, v. 10, pp. 23–4:

'Ipso quoque tempore non impar apud Ravennam exortum est malum. quidam igitur Vilgardus dictus, studio artis grammaticae magis assiduus quam frequens, sicut Italis mos semper fuit artes negligere ceteras, illam sectari; is enim cum ex scientia suae artis coepisset inflatus superbia stultior apparere, quadam nocte assumpsere daemones poetarum species Virgilii et Horatii atque Juvenalis; apparentesque illi fallaces rettulerunt grates, quoniam suorum dicta voluminum carius amplectens exerceret, seque illorum posteritatis felicem esse praeconem. promiserunt ei insuper suae gloriae postmodum fore participem. hisque daemonum fallaciis depravatus, coepit multa turgide docere fidei sacrae contraria, dictaque poetarum per omnia credenda esse asserebat. ad ultimum vero haereticus est repertus, atque a pontifice ipsius urbis Petro damnatus. plures etiam per Italiam tunc huius pestiferi dogmatis sunt reperti, qui et ipsi aut gladiis aut incendiis perierunt. ex Sardinia quoque insula, quae his plurimum abundare solet, ipso tempore aliqui egressi, partem populi in Hispania corrumpentes, et ipsi a viris Catholicis exterminati sunt.'

It may well have been the sense of such dangers as this that made the eleventh-century monk Othlo of St. Emmeram write so bitterly against those who neglected the study of religion for the classics such as Juvenal. See his *De doctrina spirituali*, c. 11 (*PL* 146. 270 A–C):

> Libros devita qui dant carnalia scita. . . .
> Forsitan ex aliquo quaerenda haec norma profano,
> ut sunt Horatius, Terentius, et Juvenalis,
> ac plures alii quos sectatur schola mundi,
> pro studio carnis carnalia dicta ferentes,
> ut per eos nobis pandatur lex pietatis,
> instinctu Satanae qui promunt pessima quaeque?
> haec ita nonnulli perverso more fatentur.

And yet he himself had loved classical poetry dearly at an earlier stage in his life (ibid. c. 14, p. 279), and in his *Life of St. Wolfkang*, c. 7 (*PL* 146. 398 D) he quotes Juv. 7. 157.

NOTES ON CHAPTER XXX

1. Most of the references in this section are due to Gabotto (*76*), Hild (*77*), and Manitius (*78*). They cite a host of other writers, besides those mentioned here: Manitius in particular is a mine of learning. But they do not usually distinguish between a quotation taken directly from Juvenal's own works and a line lifted from an anthology; nor is it always possible to do so. I have added a number of other citations from S. Consoli's two articles, 'La Satira II di Giovenale nella tradizione della cultura sino alla fine del medio evo', *RFIC* 42 (1914), 209–48, and the parallel article for Satire 9, *RFIC* 49 (1921), 79–97; some from other sources; and some from my own reading. I am also much indebted to E. R. Curtius, *Europäische Literatur und lateinisches Mittelalter* (Berne, 1948). In general see M. Manitius, *Geschichte der lateinischen Literatur des Mittelalters*, 3 (Munich, 1931).

2. M. Maas, 'Juvenal und Josephus Iscanus', *Phil* 58 (1899), 157–60, shows about thirty close adaptations, and adds the interesting suggestion that Shakespeare may have known Joseph's work and recalled it when writing of the fall of Troy in *Hamlet* (2. 2. 481 f.); but his proofs are very thin, e.g. 'the rugged Pyrrhus, like the Hyrcanian beast' ~ *Bell.Troi.* 4. 138 (*Pyrrhus ferox*) + 5. 325–6 (*tigres Hyrcanae*). Guillaume le Breton's *Philippis* is in *Œuvres de Rigord et de Guillaume le Breton*, ed. H. F. Delaborde, Paris, 1882 and 1885. Here is a good adaptation of Juv. 10. 155–6 in *Phil.* 2. 228–30:

> 'Nil,' ait, 'est actum nisi Flandro milite portas
> Parisias frango, nisi Parvo ponte dracones
> Aut medio vici vexillum pono Chalauri.'

3. Bernard of Morval, *De Contemptu Mundi*, ed. H. C. Hoskier (London, 1929). After a description of the degeneracy of his time, Bernard asks (2. 805–6):

> Flaccus Horatius, et Cato, Persius et Juvenalis—
> Quid facerent, rogo, si foret his modo vita sodalis?

A typically adroit reworking of a phrase from Juvenal appears in 2. 558–60:

Sufficientior et sibi gratior unus ocellus
Quam comes unicus, o furor ethnicus! o rea tellus!

~ Juv. 6. 53–54. Other adaptations are 2. 349 ~ Juv. 10. 22; 2. 549 ~ Juv.
2. 37; 2. 619–23 ~ Juv. 6. 300–5; 2. 751~Juv. 6. 249; and 2. 753 ~ Juv. 2. 40.

4. See *The Latin poems commonly attributed to Walter Mapes*, ed. T. Wright
(London, 1841). For example, *De Palpone et Assentatore* (pp. 106–30) is partly
inspired by Juv. 3. 58–125; note especially lines 109–24. *Contra Ambitiosos et
Avaros* (pp. 152–9) contains a number of obvious borrowings, e.g.:

quicquid agunt homines animo rebelli
gaudia discursus nostri est farrago libelli

(27–28 ~ Juv. 1. 85–86), followed by a *Cum. . .* sequence like that in Juv.
1. 22 f., and closed by

difficile est mihi satyram non scribere

(32 ~Juv. 1. 30). So also 60 ~ Juv. 14. 139, 76 ~ Juv. 3. 143, 80 ~ Juv. 6. 165,
and many more. In *De Pravitate Saeculi* (pp. 159–62), line 44 ~ Juv. 2. 88.
In *De Avaritia et Luxuria Mundi* (pp. 163–6) there is a great deal of Juvenal:
24 ~ Juv. 14. 139; 32 ~ Juv. 14. 304; and 33–36 are built up out of Juv. 10.
9–13 + 144. In Map's *De Nugis Curialium* (ed. M. R. James, *Anecdota Oxoniensia*, 12, Oxford, 1914), we find 1. 25 ~Juv. 6. 280–1; 2. 31 ~Juv. 3. 78;
4.2 ~ Juv. 1. 80; 4. 5 ~ Juv. 1. 6; and 4. 16 ~ Juv. 14. 139. On these poems
see Manitius (n. 1) 268–74.

5. On Gillebertus and his two poems see Manitius (n. 1) 910–14 and
Histoire littéraire de la France, 22 (Paris, 1895), 148–50. Their names are *De
superfluitate clericorum* and *Quispiam ad quandam virginem*: they were found in a
thirteenth-century manuscript at Brussels, and published in 1849 by L.
Tross at Hamm. The former begins:

Ad scribendum equidem hebes et piger sum;
sed cum vulgus videam vitiis immersum
clerumque conspiciam undique perversum,
si natura negat, facit indignatio versum

—which is from Juv. 1. 22 f. and 1. 79 and closely parallels the 4th stanza of
Walter of Châtillon's *Super statibus eccl. personarum* (see n. 7). It goes on to an
imitation of 1. 149 f. (*quo, vesane, navigas?*). There are one or two traces of
Juvenal in the satire on greedy priests, *Ierapigra*, by the thirteenth-century
doctor Gilles de Corbeil (*Hist. Litt. de la France*, 21. 333–62): e.g. the word
artocopus (~Juv. 5. 72) in a description of a rich bishop's banquet. The sole
manuscript of this poem was owned by Pierre Pithou, who also possessed
the best manuscript of Juvenal (see pp. 207–8).

6. On Jean de Auville see Manitius (n. 1) 805–9, and Hild (77) 9. 41–50.
The text is in T. Wright, *The Anglo-Latin Satirical Poets and Epigrammatists of
the Twelfth Century* (London, 1872), 1. 240–392. On p. 240, the first line begins *Velificatur Athos* (~Juv. 10. 174); other borrowings are *permutatque toros*
(p. 249 ~Juv. 6. 225), *ha! gula quae mundum penitus scrutatur* (p. 269 ~Juv. 5.
94–96), *vultus accommodat omni/fortunae domini* (p. 305 ~Juv. 3. 105–6), *mundi
nulla fides* (p. 307 ~Juv. 2. 8). But on the whole Jean does not borrow much
from Juvenal. Like most medieval satirists, he is engaged in trying to be

lofty, and his style is more indebted to Ovid and Lucan; in book 4, when he satirizes court life, he seems to have taken little from parallel passages in Juvenal's poems. By the way, Hild (77) asserts that Marbod of Rennes resembles Juvenal in his pieces on the harlot and on old age in the *Liber Decem Capitulorum* (*PL* 171); but the material similarities are obvious, and there are no verbal parallels worth mentioning.

7. It is hard to establish the paternity of all the songs attributed to Walter of Châtillon, but certainly he was a remarkably fine poet. In *Die zehn Gedichte des Walther von Lille, genannt von Châtillon* (ed. W. Müldener, Hanover, 1859), the dependence on Juvenal is striking. Several of them are really pastiches of lines from classical poetry and from Scripture, and Juvenal is the favourite author. So in *De Statibus Mundi*, which has twenty-seven 4-line stanzas, seventeen end with lines lifted from Juvenal, and one (104 ～ Juv. 1. 14) with an echo. It is a bit odd to hear the Pope addressed as

> inter Socraticos notissima fossa cinaedos

(ibid. 1. 28 ～ Juv. 2. 10). In a gloomy poem on the state of the church, he joins a thought from Juvenal's Sixth to the medieval image of the church as the Bride of Christ, and cries:

> sponsa Christi coniugis iussa non custodit
> saepe etenim mulier quem coniux diligit odit.

(*Contra Statum Ecclesiae Depravatum* 27–28 ～ Juv. 6. 510). Manitius (cited in n. 1, p. 924) says that a line from Walter's epic *Alexandreis* is quoted by Wilhelmus Britto and others and attributed to Juvenal.

8. See, for instance, T. Wright's edition of *The Political Songs of England from John to Edward II* (London, 1839). On p. 10, someone cries to the bishop of Norwich:

> Heu! cecidisti gravius
> quam Cato quondam tertius

(～ Juv. 2. 40, misunderstood). In a fine *Song on the Corruptions of the Time* (*Contra Avaros*), two stanzas on p. 30 end with Juv. 14. 139 and Juv. 8. 140–1, and two on p. 31 with Juv. 3. 143 and Juv. 14. 207; the singing wayfarer of Juv. 10. 22 appears on p. 35. The best stanza of all is on p. 32:

> Diligit episcopus hilarem datorem
> Fas et nefas ausus post muneris odorem,
> Nescius resumere post lapsum pudorem,
> Eiectum semel attrita de fronte ruborem . . .

which contains a parody of Scripture (2 Cor. ix 7), allusions to Juv. 13. 237–8 and 14. 204, and a quotation of Juv. 13. 242. Later, in the *Song against Scholastics*, we meet Lucan (Juv. 7. 79) on p. 209 and the black swan (Juv. 6. 165) on p. 210.

9. So in the *Carmina Burana* (ed. A. Hilka and O. Schumann, Heidelberg, 1930 and 1941), we find on p. 9 'Nobilis est ille quem virtus nobilitavit;/ Degener est ille quem virtus nulla beavit' ～ Juv. 8. 20. On p. 39, Juv. 14. 109 is cited; and on p. 38 a very poor man is said to be *Codro Codrior*, because Codrus (from Juv. 3. 208) had become a synonym for a very poor man.

Similarly, that lamentable poet Arrigo da Settimello, whose style is as dismal as his subject, says in his *Elegia* (or *De Miseria*, ed. A. Marigo, Padua, 1926) 163–4:

> Si Codrus foret hic, essem nunc Codrior illo,
> nam nichil hic habuit, ast ego plura nichil.

10. *Lamentationes Matheoli* by Jehan le Fèvre, ed. A. G. van Hamel, *Bibliothèque de l'École des Hautes Études*, 95–96 (Paris, 1892 and 1905). It is a fair conclusion that the author did not know Juvenal well, because although he adapts a number of memorable sayings, he does not use the big developments which concern subjects in which he himself was interested: e.g. the drunken woman (1733 f., cf. Juv. 6. 425–33), marriage for love (1855 f., cf. Juv. 6. 142–60), and marriage to a noble lady (2113 f., cf. Juv. 6. 161–83). Still, he knew quite a number of Juvenal's epigrams. He used *orba tigride peior* from 6. 270 at least thrice, in 1040, 1994, and 2478 (in 1039 he calls Juvenal 'quidam laudabilis auctor'); *rara auis in terris* from 6. 165 ('perito testificante tibi') in 3230; the famous Messalina line 6. 130 in 1212; and see 1432–3 ∼ Juv. 6. 199, 1555 ∼ Juv. 3. 113, 1880 ∼ Juv. 6. 347, and 1993 ∼ Juv. 6. 460.

11. 'Magis credunt Juvenali / quam doctrinae prophetali / vel Cristi sciencie'—from an anonymous poem perhaps written in the thirteenth century: see J. Wattenbach, 'Lateinische Reime des Mittelalters', *Anzeiger für Kunde der deutschen Vorzeit*, 18 (1871), 130–1, 202–3, and 231–3.

12. Alfanus, *Ad Guillelmum* (*Carm.* 39 in *PL* 147. 126 D):

> Sponte nunc coram vacuus latrone
> si volo solos per inhospitales
> canto secure, rota me nec huius
> atra revolvet

∼ Juv. 10. 22+Hor. *Carm.* 1. 22. 6.

13. See K. Rossberg's edition of Thiofrid's *Vita Willibrordi* (Leipzig, 1883). It is really a very eloquent poem. Thiofrid particularly likes odd words (*enthymema*, 3. 32 ∼ Juv. 6. 450, *xerampelinis*, 2. 368 ∼ Juv. 6. 519), and striking phrases (for the miracle of making the tide stand still in 2. 274 he uses *frangitur Ennosigaeus* ∼ Juv. 10. 182).

14. See *La 'comédie' latine en France au XIIe siècle*, ed. G. Cohen (Paris, 1931), and a thoughtful article by H. Hagendahl, 'La "comédie" latine au XIIe siècle et ses modèles antiques', ΔΡΑΓΜΑ (Lund, 1939), 222–55. William of Blois has *genialis agatur . . . ista dies* (∼ Juv. 4. 66–7) in *Alda* 291–2, and probably Matthew of Vendôme's *Lydia* 101, *uni non sufficit unus*, is built on Juv. 6. 53–4.

15. *Le Roman de la Rose*, ed. E. Langlois (Paris, 1921): in particular, note these adaptations: 8287 f. ∼ Juv. 6. 53–54; 8709 f. ∼ Juv. 6. 47–49; 8737 f. ∼ Juv. 6. 28 f.; 9142 f. ∼ Juv. 6. 133–5; 21439 f. ∼ Juv. 1. 38–39. Juvenal is actually named in most of these passages.

16. See K. McKenzie, 'Antonio Pucci on Old Age', *Speculum*, 15 (1940), 160–85, on this poem, which is the *Canzone della Vecchiezza*—esp. 162–5. Wernher von Elmendorf, ed. V. F. Hoffmann, *ZDA* 4 (1844), 284–317, 1057–62: 'Ich horte zu einē / Ein wort von Iuuenale: / Ich gedenke dick sin da bie: / Er spricht daz an dem schalke nicht erge / Is si dan die zunge an sinem munde: / Der gelichet cleinen bellenden hunde'—a memory of Juv. 9. 121. Other echoes in lines 585, 903, 913. On Wernher see Exkurse xviii in E. Curtius's *Europäische Literatur und lateinisches Mittelalter* (Berne, 1948), 508–23. The doctor is Nicole de la Chesnaye, and his play, *La Comdamnacion de Bancquet*, is in 'P. L. Jacob', *Recueil de Farces* (Paris, 1859): see p. 352: 'Le satirique Juvenal / Avoit bien tout consideré / Quant il dist qu'il vient tant de mal / De long repas immoderé; / Et après qu'il a referé / Balnea, coenas et sordes, / Quant il a tout enumeré, / Il dit, Hinc subitae mortes.' This is from Juv. 1. 143–4: *sordes* is a misunderstanding of 1. 140.

17. So in *La Bataille des .Vij. Ars*, a thirteenth-century poem printed by A. Jubinal as an appendix to the work of the Parisian Rutebeuf (vol. 3, Paris, 1875, p. 338), we see Juvenal joining in the Battle of the Books:

> Aristote, qui fu à pié,
> Si fist chéoir Gramaire enverse.
> Lors i a point mesire Perse,
> Dant Juvénal et dant Orasce . . .
> Tuit chaplèrent sor Aristote
> Qui fu fers com chastel sor mote. . . .

Again, in an anonymous Italian poem dated 1369, the poet discusses his art and says he can sing of 'il nobil Marzïale, . . . Gallo, Terensio, Persio e Giovanale'. (P. Rajna, 'Il Cantare dei Cantari', *Zeitschrift für romanische Philologie*, 2, 1878, 220–54 and 419–37.) So also in a *dezir* by Fray Miguel in the *Cancionero de Baena* (ed. F. Michel, Leipzig, 1860) p. 47:

> El buen Aristoteles, el grant natural
> Pyntagoras, Ermes, Bramis é Platon,
> Euclides, Seneca, é mas Juvenal. . . .
> Poetas perfetos é grandes astrólogos. . . .

18. The text of this play is in L. Paris, *Toiles peintes et tapisseries de la ville de Reims*, 2 (Paris, 1843), 682 f. It was first printed in 1491. See also L. Petit de Julleville, *Histoire du Théâtre en France*: *Les Mystères*, (Paris, 1880), 2. 451–60.

19. On Bernardus Silvestris, see Manitius (cited in n. 1) 205–7 and Curtius (cited in n. 16) 116–21. In his *De Vniversitate Mundi* (ed. C. S. Barach and J. Wrobel, Innsbruck, 1876), see 16. 41 ∼ Juv. 3. 203 f.; 17. 68 ∼ Juv. 5. 23; and others. There is a slip in Mr. Curtius's reference of Codrus, 'der arme Schlucker', to Juv. 1. 2, on p. 117; it should of course be Juv. 3. 208, and Cordus in 1. 2 is a different character (see p. 300 of this book).

20. Manitius gives half a page of references to the works of Ioannes Sarisberiensis (*PL* 199), showing his borrowings from Juvenal: *78*, p. 364. John's master Abelard took Juvenal's (or an interpolator's) line about rich women and applied it to domineering nuns (*Ep.* 1, c. 14 *fin.*, *PL* 178. 178 D ∼ Juv. 6. 460); but there are only three or four citations throughout his writings: *PL* 252 D ∼ Juv. 4. 9–10; 883 B ∼ Juv. 14. 139, always a favourite; and 1095 B ∼ Juv. 6. 223.

21. Petrus Cantor is in *PL* 205. His *Verbum Abbreviatum* (23 A–370 A) is curiously like Dante in mingling examples from Scripture with examples from the classics. E.g., in c. 135, against gluttony and drunkenness (*PL*

330 B), he writes: 'Vae terrae cujus rex puer est et principes mane comedunt. Exsul ab octava Marius bibit et fruitur dis iratis' (Eccl. x. 16 and Juv. 1. 49–50, to which he then attaches Juv. 11. 37–38).

22. The works of Petrus Blesensis are in *PL* 207. Hild (77) and Manitius (78) observe that his citations of Juvenal resemble those in John of Salisbury so closely that he probably got most of them second-hand. Still, a letter from him to Radulf of Beauvais, criticizing the soft life of priests attached to the suites of bishops, quotes Juvenal 5 as though it were known to both correspondents directly (*Ep.* 6 init., *PL* 207. 170 A); and in *Ep.* 79 (*PL* 245 A) he recommends Juvenal 6 with what looks like personal admiration.

23. Manitius (78) 365–6, n. 1, shows that Bacon had an independent knowledge of Juvenal; and on pp. 362–3 he gives a page of references to Vincent of Beauvais's works, observing that Satire 16 is never quoted by any medieval writer, even by Vincent.

24. This work is the *Moralium Dogma Philosophorum*, printed among Hildebert's works in *PL* 171. 1003 f. There is a useful edition of it by J. Holmberg (Uppsala, 1929) who attributes it to William of Conches; but J. R. Williams, 'The authorship of the *Moralium Dogma Philosophorum*', *Speculum*, 6 (1931), 392–411, gives reasons against this attribution, and hints that Walter of Châtillon may be the author. Juvenal's satires are freely quoted in it, sometimes two or three times in a single page, so that it is odd for Mr. Holmberg to omit his name in a discussion of the sources (p. 9). The work was very popular in the Middle Ages: Mr. Williams knows of sixty-seven manuscripts of it in Latin and thirty-eight in an Old French translation. In general see Manitius (cited in n. 1) 219, and Curtius (cited in n. 1) 510–17, to whom I am indebted for these references.

25. Cosmas, *Chronicon Boemorum* (*MGH/S*, n. s. 2, ed. B. Bretholz), 1. 9 (p. 21)~Juv. 10. 112; 3. 46 (p. 219) ~Juv. 1. 160; and an amusing citation in 1. 19 (p. 39), where, after describing how Boleslav I, 'the Mighty', commanded his chiefs to build a fortress on the Elbe, was refused, and instantly decapitated one of them, Cosmas quotes the masterful line 6. 223.

26. Vincent Kadłubek, *Kronika*, in *Monumenta Poloniae Historica* (Lwów, 1872) 2; apparently largely modelled on Justin. The prologue opens with a comparison of the author to Codrus shunning the theatre so as to avoid being laughed at (~Juv. 3. 152–9+3. 208), and brings in *scribendi cacoethes* from Juv. 7. 52 on p. 250; still, St. Vincent prefers Lucan and Horace to Juvenal.

27. In William's *Gesta Regum Anglorum* (*PL* 179), we find these quotations: 1. 49 (1006 B) ~Juv. 6. 165, adapted; 1. 52 (1010 A) ~Juv. 4. 149; in 3. 267 (1247 A) Lanfranc is compared to a third Cato fallen from heaven (~Juv. 2. 40); and 4. 381 (1335 C) ~Juv. 1. 43, of the Arab army surprised. Juvenal's name is mentioned once in *De Gest. Pont. Angl.* 3 (1558 C) ~Juv. 6. 223. But no pious writer who had read Juvenal would have applied the disgusting lines 1. 38–39 to the Cistercian Order, as William does in *Gest. Reg. Angl.* 4. 334 (1286 D–1287 A). Citations of Juvenal in Matthew Paris are given by Manitius (78) 365, and see the index in vol. 7 of *Rer. Brit. Med. Aevi Script.*, p. 57. There are several quotations also in Geoffrey of Monmouth (ed. J. Hammer, Cambridge, 1951), notably a citation of 4. 126–7 in a description of the fame of that mysterious monarch Arviragus (or Aviragus, or

Arvigarus) : see 4. 14, p. 82 in Hammer's edition. One might also list Alpert, *De Diversitate Temporum* (*MGH/S* 4, ed. G. H. Pertz), who in 2. 9 brings in Juv. 6. 460 to describe a domineering woman; and Salimbene de Adam (*MGH/S* 32, ed. O. Holder-Egger, delicious name), who on p. 144 applies Juv. 6. 223 to 'aliquis maledictus prelatus'.

28. Innocent's sermons are in *PL* 217, and the first quotation is at 684 B. He cites Juv. 8. 140–1 (with a slight textual variation) in his first, second, and fourth sermons (649 C, 659 C, and 666 D), and recurs to Juv. 14. 139 in 720 A.

29. Helinand, *Sermo* 6 (*PL* 212. 530 B) init. ∼Juv. 2. 149–53, cited in full. In his *De Cognitione Sui* 723 B, Helinand praises 'satyricus noster Juvenalis', quoting 11. 23–27 and adding that Apollo stole γνῶθι σεαυτόν from the Bible. He has a few more mentions of the satires, not always accurate.

30. Conrad of Hirsau, *Dialogus super Auctores* (ed. G. Schepss, Würzburg, 1889) p. 70: 'Iuvenalis satyricus optimus Romanorum vitia interdum fessa reprehensione confundit, cunctis divinis regularibus sanitatem hominis praelatam ostendit.' Apparently this is a faint memory of Juv. 10. 346–56; but Conrad then (not knowing the immortal apophthegm of President Routh of Magdalen College, 'Verify your references'), illustrates it by Hor. *Ep.* 1. 12. 5–6 and 2. 1. 49. On Conrad's work see Curtius (cited in n. 1) 462–3.

31. Alexander Neckam's list is given by C. H. Haskins, 'A list of textbooks from the close of the twelfth century', *HSCP* 20 (1909), 75–94, esp. 89 and 91. Neckam (who was a foster-brother of Richard Lionheart and became a professor at Paris when he was only 23) quotes Juvenal now and then in his *De naturis rerum* (ed. T. Wright, London, 1863) : for instance, the *opici mures* of 3. 207 appear (with a false derivation from *Ops* = *terra*) on p. 75; Juv. 8. 269–71 are quoted in 2. 175 (*De militibus*, p. 312); Juv. 4. 65–71 in 2. 180 (*De adulatoribus*, p. 320); and Juv. 2. 3 in 2. 185 (*De hypocritis*, p. 327). But Alexander did not really know Juvenal well, as is shown by his neglecting Satire 6 in a discussion of wives (pp. 246–7) and Satire 8 in an explanation of true nobility (pp. 243–4). For Thomas de Marleberge, see H. Rashdall, *The Universities of Europe in the Middle Ages* (ed. F. M. Powicke and A. B. Emden, Oxford, 1936), 3. 32, n. 3.

32. For Everard's *Laborintus* (= '*laborem habens intus*'!) see E. Faral, *Les Arts Poétiques du XIIᵉ et du XIIIᵉ Siècle* (*Bibliothèque de l'École des Hautes Études* 238, Paris, 1924), 336–77. On p. 359 at lines 625–6 Everard says:

> Non juvenis satura sed maturus Juvenalis
> Nudat nec vitium panniculare potest.

For his imitations of Juvenal see section 6 on the miseries of teachers: for instance, 859 f.:

> Sudoris pretium mendax astutia, primum
> Quod tibi promisit, apocopare solet.
> Hic pretium tibi dimidiat, totum negat alter,
> Vociferans natum nil didicisse suum,

which, together with what follows, is clearly inspired by Juv. 7. 157–70 and 215–29.

33. Hugo, *Registrum Multorum Auctorum*, ed. K. Langosch, *Germanische Studien*, 235 (Berlin, 1942), 158–9 (p. 166):

> Preponatur reliquis mordax Juvenalis,
> Constans et veridicus, non adulans malis,

followed by a quotation of 1. 1–2. Hugo places Juvenal in the time of Nero (p. 165).

34. S. B. Kugéas, 'Maximos Planudes und Juvenal', *Phil* 73 (1914–16), 318–19. In 10. 20 Maximos read *gladium contumque tenebis*, judging by his translation, καὶ δόρυ καὶ ξίφος ἕξῃς. Kugéas implies that he translated the whole of Juvenal, but there is really not enough evidence to show that.

35. This is in Codex 227 of the Heiligenkreuzstift; the anthology is actually headed by a quotation of Juvenal's introductory words, 1. 85–86. For a discussion, see J. Huemer, 'Zur Geschichte der classischen Studien im Mittelalter', *ŽöstG* 32 (1881), 415–22. A twelfth-century Vatican florilegium also cites Juvenal: see C. H. Haskins, *The Renaissance of the Twelfth Century* (Oxford, 1939), 113.

36. Osbern's *Derivationes*, or *Thesaurus novus latinitatis*, is in Mai, *Classici Auctores* 8 (Rome, 1836). (See also Manitius (cited in n. 1) 187–9.) The index on p. 635 lists his quotations of Juvenal. The text he uses is nearly always the inferior tradition, and his quotations are sometimes confused.

37. For this estimate see B. L. Ullman, 'Classical authors in certain medieval *florilegia*', *CP* 27 (1932), 1–42, esp. 19–21.

38. On Trivet see J. V. Le Clerc, 'Discours sur l'état des lettres', *Hist. litt. de la France au XIVᵉ siècle* (Paris, 1865²), 1. 430–1, and R. J. Dean, 'Cultural relations in the Middle Ages', *StudPhil* 65 (1948), 553. On other commentators see Knoche (*45*) 40–41, n. 6, and Sanford (*80*). For glosses, see J. F. Mountford, *Quotations from Classical Authors in Medieval Latin Glossaries, Cornell Studies in Classical Philology*, 21 (New York, 1925), who cites an enigmatic gloss on 10. 115.

39. The existing manuscripts are listed by Knoche in his edition (*58*) and discussed in his admirable *Grundlagen* (*45*). He says on 59–60 that he knows of about 80 manuscripts written between the ninth and the twelfth centuries, and of over 250 written after that. Manitius (*79*) cites over 30 mentions of Juvenalian manuscripts in Germany, about 30 in France, 12 in Italy, 9 in Britain, and 6 in Spain. Le Clerc (cited in n. 38) says on 1. 470 that in 1290 the Sorbonne had no copy of Juvenal (although it had acquired two by 1338). Still, perhaps that is less important, or even inaccurate, since the Sorbonne is said to have possessed no copy of Vergil, Horace, or Lucan either. On the musical settings for Juvenal the only evidence I know is given by F. Ludwig in G. Adler, *Handbuch der Musikgeschichte* (Berlin, 1930²), 1. 160, who says that Juvenal 8. 78 f. appears together with selections from Horace, Vergil, Statius, and Boethius in certain manuscripts written between the ninth and the twelfth centuries; but he does not particularize, and I have been unable to trace the manuscript or manuscripts. He suggests that the music was written under the impulse of the Carolingian Renaissance, which may well be true.

40. On Juvenal and Petrarch see P. de Nolhac, *Pétrarque et l'Humanisme* (Paris, 1907²), 1. 42, 1. 154, 1. 157, 1. 186, and other references in the index; and B. L. Ullman, 'Petrarch's favorite books', *TAPA* 54 (1923), 32–33. In *Fam.* 3. 15 Petrarch writes: 'loquitur experientia, . . . loquitur ueritas . . . quod si mortalem poscis auctorem, loquitur haec peritissimus rerum talium Iuuenalis, quique profundissime mores hominum nouit.' In the *Rerum Memorandarum Libri* (ed. G. Billanovich, Florence, 1943), at 2. 25, Petrarch quotes 11. 180–1 for its 'elegant' comparison of Homer and Vergil; he cites Satire 10 with respect for its wisdom at 3. 71; and he misspells *cacoethes* from Juv. 7. 52 at 3. 93, as *cacetes*, a familiar form of the inferior tradition. In the margin of his Vergil MS. he quoted Juv. 9. 102–3, and in his *Secretum*, as well as in a letter to Emperor Charles IV, he cited 9. 126–9 (so Consoli, quoted in n. 1).

41. For respectful mentions of Juvenal see Boccaccio, *Gen. Deorum* (ed. O. Hecker, *Boccaccio-Funde*, Brunswick, 1902), pp. 236. 4, 239. 13, and 253. 14; and his *Amorosa Visione*, Capitolo 5:

> Non guari dopo lui fatt' era onore
> a Giovenal, che ne' su' atti ardito
> a mondan falli ancor facea romore.

The *Laberinto d'Amore* or *Corbaccio* appears in *I Difetti delle Donne*, ed. N. Sallustio (Rome, *c.* 1947). Some of it comes from Jerome, *Adu. Iouin.* (another part of the misogynistic tradition, on which see p. 264), and some from the *Dissuasiones ad Rufinum ne ducat uxorem*, which appear in connexion with Walter Map's *De Nugis Curialium* and can be read there (see n. 4): for Boccaccio had copied passages from them both, together with the misogynistic couplet

> crede ratem uentis, animum ne crede puellis,
> namque est feminea tutior unda fide,

some time before 1350 (H. Hauvette, *Boccace*, Paris, 1914, 339–40). But passages inspired by and direct translations from Juvenal's Sixth appear throughout the work: e.g. on p. 75, 'colei, che nella moltitudine delle donne ti sembra la più casta ed onesta, vorrebbe prima avere un sol occhio che esser contenta d'un uomo solo' ~Juv. 6. 53–54; followed by 'stanche ma non sazie' ~ Juv. 6. 130, and an adaptation of the Eppia passage in 6. 92–102. On 110 we meet 'In brevissimo spazio di tempo ti dirà quel che si fa in Francia e quel che ordina il re d'Inghilterra . . .' which is from 6. 402–12, as well as from personal observation. There is an excellent comparison, point by point, of the two pieces by G. Pinelli, 'Appunti sul Corbaccio', in *Propugnatore*, 16 (1883), 169–92.

42. These are the only quotations from Juvenal in Chaucer, and in both of them Juvenal is named: they are *Troilus and Criseyde*, 4. 197–201 ~Juv. 10. 2–4 and *The Wife of Bath's Tale*, 1192–4 ~Juv. 10. 22, which Chaucer probably got from Boethius. So J. Koch, 'Chaucers Belesenheit in der römischen Klassikern', *Englische Studien*, 57 (1923), § 45. T. R. Lounsbury, *Studies in Chaucer*, 2 (New York, 1892), 260–1, adds that the name Arviragus, which first appears in Juv. 4. 127, is borne by a character in the Franklin's Tale; but that memory is very remote. The whole section about Jankyn, the

Wife's fifth husband, *WBProl* 627–828, is a reversal of the tradition of Juvenal's Sixth Satire, although the Wife does not there mention Juvenal, only the treatise of Jerome which derives from the same sources (see p. 264). The same tradition shows up again 150 years later in a book on marriage by a German moralist, the *Ehebuchlein* of Albrecht von Eyb, 1472. (See the edition by M. Herrmann, in *Schriften zur germanischen Philologie*, 4. 1, Berlin, 1890). Albrecht, who put a number of quotations from Juvenal into his *Margarita Poetica*, a Latin manual of style, here treats the Sixth Satire as a wise document on the mistakes a good wife should avoid, and frequently quotes it, e.g. 8. 2 ∽ Juv. 6. 457–60; 11. 6 ∽ Juv. 6. 92–102; 16. 27 ∽ Juv. 6. 346–8; 17. 9 ∽ Juv. 6. 144–8; and 32. 14 ∽ Juv. 6. 352–65. There is one amusing mistranslation in 11. 6 f. The lady in Juvenal who would rather have one eye than one husband was called Hiberina (6. 53–54). Albrecht does not recognize this as a proper name, and attributes this polyandrous passion to the women of Ireland, 'den frawen in dem lannde ybernia'. For all his date, he is a medieval moralist, as J. A. Hiller has shown, in *Albrecht von Eyb, Catholic University Studies in German*, 13 (Washington, 1939).

43. On Dante's knowledge of Juvenal, see E. Moore, *Studies in Dante* (1st series, Oxford, 1896), 255–8 and 353, and J. H. Sacret, cited on p. 302. In *Conv.* 4. 12. 8 Juvenal is mentioned as 'preaching against riches', a vague remark which might refer to 10. 12–27 or to the end of Satire 14, 256–331. In *Conv.* 4. 19. 12 we meet a quotation of Juv. 10. 22, attributed to 'lo Savio', which might well be Boethius (see p. 189). In *De Monarchia*, 2. 3. 4 there is a citation of Juv. 8. 20, with the addition of *animi, nobilitas animi*, which of course alters the sense drastically. Apparently Dante took that line from a medieval anthology. Juvenal carrying the message to Vergil appears in *Purg.* 22. 13 f., which situates him in Limbo. 'Desire without hope' is in *Inf.* 4. 42. Moore proposes that the adjective *dolce*, used of Statius in *Purg.* 21. 88 and *Conv.* 4. 25. 6, was suggested by Juvenal's *dulcedine* in 7. 84, which might well be true. In his *Defence of Dante* (1755) Gasparo Gozzi introduced Juvenal, Vergil, and Aristophanes chatting with Dante, and made Juvenal say, 'Dante è uno de' più cari amici ch'io mi abbia. Chi ebbe mai tanto polso nel dir male de' vizj?' By the way, Dante's contemporary Albertino Mussato (1262–1329) alludes to the Statius passage in his *Elegia ad Collegium Artistarum*:

> Carmine sic laetam non fecit Statius urbem
> Thebais in scenis [*sic*] cum recitata fuit,
> Nec minus haec tragico fregit subsellia uersu. . . .

(So R. Sabbadini, *Le scoperte dei codici* (Florence, 1914), 2. 114.)

NOTES ON CHAPTER XXXI

1. An expert typographical investigation of the earliest printed editions of Juvenal's satires remains to be made. On the evidence at present available (as far as I can analyse it), the first edition seems to be a plain text of Juvenal (without Persius), bearing the name of Vdalricus Gallus (= Ulrich Han or Hahn of Ingolstadt) but without date or place. Apparently this book was printed in Han's earliest and smallest type, which he used in Rome between the years 1467 and 1469. It is a rare book, number 9660 in Hain's *Repertorium Bibliographicum* and 280 in T. F. Dibdin's *Bibliotheca Spenceriana*. The Spencer copy is now in the John Rylands Library, Manchester, and is described on p. 32 of the *Catalogue of the Earliest Printed Editions of the Greek and Latin Classics* issued by that library in 1926; there are copies in the Bodleian, the Fitzwilliam, and the Morgan Library. If this is the first edition, then the second would be a plain text of Juvenal and Persius printed in Venice by Wendelin of Speyer. It is in his first type, which was not used until August 1470 as far as we know; but it has no date. This edition is number 9672 in Hain and appears as 4058 in R. Proctor's *Index to the Early Printed Books in the British Museum* (London, 1898). It is a quarto book, about 10 × 8 in., with some misprints (e.g. *bos* for *hos* in 13. 192). There are three copies in the British Museum, two in Bodley, one at Harvard, and one in the Marston Collection at Yale.

2. Sabino's commentary, *Paradoxa in Iuuenali* (1474), contained violent attacks on the inferior 'Cornutus' commentaries (see p. 194) and on those who believed them—particularly Calderini, who was then professor of rhetoric at Rome. Both men were lecturing on Juvenal at the same time, and one of Sabino's aims was to expose Calderini on the charge of plagiarizing his lectures. But next year Calderini published his own text and notes, *Commentarii in Iuuenalem* (the title-page says *editi Romae*, but it was printed in Venice by Jacques le Rouge), a large handsome volume dedicated to Giuliano de' Medici the elder, which drove Sabino out of the field. For details of the controversy see Sanford (*80*) 102–5, who emphasizes the fact (stressed also by Knoche, *45*, 40–41, n. 6) that there were also a number of unpublished manuscript commentaries on Juvenal in existence. Descriptions of these early printed commentaries are also given by G. L. Hendrickson in 'The Marston Juvenals', *Yale Univ. Library Gazette*, 12 (1938), 78–80.

3. See Stephan (*50*) and Wessner (*53*), pref. xx–xxiii. Valla said the commentator was 'Probus grammaticus', but he probably took the name from the life of Persius, which was written by a real Probus long before Juvenal's time; and the genuine author's name is lost. Valla's manuscript was 'very old' and broke off at 8. 198. Perhaps the monk of Verona who lamented the lack of commentaries for the last two books of Juvenal (see p. 307) was using this manuscript or one of its cousins.

4. Such are the editions of A. Mancinelli (Venice, 1492), combining the notes of Calderini, Valla, and Mancinelli himself; and of Badius Ascensius (Lyons, 1498), which is one of the least readable books I have ever handled, set up in close Gothic type full of abbreviations. It has, however, a charming woodcut on the title-page, showing Juvenal (in doctor's robes) sitting at a desk reading his works aloud, while Mancinelli and Badius sit at side desks writing notes on his words and pondering their significance. Such also is the edition produced at Brescia in 1501 by J. Britannicus, though it contains notes by Politian. It is worth reprinting Mancinelli's neat summary of the contents of the sixteen satires:

> *Prima* docet satyrae causas formamque libelli.
> Qui simulant Curios satyra patuere *secunda*.

Ex urbe Umbricii digressum *tertia* narrat.
Quarta quidem Crispinum odit caluumque Neronem.
Ganeo quae tolerat parasitus *quinta* notauit.
Sexta haec infidas mulieres pandit abunde.
Septima demonstrat Romam nil ferre poetis.
Nobilis *octaua* propria uirtute uocatur.
Turpia qui tolerant *nona* carpuntur auari.
Curae hominum *decima* rerumque libido notantur.
Arguit *undecima* uates conuiuia lauta.
Bissena arguitur satyra captator auarus.
Tertia post decimam solatur damna dolentes.
In *decima quarta* dant praua exempla parentes.
Numina diuersa Aegypti *paenultima* monstrat.
Ultima militiae felicis praemia narrat.

5. So V. Scholderer on p. xiii of his General Introduction to Part VII of the *Catalogue of Books Printed in the XVth Century now in the British Museum*. Of the editions mentioned, 8 carry the plain text of Juvenal and 14 the plain text of both Juvenal and Persius, while 25 are annotated editions of Juvenal. There is a graceful little edition by Aldus, in his characteristic italic type but without his anchor emblem, dated August 1501. Another edition, bearing the anchor and dolphin, is placed in 1512 or later by H. W. Davies, *Devices of the Early Printers* (London, 1935), 658. There is at least one forged 'Aldine' Juvenal (printed at Lyons) with the revealing mistakes *impugne* in 1. 3 and *in felicibus ouis* in 13. 142. The Elzevir Juvenal published at Amsterdam in 1651 was reproduced in 1671: it is a small, ugly, almost unreadable book. A. Willems, *Les Elzevier* (Brussels, 1880), 2. 573, notes a fake also dated 1671.

6. The idea that satire had something to do with satyrs and satyric plays persisted for a long time in the minds of the public: it even got into the French Encyclopaedia, where it appears in the Chevalier de Jaucourt's article, *Satire*; and it may not be quite dead yet.

7. Housman (*56*) xvi–xvii puts it like this: 'The difference between P [Pithou's manuscript] and [the other manuscripts] is this. Upon [the other manuscripts] there has been rained a shower of interpolation which in scores of places has obliterated the original text and overlaid it with falsehoods. In P we find the one MS. which has escaped the shower; or rather we find the shower suspended over it and only the first drops fallen.' Knoche (*45*) 230 agrees: 'Verhältnismäßig am unverfälschtesten hat sich der Juvenaltext in dem Überlieferungsstrange erhalten, der sich ziemlich rein aus dem Montepessulanus P und seinen nächsten Verwandten wiedergewinnen läßt.' P is often wrong. The manuscripts of the other tradition are often wrong. But they are much more often and more stupidly or interferingly wrong than P. The good tradition is also represented, although incompletely, by (*a*) a few pages found in bookbindings at Aarau (called *Fragmenta Arouiensia*: see H. Wirz, 'Handschriftliches zu Iuvenalis', *Hermes*, 15, 1880, 437–48, for their discovery); (*b*) some quotations in an anthology from St. Gall, the *Florilegium Sangallense*; (*c*) the lemmata—or quotations of phrases to be commented on—given by the good scholia, both in P and in the St. Gall anthology; (*d*) Parisinus 8072, an incomplete manuscript; and (*e*) Vindobonensis 107, a valuable but less pure version of the tradition. It should be remembered that, after P was written, one or more 'correctors' went over it with a manuscript belonging to the other tradition, and inserted readings from that in many passages, sometimes erasing the true ones.

8. On Lorsch see K. Löffler, *Deutsche Klosterbibliotheken* (Bonn, 1922²), 140–5, and W. M. Lindsay, 'The (early) Lorsch scriptorium', *Palaeographia Latina*, 3 (1924), 1–25. François Pithou apparently did not tell his brother how he got the book, because Pierre added a note to his edition conjecturing that it had been saved from the sack of Budapest by the Turks. He had seen the name and date *Mathias 1469* on it, and conjectured that it had belonged to king Matthias I (Hunyadi, or Corvinus) of Hungary. However, the signature is that of a keen reader, Matthias Widman of Kemnat (*c.* 1430–76), the chaplain and historian of the Palatin ruler Friedrich I, who is known to have written his name on other Lorsch books which he inspected. (See R. Beer, 'Der codex 'Budensis' des Juvenal', *WS* 8, 1886, 342–4; T. Gottlieb, 'Wer ist der im cod. Montepessulanus 125 genannte Mathias?', *Eranos Vindobonensis*, Vienna, 1893, 145–52; and Lindsay, cited above, 25. An article by J. Abel, 'A Corvina Juvenalis-codéxeről', *Egyetemes Philologiai Közlöny*, 11, 1887, 321–6, is in Magyar, which I cannot read; but it seems to be aimed at controverting Beer's article.) Löffler implies that Widman took the manuscript out of the library in 1460 (or 1469), but it is not necessary to assume that, since he quotes a chronicle saying that the Pfalzgraf Ott Heinrich (1556–9), *tanquam alter Nebucadnezar*, descended on the abbey and took the entire library away to Heidelberg—apparently on the principle *cuius regio, eius libri*. As for Pithou's edition, it was printed in Paris by M. Patisson. It is a charming little book in italic type, containing Persius and 'Sulpicia' too, and, more important for us, the good scholia on Juvenal which appear in the P manuscript.

9. The manuscript is usually called Pithoeanus after Pithou; but since it now belongs to Montpellier it is sometimes styled Montepessulanus. Its number in the catalogue is H 125. Microfilms of it can be obtained from the Institut de Recherche et d'Histoire des Textes in Paris. The Montpellier professor on the manuscript commission was C. F. V. G. Prunelle. For the work of the commission and for the rediscovery of the manuscript see the articles by the brilliant G. Libri-Carrucci, 'Notice des manuscrits de quelques bibliothèques des départements' in *JSav* 1841–2, esp. p. 438 (1841) and p. 42 (1842). Later Libri described the MS. in the *Catalogue général des manuscrits des bibliothèques des départements* (Paris, 1849), 1. 330–1. It was first used again in Jahn's edition of 1851, but the collation he employed was not always accurate.

10. See Sanford (*80*) 97, and W. H. Woodward, *Studies in Education during the Age of the Renaissance* (Cambridge, 1924²), 15. Vittorino called his school *La Casa Giocosa.*

11. Aeneas Sylvius, *De liberorum educatione*, text, tr., and introd. by J. S. Nelson (*Catholic University of America Studies in Medieval and Renaissance Latin*, 12, Washington, 1940) This quotation is from p. 184. On p. 90, in the opening passage, Aeneas Sylvius quotes Juvenal 8. 30–32, and on p. 100 Juv. 7. 210–11. He knew Juvenal very well indeed, and obviously sympathized with him. His prose satire *De Curialium Miseriis* (ed. W. P. Mustard, Baltimore, 1928) is mainly built upon Juvenal. His debt lies, first, in the themes and in the general tone of his satire—the warnings against the disillusionment of serving great men, the emphasis on the squalor which is mingled with riches (particularly at banquets ∼Juv. 5), the descriptions of hope deferred and of 'the scorns that patient merit from the unworthy takes'; and, second, in many quotations made with no attempt to disguise them—for these see Mr. Mustard's notes. There are a few amusing mistakes, such as the one about bread which cannot be chewed with *false* teeth: § 23, 'adeo durus ut uix genuinis dentibus frangi queat' ∼Juv. 5. 68–69. Some of *De Curialium Miseriis* was put into pastoral English verse by Alexander Barclay, as the first three of *Certayne Egloges* (1570).

12. 'Doctor Martin Luther sagte: Es wäre sehr von Nöthen, daß die Bücher Juvenalis, Martialis, Catulli und Priapeia Virgilii ausn Landen und Schulen ausgemustert, verwiesen und verworfen würden; denn sie schreiben so grob und unverschämbt Ding, daß man sie ohn großen Schaden der Jugend nicht lesen kann.' This is from *Luther's sämmtliche Werke*, v. 62; *Tischreden*, v. 2, ed. J. K. Irmischer (Frankfurt, 1854) p. 344, no. 2879.

13. See Sanford (*80*) 99–100 and Woodward (cited in n. 10) 43. R. Sabbadini, *La scuola e gli studi di Guarino Guarini Veronese* (Catania, 1896), 96–97, says that although Guarino is supposed to have written a commentary on Juvenal, he himself has been unable to trace it, and thinks it may be merely his metrical summary of the satires—a short poem on the same lines as that quoted in n. 4 above, and beginning 'Materiam et causam satyrarum hac inspice prima'.

14. See *Vita et mores Gregorii Sanocei, auctore Philippo Buonacorsi Callimacho*, ed. L. Finkel, in *Monumenta Poloniae Historica*, 6 (Cracow, 1893), c. 5, pp. 182–3: which tells how Gregory read Juvenal 3. 203–5 and 208–9, and then corrected a Polish scholar named Dambrowka who was editing the *History of Poland* by St. Vincent and thought Codrus was the ancient king of Athens (see p. 313). See also T. Sinko, 'De Gregorii Sanocei studiis humanioribus', *Eos* 6 (1900), 248.

15. For Peurbach see C. Bursian's *Geschichte der classischen Philologie in Deutschland* (Munich, 1883), 107, and *Das akademische Deutschland* (ed. M. Doeberl, Berlin, 1930), I. 403. Albrecht von Eyb's *Margarita Poetica* is a compendium of literary rules and models, including excerpts from many of the best books. The best epigrams from Juvenal (all satires except 11, 12, and 16, with a preponderance of 6) are cited on the six pages beginning cxxxviii: over 200 in all. Murmellius is in Bursian 100–1.

16. *Opus Epistolarum Petri Martyris* (Paris, 1670), I. 57, dated 28 Sept. 1488.

17. His schoolmaster, Pedro de Mota, said Juan was

rara avis in terra corboque simillima nigro—

which sounds like a variation of a current medieval version. The story is from V. B. Spratlin's *Juan Latino, Slave and Humanist* (New York, 1938), 10.

18. A. F. G. Bell, *Francisco Sanchez, El Brocense* (Oxford, 1925), 40, gives the facts and quotes original documents.

19. There was only one complete translation into a modern tongue until well into the seventeenth century: a free version in Italian *terza rima*, published in or after 1480 by Zorzi Summaripa. Gerónimo de Villegas translated the Tenth into Spanish in a volume published in 1515; Lodovico Dolce did a rather poor prose paraphrase of the Sixth (dedicated to Titian, with a comparison of Juvenal's clarity to Titian's colours) in 1538; Michel d'Amboyse put Satires 8, 10, 11, and 13 into French in 1544; and 'W. B.' produced an English version of the Tenth in 1617. For further translations see pp. 326–7.

20. Section 26 of *Das Narrenschiff* deals with useless wishes, and falls into these parts:

(1) introduction—wealth ∼Juv. 10. 1–27.

(2) old age ∼Juv. 10. 188–288.

(3) beauty ∼Juv. 10. 289–345.

(4) power ∼Juv. 10. 133–87.

(5) right prayers ∼Juv. 10. 346–66, with a translation of 10. 356 and a misunderstanding of 10. 361.

There are other adaptations in the *Narrenschiff*: § 21 ∼Juv. 8. 140–1; 33 ∼ Juv. 6. 345; 49 ∼Juv. 14. 41–43; 60 ∼Juv. 2. 99 f.; 64 ∼Juv. 6. 620 f., with a misunderstanding of *Belides* in 6. 655; 76 ∼Juv. 8. 20; and 83 ∼Juv. 10. 22. Brant's English or Scottish adaptor Alexander Barclay mentions Juvenal 'the noble Poete' in his *Ship of Fools* 2. 186.

21. See Skelton's works, ed. P. Henderson (London, 1948²). On p. 163, in *Against Garnesche*, he mentions Juvenal as a predecessor; and he quotes phrases from Juv. 6. 191–5 in *Speak, Parrot* (p. 297). But for more considerable mentions of Juvenal, with direct quotations of Juv. 1. 30 and 8. 140, see *Why Come ye not to Court?* pp. 343–4.

22. Régnier's Third satire deals with the same sort of theme as Juvenal's Third, and his Second and Fourth are on poverty and poetry, combining Juvenal 7 and Juvenal 3. In 2. 14–17 he writes:

> Il faut suivre un sentier qui soit moins rebattu,
> Et, conduit d'Apollon, recognoistre la trace
> Du libre Juvénal; trop discret est Horace
> Pour un homme picqué. . . .

But in 14. 103–4 he indicates his chief model by saying:

> Suivant les pas d'Horace entrant en la carrière,
> Je trouve des humeurs de diverse manière.

There are, however, several direct adaptations from Juvenal in Régnier: e.g. 3. 61 ∼Juv. 13. 141; 3. 81–82 ∼Juv. 13. 103–5; the long passage beginning at 3. 89 ∼Juv. 3. 41 f.; 5. 73–76 ∼Juv. 2. 24–28 and 34–35; 13. 9 ∼Juv. 6. 130; and 13. 210 ∼Juv. 14. 204–5. It is sometimes said that Agrippa d'Aubigné copied Juvenal in *Les Tragiques*, and there are occasional faint echoes in that remarkable poem (see pp. 249 and 265); but it is much more epic in tone, and the satiric passages are built on direct observation rather than imitation: thus, the passages about homosexual courtiers and monarchs in book 2, *Princes*, have scarcely a hint that d'Aubigné knew Juvenal 2 or 9. Montaigne, by the way, quotes Juvenal fifty times.

23. Luigi Alamanni read Juvenal (Henri Hauvette, *Luigi Alamanni*, Paris,

1903, 24), and used a few obvious quotations from him; but he concentrated more closely on newer models: thus, his fourth satire, on women, is built more on Boccaccio's *Corbaccio* than on Juvenal 6. At the opening of Vinciguerra's second satire, he calls up 'quel d'Aquino, / Che'l scettro tien in satira latina'. But although he quotes Juvenal once or twice (e.g. *marital capestro* in 5 ∼ Juv. 6. 43), his poems are far more monotonously gloomy and sermon-like. Ariosto's satires are more like Horatian epistles. In his Fifth, on marriage (not against marriage), perhaps the section 97–114 about bad mothers having worse daughters may be a reminiscence of Juv. 6. 231–41 + 14. 25–30 as well as personal observation, but there are no further traces of Juvenal in the poems.

24. Reminiscences of Juvenal are particularly noticeable in Bartolomé's Third, Fourth, and Fifth *Letters*. His Third, to Nuño de Mendoza, combines Juvenal 3 and Juvenal 14 ('Gran reverencia se le debe á un niño' ∼ Juv. 14. 47) with a version of the Messalina episode (Juv. 6. 115 f.). His Fourth, on his own retirement from the court, draws themes from Juvenal 3, 8, and 11, e.g.:

> Yo aborrezco el mentir; soneto malo
> Ni le alabo á su autor, ni se lo pido. . . .

∼ Juv. 3. 41–42. His Fifth contains this passage:

> Cuyo llanto, oh marido, y cuyas voces
> Te dirá su escritorio si son fieles,
> Si con curiosidad lo reconoces.
> ¡Oh santo Dios, qué trazas, qué papeles
> Perfidos has de hallar! (∼ Juv. 6. 276–8).

25. On Quevedo see R. Sanchez Alonso, 'Los satíricos latinos y la sátira de Quevedo', *Revista de Filología Española*, 11 (1924), 33–62 and 113–53, who shows that Quevedo (like Ben Jonson, whom he rather resembles) was a good scholar. He loved the classics, speaking of them as 'mi Seneca', 'mi Juvenal'. In a letter to Lucas van Torre dated 1628, he wrote 'Interna mentis acie perpende mei Juvenalis carmina' and quoted 6. 292–3. Among the *Sonetas Morales* (numbered as in M. Aguilar's edition of the *Obras Completas*, Madrid, 1943) the following adaptations are noteworthy:

1 ('Muestra con ilustres ejemplos cuan ciegamente desean los hombres') ∼ Juv. 10, with citations of Pompey and Marius; 5 ∼ Juv. 13; 6 and 26 ('A la violenta e injusta prosperidad') ∼ Juv. 1; 28 ∼ Juv. 13; 34 ∼ Juv. 3; 49 ∼ Juv. 10, with a particularly fine adaptation of 10. 58 f., 'Miras la faz, que al orbe fué segunda...'; 50 ('¿Tan grande precio pones a la escama?') ∼ Juv. 4; 51 ∼ Juv. 14; 53 ('La vida miserable de los palacios') ∼ Juv. 3; 55 ('Más vale una benigna hora...') ∼ Juv. 16. In addition, Quevedo's sonnet *Ruina de Roma* contains adaptations of Juv. 8. 105–7 and 6. 292–5; in his *Riesgos del matrimonio* he translates the Messalina passage from 6; and there is some Juvenalian material in his *Sermón stoico*. In section 15 of *La Hora de Todos* there is another adaptation of Juvenal 3, and in section 38 he makes King Charles I of England ruefully quote Juv. 10. 14. It was Lope, in the *Laurel de Apolo*, silva 7, who called Quevedo 'Juvenal español'. A much lighter poet, Cristóbal de Castillejo, mentions Juvenal as an authority on misogyny in his *Diálogo de*

Mujeres, a long poem in Skelton-like lyrics (*Obras*, ed. J. Domínguez Bordona, Madrid, 1926): 11. 715–19:

> Tanto mal
> No se puede en especial
> Relatar en poco espacio;
> Remítolo a Juan Bocacio,
> Torrellas y Juvenal.

(Torrellas was a Catalan poet, majordomo of the Prince of Viana.)

26. There is a good book on the entire group, and on many of their predecessors and successors, by R. M. Alden: *The Rise of Formal Satire in England under Classical Influence* (Philadelphia, 1899). Donne transformed all he borrowed, and that was little: 1. 41 ~ Juv. 1. 74; 1. 53 f. ~ Juv. 10. 219 f.; 3 init. ~ Juv. 10. 28 f.; 5. 35–36 ~ Juv. 13. 28–30; see Alden 75–90. On Marston see Alden 129–48 and M. S. Allen, *The Satire of John Marston* (Columbus, Ohio, 1920), 84–127. His early satires show no sign of Juvenalian influence, but in the *Scourge of Villainy* (1599), the opening address to the readers and the end of the third satire are both built on the same plan as Juvenal 1, with the indignant question (*Shall . . . ? shall . . . ?*), and both cite Juvenal as gloomy but valuable. In this group the first satire is called *Fronti nulla fides* ~ Juv. 2. 8, and in it lines 13–15 ~ Juv. 2. 37–44, 19 ~ Juv. 2. 95, 25–28 ~ Juv. 2. 25–28 almost word for word, with a bad mistake on *moechos* ('cuckolds'!). The second satire is called *Difficile est Satyram non scribere* ~ Juv. 1. 30, and lines 76–88 ~ Juv. 15. 9–11, neatly adapted to contemporary religious disputes. But most of this violent satirist's work is original, as he says at the end of the sixth poem in this book. On Joseph Hall see Alden 98–129, K. Schulze's *Die Satiren Halls* (*Palaestra*, 106, Berlin, 1910), and a short article emphasizing his originality, by A. Stein, 'Joseph Hall's imitation of Juvenal', *MLR* 43 (1948), 315–22. There are not many imitations of Juvenal in the first three books of Hall's *Virgidemiarum* ('Tooth-lesse Satyrs', published in 1597), the most notable being 3. 1. 1–45 ~ Juv. 6. 1–24. But in his second set of three ('Byting Satyres', issued in 1598) he evokes Juvenal often as his master, uses many of his proper names, and adapts him again and again. (It looks as though Hall had thought of it in '98 and had at once been aped by the disgusting Marston.) Thus, 4. 1. 15–16 ~ Juv. 1. 155–6 and 170–1; 4. 1. 27–28 ~ Juv. 1. 55–57; 4. 1. 134–5 ~ Juv. 3. 62; 4. 1. 144–55 ~ Juv. 6. 115–32. Juv. 8 is the model for Hall 4. 3, and its opening is a good modernization of Juvenal's initial passage. So also Hall 4. 5. 67–68 ~ Juv. 2. 16–17; 4. 6. 3 ~ Juv. 10. 1–2; 5. 2. 105–50 ~ Juv. 5, even to the names Trebius and Virro; 6. 1. 220–39 ~ Juv. 1. 7–18, amusingly Elizabethanized; and 6. 1. 243 ~ Juv. 2. 37.

27. Rabelais, *Pantagruel* 34 ~ Juv. 2. 3; *Tiers Livre* 12 ~ Juv. 6. 209–10; *Quart Livre* 59 ~ Juv. 8. 53. There is little or nothing of Juvenal in the *Epistulae Obscurorum Virorum* and the *Satyre Ménippée*.

28. Huarte de San Juan, *Examen de Ingenios* (*Biblioteca de Autores Españoles* 65, Madrid, 1873), c. 11 (p. 449) and c. 13 (p. 456) ~ Juv. 1. 79. Malón de Chaide, *Libro de la Conversión de la Madalena* (same series 27, Madrid, 1853), part 3, § 39 (p. 365) ~ Juv. 13. 193–4, reading *putas*.

29. The early English play *Fulgens and Lucres* by Henry Medwall (1497) deals with the same theme as Juvenal 8 (Nobility is Virtue), but seems to have no direct connexion with the satire. (It comes from a '*controversia*', *De Vera Nobilitate*, by Buonaccorso of Pistoja, dated 1428, which I have not seen.) In Juan de Rojas's peculiar mixture of a romance and a play, *La Celestina* (1499), the lamenting Pleberio cries 'Como caminante pobre que sin temor de los crueles salteadores va cantando en alta voz' (Aucto 21), which is Juv. 10. 22. In a college play called *Return from Parnassus* (part 2, produced at St. John's, Cambridge, in 1601), the opening soliloquy is delivered by the disillusioned Ingenioso, 'with Iuuenall in his hand':

> *Difficile est, Satyram non scribere, nam quis iniquae*
> *Tam patiens urbis, tam furens, ut teneat se?**
> I, Iuuenall: thy ierking hand is good,
> Not gently laying on, but fetching bloud,
> So surgean-like thou dost with cutting heale,
> Where nought but lanching can the wound auayle.

He goes on to say that in Juvenal's day the world was comparatively pure: then 'Vice was in his swaddling bands', but now it is a monster (contrast Juv. 1. 147–9).

30. The theory that the spirit of satire was diverted into drama by the church prohibition is worked out in O. J. Campbell's *Comicall Satyre and Shakespeare's 'Troilus and Cressida'* (San Marino, 1938).

31. There is a good analysis of this topic in K. A. McEuen's 'Jonson and Juvenal', *RES* 21 (1945), 92–104. Jonson owned a fifteenth-century MS. of the Satires, and also Lubinus's 1603 ed. (C. H. Herford and P. Simpson, *Ben Jonson*, Oxford, 1925, 1. 262–3 and 266). In *Every Man out of his Humour* the prologue parallels the themes of Juvenal 1 and 2; both Asper and Macilente are projections of Jonson–Juvenal; in *The Poetaster* too there is much Juvenal; and in *Cynthia's Revels* Crites is another such Jonson–Juvenal character. The citation in the text is from Act 3, Scene 3, and comes from Juv. 1. 73–6. *Sejanus* begins with phrases like 'We burn with no black secrets' (∼Juv. 3 49–50); 'cut men's throats with whisperings' (∼Juv. 4. 110); 'laugh when the patron laughs, sweat when he sweats' (∼Juv. 3. 100–3); 'the second face of the whole world' (∼Juv. 10. 63). In Act 5, Scene 10, most of Juv. 10. 56–107 is translated, even to 'the legs of the poor horses'; and there are many more trenchant lines well adapted throughout the play. Jonson wrote four Latin couplets as the epigraph for Thomas Farnaby's edition of Juvenal, printed in London in 1612.

32. Corneille, *Le Menteur*, 5. 3; Molière, *Dom Juan*, 4. 4 ('La vertu est le premier titre de la noblesse . . .'). Other reminiscences of Juvenal might well be found in Molière. Mr. Vincent Pascucci has suggested to me that the character of Tartuffe is partly built on the greedy Greeky of Juv. 3: his absolute authority in the house ∼ 3. 72, his attempt to seduce Orgon's wife ∼ 3. 110, his knowledge of compromising secrets ∼ 3. 113, and even his willingness to show the way to heaven ∼ 3. 78!

33. *Hamlet*, 2. 2. 195 f. In 2. 2. 160–1 Polonius says, 'You know sometimes he walks four hours together / Here in the lobby', which reminds us of Martial's vision of Juvenal (*inquietus erras*, Mart. 12. 18. 1) and of Juvenal's

---

* Juv. 1. 30–31, with *furens* instead of *ferreus*—by miscopying?

sleeplessness (Juv. 1. 77 and *Hamlet*, 2. 2. 266). Shakespeare had not read the Tenth Satire with any attention, but he had got to know the gist of some of it and had divined its spirit. In *Antony and Cleopatra*, 2. 1. 5–7 the wise Menecrates tells Pompey:

> We, ignorant of ourselves,
> Beg often our own harms, which the wise powers
> Deny us for our good; so find we profit
> By losing of our prayers. . . .

which looks like a memory of the final passage of this famous poem, 10. 346–50.

34. In 1679 Dryden was beaten by a gang hired by the earl of Rochester; in 1725 Voltaire was beaten by the servants of the duc de Rohan; in 1755 Johnson refused the patronage of the earl of Chesterfield, observing, 'Seven years, my Lord, have now past, since I waited in your outward rooms, or was repulsed from your door.'

35. This is well explained for France by J. A. Hild, 'Quelques observations à propos de Juvénal au XVIIᵉ siècle', *Mélanges Boissier* (Paris, 1903), 285–92, and for England by J. B. Emperor, *The Juvenalian and Persian element in English Literature from the Restoration to Dr. Johnson* (Cornell, 1932).

36. The capital editions of the seventeenth century are E. Lubinus (Hanover, 1603); T. Farnaby (London, 1612, often reprinted); Grangaeus (Paris, 1614); Rigaltius (Paris, 1616); Schrevelius (Leyden, 1648); the Dauphin edition, often reprinted, by Després or Prateus (Paris, 1684); Henninius (Utrecht, 1685); and an expurgated edition for Jesuit schools by the famous Jesuit teacher Jouvancy (Tours, 1687). Casaubon intended to produce an edition of Juvenal, whom he called *poetam grauissimum* (M. Pattison, *Isaac Casaubon*, Oxford, 1892, 432, and *Ep.* 523), but he was cut off too soon.

37. After Du Chesne came Denys Challine (vigorous verse, 1653); Marolles (flat prose, 1653); La Valterie (1680–1); Martignac (1682); and Tarteron (1689); as well as versions of single satires, e.g. a rambling 1,400-line paraphrase of Satire 1 called *Ivvenal bvrlesqve* by the miserable Colletet fils (see Boileau *Sat.* 1. 77–8) and a version of the Tenth by the duc de Montausier.

38. The remark about the charge of plagiarism comes from Holyday's life in the *DNB*. Two specimens will show the quality of these translators: Juv. 6. 268–72:

Holyday: The Bed, in which a wife lies, still does keep
Retorted braulings. That's no place for Sleep.
When Greif shee faighns, with secret guilt First stung,
The Tiger's less fierce, that has lost her young.
Shee's then thy Load: shee does thy Children hate:
Complains of a (faign'd) harlot.

Stapylton: Debates, alternate brawlings ever were
In Marriage-beds, no thought of sleeping there.
Fierce as a Tigress robb'd she then begins
To chide, or sigh, when guilty of close sins:
Or her own Children hates; or swears he keeps
A Wench, and as she did believe it, weeps.

They have both missed the nasty implication of *odit pueros*. Otherwise they
are equally correct; and Stapylton is much neater and more Juvenalian
(Holyday had already translated Persius, and his style was distorted by that
effort); the only word which might be borrowed is 'brawlings'.

39. Dryden himself translated 1, 3, 6, 10, and 16, and farmed out the
others to friends and relatives; but he supervised and apparently improved
their work (see T. and E. Swedenberg, *George Stepney's Translation of the
Eighth Satire of Juvenal*, Berkeley, Cal., 1948). Of the other satires, 2 and 15
were given to Nahum Tate, 4 to R. Duke, 5 to W. Bowles, 7 to Dryden's
eldest son Charles, 8 to George Stepney, 9 to S. Harvey, 11 to Congreve, 12
to T. Power, 13 to T. Creech, and 14 to Dryden's second son John. There
were a number of English renderings of separate satires in this era. In 1629
George Chapman did a version of the Fifth in heroic couplets, called
A iust reproof of a Romane smell-Feast. It has some good things in it, e.g. 5.
70–71:

> But for his bread, the pride of appetite,
> Tenderly soft, incomparably white,
> The first flowre of fine meal subdu'd in paste
> That's a peculiar for my Lords owne taste.

In 1646 Henry Vaughan, the Silurist, published a smooth translation of
the Tenth.* Anthony à Wood's nephew Thomas did a rather crabbed
modernization of Satire 1 in 1683, called *Juvenalis Redivivus*: it introduced
T(itus) O(ates) as one of the informers in 1. 35 f., and for Cluvienus in 1. 80
it used the name of the early translator Holyday (see p. 214). In 1686 and
1687 the playwright Higden produced two jolly versions of 13 and 10 in the
metre of *Hudibras*: listen—

> Who wonders at a crafty Scot,
> Or Dutchman given to the Pot?

∼Juv. 13. 162–5.
There were many more versions, nearly all superior to anything we could
write today.

40. The Spanish paraphrase is the *Declaración Magistral sobre las Satiras de
Iuuenal, Principe de los Poetas Satíricos*, by Diego Lopez (Madrid, 1642). It
looks rather like the text of Lopez's lectures: he first quotes some lines of the
Latin original, and then turns them into Spanish, occasionally expanding or
abbreviating them, and always interpolating explanatory notes and citing
parallel passages: it cannot be read as a straight translation. It has a curious
preface arguing that Castilian is not derived from Latin. The Dutch prose
version by Abraham Valentijn came out at Leyden in 1682, and includes
Persius. The verse translation, *Alle de schimpdichten van D. Junius Juvenalis in
nederduitse vaarzen overgebracht*, was published at Haarlem in 1709: it is in
alexandrines, and the translators include Christoffel Pierson, W. de Geest,
and Pieter Nuits (who did the Sixth). Silvestri's Italian rendering, published
at Padua, is very rich, putting the satires into different metres according to
their subjects. Some reference works mention a German translation by Janus

---

* Vaughan quotes Juvenal several times in his prose works: e.g. 13. 86–88 in
Mount of Olives (*Works*, ed. Grosart, 1871, 3. 101), and 15. 160–4+169–71 in
Hermeticall Physick (ibid. 276–8).

Gebhard, but it is a ghost-book: the unfortunate Gebhard's first publication was called *Juveniles Curae*, a title which someone has misinterpreted into a book on Juvenal.

41. *Macbeth* 1. 5. 53; *The Rambler* 26 Oct. 1751. Johnson made Macbeth (instead of Lady Macbeth) responsible for using the word, doubtless because he was reluctant to associate a lady with an expression so trivial and vulgar: 'we do not immediately conceive,' he adds, 'that any crime of importance is to be committed with a *knife*.' There is a fuller discussion of this subject in G. Highet, *The Classical Tradition* (Oxford, 1949), 318–20.

42. Daniel Heinsius laid down in 1608 that Horace was superior to Juvenal. But the elder Scaliger had put Juvenal above Horace; he was followed by Justus Lipsius (see his letter to Pulmann, *Epist. Quaest.* 2. 9); and Rigault in his preface expounded the merits of Juvenal so convincingly that opinion remained divided. (See Hild, cited in n. 35, 288–92.) In Britain the verdict generally was that in theory the 'laughing' satire of Horace was more admirable than the 'flaying' satire of Juvenal; yet in practice Juvenal was quite as often copied (see Emperor, cited in n. 35).

43. A complete study of Boileau's debt to Juvenal is needed—especially since so many poets in other countries took Juvenalian phrases from Boileau rather than his model. Four of his satires are built on Juvenal's: *Sat.* 1 ∼ Juv. 3 and 7 (Saint-Amant = Codrus); *Sat.* 5 ∼ Juv. 8; *Sat.* 6 ∼ Juv. 3; and *Sat.* 10 ∼ Juv. 6. (On this last there is a useful dissertation by D. Englaender, *La Xᵉ Satire de Boileau comparée à la VIᵉ de Juvénal*, Berlin, 1904: which shows that Boileau kept Juvenal's main idea, the persuasion against marriage combined with and supported by a denunciation of married women, but improved the plan. Where Juvenal's interlocutor Postumus gradually disappears like the Cheshire Cat, Boileau's friend Alcippe does not merely remain and listen, but actually argues; however, what Boileau gains in smoothness he loses in vividness.) Adaptations of single passages are scattered throughout Boileau's work: e.g. 3 init. ∼ Juv. 9. 1 f.; 4. 31–35 ∼ Juv. 10. 220–6; 5. 29 f. ∼ Juv. 8. 56 f.; 8. 3 ∼ Juv. 10. 1–2: see also O. Benecke, *Boileau imitateur d'Horace et de Juvénal* (Neuhaldensleben, 1879). Boileau himself, e.g. in *Sat.* 7, claims both Horace and Juvenal as his models. His contemporary La Fontaine has at least one pretty adaptation, in the fifth book of his *Contes et Nouvelles*, 'Philémon et Baucis', where the old peasant says (to Jupiter himself!):

> Saluez ces pénates d'argile:
> Jamais le ciel ne fut aux humains si facile,
> Que quand Jupiter même était de simple bois;
> Depuis qu'on l'a fait d'or, il est sourd à nos voix.

Cf. Juv. 11. 114–15.

44. *Discourse concerning Satire*. On the preface to Dryden's *All for Love* see p. 272.

45. Oldham's 'Satyr in Imitation of the Third of Juvenal' and his imitation of Juvenal 13 are direct adaptations; he also adapted Juvenal 8 'out of Monsieur Boileau' in 'A Satyr touching Nobility'; and in 'A Satyr address'd to a Friend that is about to leave the University, and come abroad in the World' he used the Fifth Satire very skilfully. Fragments of other poems by Juvenal often appear in his work.

46. In his preface to *Love of Fame* Young says: 'Juvenal is ever in a passion: he has little valuable but his eloquence and morality: the last of which I have had in my eye; but rather for emulation, than imitation, through my whole work. But though I comparatively condemn Juvenal, in part of the sixth satire (where the occasion required it), I endeavoured to touch on his manner . . .' In fact, at the climax of his sixth book, after mentioning a number of harmless if irritating foibles, Young cries:

> O Juvenal! for thy severer rage!
> To lash the ranker follies of our age.
> Are there, among the females of our isle,
> Such faults, at which it is a fault to smile?

and replies gloomily:

> There are.

In his *First Epistle to Mr. Pope* Young adapts the opening of Juvenal 1.

47. Atterbury said Pope was *mens curua in corpore curuo* ∼ Juv. 10. 356. There are not many readily apparent adaptations of Juvenal in Pope: he himself signalizes *Moral Essays, Epistle III*, 394 ∼ Juv. 3. 3; Codrus appears in *Prologue to the Satires*, 85, not as a poor man but as a scribbler, apparently understood as Cordus of Juv. 1. 2; and there are two or three other possible borrowings, but Pope, like other eminent satirists, appears to have refrained from studying his predecessor.

48. Johnson's adaptation of Juv. 10, *The Vanity of Human Wishes*, was the first work to carry his name on the title-page. It came out in 1749, and the publisher paid him 15 guineas for it (Boswell's *Life*, Oxford, 1924, 1. 129–30). *London* (∼ Juv. 3) was written in 1738, and brought him 10 guineas (Boswell 1. 82, 85). 'I remember', says Boswell, 'when I once regretted to him that he had not given us more of Juvenal's *Satires*, he said he probably should give more, for he had them all in his head. . . . Some of them, however, he observed were too gross for imitation' (1. 130). He quoted Juvenal often, and on his deathbed corrected Dr. Brocklesby for falsifying the metre of 10. 358 by substituting *supremum* for *extremum* (Boswell 2. 634). And really, he *believed* Juvenal. See him repeating 8. 79–84 and praising the passage (*Tour to the Hebrides*, ed. F. A. Pottle and C. H. Bennett, New York, 1936, 338); breaking into 'a passion of tears' when repeating the passage about the scholar's life in his own version of the Tenth (H. L. Piozzi, *Anecdotes*, London, 1786⁴, 30); and pessimistically denying that life would be worth living over again (Boswell 2. 556–9 ∼ Juv. 10). Only his handling of the contrast between city and country is forced, for he really loved the city and knew little of country life: E. Walford, *Juvenal* (London, 1872), 150–4, points out that he wrote the adaptation of Juvenal 3 while staying in the then quiet village of Hampstead, and may there have persuaded himself that he hated the city. In his library there were at least four editions of Juvenal: one printed at Amsterdam in 1626, which passed to his negro servant Frank (A. L. Reade, *Johnsonian Gleanings*, 2, 1912, 80), Henninius's edition as reissued in 1695, and two or three more (P. H. Houston, *Doctor Johnson*, Cambridge, Mass., 1923, 264).

49. See *Joachim Rachels satyrische Gedichte*, ed. K. Drescher (Halle, 1903).

The first satire is modelled on Semonides, which does not seem to have been generally noted. The fourth, *Kinder-Zucht*, is a paraphrase of Juvenal 14, even to the proper names; the sixth, *Gut und Böse*, of Juvenal 10; the opening of the seventh, *Freundt*, is based on the opening of Juvenal 6, and the eighth, *Der Poet*, has some of Juvenal 1 in its indignation.

50. Salvator Rosa has other adaptations too: 2. 172–4 ∼ Juv. 7. 34–5 and 5. 106 f. ∼ Juv. 3. 41 f. On Sergardi see V. Cian, *La Satira* (Milan, 1945²) 2. 433 f., and R. Battignani, *Studio su Quinto Settano* (Girgenti, 1894). His satires are full of phrases adapted from Juvenal and Horace: the first begins 'Ibam forte . . .' ∼ Hor. *Serm.* 1. 9. 1, and the third, 'Ecce iterum ventosus adest Philodemus...' ∼ Juv. 4. 1. They are rather good, full of energy and not unoriginal despite their borrowings. The Italian satires of Benedetto Menzini (1646–1704) contain a few allusions to Juvenal and a few passages inspired by his work, e.g. in 7 'Splenderon gli avi, come face eterna / in candelabro d'oro' ∼ Juv. 8. 138–9; but they are much more Bernesque in tone than Juvenalian. The elegant Cavaliere Marino has a neat baroque picture of Juvenal in his *Galeria* (Venice, 1667), 180:

> Del satiro d'Aquino
> E' la penna pungente,
> Medico ferro, che con arte estrana
> Di spietata pietà ferisce, e sana.
> Lancia, la cui virtù fatale, e maga
> E salubre, e nocente,
> Vipera, che col dente
> Morde, ma con le polpe unge la piaga;
> Però che la sua Musa
> Corregge i vitij altrui mentre gli accusa.

The finest modern Italian satire, Parini's *Il Giorno*, owes practically nothing to Juvenal: G. Carducci, in 'Studi su Giuseppe Parini', *Opere* (Bologna, 1892), 14. 89–95, says that Parini has the intensity of Juvenal's sarcasm, but is not really a regular satirist at all: 'è l'epica della satira.'

51. e.g. Abraham's sermon on the 11th Sunday after Pentecost, in *Judas der Erzschelm*. The text is *Et apprehendens eum de turba seorsum* (Mark vii. 33), and the outline of the sermon is this:

'Instruit nos sacer iste textus ut pari pacto de turba seorsum ducamur, cum turbae ut plurimum mentem turbare soleant, quia quoties bonus malo conjungitur, raro ex bono malus melioratur sed quasi semper ex malo bonus contaminatur. QVI TETIGERIT PICEM INQVINABITVR AB EA, ET QVI COMMVNICAVERIT SVPERBO, Ecclus. xiii. 1. . . .

> sicut grex totus in agro
> unius scabie cadit et portigine porci [*sic*]
> uvaque conspecta livorem ducit ab uva (Juv. *Sat.* 2).'

52. Gracián, *El Criticón* 2. 12: 'No ai otra honra sino la que se apoya en la virtud' ∼ Juv. 8. 20. Still, M. Romera-Navarro, 'Autores latinos en *El Criticón*', *Hispanic Review*, 2 (1934), 102–33, shows that Gracián did not use Juvenal much.

53. On p. 44 (ed. J. Fabre, Paris, 1950), Rameau says, 'On loue la vertu; mais on la hait; mais on la fuit; mais elle gele de froid, et dans ce monde, il faut avoir les piés chauds' (∼Juv. 1. 74). Rameau himself is a cross between Naevolus and Trebius. Elsewhere, in his *Essai sur les Règnes de Claude et de Néron*, c. 102 (*Œuvres complètes*, Paris, 1875, 3, pp. 155–6), Diderot has a spirited paraphrase of Juv. 5. 108–11 and 8. 211–12.

54. In § 71 of the same book Locke cites Juv. 14. 47 (reading *pueris*) and 14. 49; and in his peroration, § 200, he quotes 10. 365 (with *abest*). J. Parmentier, 'M. Berthelot et Locke, interprètes de Juvénal', in *Bulletin de la Faculté de Poitiers*, 6 (1888), 382, suggests that Locke was the first to apply Juv. 10. 356 to *education*.

55. For a discussion and details, see Emperor (cited in n. 35). W. H. Irving, *John Gay's London* (Cambridge, Mass., 1928), shows how many poets drew on Juvenal for their bitter or comical accounts of city life: see esp. 91–109. Voltaire—by a paradox which we have seen elsewhere—knew little of Juvenal, and merely scolded him for laughing at Cicero (*Œuvres complètes*, Paris, 1877–85, 5. 207) and at Alexander (ibid. 6. 102, 22. 244). His only other mention of him is an unimportant reference to 15. 9 (ibid. 11. 67). The motto of the first issue of the *Tatler* is Juv. 1. 86.

56. Swift's epitaph: HIC DEPOSITVM EST CORPVS JONATHAN SWIFT, S.T.P., VBI SAEVA INDIGNATIO VLTERIVS COR LACERARE NEQVIT—which sounds like an inscription over the body of the speaker of Juvenal 1. See M. Johnson on it in *PMLA* 68 (1953), 814–27. Swift quotes Juvenal about twenty times in extant works, and once (after citing 7. 53–56) exclaims 'Excellent, by my soul!'

57. See Gibbon's *Journal à Lausanne*, ed. G. Bonnard (Lausanne, 1945): e.g. on pp. 22–23:

'Je distinguerois . . . entre les caractères de Boileau et de Juvenal. L'un et l'autre paroissent avoir peu connû les sentimens tendres. Mais c'etoit dans le premier une secheresse de cœur. . . . Juvenal avoit l'imagination ardente, et un cœur qui y repondoit: mais tous les deux portoient plutot leur energie sur les passions fortes, sombres, et elevées; que sur celles qui sont douces et aimables.'

58. Richardson, *Clarissa*, 4 (Oxford, 1930), Letter 51, p. 339: 'These lines translated from Juvenal by Mr. Tate, I have been often pleased with. . . .' ∼Juv. 15. 131 f.

59. Casanova, *Mémoires* (ed. R. Vèze, Paris, 1928), 8. 216 ∼ Juv. 10. 22. For further details on Juvenal's influence at this time see R. C. Whitford, 'Juvenal in England 1750–1802', *PQ* 7 (1928), 9–16. Many of the political poems of the period are best understood through Juvenal: e.g. a Whig piece by an anonymous Scotsman, dated 1781, dedicated to the Earl of Mansfield, and called, with a ghastly infection of Sternian whimsy, *XSMWPDRIBVN-WLXY, or The Sauce-Pan*—which is a huge paraphrase of Juvenal 1.

NOTES ON CHAPTER XXXII

1. In this chapter I am indebted for many hints to de Labriolle (*4*). (See his *Appendice III* for the reference to Marat, which he in turn owes to M. Gérard Walter.) The issue of *L'Ami du Peuple* in question is no. 539 of 27 August 1791: one could hardly find a better example of the timeliness of

Juvenal and of his power to canalize the bitterness of his admirers. After mentioning Satires 6, 7, and 8, as true pictures of contemporary Paris, Marat goes on:

'Mais c'est dans la satyre XIII que les Parisiens peuvent se reconnaître, au tableau qu'il fait de l'avarice, de la rapacité, de la fraude, de la friponnerie, de la perfidie, du brigandage et des crimes de tout espèce qui soullaient [*sic*] Rome. Je passerai sous silence ces traits caractéristiques, pour tracer le portrait qu'il fait de la soldatesque romaine; nous y reconnaîtrons, trait pour trait, nos gardes nationaux: même insolence, même licence, même impunité et mêmes privilèges.'

This is follcwed by paraphrases of 16. 8–34 and 42–50. Another Juvenal enthusiast was deeply involved in the French Revolution: Jean Dusaulx (1728–99). He became devoted to Juvenal in his youth, announced a translation of the satires in 1757 and published it in 1770. It is rather inaccurate, but it is in clear, graceful prose. During the Revolution Dusaulx held several important posts, and was a Girondin. He was imprisoned from 1792 to 1794 (Marat defended him) and apparently just escaped the guillotine. When released, he was asked to produce a third edition of his translation, and did so without much interest because he was sunk in the gloom of the disillusioned political idealist. But, when he received his proofs—

'Le croira-t-on? Le texte de Juvénal, reproduit sous mes yeux après six années d'anxiétés, ce texte brûlant m'électrise tout-à-coup. Le cœur me bat; les sensations et les idées renaissent. Sorti de ma profonde léthargie, je m'élance à la tribune nationale. . . .'

And after telling how he reaffirmed his belief in lofty political aspirations and proposed the erection of a monument to the martyrs of the revolution, he cries:

'O Juvénal! ton ombre m'en a su plus de gré que de mon enthousiasme pour tes vers immortels.'

These passages are from the preface to his third edition; see the *Éloge* by Villeterque in the fourth edition (Paris, 1803). One should also mention a graceful translation of Juv. 10. 270 by André Chénier (*Œuvres*, ed. P. Dimoff, Paris, n.d., 3. 171), and a paraphrase of parts of 1 and 6 in his brother's *Essai sur la Satire* (*Œuvres posthumes*, Paris, 1825), 2. 287–8.

2. The text of Wordsworth's version (which is really more of a free paraphrase and improvisation than a translation) appears in W. Knight's *Letters of the Wordsworth Family* (Boston and London, 1907), 1. 87–98. For a discussion, see C. V. Tuckerman, 'Wordsworth's plan for his imitation of Juvenal', *MLN* 45 (1930), 209–15, who cites *The Prelude*, 8. 340–686 and 13. 206–20 to illustrate the feelings which impelled Wordsworth towards Juvenalian satire. There are some good lines, e.g. 8. 211–12:

> What fool, besotted as we are by names,
> Could pause between a Raleigh and a James?

3. e.g. 'Monk' Lewis translated Juv. 13 as 'The Love of Gain' in 1799; the Marquis de La Châtaigneraye translated 4, 'Le Turbot', in 1812. The most effective poem of this kind is an anonymous version of the Eighth called

'High Birth' (London, 1821), evidently written by a Whig who knew the people and the milieu he was satirizing. Thus 8. 87–88 becomes:

> If the long-wished for, long-expected call
> At length shall hail thee, Viceroy of Bengal . . .

and 8. 171 f. is turned into something worthy of Hogarth:

> Just bend your footsteps to St. Martin's Lane:
> Stripped to the skin, behold the British Peer!
> 'The Fancy' owns its kindest patron here.
> Some base-born bruiser ventures to the list,
> And gives, and takes the glove-attempered fist.
> Rogues, vagrants, navigators shout around,
> And Jews and Gipsies swell the plausive sound.
> Another scene succeeds—the champion's bawl
> Invites their Lordships to his 'house of call'.
> There portly freedom sits, and freely there
> Pots, plates, and knives the motley comrades share;
> With equal zeal the ivyed god adore,
> And roll in drunken concert on the floor.

See also R. C. Whitford, 'Juvenal in England 1750–1802', *PQ* 7 (1928), 9–16.

4. See Coleridge's letter to Godwin, 25 March 1801; *The Friend*, Second Section, Essay xi (1818); and the poem *Self-Knowledge* (1832), which bears Juv. 11. 27 as an epigraph.

5. *A New Translation of the Third Satire of Juvenal* (New York, 1806) is fairly rare. It is anonymous; but the *Index to American Poetry and Plays in the Collection of C. Fiske Harris* (Providence, 1874), p. 41, attributes it to John Duer, I know not on what grounds. Duer (who rose to be a leading lawyer and whose brother became President of Columbia College) was 24 when the translation was published; but the biographers say his education was 'irregular', and it is not clear whether he was qualified to translate Juvenal. The style is heavy baroque:

> Umbritius then (while forrow fwell'd my breaft)
> His rage and grief in manly ftrain expreft.

The volume also contains poems by Clement Moore, who later wrote 'The Night before Christmas'. The first Danish translation, by Frederik Plum (later Bishop Plum), appeared in 1790.

6. See pp. 125 and 277 for quotations. *Sardanapalus* 3. 1. 145 f. is modelled on Juv. 2. 93–109 (see Byron's letter to Murray, 30 May 1821); the story of the silver urn appears in a letter from Scott himself, given by Moore, *Works of Byron* (London, 1832), 3. 164; the citation is Juv. 10. 147–8 + 172–3.

7. B. Dobell, in *The English Review* (August, 1915), 1–24, reprints *A Farrago Libelli* and points out coincidences of phrasing between it and Byron's early work. Messrs. Hatchards's archives were largely destroyed during the 1940 blitz, so that they have been unable to trace the provenance of the poem. However, S. C. Chew, 'Did Byron write *A Farrago Libelli*?', *MLN* 31 (1916), 287–91, declares that the parallels are slight, the possibility of Byron's authorship slim, and the poem by a weak imitator of Pope. And in a letter to me Mr. Leslie A. Marchand of Rutgers University, who is engaged on a biography of Byron, adds these facts, which appear conclusive: that Byron never mentions this poem, although at that time of life he was proud enough to have referred to anything so ambitious if he had written it; that he never mentioned Juvenal before his second residence at Cambridge in 1807, and that Juvenal is not named in the extensive catalogue of his reading compiled by Moore (*Life*, 1. 95–98) from Byron's memorandum-book of 1807; that among his early poems of 1806 and 1807 there are a number of imitations and translations of other classical poets but none from Juvenal, although later Byron recognized him as a congenial spirit and quoted him extensively; and that in 1806 Byron knew little or nothing about publishing, and had his early poems privately printed by Ridge or Newark, while there is no indication that he was ever connected with Hatchards.

8. J. C. Hobhouse, *Imitations and Translations from the Ancient and Modern Classics Together with Original Poems* (London, 1809), opens with a really charming modernization of Juvenal 11 in heroic couplets. *Curius paruo . . . horto* (11. 78) becomes Sir William Temple; *Gallis uenientibus* (11. 113) the Armada; and the last epigram is gracefully rendered

> 'Tis after sickness, health looks doubly fair,
> And pleasure then most pleases, when most rare.

Apparently it was Hobhouse, together with Francis Hodgson, who introduced Byron to Juvenal, of whom he became a lifelong admirer.

9. Lessing, *Sämtliche Schriften*, ed. K. Lachmann and F. Muncker, Stuttgart, 1886[3]: Hispulla, Hippia (= Eppia), &c. are on 2. 30; Letter 77 of the *Briefe, die neueste Litteratur betreffend* (8. 201), begins with *Ecce iterum Crispinus* (~Juv. 4. 1) and follows it with other citations of 4; Juv. 11. 100–7 is discussed in *Laokoon*, 1. 7 (9. 52–56), 12. 43–47 and 7. 125–8 on pp. 13–14 of vol. 15.

10. Herder, *Werke*, ed. B. Suphan, Berlin, 1877, 1. 492–7: 'Von der horazischen Satyre', part of his 'Ueber die neuere deutsche Litteratur' (1767).

11. Schiller, *Werke*, ed. C. Höfer, Munich, n.d., 12: 'Ueber naive und sentimentalische Dichtung', p. 87:

> 'Die pathetische Satire muß also jederzeit aus einem Gemüte fließen, welches von dem Ideale lebhaft durchdrungen ist. Nur ein herrschender Trieb nach Uebereinstimmung kann und darf jenes tiefe Gefühl moralischer Widersprüche und jenem glühenden Unwillen gegen moralische Verkehrtheit erzeugen, welcher in einem Juvenal, Lucian, Dante, Swift, Young, Rousseau, Haller, und andern zur Begeisterung wird.'

12. Goethe, *Werke* (Weimar ed.): 3. 357 shows him reading Juvenal 1; 37. 92 shows him copying out Juv. 10. 324–5 in his *Ephemerides*; and 46. 192 contains, in *Philipp Hackert*, a transcription of 8. 105–11, with the remark: 'Dieß sind die Worte eines Dichters, auf dessen Sittenschilderung wir uns verlassen können.'

13. The date of the speech was 1809. See C. A. Vince, 'Latin poets in the British Parliament', *CR* 46 (1932), 97–104, who gives another amusing example, Canning's quotation of Juv. 13. 38 on Napoleon's alliance with the Pope. He adds that over a long period Juvenal was one of the four poets most frequently cited in Parliament.

14. Ribbeck's text was published at Leipzig in 1859, and his justification of it (*49*) in 1865. See also his 'De Iuvenalis satira sexta' in *Symbola Philologorum Bonnensium in honorem F. Ritschelii collecta* (Leipzig, 1864–7), 1–30. His methods were pushed farther by other scholars, e.g. X. Prinz, 'Quelques passages de Juvénal', *RIPB* 9 (1866), 1–9, 69–79, and 10 (1867), 1–20 and 85–103; and H. Wirz, *Zur Kritik der fünften Satire Juvenals* (Aarau, 1868).

15. The most cogent of these rejoinders are P. Doetsch, *Vindiciae Juvenalianae* (Munster, 1870); M. J. Hofmann, *Zur Kritik und Erklärung einiger Satiren des Juvenal* (Amberg, 1878); B. Lupus, *Vindiciae Juvenalianae* (Bonn, 1864); O. Meinertz, *Vindiciae Juvenalianae* (Königsberg, 1866) and his *Zur Kritik und Erklärung der Satiren des Juvenal* (Konitz, 1871); G. Mosengel, *Vindiciae Juvenalianae* (Leipzig, 1887); G. Palm, *De Juvenalis satira quinta decima* (Nordhausen, 1882); G. Schönaich, *Quaestiones Iuvenalianae* (Halle, 1883); W. Schulz, *Quaestionum Juvenalianarum capita tria* (Leipzig, 1885); Sydow (*37*); Vahlen (*51*); and one of the best, Weise (*39*).

16. It has several times been proposed that some or all of these variants were the remains of a second edition of Juvenal's poems—that they were new versions of passages which he had already written but thought he could improve, or else new material he meant to insert. The theory is said to go back to Karl Otfried Müller, but I have been unable to trace the paper in which he may have advanced it. It was upheld later by Ribbeck in his text (pref. xii), Teuffel (*38*) 349–60, H. L. Wilson, 'The Codex Canonicianus Lat. XLI and the tradition of Juvenal', *TAPA* 34 (1903), xix, and finally Leo (*46*). But there is really not enough evidence to make us believe in anything so extensive as a second *edition*, which, judging by what we know of editions in antiquity, would go much farther than variations of a few lines here and there. It is much more probable that the variants were composed by readers in the generations following Juvenal's death. See R. Clauss, *Quaestiones Criticae Juvenalianae* (Leipzig, 1912); Jachmann (*43*); Knoche (*45*) 68–69; and G. Schönaich, cited in n. 15.

17. One lone exception was A. Haeckermann, who went to the other extreme, and wrote bitterly but uselessly for forty years against 'die Pithöanische Schwindel' (as he calls it in *Zur Kritik und Erklärung Juvenals*, Greifswald, 1877, 36). He brought out a text based largely on the 'vulgate' tradition in the same year as Jahn's; and he says it was sabotaged by Jahn's anonymous review in *LZ* for 1852. His many papers on Juvenal are ingenious but ill-tempered and often wrong-headed. N. Bob, in two essays called *Zur Kritik und Erklärung der Satiren des Juvenal* and *Zur Kritik und Erklärung der Satiren Juvenals* (Kaiserslautern, 1874 and 1889) also challenged the authority of P.

18. E. O. Winstedt, 'A Bodleian MS. of Juvenal', *CR* 13 (1899), 201–5, is the first report. He then published a facsimile, *Juvenalis ad satiram sextam in codice Bodl. Canon. XLI additi versus XXXVI* (Oxford, 1899). The passages are 34 lines following 6. 365 and 2 lines following 6. 373. The main passage, the 'O fragment' as it is called from being found in an Oxford manuscript, complains that married women often keep passive male homosexuals as secretaries and confidants (cf. 14. 30), and that for all their soft appearance these creatures are potential adulterers: they are both disgusting and dangerous. This type of satire, which cuts first one way and then another, seems to be peculiar to Juvenal. The manuscript itself is in Beneventan script of the eleventh or twelfth century: E. A. Loew, *The Beneventan Script* (Oxford, 1914), 17.

19. Notable papers on the O fragment are B. Axelson, 'A problem of genuineness in Juvenal', *Δράγμα M. P. Nilsson dedicatum* (Lund, 1939), 41–55; F. Buecheler, 'Der echte oder der unechte Juvenal?' *RhM* 54 (1899), 484–8; R. Clauss, *Quaestiones criticae Iuvenalianae* (Leipzig, 1912), 1; R. Ellis, *The New Fragments of Juvenal* (London, 1901); A. E. Housman, 'The new fragment of Juvenal', *CR* 15 (1901), 263–6; U. Knoche, 'Ein Wort zur Echtheitskritik', *Phil* 93 (1938), 196–217; F. Nougaret, 'Juvénal: omission du fragment Winstedt', *Mélanges E. Chatelain* (Paris, 1910), 255–67; R. Vianello, 'La sesta satira di Giovenale: note esegetiche e critiche', *Historia*, 4 (1930), 747–75; H. L. Wilson, 'The Bodleian fragments of Juvenal', *AJP* 22 (1901), 268–82; P. von Winterfeld, 'Zu den Oxforder Juvenalversen', *BPW* 19 (1899), 793–4, and his review in *GGA* 161 (1899), 895–7. The arguments against accepting the fragment as Juvenal's are that (1) if it were it would be part of the regular manuscript tradition; (2) its subject is too dirty and its composition too confused to fit into the Sixth Satire; (3) its language and metre are unlike Juvenal's. The counter-arguments to these are that (1) we do not know enough of the tradition to be sure that *all* Juvenal's authentic work came down the main channels and none elsewhere; (2) the subject suits Juvenal very well, even the comparison of net-casters to homosexuals which occurs elsewhere; (3) the language and metre are no more unlike Juvenal's (apart from scribal errors) than many a powerful and authentic passage. I myself believe it is Juvenal's work because I cannot think of any other poet who could have written it, esp. such lines as O14–16 and O25–29, and remained unknown to fame, and because the rest of the passage blends well with his ideas. Even the new version—O29–34—of the former 346–8 looks to me like Juvenal, and the previously accepted abbreviation like the work of an editor. Mr. Knoche (*45*) has shown us so much of the interference of editors that it is easy to accept the excision of this passage as another, much earlier, example; and yet traces of its existence were known to the P scholiast, just as he knew of two lines of Martial which occur in no official edition. I should not be surprised if a new manuscript of Juvenal turned up tomorrow with half a dozen new passages (several of them shocking) and with a totally irregular provenance and descent. The Dark Ages were a time of confusion.

20. Browning, *Pacchiarotto*, § 9. The couplet means 'those charges which no one could repeat fully unless, upon my word, with an unwashed mouth', and *Apage!* means 'away with it!'

21. G. Flaubert, *Correspondance*, 2ᵉ Série (Paris, 1889), 332, to Mme X, autumn 1853: 'J'ai en ce moment une forte rage de Juvénal. Quel style! quel style! et quel langage que le latin!'

22. The two sonnets neighbour each other in the series *Rome et les Barbares*. One is *Après Cannes*, which ends with a description of the Roman mob pouring out to watch for the advance of the Carthaginian army:

Tous anxieux de voir surgir, au dos vermeil
Des monts Sabins où luit l'œil sanglant du soleil,
Le Chef borgne monté sur l'éléphant Gétule.

This was meant by Juvenal (10. 157–8) to be a farcical picture; but Heredia has magically made it sinister, by making the sun's single red eye glare over the elephant-backed hills like the eye of the Punic conqueror on his beast. (*Media . . . Subura* in 10. 156 is echoed earlier in the sonnet.) The other is *A un Triomphateur*, a brief meditation on the theme of military glory—which is the subject of Juv. 10. 133–87.

Fais sculpter sur ton arc, Imperator illustre,
Des files de guerriers barbares, de vieux chefs
Sous le joug, des tronçons d'armures et de nefs,
Et la flotte captive et le rostre et l'aplustre. (∼ 10. 133–40).
Quel que tu sois, issu d'Ancus ou né d'un rustre,
Tes noms, famille, honneurs et titres, longs ou brefs,
Grave-les dans la frise et dans les bas-reliefs
Profondément, de peur que l'avenir te frustre. (∼ 10. 140–4).
Déjà le Temps brandit l'arme fatale. As-tu
L'espoir d'éterniser le bruit de ta vertu?
Un vil lierre suffit à disjoindre un trophée; (∼ 10. 144–5)
Et seul, aux blocs épars des marbres triomphaux
Où ta gloire en ruine est par l'herbe étouffée,
Quelque faucheur Samnite ébréchera sa faulx. (∼ 10. 146).

23. Juv. 6. 292–3. The picture is in the Louvre, and another version of it is in the Fogg Museum at Harvard. Someone like Juvenal himself appears in it, watching the debauch with grim thoughtfulness. Probably it was inspired by the gay parties of Couture's own time, which prompted several critics to draw parallels between imperial Rome and Paris, imperial and bourgeois.

24. For a full discussion see A. Collignon, 'Victor Hugo et Juvénal', *Revue d'Histoire littéraire de la France*, 16 (1909), 259–84, and A. Guiard, *Virgile et Victor Hugo* (Paris, 1910). In 'Fulgur', *Les Quatre Vents de l'Esprit*, 1. 44, Hugo says: 'On est beau par Virgile et grand par Juvénal.'

25. 'Et j'ajoute à ma lyre une corde d'airain': the last line of the last poem in *Feuilles d'Automne*. P. Stapfer, *Victor Hugo et la grande poésie satirique en France* (Paris, 1901³), calls Hugo the greatest French satiric poet, and compares him with Agrippa d'Aubigné, but does not draw parallels with Juvenal; but the conception of 'lyric satire' is well worked out.

26. P. Stapfer, *Victor Hugo à Guernesey* (Paris, 1905), 144–5, reports that Hugo said he had read and re-read some of the satires till he knew them virtually by heart. Stapfer also gives an odd story about Hugo's unconscious memory. Hugo said he had written, for *Les Châtiments*, the sentence

Personne ne connaît sa maison mieux que moi
Le Champ de Mars . . .

and had then been astonished to find that Juvenal had said the same thing in 1. 7–8. Since he did not know the passage in Latin, it followed that Juvenal had stolen it from him. Stapfer reflected that Hugo could hardly avoid knowing the first page of Juvenal; but . . . Anyhow, the line never appeared.

27. *Les Châtiments* (introduction) : 'Nox' ix:

> Toi qu'aimait Juvénal gonflé de lave ardente,
> Toi dont la clarté luit dans l'œil fixe de Dante,
> Muse Indignation, viens!

28. *Les Châtiments*, vi, xiii, 'A Juvénal'; 'l'âme vieille libre des républiques mortes' (almost an alexandrine) is from *William Shakespeare*, Première Partie, Livre Deuxième, ii, § vii, where Hugo adds the penetrating remark, 'il y a de l'épopée dans cette satire'.

29. *L'Art d'être Grand-père*, viii, 'Les Griffonnages de l'Écolier'. Note the citation of Juv. 2. 1 at the opening. The joke on Nisard may have been suggested by the sound of his name, the French for a bray being *hihan*.

30. The first poem in *Le Livre Satirique*, book I of *Les Quatre Vents de l'Esprit* (saying that the emotion which makes a hymn, when darkened and reversed, creates satire), is called 'Inde irae' ∼ Juv. 1. 168. *Les Misérables*, part 3, book 4, c. 6, describing young Marius starving, is called 'Res angusta' ∼ Juv. 3. 165.

31. *William Shakespeare*, Deuxième Partie, Livre Sixième, ii. See also Première Partie, Livre Premier, ii, on the 'hommes océans', and the last page of Deuxième Partie, Livre Quatrième on the great exiles.

32. See Ventura Ruiz Aguilera, *Libro de las sátiras* (Madrid, 1874); most of them are rather Horatian in tone, but in the eleventh, *Los Caracteres* (p. 58), there is a fine invocation of Juvenal:

> Amarrabas perversos á perversos,
> De la historia sublimes galeotes,
> Marcados en la espalda y en la frente
> Con tu sátira ardiente
> Y el negro verdugón de tus azotes.

Roy Campbell's *Georgiad* (1931) has no direct influence of Juvenal, but is in the Juvenalian tradition without a doubt.

33. Myron Grindea, 'Blum: the man of letters', *Time and Tide*, 15 April 1950: expanded in a letter to me from Mr. Grindea, who heard the story from a contemporary of Blum and had it confirmed by Blum's son.

SELECT BIBLIOGRAPHY

Since 1800, well over a thousand books and articles on various aspects of Juvenal's life, work, and influence have appeared. I have selected the following list, which covers the most important of them, as a working bibliography for readers who wish to learn more about Juvenal and his satires. References to this bibliography in the text and in the notes are given simply by author's name and number—the numbers being set in italics: thus, page 12 of Pietro Ercole's book is simply Ercole (*3*) 12.

(A) WORKS OF GENERAL INTEREST

1. G. BOISSIER, 'Juvénal et son Temps', in his *L'Opposition sous les Césars* (Paris, *c.* 1921⁹), c. 6, §§ 3 and 4.
   A cool and rather unsympathetic analysis of Juvenal's character, suggesting that he had no profoundly felt ideals but was simply a gifted malcontent.
2. J. W. DUFF, 'Juvenal and other satirists', c. 8 of his *Roman Satire* (*Sather Classical Lectures*, 12, Berkeley, Cal., 1936).
   Brief and sensible introductory discussion.
3. P. ERCOLE, *Studi Giovenaliani* (ed. E. Paratore, Lanciano, 1935).
   Learned but often inaccurate articles on the chronology of Juvenal's life and work, the manuscripts, and other problems; poorly edited after the author's death.
4. P. DE LABRIOLLE, *Les Satires de Juvénal: étude et analyse* (Paris, 1932).
   Gracefully written but sometimes superficial essays.
5. A. H. MABLEY, 'Bibliography of Juvenal', *Western Reserve University Bulletin*, 1 (1895), 2. 3–31.
   A rich but uncritical list of editions, translations, and special studies.
6. H. NETTLESHIP, 'Life and Poems of Juvenal', c. 5 of his *Lectures and Essays, 2nd Series* (Oxford, 1895).
   A good survey, emphasizing Juvenal's close relationship to Martial.
7. M. SCHANZ, *Geschichte der römischen Literatur* (Munich, 1913³), 2. 2, §§ 418, 419, 420, and 420*a*.
   A thorough discussion covering almost every problem, with large bibliographies.
8. F. SKUTSCH, in W. S. Teuffel's *Geschichte der römischen Literatur* (ed. W. Kroll and F. Skutsch, Leipzig, 1913⁶), 3. §331.
   A competent study on the same lines as 7, but much shorter.
9. F. VOLLMER, 'D. Iunius Iuvenalis' ('Iunius' 87) in Pauly–Wissowa, *Real-Encyclopädie der classischen Altertumswissenschaft*, 10. 1041–50.
   Well-balanced but not very penetrating account of the poet's life and work.

(B) THE LIFE OF JUVENAL

10. G. BOISSIER, 'Relations de Juvénal et de Martial', *Revue des Cours et Conférences*, 7 (1899), 2. 443–51.

An able comparison of the two poets, showing resemblances and differences.

11. H. J. DE DOMPIERRE DE CHAUFEPIÉ, *De titulo I.R.N. 4312 ad Iuvenalem poetam perperam relato* (The Hague, 1889).
Argues that since the poet was poor and the Juvenal of the Aquinum inscription was rich, the two cannot have been identical.

12. J. DÜRR, *Das Leben Juvenals* (Ulm, 1888).
One of the best-balanced attempts to make sense out of the ancient biographies, printing them all and extracting their common elements.

13. J. DÜRR, *Die zeitgeschichtlichen Beziehungen in den Satiren Juvenals* (Cannstatt, 1902).
Valuable survey of many of the datable facts in Satires 1–9.

14. G. HIGHET, 'The life of Juvenal', *TAPA* 68 (1937), 480–506.
Reconstruction of the career of the poet.

15. J. A. HILD, *Juvénal, Notes biographiques* (Paris, 1884).
Builds on the Aquinum inscription to show that the poet must have been well off and that the story of his exile was therefore a medieval invention.

16. J. VAHLEN, 'Juvenal und Paris', *Gesammelte philologische Schriften*, 2 (Leipzig, 1923), 181–201.
Closely argued paper attacking the tradition that Juvenal was banished for the sneer at Paris in 7. 88–92.

(C) JUVENAL'S POETRY

17. R. E. COLTON, *Juvenal and Martial* (Columbia University doctoral dissertation, 1951).
Shows in detail how Juvenal adapted the themes and stylistic tricks of Martial's epigrams.

18. J. DE DECKER, *Juvenalis declamans* (*Recueil de Travaux publiés par la Faculté de Philosophie et Lettres*, 41, Ghent, 1913).
Useful but sometimes over-scrupulous analysis of the rhetorical elements in the satires.

19. F. GAUGER, *Zeitschilderung und Topik bei Juvenal* (Bottrop, 1936).
A painstaking attempt to distinguish genuine observation from philosophical and rhetorical commonplaces throughout the poems.

20. J. A. GYLLING, *De argumenti dispositione in satiris I–VIII Iuvenalis* (Lund, 1886) and *De argumenti dispositione in satiris IX–XVI Iuvenalis* (Lund, 1889).
A structural analysis of the poems, mainly intended to combat Ribbeck's rearrangement of them.

21. A. HARTMANN, *De inventione Iuvenalis* (Basel, 1908).
A detailed study of the construction of Satires 1, 3, and 5.

22. G. HIGHET, 'The philosophy of Juvenal', *TAPA* 80 (1949), 254–70.
Suggests that Juvenal was converted to Epicureanism in later life.

23. G. HIGHET, 'Juvenal's bookcase', *AJP* 72 (1951), 369–94.
Lists Juvenal's favourite authors and discusses his debts to them.

24. A. KAPPELMACHER, 'Studia Juvenaliana', *Dissertationes philologicae Vindobonenses*, 7 (1903), 159–99.

An essay on Juvenal's relation to the professional schools of rhetoric, arguing rather convincingly that he was a pupil of Quintilian.

25. L. O. KIÆR, *Sermonem D. J. Juvenalis certis legibus astrictum demonstrare conatus est* (Copenhagen, 1875).
   A masterly analysis of the grammatical and syntactical aspects of Juvenal's style.

26. C. MARTHA, *Les Moralistes sous l'empire romain* (Paris, 1865), 315–412.
   Corrects the exaggerations of Victor Hugo, emphasizing that Juvenal was neither a Stoic nor a republican; but also acknowledges his penetration and the breadth of his vision.

27. D. NISARD, *Études de Mœurs et de Critique sur les poëtes latins de la décadence* (Paris, 1888⁵), 2. 1–70.
   Unsympathetic but penetrating criticism of Juvenal as a poet powerful but insincere.

28. H. PETER, *Die geschichtliche Litteratur über die römische Kaiserzeit* (Leipzig, 1897), 2. 77–83.
   Discusses Juvenal's veracity and concludes he reflects only the senatorial view of politics, society, and morals.

29. J. RAHN, *Selecta capita de syntaxi Juvenaliana* (Halle, 1875).
   Useful tabulation of syntactical usages.

30. K. SCHNEIDER, *Juvenal und Seneca* (Würzburg, 1930).
   Rather uncritical list of parallel passages.

31. R. SCHUETZE, *Juvenalis ethicus* (Greifswald, 1905).
   Valuable collection of the philosophical commonplaces used by Juvenal, with notes on their appearance elsewhere.

32. I. G. SCOTT, *The grand style in the satires of Juvenal* (*Smith College Classical Studies*, 8, Northampton, Mass., 1927).
   A good exposition of Juvenal's (mainly parodic) use of lofty phraseology.

33. E. SMEMO, 'Zur Technik der Personenzeichnung bei Juvenal', *Symbolae Osloenses*, 17 (1937), 77–102.
   An interesting analysis of the methods Juvenal uses to make his characters seem real and vivid.

34. W. STEGEMANN, *De Juvenalis dispositione* (Weyda, 1913).
   Careful dissection of six of the satires, rather spoilt by the author's efforts to find symmetry everywhere.

35. J. STREIFINGER, *Der Stil des Satirikers Juvenalis* (Regensburg, 1892).
   A list of Juvenal's figures of speech.

36. E. STRUBE, *De rhetorica Juvenalis disciplina* (Brandenburg, 1875).
   Painstaking collection of the imitations of other poets in Juvenal and of his figures of speech.

37. H. SYDOW, *De Juvenalis arte compositionis* (Halle, 1890).
   Analyses Juvenal's methods of composition in order to refute the theories of Ribbeck and Teuffel.

38. W. S. TEUFFEL, *Studien und Charakteristiken zur griechischen und römischen Litteraturgeschichte* (Leipzig, 1889²), c. 20.
   Discussion of Juvenal's life and poetry with some penetrating criticisms of his weaknesses; restates the theory that Juvenal issued two different editions of the satires, which later got mixed up.

39. R. Weise, *Vindiciae Juvenalianae* (Halle, 1884).
A competent analysis of the chief characteristics of Juvenal's style, showing that they recur throughout his poems.

40. H. L. Wilson, 'The literary influence of Martial upon Juvenal', *AJP* 19 (1898), 193–209.
A fundamental study of the relationship.

(D) The Text and the Scholia

41. R. Beer, *Spicilegium Iuvenalianum* (Leipzig, 1885).
The first close study of the P manuscript and of its tradition; now partly obsolete but still well worth reading.

42. F. Cremer, *De grammaticorum antiquorum in Juvenalem arte critica* (Munster, 1913).
Shows how many of the variations in the text were introduced by scholars who intended to improve Juvenal's style and metre.

43. G. Jachmann, 'Studien zu Juvenal', *Nachrichten von der Akademie der Wissenschaften in Göttingen, philologisch-historische Klasse*, 1943, 187–266.
Brilliant dissection of many difficult passages, showing that a number of apparently hopeless problems were created by interpolators.

44. L. Kelling and A. Suskin, *Index verborum Iuvenalis* (Chapel Hill, N. Carolina, 1951).
A full lexicon listing all word-forms and notable variants.

45. U. Knoche, *Handschriftliche Grundlagen des Juvenaltextes* (*Philologus* Supplement 33. 1, 1940).
The result of Knoche's collation of scores of manuscripts, this is a fundamental reconstruction of the history of the text. It completes and complements his *Überlieferung Juvenals* (Berlin, 1926), and is the basis of his 1950 edition of the satires, no. 58 in this list.

46. F. Leo, 'Doppelfassungen bei Iuvenal', *Hermes*, 44 (1909), 600–17.
Proposes to take the Oxford fragment and other passages in Satires 6, 8, and 9 as evidence that Juvenal's poems were issued in two editions, the second posthumous.

47. E. Lommatzsch, 'Quaestiones Iuvenalianae', *Jahrbücher für classische Philologie*, Suppl. 22 (1896), 373–506.
A searching analysis of the notes and additions in the P manuscript.

48. E. Matthias, *De scholiis Iuvenalianis* (Halle, 1875).
A clear description of the better scholia.

49. O. Ribbeck, *Der echte und der unechte Juvenal, eine kritische Untersuchung* (Berlin, 1865).
A bold attempt to prove that the later satires were forged and many of the genuine satires distorted by interpolation: misguided but stimulating.

50. C. Stephan, *De Pithoeanis in Iuuenalem scholiis* (Bonn, 1882).
A useful account of the better scholia.

51. J. Vahlen, 'Quaestiones Iuvenalianae', *Opuscula academica*, 1 (Leipzig, 1907), 223–53.
Explains Juvenal's habits of digression and expansion, misinterpreted by Ribbeck as interpolation and by Leo as evidence of a double edition.

52. N. Vianello, 'Il testo delle satire di Giovenale', *Atti della società ligustica di scienze e lettere*, n.s. 12 (1933), 81–123.

Valuable discussion of the history of the text, emphasizing the frequency of interpolations.

53. P. Wessner, *Scholia in Iuuenalem uetustiora* (Leipzig, 1931).

A priceless edition, with admirable introduction and notes.

(E) Editions

54. J. D. Duff, *D. Iunii Iuuenalis saturae XIV* (Cambridge, 1898, often reprinted).

Annotated and expurgated edition omitting 2, 9, and parts of 6: the handiest work in English on the subject for school and college use.

55. L. Friedländer, *D. Junii Juvenalis saturarum libri V mit erklärenden Anmerkungen* (2 vv., Leipzig, 1895).

Full, sensible, and generally useful commentary, with uneven introductory essays, all in German.

56. A. E. Housman, *D. Iunii Iuuenalis saturae, editorum in usum edidit* (Cambridge, 1931).

Text, with introduction in English and no commentary: the text is based on an inadequate number of manuscripts but is intelligently, if acrimoniously, edited.

57. O. Jahn, F. Buecheler, F. Leo, *D. Iunii Iuvenalis saturae* (Berlin, 1932[5]).

A conservative text with introduction in Latin, selected scholia, and brief apparatus criticus: a revision of the first good modern edition produced by Jahn in 1851.

58. U. Knoche, *D. Iunius Juvenalis saturae* (Munich, 1950).

The best-edited modern text, with the first full critical apparatus.

59. P. de Labriolle and F. Villeneuve, *Juvénal, Satires* (Paris, 1932[2]).

Text, with introduction, translation, and notes in French.

60. J. E. B. Mayor, *Thirteen satires of Juvenal with a commentary* (2 vv., London, 1880–1[2]).

A text with very learned notes on all satires except 2, 6, and 9; the comments consist chiefly of parallel passages, and do not go deeply into problems of text and interpretation.

61. S. G. Owen, *A. Persi Flacci et D. Iuni Iuuenalis saturae, cum additamentis Bodleianis recognouit breuique adnotatione critica instruxit* (Oxford, 1907[2], often reprinted).

Text with introduction and apparatus criticus in Latin, not very percipient.

62. N. Vianello, *D. Junii Juvenalis saturae* (Turin, 1935).

Unenterprising but useful text, with rich but careless bibliography.

63. A. Weidner, *D. Iunii Iuuenalis saturae, erklärt* (Leipzig, 1889[2]).

An ambitious edition with notes in German: the best before Friedländer, but marred by errors of judgement.

64. H. L. Wilson, *D. Iunii Iuuenalis saturarum libri V, edited with introduction, commentary on thirteen satires, and index* (Boston, 1903).

A very sensible edition, nearly as good as Duff, and a useful complement to his work.

(F) Translations, with Specimen Renderings of i. 1–4

65. A. Berg (Berlin, 1863).
German hexameters, with explanatory notes and short introduction.

> Stets Zuhörer nur sein sollt' ich? nie sollt' ich's vergelten,
> Welchen so häufig geplagt des heiseren Cordus Theseïs?
> Straflos hatte mir denn d e r Togastücke gelesen,
> D e r Elegieen?

66. F. Díaz Carmona (Biblioteca Clásica 158, Madrid, 1892).
Spanish verse, sometimes terza rima and sometimes freely rhyming;
with introduction opposing Nisard. This is a good translation, gay and
free.

> ¿Siempre he de ser oyente? ¿Atormentarme
> Codro, con su Teséida cada día
> Podrá y no he de vengarme?
> ¿Impune un drama éste, una elegía
> Aquél me habrá de recitar?

67. J. Dryden 'and several other eminent hands' (see n. 39 on c. 31, p. 327)
(London, 1693, often reprinted).
Clear and often brilliant version in English heroic couplets, with an
eloquent explanatory letter and dedication. A free adaptation rather than
a close translation.

> Still shall I hear, and never quit the Score,
> Stunn'd with hoarse *Codrus' Theseid*, o'er and o'er?
> Shall this Man's Elegies and t'other's Play
> Unpunish'd murther a long Summer's Day?

68. W. Gifford (London, 1802).
English heroic couplets, slower and more pompous than Dryden's but
closer to the original meaning.

> What! while with one eternal mouthing hoarse,
> Codrus persists on my vex'd ear to force
> His Theseid, must I, to my fate resign'd,
> Hear, ONLY hear, and never pay in kind?
> Must this with farce and folly rack my head
> Unpunish'd? that with sing-song, whine me dead?

69. C. Giussani (Milan, 1947).
Long version in Italian blank verse with brief notes.

> Sempre e soltanto ascoltator? Di questo
> sfiatato Codro, la 'Teseide' afflitto
> tante volte m'avrà, senza ch'io n'abbia
> vendetta mai? Le sue commedie l'uno,
> le sue liriche [*sic*] un altro impunemente
> recitato m'avranno?

70. M. Guérin (Paris, 1887).
French Alexandrines, bold and accurate, with an introduction defending Juvenal against the charge of being a mere declaimer.

> Quoi! toujours écouter et ne jamais répondre,
> Par l'enroué Codrus (Puisse un dieu le confondre)!
> Et par sa Théséide excédé tant de fois?
> C'est donc impunément qu'un poète, à sa choix,
> Vient m'assommer du faix de sa verve comique,
> Ou du récit dolent d'un amour chimérique?

71. U. Knoche (Munich, 1951).
Brisk German hexameters, very careful and close to the original. Introduction and brief notes in German. Companion to 58.

> Immer soll ich nur der Zuhörer sein? Nie soll ich's vergelten,
> Oft von des Cordus Theseis gequält, der sich heiser geredet?
> Straflos soll Lustspiele dieser, ein anderer mir Elegien
> Lesen?

72. P. de Labriolle and F. Villeneuve (Paris, 1932[2]).
French prose, clear and rather dull, with text, introduction, and notes: same as 59.

> Faut-il donc n'être qu'auditeur, toujours? Ne les paierai-je jamais de retour, excédé tant de fois de la *Théséide* d'un Cordus enroué? Est-ce impunément que l'un m'aura récité ses *togatae*, l'autre ses élégies?

73. S. G. Owen (London, 1924[2]).
English prose version excluding 2, 6, and 9; written to accompany 61 and to supplement a commentary which (for fear of Housman) Owen never published. Rather stilted.

> A mere listener shall I always be? Shall I never take revenge for all the torment of bawling Cordus' Tale of Theseus? What! without punishment shall one have read to me his comedies, another his love-ditties?

74. G. G. Ramsay (Loeb series, London and New York, 1918: often reprinted).
Vigorous though old-fashioned English prose, with introduction and notes.

> What? Am I to be a listener only all my days? Am I never to get my word in—I that have been so often bored by the Theseid of the ranting Cordus? Shall this one have spouted to me his comedies, and that one his love ditties, and I be unavenged?

75. G. Vitali (Bologna, 1947).
Italian blank verse, very leisurely (Satire 1 takes 274 lines), with introduction and notes in Italian.

> Sempre a udir gli altri starò io? Non mai
> mi rivarrò del tedio onde mi assilla
> con la *Teseide* lo sfiatato Còrdio?
> E mi avran recitato impunemente
> chi elegie, chi commedie?

(G) Juvenal's Survival and Influence

76. F. Gabotto, 'Appunti sulla fortuna di alcuni autori romani nel medio evo', *Biblioteca delle scuole italiane*, 3 (Verona, 1891), 40–54.
Interesting collection of references to Juvenal from the fifth to the fifteenth century, with a discussion of the reasons for his popularity.

77. J. A. Hild, 'Juvénal dans le moyen âge', *Bulletin de la Faculté de Poitiers*, 8 (1890), 177–89 and 9 (1891), 39–54, 106–22, 235–52.
Good description of the use made of Juvenal by medieval poets and thinkers, especially Hildebert, John of Salisbury, Peter of Blois, and the satirists.

78. M. Manitius, 'Beiträge zur Geschichte römischer Dichter im Mittelalter', *Phil* 50 (1891), 354–68.
A huge collection of quotations and adaptations of Juvenal's poetry in medieval authors, made with fabulous industry but unclassified.

79. M. Manitius, 'Handschriften antiker Autoren in mittelalterlichen Bibliothekskatalogen', *Zentralblatt für Bibliothekswesen*, Beiheft 67 (Leipzig, 1935), § 58.
Lists about a hundred mentions of manuscripts of Juvenal in medieval catalogues.

80. E. M. Sanford, 'Renaissance commentaries on Juvenal', *TAPA* 79 (1948), 92–112.
Excellent survey of Juvenalian scholarship in the age of the humanists.

81. P. Wessner, 'Lucan, Statius und Juvenal bei den römischen Grammatikern', *Phil. Woch.* 49 (1929), 296–303, 328–335.
Conclusive proof that Juvenal was virtually forgotten till the fourth century and then was brought back to the notice of scholars, chiefly through Servius.

SVMMI PLENA IAM MARGINE LIBRI
SCRIPTVS ET IN TERGO NECDVM FINITVS AQVINAS

Persons, Places, and Things Discussed in the Text and Notes

Figures in bold type indicate an important reference. Figures within brackets mean that the subject of the note is not actually named in the passage cited.

INDEX II

Passages of Juvenal's Poetry mentioned in the Text and Notes

Satire Four: character and subject, 4, 5, 11, 39, 44–45, 57, **76–82,** 85, 87, 89–90, 119, 168, **235, 256–62,** 270, 279, 319; date, 39, 89–90, 168, **235, 257–8;** length, 245; sources, 79, 89–90, 256–8; structure, 44–45, 76–79, 82, 84, 93, 106, **256–7,** 275; translations, quotations, adaptations, 219, 323, 327, 332, 334.

Satire Eight: character, 38, 105, **113–16,** 168, **272–3,** 319; date, 104–5, 240–1, 293; length, 245; sources, **272;** structure, 44–45, 93, 114, 270, **273,** 275; translations, quotations, adaptations, 212–13, 216, 219–20, 227, 272, 306, 314, 322, 323, 324, 325, 327, 328, 329, **332, 333.**

Satire Fourteen: character, 44–5, 138, **145-8,** 168, 208, 240–1, **282-4,** 319; date, 240–1; length, 145, 245; sources, 148, **284;** structure, 44–45, 93, 145, 146, 147, 170, 266, **283-4;** translations, quotations, adaptations, 216, 323, 327, 330.

Satire Fifteen: character, **28-31,** 41, 44–45, **149-53,** 168, 240–1, 279, **284-6,** 288, 319; date, 240–1, 284, 294; length, 245; sources, 149, 152, **284-5;** structure, 44–45, **285;** translations, quotations, adaptations, 327.

INDICE COMPLETO SALTAT SCRIPTOR PEDE LAETO

PRINTED IN
GREAT BRITAIN
AT THE
UNIVERSITY PRESS
OXFORD
BY
CHARLES BATEY
PRINTER
TO THE
UNIVERSITY